HB&W·HB&W·HB&W·HB&W·HB&W·HB&W·HB&W·HB&W·HB&W·HB&W·HB&W·HB&W·HB&

Examination Copy

MICROSTATICS

We are pleased to send you
this book, with our compliments,
so that you may have an
opportunity to review it for
possible class use. We hope you
will enjoy examining it.

Price $9.50

Harcourt, Brace & World, Inc.

757 Third Avenue, New York, New York 10017
7555 Caldwell Avenue, Chicago, Illinois 60648
Polk and Geary, San Francisco, California 94109
1372 Peachtree Street, N.E., Atlanta, Georgia 30309

HB&W·HB&W·HB&W·HB&W·HB&W·HB&W·HB&W·HB&W·HB&W·HB&W·HB&W·HB&W·HB&

MICROSTATICS

WILLIAM S. VICKREY
COLUMBIA UNIVERSITY

Microstatics

HARCOURT, BRACE & WORLD, INC.
New York · Chicago · Burlingame

TO THE MEMORY OF
ROBERT MURRAY HAIG

CONTENTS

PART III *Monopoly and*
Imperfect Competition

PREFACE

THIS *work, with its companion volume,* Metastatics and Macroeconomics, *has grown so gradually over the course of the years during which it has served, in its various stages, as a text for a basic course in economic theory that it is a little difficult to capture in any brief statement exactly what it has become. Essentially, the objective is to place in the hands of the student an exposition of the basic structures of current economic theory. The emphasis is on the logical structure of the various theoretical tools, and I have made a special attempt to show how theories are developed from the underlying, basic postulates and concepts upon which they are built. I have also tried to keep the treatment at a fairly elementary mathematical level, through the use so far as possible of graphical illustration rather than algebraic representation.*

The complete work has been separated into two volumes, in order more nearly to suit the needs of those who may be interested primarily in neoclassical microeconomics, which is covered in the present volume, as well as those who may be primarily interested in macroeconomics and dynamics, which are treated in a second volume, entitled Metastatics and Macroeconomics. *The coverage of the two volumes, taken together, is considerably broader at the theoretical level than that of the usual textbook of economic theory, while at the same time the discussion of the framework of institutions has been limited to that necessary to motivate the theoretical model.*

In the present volume the usual topics of consumption, production, competitive equilibrium, monopoly, and imperfect competition are covered from an analytical point of view. Indifference curves and associated techniques are developed in considerable detail, in spite of the tendency recently to disparage this technique in favor of such concepts as revealed preference and set theory; indifference curves are likely for some time to remain one of the best available tools both for introducing the student to the "plausible topology" of economic theory and for initial explorations into new areas. Considerable attention is given to welfare economics as a source of motivation for the study of economic theory. The student is also introduced to the basic notions of the theory of games, not so much because a student is likely to find very much use for the theory directly, but because in no other way can the difficulties encountered in precise theorizing concerning imperfect competition be so clearly exposed. On the other hand, relatively little space is given to the elaboration of the more institutional aspects of imperfect competition: these are adequately treated elsewhere insofar as a less rigorous treatment suffices; while if we push a rigorous theoretical analysis very much further in these areas we encounter rapidly increasing complexity and diminishing returns in significant results.

There is probably more material in the two volumes combined than can be adequately covered in the ordinary two-semester course. It would be presumptuous to attempt to indicate what should be left out; this will differ widely according to the way in which the course fits into the over-all curriculum. In any case, even though such topics as the theory of games or the more intricate examples of welfare economics might be omitted, it is well worth while to place in the hands of the student an introductory treatment of these out-of-the-way topics so that he at least becomes aware of their nature and can pursue them further if his interests lie in that direction.

This preface would not be complete without an expression of gratitude for the patience with which successive classes of students have borne with this work in its various preparatory stages, and for the many suggestions and corrections that have been made. My especial thanks go to Professors Bonbright, Hart, and Shoup for their help and encouragement.

WILLIAM S. VICKREY

Columbia University
October 1963

PART I

Introduction

CHAPTER ONE

The Nature and Role of Economic Theory

What Is Economics?

To DEFINE precisely the general area of investigation known as economics poses something of a problem, as the ramifications of economics are many and the limits often obscure. Indeed, economics has been defined somewhat facetiously as "what economists do." One of the most illustrious economists of recent times defined economics in one breath as "a study of mankind in the ordinary business of life" (a definition most would regard as too broad), and in the next as the study of "action which is most closely connected with the attainment and with the use of the material requisites of well-being" (which could be considered too narrow on the one hand as excluding nonmaterial elements, and as too broad on the other as tending to include mere technology) [2.71, p. 1]. In fact it may be almost impossible to comprehend in a brief definition all that goes on under the name of economics.

If we confine our attention to that branch of economics known as economic theory or economic analysis, we may perhaps be more successful. For this purpose economics can be defined as the study of the processes by which scarce resources are or might be allocated toward the achievement of diverse competing objectives. In addition, it is appropriate to specify that for the process to be of interest to economic analysis, it is usually necessary that it involve at some point resources that are transferable and measurable.

The consideration of diverse objectives is needed to set off economics from engineering, for example. If we are given a certain supply of wood, steel, and cement and asked to build a bridge meeting certain requirements, the problem is one of engineering, not of economics. On the other hand, if there were unlimited quantities of wood, steel, and lumber available, there would be no need to economize in their use, and again no economic problem, even though there might be many uses to which they could be put. Or if we have multiple ends but the resources cannot be transferred from one objective to another, as, for example, if we have materials for a bridge and the makings of a stew; then unless the one can in some way be converted into the other there is still no economic problem but merely a number of separate technological problems.

It is only when the wood, steel, and concrete might be diverted to other uses if not used for the bridge that the necessity arises for the kind of choice we term economic, typically expressed through the influence that the prices at which the materials are valued have on how much of each material is to be used in the structure.

While in a sense any problem containing the elements of limited resources and competing ends can be called economic, or perhaps better may be said to have economic aspects, economics is chiefly interested only in those cases involving at least the possibility of a transfer of resources between individuals or groups, as in exchange. Thus the study of the actions of a Robinson Crusoe, while it may serve to illustrate principles, is in itself more of an exercise in hypothetical psychology than one in economics. And while it is not absolutely necessary that the resources involved be measurable, ordinarily it is difficult or impossible to bring the apparatus of economics effectively to bear on a problem unless these resources are at least indirectly measurable. Indeed, for purposes of analysis it very greatly facilitates matters to assume not only that resources are measurable, but that they are "fungible"; i.e., that an aggregate amount of a given resource can be subdivided without changing its essential qualities, in somewhat the same degree that a gallon of gasoline may be divided into quarts and pints without losing its properties.

Indeed, this fungibility, or divisibility, is often so important that in cases where it does not exist of itself it is often introduced by an artificial device in order to render the problem under discussion more amenable to the manipulations of the economist. Thus a house, from the point of view of the occupant, is certainly not a fungible resource (though to a contractor or real estate operator dealing in large numbers of houses, "housing" might approach a certain degree of fungibility); the economist, however, instead of talking separately about housing units of different kinds, may attempt to substitute for them all a common fungible denominator in the shape of the number of dollars spent for rent or the "dollars' worth of housing." Some of the pitfalls necessarily involved in such convenient devices will be examined later.

Of course, fungibility is in a sense only a matter of perspective. If one begins to deal in gasoline by the molecule, fungibility vanishes. Nails by the pound are reasonably fungible, if of small size; for large spikes and bolts it may be another matter. As one approaches the scale for which the fungibility begins to be imperfect, special care must be taken to consider the effects of these "indivisibilities." Man himself is the greatest source of indivisibilities, and yet the economist often persists in treating labor as a perfectly divisible resource. Paradoxically, though, the identity of the firm or the consumer is intimately tied up with this matter of indivisibility, so that in a sense the economist who persists in treating resources as though they were perfectly fungible is indulging in a basic inconsistency. Complete consistency, unfortunately, is often only available at the cost of considerable added complexity,

4]

or even of complete frustration, and to be completely consistent in this matter, as in many others, would make economic analysis an almost hopelessly complicated subject. But if we are to be inconsistent, it is better to be consciously so.

The Role of Economic Theory

ECONOMIC theory bears somewhat the same relation to other branches of economics, such as economic history or the study of economic institutions, as geometry [1] does to surveying: it provides a logical framework or skeleton in relation to which the necessarily inexact and incomplete observations of the real world can be apprehended with greater insight.

Economic theory proper, indeed, is nothing more than a system of logical relations between certain sets of assumptions and the conclusions derived from them. The propositions of economic theory are derived by logical reasoning from these basic assumptions in exactly the same way as the theorems of geometry are derived from the axioms upon which the system is built. The difference between economic theory and geometry is that while in geometry the axioms are intended to have some approximate relation to the real space of ordinary experience, in economics the axioms are intended to have some approximate relation to the properties of the real economic world. In addition, there is a marked difference in the care and rigor with which economists have typically stated their assumptions and deduced their conclusions, and the great complexity of the real economic world has called forth a relatively large number of different theoretical systems in an attempt to aid in the understanding of various aspects of reality. But this is essentially a matter of degree rather than of kind.

The validity of a theory proper does not depend on the correspondence or lack of it between the assumptions of the theory or its conclusions and observations in the real world. A theory as an internally consistent system is valid if the conclusions follow logically from the premises, and the fact that neither the premises nor the conclusions correspond to reality may show that the theory is not very useful, but does not invalidate it. In any pure theory, all propositions are essentially tautological, in the sense that the results are implicit in the assumptions made. The proposition that under perfect competition minimum average cost, marginal cost, and price are all equal is implicit in the definitions given to these various terms, in the same sense that the proposition $12 \times 12 \times 12 = 1,728$ is implicit in the definition of the decimal notation and the operation of multiplication, or that the proposition that the angles of a triangle add up to $180°$ is implicit in the parallel postulate.

The fact that the propositions of economic theory are tautologies does not mean, however, that they are not useful. Of course, if man were a perfect,

1. Etymologically, indeed, geo-metry is "earth measurement."

logical thinking machine so that immediately upon defining the terms and assumptions all the logical implications of those assumptions would be apparent, there would be no need to study economic theory, just as there would be no need to study arithmetic if it were intuitively obvious as soon as one defined the decimal notation that 12 × 12 × 12 = 1,728, or that a 12-inch cube contains 1,728 cubic inches. It would then be quite obvious what theoretical assumptions correspond to reality, and there would be no need to go through the tedious process of elaborating the structure implied in a set of assumptions.

Indeed, a fairly sharp distinction can be drawn between the "tautological" nature of the propositions of economic theory and the inductive propositions derived from observation on the basis of whether the proposition is conceivably falsifiable by any possible hypothetical observation. In the case of theoretical propositions, if an observation does not conform to the prediction given by the model, one will merely deduce that the assumptions upon which the proposition is based are not met in fact. An observation that price is different from marginal cost does not disprove the proposition that perfect competition would achieve this result, but rather indicates that in this particular case the conditions of perfect competition are not fulfilled. Indeed, no set of observations would persuade us to discard this proposition: in any instance, some means would be found for declaring that the conditions do not correspond with those postulated by the theory (assuming, of course, that there is no logical flaw in the process by which the result was deduced from the assumptions). Similarly, if one were to fill a one-foot cube with water by means of a dipper containing one cubic inch, and found that it would take more or less than 1,728 dippers to fill the cube, one would not discard the multiplication table (though one might go over and check the arithmetic), but would conclude that the measurements were a little off, or the method of constructing the cube was incorrect, or that the dipping process was inaccurate, or perhaps that space was warped, rather than Euclidean. On the other hand, Gresham's law, to the effect that bad currency drives out good, is a generalization from observation that would have to be abandoned or modified if an instance were adduced in which bad money failed to drive out good, just as the proposition that "Steel rusts when exposed to the elements" would have to be modified upon the exhibit of stainless steel to read: "Ordinary steels rust when exposed to the elements."

Nevertheless, the putting together of a logical economic theory is more than a mere intellectual exercise, although sometimes some of the more abstruse and hypothetical constructions seem to yield their chief utility in terms of the artistic appreciation of the adept. For example, some aspects of the theory of games seem for the moment to be at this stage. (Mathematics is not without cases of this sort. One famous mathematician, upon completing the proof of a theorem in the theory of numbers, is said to have remarked: "And the peculiar beauty of this theorem, which will particularly endear it to the hearts of all true mathematicians, is that under no conceivable circumstances can it be of any possible practical value!"). One approach to the application of economic theory is to use it as a first approximation, or skeleton, to which modifications may be added which will, it is hoped, permit successively closer approximations to reality. This has been termed, not without a touch of irony, the "optimistic approach." It is indeed a method with which the physical sciences have had eminent success. Kinematics starts with concepts such as the perfectly rigid body, the weight concentrated at a point, frictionless motion, and the like, though in fact all bodies are more or less flexible, weight is distributed, and friction is inescapable. Thermodynamics makes use of the "perfect gas," and hydrodynamics has its "perfect fluid." By setting up systems on the basis of these abstract and impossible assumptions, models are built up which not only give insight into the operation of the real world but are capable of modification so as to permit prediction of real phenomena with reasonable accuracy, whereas to have attempted to build up a science by taking into account all of the factors from the beginning would have been an impossible intellectual achievement, both for the original investigator and for the student.

It is moreover necessary at times to set up a simplified abstract model in order to understand fully the operation of the factors that produce a departure from the model. The operation of friction can be understood, for example, only when one considers what would happen in the absence of friction. Similarly, only by considering a system in which there is perfect competition can the nature of monopoly and the various types of imperfect competition be fully understood.

Abstract models are also useful in deducing boundaries or limits that cannot be surpassed by the real world. For example, in thermodynamics, from the empirically validated premises of the conservation of energy and the tendency of heat to flow only from hotter to cooler media (the second law of thermodynamics), and consideration of a hypothetically perfect Carnot cycle engine, perfectly insulated and operating infinitely slowly, one can deduce a maximum limit on the proportion of the heat of combustion of a fuel that can be turned into mechanical energy when operating between given extremes of temperature. Practical engines differ greatly from the Carnot engine, and the theoretical limit cannot be reached or even in many cases very closely approximated in practice, but the theoretical relation between the temperature extremes and the efficiency is useful as a guide in the design of power plants. Similarly, a hypothetical state of perfect competition in economics can be shown (and will be, in Chapter 5) to produce results that are in a certain sense an optimum. Perfect competition does not exist, and indeed cannot be approached at all closely in many areas, but from this theoretical result we can derive some ideas as to how to proceed in improving the

[7

operation of the actual economic system. Again, with some care, perfect competition and complete monopoly can be set up as extremes, within which the real world may be expected to lie, although here one must be somewhat careful as it may be difficult to show conclusively that assumptions which lie between two extremes will produce results that in some relevant sense lie between the results of the extreme assumptions.

The Selection of Assumptions

IN CONSTRUCTING an economic theory, the logical sequence starts with the selection of a set of assumptions. In practice, of course, the basic assumptions or postulates are often added to or modified as indicated by the way the logical superstructure develops. But the initial foundation will strongly influence the way the superstructure develops, and it is indeed in the selection of these initial assumptions that much of the art of economic theory lies, as contrasted with the more determinate and mechanical procedure of erecting the logical consequences. For in the selection of initial assumptions one is faced with a dilemma. On the other hand, one can attempt to make quite realistic assumptions, only to find that no interesting corollaries can be deduced from them. One could, for example, postulate that business executives determine their actions by a compromise between the ethics or mores of their class, their past habits, and their own self-interest. But without more details being supplied, this is too vague to enable us to predict with any accuracy the behavior of such persons. And if one goes on to specify in detail the ethics, the past habits, and the nature of the entrepreneur's own interest, as well as the mechanism of compromise, the result is immediately too complicated to be manageable.

On the other hand, one can make assumptions that are extremely simple and tractable, and from which a long chain of interesting corollaries may be drawn. But often these assumptions differ so significantly from reality that the corollaries likewise fail to give much insight into the real world. For example, the classical quantity theory of money was based tacitly on the assumption that individuals would spend or invest their income as fast as they conveniently could, so that the velocity of circulation of money was virtually a constant. A system of theory based on such an assumption proved incapable of developing an adequate theoretical counterpart to the business cycles and depressions actually observed, and thus while the superstructure built on this assumption was logically sound, it failed to provide helpful insights into some of the important problems of the real world. A slightly more elaborate assumption, that cash holdings and the velocity of circulation would vary with the rates of interest obtainable, proved capable of supporting a more realistic superstructure, and after some difficulty found an important place in some of the variants of the Keynesian system.

The problem then is to select basic assumptions that will be at once tractable, in the sense of being easy to handle and capable of producing a substantial superstructure of logically deduced propositions, and sufficiently realistic so that the superstructure thus built up will have an illuminating resemblance to reality. The value of an economic theory will depend very heavily on the selection of assumptions that prove successful in approaching reality without too great a sacrifice of tractability.

The feat is the more difficult in that the "realism" of the assumptions is often not apparent in the assumptions themselves, but only becomes apparent after the superstructure has been built and compared with reality. Kelvin's concept of matter as built up of vortex rings in the ether proved fruitless as a means of approaching the real world; on the other hand, although the basic elements of Maxwell's electromagnetic interaction theory appeared to be merely mathematical abstractions that seemed at first even less "realistic," nevertheless out of them came Hertzian waves and radio. Similarly, in monetary theory, one might be hard put to determine, on the basis of immediate observation, whether a fixed velocity of circulation or a liquidity-preference theory would be more "realistic," in the relevant sense, but as the one did not, and the other did, provide a satisfactory model for depressions, one is inclined to return and ascribe some of the evident realism of the superstructure to a corresponding underlying realism in the foundation.

This imputation of realism to the underlying assumptions cannot, however, be taken too literally. One might argue, for example, that although the assumption that firms act to maximize profits by equating marginal cost and marginal revenue yields a reasonably good picture of over-all business behavior, this need not necessarily indicate that businessmen consciously consider either marginal cost or marginal revenue in making decisions. The "Darwinian" economist may argue that various business policies have survival value in proportion to the closeness of the behavior they produce to that predicted by the classical theory, so that in competition only those firms survive whose policies in fact produce a close approach to the theoretical behavior. We could thus observe results that agree very well with those predicted by the classical assumptions without these assumptions being themselves any very close reflection of the actual decision process, just as evolutionary developments may appear to have teleological origins, and may even be described, for the sake of brevity, in teleological language, even by those who reject completely any teleological concept of the evolutionary process itself.

On the other side of the problem, it is often difficult to foresee just how far one can go in making assumptions realistic without destroying their tractability. For this reason it is often convenient to start with more drastically unrealistic assumptions than is absolutely necessary, in order to be sure of having a satisfactory degree of tractability, without which one is blocked

[9

from the start. Then after the superstructure has been built, one can often go back and see to what extent the foundation can be modified in the direction of greater realism or greater generality without undercutting the superstructure. For example, one may start with a notion of competition that requires an infinitely large number of buyers and sellers in each market, but having built a theory on this foundation, it may be possible to go back and find that the theory will still hold if one assumes merely that buyers and sellers are numerous enough so that the influence of each upon the price is actually negligible. Or one may go further and stipulate merely that each buyer or seller thinks that his individual influence on the price is too small to be given any weight in determining his action; or even to specify merely that each acts as though his action would not influence the price, even though he may actually believe that it does. The analysis in this last case would then become applicable to a system of socialist managers instructed to follow a "rule" designed to simulate perfect competition.

Or again, in the analysis of monopoly, it is often convenient, for the sake of simplicity in the original investigation or exposition, to assume that the marginal cost of production is zero. Application of the results to cases where the marginal cost is not zero can then often be made merely by a shift of the axes so that the former origin of the diagram now falls at a point on the scale equal to the marginal cost. Thus one should not become impatient with a theoretical structure merely because the assumptions are unrealistic: if only the assumptions are sufficiently tractable to produce an interesting superstructure, ways may often be found to modify the assumptions so as to bring the results into a more illuminating relation to reality. It is indeed often necessary to start with oversimplified cases just to acquire the necessary skill in handling the type of problem being attacked.

Prescriptive Uses of Theory

ECONOMIC theory can also be useful in showing in what direction changes would be beneficial, even where it is not very successful in making predictions about the precise absolute outcome. In particular, the analysis of perfect competition may be used as a point of departure for devising a host of measures which might make the real world approach more closely this ideal. Unfortunately, this branch of theory has often been seriously misused as an apologia for the status quo, or for the promotion of a policy of laisser faire, in that the beneficial aspects' of the perfect competition model were ascribed to the real world of laisser faire without adequate attention to the very substantial differences that in fact separate a laisser faire system from the perfect competition of the economist. Far from being an apologia for the status quo, this part of economic theory can be made the basis for prescribing very definite and substantial interference with the free play of anarchic economic forces. Indeed, as a prescriptive theory, classical economics may be said to be the economics of socialism, in that it has a great deal to say, rightly or wrongly, about how a socialist regime ought to be run—even more, perhaps, than about how a capitalist regime actually operates; Marxist economics, on the other hand, can be said to be the economics of capitalism rather than socialism: it has a great deal to say, rightly or wrongly, about the workings and especially the development of capitalist regimes, but is of little or no help and may actually be misleading in the running of a socialist economy.

Finally, it may be noted that without the aid of some sort of economic theory to fall back on, even a community of complete altruists would probably fail to come to the most satisfactory arrangements. The complexities of the modern industrial community are such that no individual can trace the specific consequences of the various alternative courses of action open to him through all their repercussions. Nor would it be sufficient for each individual to attempt to act in the common interest subject to those economic institutions which happen to exist at the time. Rather it is necessary to find that set of economic institutions within which individuals can achieve the best results. Even if through some mass religious conversion or through the reforming influence of a utopian socialism the problem of incentives were swept away, it would still be necessary to provide some method by which individuals could determine what action would be in the general interest of the community, even though it might no longer be necessary to provide a specific incentive for them to act in the way indicated.

More realistically, while it may be possible to postulate some gradual improvement in the degree to which individuals can be persuaded to act in the common interest instead of or as well as in their own individual interests, and even to hope for an eventual far-reaching change in this direction, it appears likely that for the foreseeable future altruism will continue to be a scarce resource to be relied on as far as possible only where economic incentives alone cannot do the job. For the very large area where economic incentives can be made to work effectively, economic theory will still be important. Indeed, an appreciation of some of the simpler propositions of economic theory may well be essential if the individual is to determine the boundary line between the areas where he may pursue his own economic self-interest without detriment to the common welfare and those areas where he may be expected to draw upon his resources of altruism. As Sir Dennis Robertson puts it, it is the business of the economist to economize the "greatest thing in the world, love" [1.5].

PART II

Competitive Microeconomic Statics

CHAPTER TWO

Consumption

The Framework of Static Theory

A LARGE and fundamental part of economic theory falls into a broad category known as statics, or the economics of stationary states. In this branch of economics, we investigate the results that will obtain if an economic system is allowed to come to an equilibrium without being continuously subjected to changes. Here we are interested in the point toward which the economy at a given moment may be thought to be moving, often (too often, perhaps) without inquiring how rapidly the economy gets to that point, or indeed whether it ever does get anywhere near it.

There are several ways of setting up the basic assumptions upon which the static theory will be constructed. Perhaps the simplest is merely the assumption that everything keeps happening in the same way day after day: i.e., the same things get produced in the same way, and get consumed by the same people, or at least by people of the same characteristics.

This assumption is a very powerful one, for it implies immediately that if the situation is thus to continue, no individual must be left with any effective incentive to change his behavior. (The possibility that different persons might be under incentives to change their behavior in exactly opposite amounts and directions, so as to cancel out and in effect change places, may be ruled out as too improbable or as requiring persons in approximately the same positions and affected by the same influence to behave in opposite fashion.) For if a person has both opportunity and incentive to change his behavior, it may be assumed that he will do so and the situation changes contrary to the basic assumption.

It is immediately apparent that this assumption that the situation is stationary (or perhaps better, "steady") is rich in corollaries, and that in conjunction with other basic assumptions a fairly complete yet relatively simple structure can be erected on this basis. This goes far to explain why economists have devoted so much thought to the analysis of the "steady state" in spite of the fact that this basic assumption also has some other corollaries which imply fairly drastic restrictions upon the realism that can be achieved. For example, we must obviously have a constant supply of basic resources: if the supply of resources can be exhausted, the conditions of production will undergo a gradual change. While this change can be allowed for in subsequent

[15

modifications of the theory, in strictly static analysis such developments must be ruled out. Accordingly, in the strictly static economy there can be no mining or other extractive industries (although in the case of coal mining, quarrying, and industries such as the extraction of bromine from sea water, the rate of extraction relative to the total supply is so small that the nonstatic elements of the situation may be negligible). Similarly, technology must remain constant, and there can be no research or innovation.

The population must also remain constant. This need not necessarily mean that no change takes place in individuals, but that the age composition of the population, for example, remains the same; similarly, tastes at a given age must remain the same, though they may change for a given individual as he grows older. In such a stationary population the death rate at each age must be exactly equal to the decline in numbers between successive age groups at a given point in time. Accordingly, certain types of population patterns encountered in the real world are ruled out; for example, there cannot be more ten-year-old persons in the population than nine-year-olds, though in a dynamic population this could occur, as has happened in periods following wars and other catastrophes.

Finally, and perhaps most significant, the amount of capital available for use in production must remain constant. This does not necessarily mean that no wear and tear takes place (any more than that the individuals were required not to grow old), but rather that this wear and tear is made good, either by repairs or by replacement of worn-out equipment with new. Thus at any one time there will be in use equipment of varying ages, each unit getting older but the aggregate composition being the same, just as the population continues unchanged in the aggregate, although individuals change as they age.

It is sometimes claimed that this constant total capital implies a zero rate of interest, but further consideration indicates that this is not necessarily so. If it were, then one would be faced with the absurdity that an asset such as a piece of land which yields valuable services but does not depreciate would have an infinite price. Actually, there is no reason why the aggregate rate of net saving should not be zero at a positive rate of interest. One can indeed imagine that even under the incentive of a positive rate of interest individuals might dissave as much in their years of retirement as they saved in their period of maximum productivity, so that dissavings would balance the savings and the net be zero.

The above implications of the stationary state impose limitations on the scope of the theory, which will have to be removed later by considering the implications of deviations from the prescribed conditions. Another implication which also imposes a limitation but is at the same time a source of tractability is that uncertainty is absent. For with the same thing going on day after day, individuals eventually become aware of what is happening, and after all adjustments to such knowledge have taken place and the economy comes to a static condition, there will necessarily be absence of uncertainty on the part of individuals about such matters of current occurrence as concern them. This is not the same thing as perfect knowledge, however, in that nothing is said about knowledge of opportunities, or of things that might happen or be made to happen but do not in fact occur, except insofar as such knowledge is implicit in the knowledge of such things as market prices, which imply the ability of individuals to buy more or less of the various goods at those prices. Thus if further analysis depends on knowledge of such exotic potentialities, this must be made the subject of an additional express assumption.

Indeed, assumption of too perfect knowledge can easily lead to the collapse of the entire structure. For example, the knowledge that by combining together in certain ways monopolistic advantages could be secured might produce a breakdown of the competitive equilibrium, no matter how numerous the participants were. At the very least, the existence of such knowledge would open the door to a very wide range of possibilities among which it would be very hard to select the most reasonable outcome, as has been discovered in the development of the theory of games. Or perfect knowledge may destroy the identity of the firm, since in many cases that identity arises from a superior knowledge of some sort (if only of the special properties of certain physical assets) possessed by the entrepreneur or controlling group at the head of the firm.

Thus at this point economic analysis is subject to a rather disquieting paradox. Prediction of how a given system will operate often depends on the making of assumptions which, if strictly true, would dissolve the structure itself. The question may be compared to that of determining the derivative in calculus: the value of the derivative is approximated by the ratio of differences in an argument and in a function depending on it; theoretically, the differences should be made vanishingly small if the approximation is to be capable of any desired degree of accuracy, but they cannot be made zero without making the ratio indeterminate. The solution is to take as the derivative the limit of this ratio as the differences approach but do not reach zero. Similarly, one could regard the solutions reached in economic analysis as being the limits approached as the assumptions are approached but not perfectly realized. The logical difficulty here is that while in calculus the ratio of differences remains determinate and normally behaves quite regularly as the limit is approached, in the economic realm the breakdown may come with some suddenness substantially before the limit of perfect knowledge (or whatever the critical assumption is) is reached. At best, then, the approximations of economics will remain approximations with substantial margins of error, and not, as in calculus, "approximations" that can be considered as exact as we please. The situation can perhaps better be compared to that obtaining with certain "quasi-convergent" series, in mathematics, where after appearing to converge for a certain number of terms, the series, instead of continuing to converge to a limit, suddenly becomes divergent.

[17

It is important to distinguish here the absence of uncertainty in this restricted sense from the absence of risk. Risk is distinguished from uncertainty by the fact that the respective probabilities of the various outcomes are known to the one who is subject to risk, whereas uncertainty involves ignorance of at least some of these probabilities, and may even involve a lack of knowledge of some of the possible outcomes. Thus honest gambling on the toss of a coin or a throw of dice involves risk without uncertainty. The possibility of loss by fire is largely a matter of risk rather than uncertainty, though here there may be some uncertainty as to what effect various special features of a particular building have on the fire hazard, and for the individual, particularly in the nonstatic case, there may be uncertainty as to the rate of loss experienced with buildings of a given general type. Such elements as fire hazard may be admitted to the static state in that, though there may be fluctuations in the positions of individuals as a result of fires, when the aggregate economy is considered the number of fires during the year may be considered constant and the aggregate pattern of the economy may thus remain the same from year to year.

There are, of course, other approaches to static analysis. For some purposes it is sufficient to specify merely that one is studying states in which there are no unbalanced internal forces tending to produce change. Or again one may consider static analysis as the study of that state which the system will tend to approach provided no further shocks or disturbances impinge on it from outside. In some ways the study of comparative statics—i.e., the comparison of alternative static systems—may be described in terms of considering the administration of some specific disturbance to a system previously in static equilibrium, and comparing the original state with the state approached by the system subsequently, on the assumption that it is allowed to come to this equilibrium without further disturbance. However, it would seem more or less implicit in the idea of thus reaching an equilibrium that sources of continuing change should be eliminated or neglected.

Another alternative notion of statics is to consider it the study of what would happen if various types of adjustments could be made instantaneously instead of requiring more or less time, and if the effects of the movements involved in this adjustment process could be ignored. The notion of instantaneous adjustment is at best unreal, however, so that following this line is very likely to lead to some rather uncomfortable paradoxes. It can be modified, however, by assuming that the time required for adjustment is small compared with the time interval between disturbances to the system, so that there is actually time for an equilibrium to be reached, or at least approached reasonably closely, before the system is again disturbed.

The much-used distinction between short-run and long-run equilibrium is related fairly closely to this latter approach to statics. Formally, the distinction between the two can be expressed in terms of assuming for the short-run equilibrium that certain specified elements are not free to adapt themselves, while for the long-run equilibrium these factors are adaptable. One may indeed have several types of "short-run" equilibrium, depending on which factors or elements in the situation are assumed to be fixed. Moreover, in the pure logic of the structure the difference is not a matter of time period at all, but merely of the fixity or variability of the various elements. Even where the difference is expressed in terms of a time period the relevant lapse of time is often not that between the occurrence of the disturbance and the consequent adjustment, but rather between knowledge of the disturbance and the adjustment. What may appear to be a prompt reaction to a disturbance may have in fact involved considerable anticipation of the disturbance and advance planning. The planning of changes, however, lies somewhat outside the usual scope of static analysis.

To a considerable extent the selection of an approach to the assumptions of statics is a matter of taste. The essential is that we somehow derive the condition that no individual be under any effective incentive to change his behavior. This is the condition upon which the superstructure depends, and provided that this condition is justified in some adequate way, the rest will follow.

The Simple Catallactic System

HAVING established the static assumptions under which we are for the time being to operate, we can now set up a system under these assumptions and see how it works. The simplest model that it is possible to set up and yet that will exhibit some of the significant characteristics of an economic system is one consisting merely of exchange and consumption.

In this pure exchange model we will not be concerned with production. That is, we will assume either that flows of commodities and services arise automatically and become subject to the control of various individuals in fixed and unchangeable amounts, or that the production of each individual or group is fixed and determined by immutable custom or the overwhelming force of circumstance. This assumption will then later be modified to admit of changes in production patterns, but for the time being we will consider production as fixed. The problem is to discover how this fixed flow of goods and services might be redistributed among the members of the community by exchange. This can be done either from a "positive" standpoint, by postulating in sufficient detail the characteristics of the exchange process, presumably in a way that bears some resemblance to the real world, and studying the logical consequences; or it can be done from a normative point of view, by attempting to determine what types of exchange patterns are "good" by some standard of evaluation, and attempting to define institutional arrangements that would tend to bring such patterns about. In either case, we expect that

[19

the eventual consumption patterns of individuals arrived at through the exchange process will in some way be more in line with their respective needs than was the original pattern.

Very often the study of economic theory begins with the study of production; this does have certain advantages, since in some respects the theory of production is less abstruse than the theory of consumption. However, in the absence of a theory of consumption, a study of production would lack objectives. While one could assume some system of market prices for which production is undertaken, this would be an incomplete model as there would be no indication of what lies behind the assumed prices. Or one could take some fixed set of consumption requirements, but again unless the supply of such factors as labor is to be brought in, which in turn would involve the negative aspects of consumption (i.e., labor can be considered as the giving up of leisure), there would be nothing to economize. The pure exchange model, though highly restricted, contains within itself its own motivation and rationale.

Homo Oeconomicus: The Household

THE ACTING units in this world of exchange and consumption are variously termed "consumers," "individuals," "households," or "economic men." From the point of view of theory, what is assumed of these units is that they buy, sell, and consume in accordance with their own preferences, without direct regard for the desires of others. In the real world there is nothing that corresponds exactly to this theoretical concept, although perhaps in the case of some unattached single individuals who happen to lack even a minimum of normal consideration for others, the approximation is fairly close. Such individuals are more likely to be rather dubious members of the community than typical or useful citizens. Usually, however, there will be found significant areas within which even average citizens will feel free to consult only their own self-interest in the making of choices, so that within this area the "economic man" may be considered a reasonably close approximation. More serious a difficulty is the fact that most individuals form parts of households or families, but provided that these households act for economic purposes as a harmonious unit, they may also be considered a reasonably close counterpart of the economic unit of theory.

Whether the economic unit is a single individual or a more or less cohesive group, our economic theory will assume for the time being at least that there is some valid and worthwhile objective which the behavior of the unit is intended to secure and in terms of which this behavior can be rationalized. By this we mean that the unit is capable of judging which of the alternatives open to it will come closest to achieving this objective, and that the unit will actually behave as indicated by such a judgment. Among other things, this implies that one should never find a unit choosing alternative A when B was available, while on other comparable occasions choosing B when C was available and C when A was available. In general, the larger the group that is being considered as an economic unit or "household," the more likely it is that the opposition of interests within it will lead to such "intransitive" choice patterns.

We will call the degree to which a unit achieves its objectives the "satisfaction" or "utility" of this unit. For the sake of tractability, we will consider that this utility or satisfaction is determined as soon as we specify certain economic parameters relating to this unit, and for present purposes these parameters will consist of the amounts of the various commodities and services consumed per unit of time. Each unit is assumed to know what degree of satisfaction will be derivable from various flows of consumption goods in all the possible combinations that might be relevant at any given time.

One need not actually exclude stocks entirely from the discussion, but they enter the consumption patterns only insofar as they are conceived to provide a flow of services of some sort. Thus the use of a house may provide satisfactions, but it is the flow of "uses" of the house—the counterpart of the rent paid by a tenant—that is to be considered and not the value of the house itself. Indeed, for present purposes it makes no difference whether the consumer owns the house outright and enjoys its services as imputed income or pays rent explicitly to a landlord for the use of the house over a period of time.

Given that the unit knows the results for itself of the various consumption combinations, it is assumed to choose that combination among those available to it that gives the greatest satisfaction. Objectively, one can observe that in fact individual units will make certain choices, but as there is no objective measure of satisfaction available, how much content is read into the proposition that choice is made in such a way as to maximize satisfaction is to a large extent a matter of taste. An extreme operationalist might simply define satisfaction, or "utility," as that quantity which is maximized by the individual choices (assuming that the choices are sufficiently consistent to admit of such an explanation in terms of the maximizing of such a "potential"), in somewhat the same way that one could define "height" or "gravitational potential" as that which is minimized by a body allowed to move under the influence of gravity. At the other extreme, one can adopt an individualistic point of view and consider that the individual (or the head of the household, or the deciding voice in whatever unit is being considered) is the final judge of what is good insofar as his own interests and experiences (or those of his unit) are concerned, and consider that these individual judgments provide the only basis for judging the performance of the economy as a whole. In general, there is a strong tendency for economists belonging to the democratic and individualistic tradition of Western countries to adopt this maxim that each individual

[21

is the best judge of his own welfare, if not as an inviolable principle, at least as a working first approximation. Some indeed go even further than this and assert that no one else can possibly know anything about the feelings of satisfaction experienced by others, and that, accordingly, interpersonal comparisons of satisfaction are inadmissible. Or in a less extreme form, interpersonal comparisons are considered to involve more uncertainty and to provide greater room for differences of opinions and individual bias than comparisons of situations experienced, successively or hypothetically, by a single individual or "unit."

Attractive as the simplicity of the extreme individualistic interpretation is, many qualifications must at least be kept in mind, even though one may not wish to insert them explicitly into the theoretical structure for fear of making it overcomplicated and intractable. To begin with, one is faced with the fact that within the household interpersonal comparisons are in fact made and given effect. For example, few would assert that the children in a family should be permitted to exercise their own choices freely among available alternatives; the choices as to what the family will eat are in practice made predominantly by the wife; other choices may be made more or less in consultation with a considerable amount of interpersonal evaluation. The difference between the head of the family making decisions as to the consumption of the entire family, or decisions in particular areas being made by one member for the whole, and a commissar making decisions as to what the entire population of a district shall consume may be great and even revolutionary, but in principle it is merely a difference of degree. In various civilizations at various times different persons—patriarch, chief, squire, prince, mayor, or president— have taken it upon themselves to make decisions on behalf of their constituency in ways that do implicitly involve the making of interpersonal comparisons. And in fact it is not possible to imagine a society, no matter how individualistic its philosophy, where there are not at least some decisions that have to be made on a collective basis in a manner that will involve interpersonal comparisons.

Again, even on a completely individualistic basis, "households" must make decisions involving comparisons between future and present satisfactions: the classical theory of interest depends on such comparisons. Such comparisons have frequently been questioned by economists and others on the ground that future satisfactions may be less vivid and therefore may be subjected to some sort of discount by reason of the long perspective in which they are viewed. Some have even argued that the discount operates in both directions and that past satisfactions are likewise discounted, though it is not clear just what practical conclusions would follow from such a proposition. More important here is the fact that a household does not permanently retain the same identity and composition, and that to compare satisfactions in the "same" household at different times may in fact be comparing the satisfactions of more or less different units. There can even be a question as to how far a single person is the "same" person at different times. And of course the decisions of individuals often involve questions of how much of a heritage is to be left for the succeeding generation, a decision that will often involve comparisons between satisfactions obtained by persons in different generations.

All of this would indicate that to eschew interpersonal comparisons absolutely is to limit unduly the scope of economic theory as a normative discipline, even though for descriptive and predictive purposes indulgence in interpersonal comparisons by economists *qua* economists may be irrelevant. Yet since interpersonal comparisons will usually involve a much greater degree of subjective variation according to the person doing the comparing, it is still entirely proper to treat propositions not involving such comparisons as having a higher order of objectivity, if not a higher order of validity.

Yet even where interpersonal comparisons are unnecessary, there are grounds for questioning the proposition that the choice of the individual is the final arbiter of value. At the very least, phenomena are observed that are somewhat difficult to reconcile with an absolute principle of "consumer sovereignty." For example, much consumption is not determined as a result of deliberate choice, but is more nearly the result of using conventional patterns of behavior. To some extent this represents nothing more than a rational decision to economize in the effort of choosing, being willing to go along with the established pattern on the assumption that whatever deviation it may involve from what would have been selected on the basis of more deliberate and strictly individual choice will produce less loss of satisfaction than that involved in making the effort to choose independently. Of course, not all choosing is irksome: deliberate shopping around is a source of satisfaction in itself to many, while others put a value on the mere existence of open alternatives, even though their actual selection may be of an item identical to what would have been available had the wider range of choice not been offered. On the other hand, there is often a sort of social tyranny involved in which an established pattern of behavior or consumption is adhered to because of the penalties of one sort or another attached to nonconformity. Or consumption may become competitive in nature, involving "keeping up with the Joneses." In some contexts this phenomenon can be dealt with by treating it as a sort of external diseconomy of consumption whereby added consumption by one person adversely affects the level of satisfaction achieved by others, but often the phenomenon is more complicated than this.

Again, the picture of the individual or household as having unchanging tastes (i.e., not necessarily unchanging consumption requirements through time, but rather unchanging ideas about what the consumption requirements will be at a given future point in time) fails to allow for the fact that tastes obviously do change. Changes may be of a purely accidental and random

[23

character, as when one tires of one item and shifts to another, or discovers something new; they may be consciously developed by the consumer himself, as when learning to play golf, or becoming a connoisseur of this or that, or studying literature. Or more disturbing to the theorist, the consumer may have his tastes distorted or at least influenced by advertising and other wiles of those having an interest in increasing the sales of some commodity. Whatever the source of such changes in taste, one is immediately faced with the problem of deciding with respect to which set of tastes shall the relative desirability of two "baskets" of consumption goods be appraised? One basket may be preferred from the point of view of one set of tastes, but from the point of view of another equally valid set of tastes, the second basket may be preferred. Tastes may depend on the current consumption experience or on the past consumption history of the individual. It will not do simply to take the more recent set of tastes as the more valid one: consider the case of the man who becomes an alcoholic. This problem seems insoluble on an a priori basis, and indeed most economists have simply ignored it, as we shall also, except for this brief mention.

Another qualification to be kept in mind is that individuals do not have complete knowledge of the results to be expected from various types of consumption, as is evidenced in particular cases by the fact that consumers turn to doctors, teachers, architects, and others to secure advice as to what to consume. Indeed, the purchase of this sort of advice is in itself a transaction that fits very awkwardly into the theoretical scheme, for by hypothesis the consumer cannot know with any precision how much good the advice he is about to get will do him, and in some cases will not know how good the advice was even after it has been followed and the results observed.

Again, some values can be achieved only collectively and where individual deviation from the norm cannot be (or at least is not) permitted. Thus a certain minimum amount of clothing may be prescribed for all, as is also a certain minimum amount of education, with some exceptions. In such broad and widely approved standards there may be no serious problem, but where the decisions to be made on an over-all basis become numerous, the degree of unanimity diminishes, and there may be a tendency to substitute the values of the planner or administrator for those of the people whose pattern of life is being determined. Where the values of the planner are individualistic, this may merely mean the substitution of an expert appraisal of the results of an action combined with imperfect evaluation of the satisfaction derived by individuals from the more definitely predicted results ("you'll like it when you see how it works out") for relatively ignorant forecasting of the results coupled with a closer experience of them ("it wasn't quite what I expected, but I liked it just as well"). But where the planner becomes enamored of his schemes for their own sake, there may be a substitution away from individual values entirely and in the direction of centering values in the social organization such as finds its extreme expression in various forms of totalitarianism.

But one need not go to the extreme of totalitarianism in the search for social values: such values can be related to individual preferences in the sense that individuals as such would attach a value to the results of action designed to achieve social values. There are values attached to living in a community in which income is not too unevenly distributed, even apart from the better utilization of that income through its being more evenly distributed. Values may be attached to the presence or absence of various social patterns. Individuals who might not dare individually to decline to wear formal dress might consider the abolition of such a fashion as a great boon. The practice of tipping is another example of an economic arrangement that is very hard to modify by individual choice. In some instances, such phenomena may be dealt with under the general heading of external economies and diseconomies of consumption, and yet it is not possible to rule out such social values out of hand or even to consider them adequately as merely "neighborhood effects."

Nor is it possible, even if we take such a small unit as the household, to ignore completely the possibility of a conflict of interests within the unit. Divorce statistics indicate that in some instances at least the household is not the harmonious unit that the theory would require, and the records of child-welfare agencies bear this out from another direction. Specific legislation on child welfare and school feeding programs testify to a reluctance on the part of the community to leave the welfare of children entirely in the hands of the head of the household.

An even more disturbing difficulty with the notion of economic behavior as determined so as to maximize satisfaction is the possibility that the consumption pattern may not itself be the source of satisfaction so much as the striving toward it. If economic behavior be viewed as a sort of game, then a too easy achievement of the nominal goal of maximum satisfaction might itself prove unsatisfactory. Complete satiation with economic goods may prove to be completely boring, as is a game that proves too easy to be interesting. If the game of golf could be completely described as the driving of a ball into 18 cups in succession, there would be no explanation for the fact that great expense is often devoted to the preparation of bunkers. The nominal goal may become unimportant and the method of reaching it the important thing.

Yet while it may be necessary to pay attention to the means as well as to the nominal end, there are dangers in turn in the substitution of means for ends. If we consider consumption as the nominal end and the acquisition of money the means of attaining that end, to convert the acquisition of money into an end in itself is dangerous for the individual and the economist alike. For individuals it leads to the "money illusion" and a false sense of security in periods of inflation, an unwarranted panic in periods of depression, and a

[25

degree of deception about all transactions involving the future; the economist is usually more wary, but he too often gets trapped in dangerous over-simplifications. Again, in an economy in which there is production, work may for many be a prerequisite to consumption and thus a means to a desirable end. To a considerable extent, also, productive work can be a source of satisfaction in itself and thus become both means and end. But to lose sight of the ultimate end of consumption and to convert the provision of work of any sort into an end in and of itself regardless of its productivity is to pervert this phenomenon: the kinds of work provided by "make-work" policies, whether of monopolistic unions or of public-works authorities, are seldom such as to provide much real satisfaction in the mere performance.

For the present, however, the dangers of satiation on any grand scale seem to be sufficiently remote so that it is not too far from the mark to consider consumption as the final goal and to permit the economist to assume without further investigation that for the present at least and for the great bulk of the population of the world he does not have to worry very much about supplying additional obstacles in order to make the game of economic life interesting to the participants. He should nevertheless realize that for some fortunate individuals, many of them very strategically placed, the patterns of behavior to be expected may differ somewhat from those predicted on the basis of the usual economic assumptions. However, the theorist is fortunate to some extent in that while some individuals may have passed the point at which the increase in their own standard of living is of much importance to them, nevertheless the rules of the economic game have by habit and tradition become so much a part of the established standards that the acquisition of wealth has frequently enough remained an objective as a symbol of success at the game long after it ceased to be a means to the end of increased consumption.

These are some of the many points at which our theory will necessarily depart from reality because of the inherent oversimplification of our assumptions in the interests of tractability. Having noted them, we now turn to see what kind of an abstract structure can be built from our assumptions.

The Analysis of Consumers' Preferences

WE CAN START by restating our basic assumptions as follows: We assume that each individual would be able to tell us, if we describe any two alternative situations to him, whether he prefers the one or the other or considers them both equally satisfactory. We also assume that these potential choices are consistent; by this we mean not only that the same answer would always be given to the same question, but that if A is preferred to B, and B is preferred to C, then A must necessarily be preferred to C, and similarly, if A and B are equally satisfactory, and B and C are likewise equally satisfactory, then A

and C must be equally satisfactory. This is sometimes described by saying that the relations "is preferred to" and "is as satisfactory as" are transitive. For the sake of tractability we further assume that each of the situations to be compared may be completely described by assigning numerical values to a certain number of parameters; in economic discussions these parameters will be the amounts of various goods and services consumed per unit of time, and possibly the amounts of various services performed for others per unit of time.

In principle, there will be as many of these parameters as there are goods and services involved in the economic life of this individual. But to permit the use of diagrams drawn on a two-dimensional surface, we must restrict our attention largely to two of these parameters at a time. Once we have become familiar with the two-commodity case, we will find it easier to grasp the more general cases. For the time being, then, we may consider either that the two commodities to which our two parameters relate are the only ones in existence, thus assuming a drastically oversimplified sort of economy or, alternatively, that we are going to vary only these two parameters while keeping all others constant. In either case, we can construct a diagram, as in FIGURE I, where

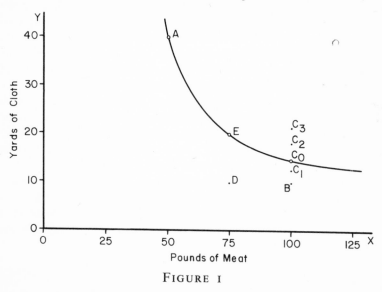

FIGURE I

the abscissa, or distance along the horizontal x axis, represents the consumption of commodity x, say pounds of meat per year, and the ordinate, or distance along the vertical y axis, represents the consumption of commodity y, say square yards of cloth per year. Thus the point A in FIGURE I would represent the consumption of 50 pounds of meat and 40 yards of cloth per year.

Similarly, the point B might represent an annual consumption of 100

[27

pounds of meat and 10 yards of cloth. We assume that our consumer is able to tell us whether he prefers A or B, or considers them both equally satisfactory. Let us suppose that A is preferred to B. Then we can select a point C_1 just a little above B, with the same amount of meat and just a little more cloth— 12 yards, say. We will assume that if one of two baskets has a little more of one commodity and the same amount of all other commodities as the other basket, then the consumer will always choose the one with more. In this case, the first basket will be said to "dominate" the second. In effect, this is not so much an assumption as a definition of an economic good, for if we were to find that the basket with less of the good was selected, we would consider this commodity a nuisance or a "discommodity." Thus economic goods can be defined as those of which a little more makes the consumer better off. Accordingly, C_1 will be preferred to B. C_1 may or may not be preferred to A. If C_1 is still not preferred to A we can add a little more cloth to the combination, until we find a point C_2 which is preferred to A. By further exploration we can determine a point C_0 such that all points above it are preferred to A, and A is preferred to all points below it. As between this point C_0 and A, we say that the consumer is indifferent; the addition of any slight amount of any commodity to either basket would tilt the balance in its favor.

Similarly, starting from, say, 75 pounds of meat and 10 yards of cloth at D, and adding a little more cloth at a time, we can find another point E, corresponding to, say, 75 pounds of meat and 20 yards of cloth, which will also give the same satisfaction as A. Or perhaps we could consider asking directly, "How much cloth would you have to have in combination with 75 pounds of meat to make you feel just as well off as at A?" Similarly, for each quantity of meat, within a reasonable range, an amount of cloth could be found which would bring the total satisfaction to the same level as at A, and a corresponding point on the diagram determined. If we then draw a line through all of these points, this will be the boundary such that all points above it are preferred to A, and A is preferred to all points below it. Ordinarily we think of the consumer as being indifferent as to which one of all the combinations lying on this curve he is provided with, and, accordingly, this curve is called an indifference curve.

This notion of the indifference curve as a definite line is sometimes objected to on the ground that the consumer is not, in practice, always able to pick out a single point C_0 as the point that gives the same satisfaction as A, but may have a whole range of points, say from C_1 to C_2, for which he is unable to tell consistently whether he is better or worse off than at A. This is no reason for abandoning the concept, however, any more than the fact that all approximations to a straight line are imperfect would be reason for abandoning Euclidean geometry, or the fact that it may not be possible to ascertain the relative weight or hardness of two very similar objects would be reason to reject these concepts in physics or engineering. All that is implied by this range of uncertainty is that our results will themselves involve a certain range of uncertainty or of unpredictable variation. For the time being, we merely assume for the sake of simplicity that whether because we normally take the sum of a large number of individual actions or for some other reason, this range of uncertainty can be neglected. Indeed, in a purely formal sense, such a range of uncertainty would be inconsistent with the assumption of transitivity, since if C_1 and C_2 are each equally satisfactory with A, they must be equally satisfactory with each other, which contradicts the assumption that cloth remains an economic good and that therefore C_2 must be preferred to C_1.

A more subtle objection is that it is conceivable that an individual might consistently always express a preference one way or the other between any two alternatives, so that it would not be correct to say that an individual is indifferent as between any two points on an indifference curve. Given that the system of preferences is transitive and that if a basket A dominates another basket B, B is never preferred to A, however, it will always be possible to construct a boundary, as above, such that all points above it are preferred to and all points below it are inferior to a given point, and as this boundary will have all the properties we need, it will still be referred to as an indifference curve even though it is not necessarily implied that an individual is strictly indifferent as between any two points on the curve. And in any case this objection depends on a degree of mathematical exactness quite out of line with the necessary imprecision of an actual application.

In a similar way, by starting with another reference point F not on this first indifference curve, one can construct another indifference curve through F. This indifference curve cannot intersect the first, otherwise the transitivity condition would be violated. Continuing in this way, one can construct a whole series of nonintersecting indifference curves for the given individual, which taken together will constitute his indifference map, which may look something like that shown in FIGURE 2.

Such an indifference map is somewhat similar in appearance to the familiar contour map used to depict the topography of a region, with the exception that it is ordinarily much more regular in general appearance than a topographic contour map, or at least than one representing a section of fairly uneven terrain. There is one very important difference in kind, however, and that is that while on the topographic map the contours are taken to represent definite heights above sea level, and are ordinarily labeled accordingly, on the indifference map nothing is said about the "height" of each of the curves, or about any measure of the intensity of satisfaction that each of them represents. All that we know about the "height" of the indifference curves is their ranking; i.e., we are able to tell which of two indifference curves is the higher one, but not *how much* higher it is.

[29

One can think of an indifference map as a contour map of a "utility surface" or "hill of satisfaction" (Vilfredo Pareto's "colline de plaisir") in which the height of a point on the surface above the base plane ("sea level") is an index

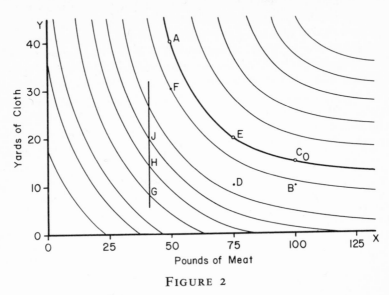

FIGURE 2

of the degree of satisfaction derived from the consumption pattern indicated by the "latitude" and "longitude" of the point. The consumer may then be considered to be striving to reach the highest point possible on this utility

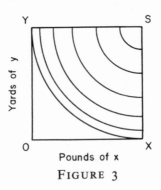

FIGURE 3

surface. However, the hill of satisfaction or utility surface corresponding to a given indifference map may have any of a number of different shapes and still conform to all of the information contained in the indifference map. For example, if, as in FIGURE 3, we take for simplicity an indifference map composed of indifference curves that are arcs of concentric circles, the

30]

corresponding utility surface might have any of the shapes shown in FIGURE 4: part of the surface of a cone, as in 4a; part of the surface of a sphere, as in 4b; part of the surface of a paraboloid of revolution, as in 4c; or part of a trumpet bell, as in 4d. In fact, in this case any of a wide variety of "surfaces of revolution" would furnish a utility surface that could correspond to the indifference map of FIGURE 3. Actually, one is more inclined to think of the utility surface as like the shapes shown in FIGURE 4b or 4c, rather than those in 4a or 4d, since in the former two cases successive additional units of either commodity always produce progressively smaller increases in height or utility; this is in accordance with notions of "diminishing marginal utility" that we derive from more or less introspective and intuitive considerations. But on the basis of the objective behavior of consumers in choosing between alternatives that are certain, there is no way of determining which of these

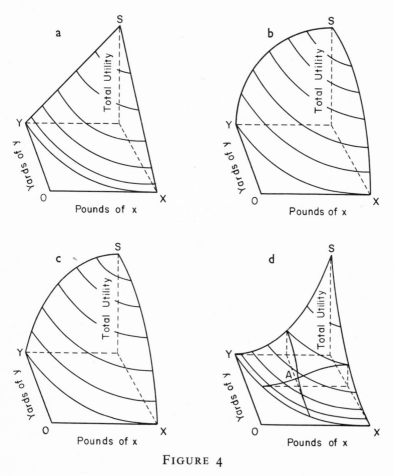

FIGURE 4

surfaces is more nearly correct: the consumer attempting to reach the highest point on his indifference map will select exactly the same combination of goods if he is acting on the basis of one of the surfaces of FIGURE 4 as he would on the basis of any other. As we shall see later, it is only when some of the choices involve risk that there is any need to distinguish between the different possible utility surfaces. And since risk brings with it a host of added complexities, we will postpone its consideration for the time being. As long as we are excluding alternatives that involve risk, it will be sufficient to leave undetermined the exact shape of the utility surface. This is in accordance with the general logical principle known as Occam's razor, or rule of parsimony, which cautions against the introduction of extra assumptions or concepts where they are not needed.[1]

Since we can thus predict the behavior of the consumer under riskless conditions from the indifference curves alone, without specifying their height, it follows that the information we can get from studying such consumer behavior is all contained in the indifference map. Thus no experiment under riskless conditions could give us any information not contained in the indifference map, and in particular no experiment not involving risk will enable us to determine the specific shape of the utility surface. This is sometimes expressed by saying that utility can be determined ordinally but not cardinally.

In practice, we find that even though utility cannot be cardinally defined, and, accordingly, marginal utility, which is the increment of utility associated with a small-unit increment in the consumption of some commodity, is dependent on the arbitrary selection of a particular utility surface, it is often much easier to talk about relations in terms of utility and marginal utility than in the more cumbersome and sometimes ambiguous language of indifference curves. (Indeed, to the distress of the student, different writers have often defined terms associated with indifference curves in diametrically opposite fashion.) In a certain class of cases, however, the marginal-utility language can be used without implying any knowledge not found in the indifference map. In particular, it is always safe to talk about the ratio between the marginal utilities of two goods for a given consumer at a given point on his indifference map, or at different points on the same indifference curve.

For example, in FIGURE 5 we have a very much magnified representation of a small portion of the indifference map, with one indifference curve passing through A and a second indifference curve just a little higher than the first. From A it will then take an additional AB of commodity x to increase the level of satisfaction from that of indifference curve U^1 to that of curve U^2. If we call the difference in utility between the two curves, whatever it may be considered to be, ΔU, then the marginal utility of x will be the change in

1. William of Occam was a fourteenth-century philosopher and theologian who fought against the elaborate multiplication of concepts practiced by his contemporaries.

utility divided by the change in the quantity of x, or $\Delta U/AB$ (strictly, the limit approached by the ratio $\Delta U/AB$ as we take indifference curves U^2 successively closer to U^1 so that both ΔU and AB approach zero). Similarly, the marginal utility of y would be $\Delta U/AC$. Accordingly, the ratio of the marginal utility of x to that of y will be

$$\frac{U_x}{U_y} = \frac{\dfrac{\Delta U}{AB}}{\dfrac{\Delta U}{AC}} = \frac{AC}{AB}$$

so that the ratio of the marginal utilities is independent of the value assigned to the difference in utility ΔU between the two indifference curves, and can be

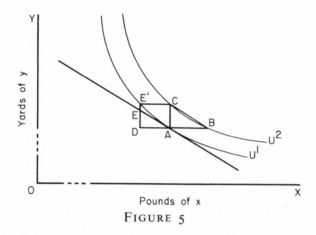

FIGURE 5

determined from the indifference map itself. In fact, this ratio is nothing more than the slope of the line CB. If we select the two indifference curves closer and closer together, the slope of the line CB approaches the slope of the indifference curve at A, and corresponds to the marginal rate of substitution of y for x, which can be defined as the ratio of the amount of y which would be required to bring an individual back to the original level of satisfaction after the loss of a given small quantity of x, to the quantity of x lost. Thus starting from point B, the loss of AB of x would require the addition of AC of y to bring the individual back to U^2, and the ratio AC/AB is the marginal rate of substitution of y for x. In a similar fashion, ratios of marginal utilities for different points on the same indifference curve may be deduced from the indifference map.

Thus in many cases it is possible to arrive at the same results by either the utility approach or the indifference approach. The indifference approach, however, seems for many purposes to possess sufficient advantages to justify

[33

keeping to the slightly more cumbersome form. In the first place, it helps to safeguard against expressing postulates and definitions in terms that are not objectively verifiable or are not conceptually operational. Even Pareto, who was one of the first economists to use indifference curves extensively, allowed the older habits of thinking in terms of a measurable utility to lead him into errors of this sort, as in his definitions of complementarity and substitution. More important, indifference curves present a clearer picture of the relation between two commodities than is readily possible by analyzing solely in terms of utility, and permit a clearer analysis of consumer reactions to changes in incomes and prices. Nevertheless, it will often be convenient to speak in terms involving utility, as in speaking of relative marginal utility rather than in terms of marginal rates of substitution, in order to avoid complicated and confusing expressions that are more easily misinterpreted.

We have developed our theory of indifference curves in terms of only two commodities, and for most purposes we will have to be satisfied with such two-commodity maps for the simple reason that the surface of a sheet of paper has only two dimensions. But there is no reason in principle why the concept of an "indifference locus" should not be extended to any number of commodities. One can in fact visualize indifference surfaces involving three commodities in three dimensions, looking something like a nest of bowls tilted against a corner of a cupboard, the amounts of the three commodities being represented by the distances from a given point to the two walls and the floor, the points on the inmost bowl representing a higher level of satisfaction than those on the outer bowls. Or another picture might be the successive layers of an onion, the tenderest part of the onion appropriately representing the highest level of satisfaction. For four commodities we would need four-dimensional space for a concrete representation of the indifference loci; although we would not be able to construct a physical model of such a concept, there is no particular difficulty in handling this concept analytically, nor indeed of the indifference loci in n-dimensional space which would be involved in the analysis of choice among n commodities. Fortunately, most of the interesting phenomena can be illustrated in two dimensions, and even as many as three dimensions are required only in the case of one or two fairly abstruse relationships.[2]

If for the moment, however, we limit ourselves to two dimensions for the sake of simplicity, it becomes desirable to examine in some detail the various

2. Mathematically, the case of n commodities is treated by considering a utility function $U(q_1, q_2, q_3, \ldots q_n)$, and the indifference loci will then be obtained by putting $U = k$, a different locus being obtained for each value of k. The ordinal nature of utility is given effect by requiring that all propositions established with respect to U shall also be true for any other utility function $V = F(U)$, provided that $F(U)$ is a monotonically increasing function, i.e., a function such that increasing U always produces an increase in V (for example, $V = U^3$; $V = \log U$). Such propositions are then said to be invariant under monotonic transformations of U. In particular, propositions involving the ratios between marginal utilities at given levels of utility will be invariant under such transformations.

ways in which such a two-dimensional oversimplification might be interpreted. The possibility already mentioned of assuming that there are only two economically significant commodities in existence is logically unexceptionable, but it may involve an unnecessarily great sacrifice of realism. The other previously mentioned method of considering that the consumption of all but two commodities is frozen at a fixed level can be seen to be equivalent to taking a two-dimensional cross section of a multi-dimensional set of indifference loci. For example, if altogether there were three commodities, keeping one of them constant and plotting the indifference curves between the other two would be equivalent to looking at only one slice of the three-dimensional onion and considering only movements within this slice.

There are, however, other more significant ways of reducing a problem to two dimensions. We can, for example, measure along either or both axes whole categories of consumption rather than particular strictly defined commodities. A completely general and strict analysis, indeed, would require us to consider every good for which a separate price can be quoted as a separate commodity, and to provide a distinct axis along which its quantity can be measured; in other words, in principle a commodity must be defined strictly enough so that a price can be quoted for it. But at the cost of some loss of precision or alternatively of making some further assumptions about prices, it is possible to combine groups of commodities into an aggregate or index of quantity, so that instead of having to talk about pounds of a particular cut and quality of meat we can talk about dollars' worth of meat evaluated at some selected fixed set of prices, and similarly instead of restricting our discussion to yards of cloth of a particular kind we can talk about an aggregate quantity of fabric, also measured by some sort of index. Similarly, variations in the relative prices of meat and fabric will be expressed by some sort of relative price index. As will be seen later in the discussion of index numbers, the use of index numbers will in general involve some loss of accuracy. If, however, we can stipulate that the relative prices within each commodity group remain unchanged (for example, percale always costs 50 per cent more than muslin), then the analysis will still be exact subject to this restriction. One can imagine, in effect, that all varieties of meat are sold for some special currency, say "simoleons," at fixed prices, while all varieties of cloth are sold similarly at fixed prices but for "mazuma." A given combination of mazuma and simoleons will then be capable of producing a well-defined level of satisfaction for an individual, and we can thus construct an indifference map between "mazuma" and "simoleons" which will become the measures of cloth and meat, respectively, with changes in the relative price of meat and cloth reflected in changes in the rate of exchange between mazuma and simoleons. We do in fact find that within some categories of commodities there is a tendency for prices to remain in nearly the same proportions, so that assumptions of this sort may be fairly closely

[35

approximated in the real world. To the extent that these assumptions are not fulfilled, some loss of accuracy will result.

One particular type of such aggregation deserves special mention: it is often convenient to take one more or less strictly defined commodity on the x axis, and on the y axis a composite of all other commodities represented by the amount of money spent on these other commodities at prices that are assumed to remain fixed. This constancy of all other prices then becomes the essential *ceteris paribus*[3] of such an analysis.

In any case, the two-dimensional diagrams are used to a considerable extent as illustrative of the principles applicable to the more general n-dimensional cases, and the fact that no two-dimensional diagram can completely represent a situation is not a serious limitation for purposes of developing the simpler basic concepts.

Characteristics of Indifference Maps

BEFORE continuing with the analysis proper, it is worthwhile to examine some of the properties of indifference maps, and observe how different relationships between commodities can be reflected in such maps. To begin with, it is ordinarily assumed that the commodities depicted on the indifference map are perfectly divisible, so that we can have smooth indifference curves rather than a scattering of discrete points or curves that jump from one number of units to the next. Actually, this assumption does not involve such a drastic departure from reality as might seem at first glance: even though one would never purchase half a shirt or a third of a pair of shoes, if we remember that we are concerned with a flow of consumption over time, there can be a continuous gradation between purchasing a pair of shoes on the average every eight months and purchasing a pair on the average every six months, even without considering the possibility of relaxing the strictness of the definition of the commodity and including in the general category "shoes" shoes of varying quality. In any case, allowing for discontinuities in an indifference map would in general make the analysis more tedious and complicated without in most cases introducing any significantly new principles.

We further note that in the significant region of the indifference map where both commodities are goods rather than discommodities or nuisances, the curves have a negative slope: i.e., as the quantity of x increases along an indifference curve the quantity of y decreases. This is obviously an immediate corollary of the assumption that both goods are economic goods and hence an increment of either or both of them must make the consumer better off. However, it is possible to depict on the same indifference map situations where the consumer is satiated with one or both of the commodities: i.e., situations

3. "Other things being equal."

where giving the consumer additional amounts of a commodity will yield no increase in satisfaction. Where the consumer is satiated with x but not with y, the indifference curves will be horizontal, and where he is satiated with y but not with x the curves will be vertical. There can also be regions or situations where commodities have become discommodities or nuisances; if one of the two commodities has become a nuisance, the curves will have a positive slope. This is shown in FIGURE 6, which may be taken to represent an

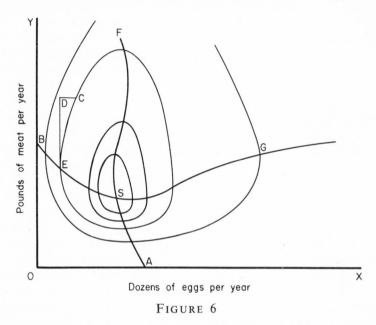

FIGURE 6

indifference map of an individual with respect to meat and eggs. In the region $oASB$ both commodities are desirable goods, and this is the normally significant region of this indifference map. Along the line AS the individual has as many eggs as he can make use of (in combination with the various indicated quantities of meat: the more meat he has, obviously, the fewer eggs he can use) and the indifference curves are horizontal; along the line BS the individual is satiated with meat and the curves are vertical. Above BS the excess of meat begins to be a nuisance, and if it is dumped willy-nilly on the consumer's doorstep, he may have to spend some effort in burying it or carting it away in order to avoid a stench. Thus at point C the individual would be willing to pay someone CD of eggs (which are still at that point a desirable commodity to him) for carting away the excess DE of meat. At the satiation point S the individual has exactly that quantity of meat and eggs that will give him the maximum of satisfaction. The curves extend much further above and to the right of S than below and to the left, indicating that on the whole

[37

the trouble of getting rid of a given surplus is much less onerous than would be the lack of an equal amount. In the region *SFG* the curves are again negatively sloped, indicating that the individual would be willing to dispose of more eggs if he could be burdened with less meat, or vice versa.

Actually, of course, we are almost exclusively concerned with the area o*ASB*, and the remainder is filled in only as a piece of analytical supererogation. The few items that do in practice become alternately desirable goods and nuisances usually present quite different characteristics under the two conditions such as to call for separate treatment rather than being included in a single diagram. Water may be alternatively carefully husbanded for irrigation and drained from flooded areas, but the mechanics of the two processes are entirely different. The nearest approach to the type of situation illustrated in FIGURE 6 is perhaps in certain types of labor, where the line between labor that is paid wages and labor that pays in one way or another for the privilege of gaining experience, or the line between working for an income and spending money on a hobby may become somewhat obscure.

Somewhat more frequent is the case where one is primarily concerned with one of the quadrants other than o*ASB*, as when an indifference map is drawn with one axis representing labor and the other income. But even in this case it is sometimes more convenient to assimilate it to the more usual type of case by speaking in terms of leisure as a "good" sacrificed rather than of labor performed as a "discommodity."

Another usual characteristic of indifference curves is that they curve away from the origin, or, more briefly, that they are "convex," at least in the significant quadrant. This is what is sometimes called the law or hypothesis of the "increasing marginal rate of substitution" (of y for x, as successive amounts of y are substituted for x). That is, as we move along an indifference curve by substituting y for x (moving upward to the left on the indifference map), we find that it requires increasing amounts of y to compensate the individual for successive equal losses of x, as he comes to have less x left and y becomes more and more abundant. Thus in FIGURE 7 if starting from a point A we deprive the individual of an amount of x equal to AB, it will require BC of y to bring him back to the same level of satisfaction. If we then deprive him of a further like amount of x, say CD, equal to AB, the amount of y needed to compensate him will now be DE, which is greater than BC, and a third similar decrease in x, EF, will require a still larger increment of y, FG.

It is necessary to note here that some writers have defined the marginal rate of substitution of y for x as the ratio of the increment of x required to compensate for the loss of a small amount of y, to the amount of y lost, or $- dx/dy$, which is the reciprocal of the quantity as defined above. From this follows a law or hypothesis of diminishing marginal rate of substitution, corresponding to the increasing marginal rate of substitution defined above. This alternative has the advantage of corresponding verbally with diminishing marginal utility, of which it is the approximate counterpart, as we shall see below, but it may be doubted whether this advantage is sufficient to justify departing from the literal meaning of the more natural expansion of the phrase. In any case, usage has not been at all consistent, and the student will have to be sure on each occasion that he understands the sense in which the term is being used. Normally, the context will settle the matter unambiguously.

If we adopt the additional assumption, usual in marginal-utility analysis, that the marginal utility of one commodity is independent of the quantity of the other commodity consumed, then the principle of increasing marginal

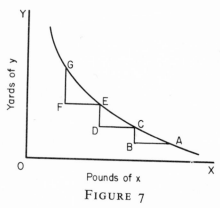

Pounds of x

FIGURE 7

rate of substitution follows directly from that of diminishing marginal utility. For as the amount of x decreases, the law of diminishing marginal utility, applied in reverse, implies that the marginal utility of x increases, while similarly the marginal utility of y decreases as its quantity increases; hence the ratio of the marginal utility of x to the marginal utility of y increases, which as we have seen is the same as the marginal rate of substitution of y for x.

The converse does not necessarily follow, however, for even if we make the assumption that the utilities of the two commodities are independent, the utility of one commodity may be increasing while the utility of the other is decreasing rapidly enough to offset this and produce an increasing rate of substitution, as in FIGURE 8a. And if the assumption of independence is not made, we can have diminishing marginal utility for both commodities and yet have a decreasing marginal rate of substitution, as in FIGURE 8b, where the utility surface is given the shape of part of the inside surface of a doughnut; or, conversely, we may have increasing marginal rate of substitution and increasing marginal utility to both commodities, as at point A in FIGURE 4d, if the flare is made sharp enough.

Though this hypothesis of increasing marginal rate of substitution is plausible enough in many instances, it cannot properly be treated as a law of

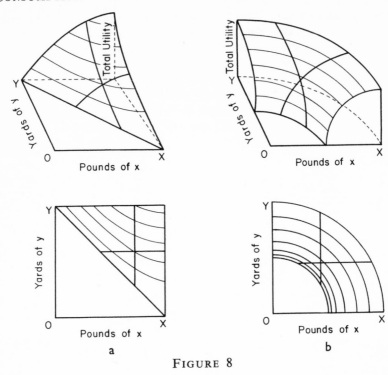

FIGURE 8

human behavior. At best it is merely characteristic of a large part of such behavior, and "normal" behavior might perhaps be usefully defined as behavior that conforms to this rule. We shall see later that increasing marginal rate of substitution is a necessary condition if a stable equilibrium is to exist in situations where a consumer is faced with prices over which he has no influence. Accordingly, most of the points we will be interested in will be points at which this "law" holds. But this does not validate the proposition as a law generally applicable to other points on the indifference map. Indeed, one can point to a considerable variety of patterns of behavior that are most easily interpreted as involving contradictions of this "law." The alcoholic, for example, finds it difficult to follow the counsel of moderation implied in the principle of increasing marginal rate of substitution: he either stays on the wagon or falls all the way off. One or two lone phonograph records may gather dust, while a substantial collection may produce much more satisfaction per record. Or a student may find himself in a position where it seems more worthwhile to concentrate his book purchases on either law or economics than to try to divide his purchases between the two disciplines. However, most such cases involve fairly narrowly defined categories of goods, and for broad analysis we can perhaps treat such cases as unusual and consider that increasing marginal rate of substitution is, if not a law of human behavior, at least a pattern that can be expected to exhibit itself in most cases where there are not special reasons to suppose otherwise.

The principle of increasing marginal rate of substitution along an indifference curve should not be confused with the hypothesis of increasing rate of substitution as the consumer moves parallel to an axis. It is not necessarily true, for example, even in fairly normal circumstances, that the marginal rate of substitution of y for x should increase as y is increased while x remains fixed. In FIGURE 2, to be sure, it so happens that the curves become steeper

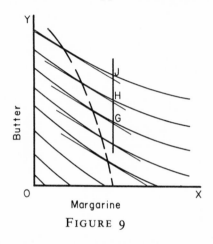

FIGURE 9

as we go from G to H to J. In his earlier work Pareto assumed that this would be true in general; he later corrected this, but as long as the assumption remained unchallenged, the interesting case where one of two commodities is an "inferior good" was excluded, as will be seen later. For example, FIGURE 9 shows an indifference map intended to represent a relation between butter and margarine; it will be noticed that the marginal rate of substitution decreases as the amount of butter is increased while keeping the amount of margarine constant: the indifference curve at J is flatter than that at H, flatter at H than at G, and so on. This indicates that margarine is an "inferior good," as will be explained further on.

A fairly wide variety of relationships between commodities can be reflected in indifference maps, even in the two-commodity case. For example, in the lower portion of FIGURE 9 the indifference curves are very nearly straight lines: in this region of the map, butter and margarine are very close substitutes. The consumer may be thought of as interested in obtaining a certain amount of table fat, and at this low level he cannot afford to be very choosy about the particular form in which it comes, so that he will not sacrifice very much in terms of total amount to have it in the preferred form or preferred assortment of forms. The marginal rate of substitution is very close to pound for pound. As the income rises and the level of satisfaction increases, the preference for a certain minimum proportion of butter has a chance to show itself in a willingness to give something more than a pound of margarine in exchange for a pound of butter, especially in regions where the amount of butter is small, in order to have at least some of the superior commodity. In FIGURE 9 the satiation points for both butter and margarine are assumed to be beyond the range of the diagram.

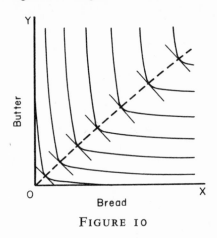

FIGURE 10

Conversely, the relation between two commodities may be such that the fullest satisfaction from one cannot be obtained without the presence of a suitable quantity of the other. Bread and butter might be such a combination, or paper and pencils; or, as an extreme case, left shoes and right shoes. In extreme cases, indeed, complementary commodities are often only traded in combination so as to be in effect but a single commodity. Indifference curves between such complementary commodities will be fairly sharply bent in the region representing the most favorable combinations, as is illustrated in FIGURE 10; adding more of either commodity is then much less effective in providing satisfaction than adding a suitable combination of both.

A precise drawing of the line between complementary and substitute pairs of commodities is a fairly difficult and subtle matter, however. A definition, to make sense, should be independent of the units of measurement and scales used in plotting the indifference map, which suggests plotting the indifference curves using a logarithmic scale on both axes, and terming the commodities complementary or substitute according to whether these curves are convex or concave. Another way of expressing this criterion is to ask whether the curves are more or less convex than the curves of the form $x^a y^b = k$ with the constants so chosen as to make the two sets of curves tangential to each other at the point in question; as we shall see later, these "standard" curves are of the form which for demand curves would be termed curves of constant elasticity. This definition of complementarity has some interesting properties, but it does become inconsistent with "potential independence" as we shall define it below; moreover, it depends on the choice of the origin, and while for most commodities the origin can be thought of as well defined, there are cases in which the origin is somewhat arbitrary, as is the case, for example, with leisure, or where the consumer also has a certain amount of other commodities that are close substitutes for the ones shown on the diagram. Some writers, notably Hicks, have considered that no meaningful definition of complementarity is possible without reference to some third "background" commodity. This approach is a development of an earlier definition in terms of utility proposed by F. Y. Edgeworth and Pareto, according to which two commodities are complementary if an increase in the quantity of one tends to increase the marginal utility of the other. Such a definition would not, however, be independent of the way in which utility values are assigned to the indifference curves, and J. R. Hicks in effect proposes to substitute in this definition the "marginal rate of substitution of the background commodity, z, for x" in place of the "marginal utility of x." Such a definition also has some interesting properties, though it has the awkward effect of making complementarity depend on the choice of the background commodity. Presumably, however, two commodities that are complementary in the everyday sense of the term would preserve this complementarity in the Hicksian definition in relation to a wide range of background commodities. But it is not at all certain that there is any precise definition of complementarity that will serve adequately for all purposes.

Commodities may also be necessities or dispensables. If a given minimum amount of a commodity is required for survival, then the part of the map representing less than this minimum amount will be out of the range of significance. For example, if we draw a map between food and clothing, as in FIGURE II, we may consider that a certain minimum amount of food is necessary to avoid starvation, but that, in warm climates at least, a certain minimum amount of clothing may be customary but not vital, and sometimes even the customary minimum may be quite small. Here the region to the left of the ordinate AB will represent starvation. One could interpret these indifference curves as representing a utility surface that becomes progessively steeper as AB is approached, terminating in a drop to minus infinity. Or if one is willing to admit a preference as between slow and rapid starvation, then the area of starvation to the left of AB might be considered to be covered with indifference curves that are substantially vertical lines, the interest of the consumer at such points being entirely with securing more food, with clothing by comparison being irrelevant. In general, where a commodity is a necessity, indifference curves will not cut the axis representing none of such a commodity, and will normally be asymptotic to the line representing the minimum required amount. On the other hand, the indifference curves will in general cut the axis along which the amount of a dispensable commodity is zero.

It is of course difficult to find a strictly defined commodity that is a necessity in this sense unless one assumes at the same time that the quantities of all close substitutes are zero, which involves treating an extremely special case, indeed one that may not be very interesting. On the other hand, a broadly defined commodity is usually defined in terms that permit of a wide

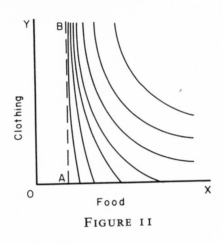

FIGURE II

range of ratios between the physically necessary amount and the economically significant measure. For example, a certain minimum number of calories of food may be a necessity, but ordinarily a food quantity index will be weighted according to the market prices of the various types and varieties of foods, so that by changing the composition of the food basket the cost of the minimum number of calories may vary greatly. Thus in this case the limit of starvation in terms of an economic index of consumption of food may be a much fuzzier region than when food consumption is expressed in calories. If such fuzziness is to be avoided, it is necessary to specify some internal constancy in the food complex, such as keeping to a given pattern of food purchases, or purchasing food at prices that always stay in the same ratios to each other.

In the very useful case where a selected commodity is placed on the x axis and "all other" commodities, represented by aggregate money expenditure on them at prices assumed to remain constant, placed on the y axis, this "all other" commodity, often called for brevity "money" will usually be a necessity in that the selected commodity by itself will usually be insufficient to support life, however abundant it may be, and at least some money will be required to purchase the supplementary needs. Thus the indifference curves will not normally cut the x axis, while in the usual case where the commodity x is not an absolute necessity, the curves will cut the y axis, as shown in FIGURE 12. "Money" in this case being a very broadly defined commodity, there will ordinarily be no satiation with money, or at least if such a point exists it will be far beyond the scope of any normal diagram. On the other hand, if the commodity x is fairly strictly defined, there will ordinarily be a satiation point for x not too far removed from the area of immediate interest, as shown in FIGURE 12 along the line AB. In general, the more money one has

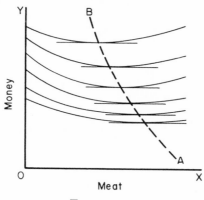

FIGURE 12

to spend on things other than x the smaller will be the satiation quantity of x, as is illustrated by the negative slope of the line AB.

Indeed, where a commodity is strictly enough defined to have a single price (or a set of prices in fairly rigid relationship with one another, e.g., one-pound packages of sugar and five-pound packages of sugar, where the price of the five-pound packages will ordinarily be a fixed amount or percentage less than the price of five one-pound packages) there will almost always be a satiation point not too far from the point of actual consumption (for example, almost certainly within a range of, say, ten times the normal consumption of any fairly important commodity). The traditional assumption of the insatiability of human wants is then fulfilled only by the introduction of new commodities. These new commodities may be merely better qualities of the old, but since they presumably command different prices that may not be rigidly tied to those of the old commodities, they must be treated for strict analytical purposes as separate commodities. Thus if one starts with two strictly defined commodities and comes to the satiation point for both (which may be pictured as the center of a slice of an onion, the slice itself being off-center), further increases in satisfaction must be sought by intro-ducing a third commodity and moving in a third dimension (i.e., out of the

[45

original slice toward the center of the entire onion). Having reached the center of the three-dimensional indifference map, further improvement would involve escape into a fourth dimension, and so on. Complete satiation would thus involve running out of new commodities and new dimensions; this result can be avoided, if not indefinitely, at least for a long time for the bulk of individuals. Actually, whether satiation can be indefinitely deferred in this way or whether a complete satiation with economic goods is possible is to a large extent irrelevant if in any given case the point of satiation would be far removed from the point representing the situation under consideration. General satiation may indeed occur in individual cases: for example, in the case of ascetics whose material wants are more restricted than those of the bulk of the population, and in the case of the very wealthy who, whether from fear of criticism or other reasons, find difficulty in consuming their entire incomes. The mere fact that a large part of an individual's income is saved and not spent is not, however, necessarily evidence of satiation: savings may be accumulated for future consumption, or for the sake of the power that comes with the possession of capital, and may thus be undertaken on a substantial scale even when additional satisfaction could be obtained from further immediate consumption.

Another somewhat more abstruse property that indifference maps may have is that of potential independence. Early theorists, in thinking about utility and marginal utility, were prone to assume that utility derived from different commodities would be independent and additive, and that the marginal utility of one commodity would depend only on the amount of that commodity consumed and would be unaffected by variations in the consumption of other commodities. In mathematical terms, this would mean a utility function of the form $U(x, y) = F(x) + G(y)$, with marginal utilities $U_x = \partial U/\partial x = dF/dx$ and $U_y = \partial U/\partial y = dG/dy$, for the case of two commodities. In terms of Edgeworth's definition, this form of utility function precluded complementarity or substitution relationships between commodities, and Edgeworth was largely responsible for generalizing the utility function to permit the analysis of such relationships.

If two commodities are actually independent in this sense, however, this property will be reflected in certain properties of the indifference map. For such independence means that at any point the marginal rate of substitution shown by the indifference map must be capable of being expressed as the ratio of a marginal utility of x depending only on the quantity of x, to a marginal utility of y depending only on y. If then we take the marginal rates of substitution at the four corners of a rectangle oriented parallel to the axes of the indifference map, these four quantities must form the elements of a proportion. Thus in FIGURE 13 if $ABDC$ is a rectangle with sides parallel to the axes and utilities are independent, the marginal utility of x must be the same at A as at B: $U_x(A) = U_x(B)$ and, similarly, $U_x(C) = U_x(D)$, $U_y(A) = U_y(C)$, and $U_y(B) = U_y(D)$. If we write $S_{y/x}(A)$ for the marginal rate of substitution of y for x at the point A, then we have:

$$S_{y/x}(A) = \frac{U_x(A)}{U_y(A)}$$

and

$$\frac{S_{y/x}(A)}{S_{y/x}(B)} = \frac{\dfrac{U_x(A)}{U_y(A)}}{\dfrac{U_x(B)}{U_y(B)}} = \frac{\dfrac{I}{U_y(A)}}{\dfrac{I}{U_y(B)}} = \frac{\dfrac{I}{U_y(C)}}{\dfrac{I}{U_y(D)}} = \frac{\dfrac{U_x(C)}{U_y(C)}}{\dfrac{U_x(D)}{U_y(D)}} = \frac{S_{y/x}(C)}{S_{y/x}(D)}$$

Whether the marginal rates of substitution do form such a proportion in any particular case can be tested geometrically by drawing the four tangents

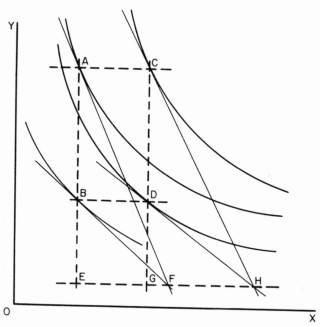

FIGURE 13

and seeing whether the intersection of the left-hand pair lies on the same horizontal line as the intersection of the right-hand pair. Thus in FIGURE 13 the tangents from A and B meet at F, while the tangents from C and D meet at H, with FH being parallel to the x axis. We then have:

$$\frac{S_{y/x}(A)}{S_{y/x}(B)} = \frac{\dfrac{EA}{EF}}{\dfrac{EB}{EF}} = \frac{EA}{EB} = \frac{GC}{GD} = \frac{\dfrac{GC}{GH}}{\dfrac{GD}{GH}} = \frac{S_{y/x}(C)}{S_{y/x}(D)}$$

[47

Conversely, if an indifference map has the property that for all rectangles the marginal rates of substitution at the four corners always form a proportion, then it will be possible to fit a utility surface to this map that is the sum of independent elements. For example, it is possible to do this in the case of an indifference map composed of concentric circles, and in fact the utility surface that results in this case is a paraboloid of revolution, shown in FIGURE 4c. Such a surface has the property that all vertical cross sections parallel to the x axis are similar, differing only by a vertical displacement, as are also all cross sections parallel to the y axis. In effect, the utility surface can be traced out by taking one of these vertical cross sections parallel to the x axis and moving it, keeping it vertical, so that one of its points traces out one of the vertical cross sections parallel to the y axis. For the other possible utility surfaces shown in FIGURE 4 that correspond to the circular indifference curves of FIGURE 3, the utilities of the two commodities are not independent.

Indeed, for an indifference map that has this property of potential independence there is only one independent utility function in general, aside from variations in zero point and unit of measurement. That is, if we are given such an indifference map, conceptually derivable from observations on the choices of an individual or groups of individuals, and make the additional assumption that the utilities of the two commodities are independent, then we can determine uniquely the corresponding utility function, except for arbitrary choice of a zero point and unit of measurement (i.e., "to within linear transformations"). This principle has been used by Irving Fisher and Ragnar Frisch in attempts to determine a "cardinal" utility function, and with it a curve of marginal utility of money, by studying data on the consumption patterns of families at different income levels and under two or more different sets of prices. Indeed, if we do make this assumption of independence, it suffices to determine two indifference curves (or two Engel curves, as defined on p. 56) in order for the entire map and its utility function to be determined. However, actual attempts yield widely different estimates, and seem to indicate that it is not in practice possible to pick out commodities, whether narrowly or broadly defined, that in fact have the property of independent utility. Indeed, no indifference map has been determined in practice in sufficient detail and with sufficient accuracy to provide any direct evidence that the above "rectangular" test of potential independence is satisfied. Independence of utility, actual or potential, is, accordingly, more of a convenient assumption or standard than a frequent phenomenon in practice. Even for an indifference map that has the property of potential independence, there seems to be no strong reason for considering that the independent utility surface has any closer relation to a subjective satisfaction, however defined, than any of the nonindependent utility functions corresponding to the same indifference map.

48]

Potential independence, indeed, as distinguished from actual independence, neither implies nor is implied by any specific degree of partial substitutability or complementarity, whether of the Edgeworth type or the elasticity type. Perfect substitutability, with straight lines for an indifference map, does indeed imply potential independence, but the utility function that preserves this independence is the one for which the marginal utility of both commodities is constant, which is hardly admissible. Failure of the potential independence criterion to hold is reflected in the indifference curve at a point C being either too steep or not steep enough relative to the slopes at the other three corners A, B, and D of an arbitrary rectangle; such deviations are not symmetrical with respect to x and y, whereas the concepts of complementarity and substitutability are symmetrical with respect to x and y. In general, potential independence and deviations from it seem to offer little help in the analysis of the properties of indifference maps.

One case, however, deserves special mention because of its importance in relating analysis in terms of indifference maps to the older analysis in terms of utility. In many types of partial equilibrium analysis, the assumption is made that the marginal utility of money is constant, or at least that variations in its marginal utility are small enough to be neglected, within the range under discussion. Now it follows immediately that if variations in commodity x (within the prescribed limits of both x and money) cannot affect the marginal utility of money, then changes in the amount of money or income do not affect the marginal utility of x, and this marginal utility of x will therefore depend only on the quantity of x. This can be shown by reference to FIGURE 13: as we go from B to A, the increase in utility resulting from this increase in y (which now stands for "money") must be the same as the increase in utility in going from D to C, since the marginal utility of y does not change with the change in x. This implies that the change in utility from B to D is the same as that from A to C, and since the rectangle can be selected with the change in x as small as we please, this means that the marginal utility of x is the same at B as at A, i.e., it does not depend on the quantity of y.

Now if the marginal utility of money is constant everywhere within a given region, the marginal rate of substitution of money for x will be proportional, within this region, to the marginal utility of x, which in turn can depend only on the quantity of x. Thus the slope of the indifference curves will depend only on x, and will be the same at all points within the region along any vertical ordinate. In other words, the indifference curves will all be similar to each other, one being obtainable from the other by a simple displacement parallel to the y axis.

It is of course absurd to make this assumption of constant marginal utility of money for a whole indifference surface. But if the amount that would ever be spent on commodity x is only a small part of the total budget of an individual, the relevant part of the indifference map, over the small range of

[49

levels of satisfaction possible with variations in the price of this one commodity, will be small enough, relative, say, to the entire area between this part of the indifference map and the origin, so that within this range the assumption of constant marginal utility of money may be closely enough approximated to give a degree of realism to any conclusions reached on the basis of such an assumption. Thus if we are considering an individual with an income of $3,000, and his indifference map as between money and, say, travel, and if we consider that under no circumstances would he spend more

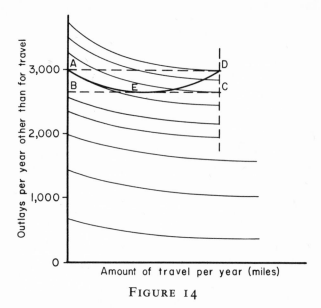

FIGURE 14

than $200 for travel, then for this person and for this income level, we are concerned only with that part of the indifference map lying between $3,000 and $2,800 on the income axis, though we may be considering points all the way from zero to the satiation line in the direction of the travel axis. Thus in FIGURE 14 we would be concerned only with the area within the dotted rectangle *ABCD*.

For such a restricted area of an indifference map, it would be quite possible, however improbable prima facie, for the indifference curves to be all parallel in the sense here relevant, and in many cases it would not be too gross an exaggeration to assume that they were exactly parallel. If this is the case, then, as we shall see shortly, the amount of *x* purchased at a given price will be independent of income within the given range, and the willingness to buy another unit at a given price will not be affected by the amount paid for the preceding units. Many useful propositions then present themselves as corollaries.

It should be noted, however, that while this property of a portion of an indifference map is most commonly and indeed most conveniently described as representing a constant marginal utility of money, it is possible to have an indifference map of this sort, and with it most of the interesting propositions that depend on this property, without going so far as to assume constant marginal utility of money. All that is necessary is that the marginal rate of substitution between x and money be independent of the amount of money, and this may be true if both the marginal utility of x and the marginal utility of money diminish in the same proportion as the amount of y is increased.

Consumer Choice with Fixed Prices and Fixed Resources

WE NOW TURN to see how indifference maps can be used in the analysis of consumer behavior. In general, a consumer will be faced with a situation in which he is to make a choice among alternatives which may be represented as points on the indifference map. There will be certain points on the indifference map that are unattainable for one reason or another; ordinarily the attainable and the unattainable points will form contiguous regions, separated from each other by a boundary. Since ordinarily when we are talking about economic goods an individual will not choose less of some good when he can obtain more of it without sacrificing something else, the point selected by the consumer will be on this boundary that separates the attainable from the unattainable. This boundary may then be called the opportunity path (in a three-variable case we may speak of an opportunity surface, or in more complicated cases of an opportunity locus). It represents the various opportunities open to an individual among which he is to choose.

In general, this opportunity path is curved. In many cases, however, and particularly in the case where the opportunities consist of the freedom to buy or sell as much as is desired at a fixed price, the opportunity path is linear; i.e., in the case of two commodities it is a straight line, in the three-variable case a plane, and in the general case a linear constraint or "hyperplane." For example, in FIGURE 15 if an individual starts out with an initial endowment of 20 pounds of meat and 30 yards of cloth, we can indicate this in the figure as his "starting point" S. If there is a market in which meat may be traded for cloth in the ratio of three yards of cloth for ten pounds of meat, then by giving up all his meat the individual could secure a total of 36 yards of cloth and so arrive at point B, or by giving up all his cloth he can obtain 120 pounds of meat and so arrive at point C. Or by varying the amount purchased or sold, he can arrive at any point on the line BC. BC is called the "budget line" or "price line."

Among these various points that are attainable, he will select that one which lies on the highest indifference curve, in this case the point E, representing a final consumption of 80 pounds of meat and 12 yards of cloth. In

[51

moving from S to E, he has given up or paid 18 yards of cloth, or SF, and obtained in exchange 60 pounds of meat, represented by FE.

If the equilibrium point E lies within the quadrant containing the indifference map, and if the indifference curves are smooth, the price line will be tangent at the point E to some indifference curve. (If it is not tangent to one of the indifference curves already drawn, then remembering that the indifference curves actually shown are always only a sample of the continuous series of curves that could be drawn, another curve can always be drawn in which

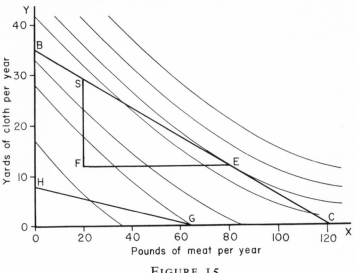

FIGURE 15

will pass through E and be tangent to the price line. We may think of the price line as a path over the shoulder of the utility "hill"; the point E represents the point at which the path ceases to climb and starts to go down again. The slope of the price line represents the price of the commodity on the horizontal axis in terms of the commodity on the vertical axis: the higher the price the steeper the line. The slope or "steepness" of the indifference curve at E is the marginal rate of substitution. Thus at the point of equilibrium the marginal rate of substitution of y for x must be equal to the price of x in terms of y. Or stated in terms of marginal utility, the marginal utilities of the two commodities must be proportional to their prices. Or, the marginal utility of a "dollar's worth" of one commodity must be equal to the marginal utility of a dollar's worth of the other. It is easy to see that at any point where this condition is not fulfilled, within the quadrant, it is open to the consumer to improve his lot by moving in one direction or the other along the price line BC.

It is important to note, however, that the equilibrium point may lie not within the positive quadrant, but on one of the axes, and that in this case the tangency condition may fail, or at least must be reinterpreted. Instead of the marginal rate of substitution being equal to the price, the marginal rate of substitution of any consumed commodity x for any commodity not consumed (for example, $y = 0$) must be less than or equal to the price of the non-consumed commodity (y) in terms of the consumed article (x). In FIGURE 15 this is illustrated by the case where the consumer starts out at H with eight yards of cloth and no meat, and finds that the price of meat is one yard of cloth for eight pounds of meat. He then trades all his cloth for meat, arriving at G with 64 pounds of meat and no cloth, and can go no further even though the marginal rate of substitution at G is one yard of cloth for four pounds of meat.

It is ordinarily convenient to adopt the convention of speaking of the commodity on the x axis as the one which is being bought or sold, and of the commodity on the y axis as the commodity being used in payment and in terms of which the price is quoted. This is sometimes expressed by saying that the y commodity is a "numéraire," or yardstick commodity. The slope of the price line is then the price of x in terms of this numéraire. This does not imply that y is actually used as a money commodity or a medium of exchange, but merely that y serves as a conventional standard of measurement and comparison, without the selection of one commodity rather than the other for this purpose being deemed to affect the result in any way. Indeed, the pure theory of exchange has no place for money as such, and if some kind of money is actually used as an intermediary in the exchange process, it is necessary to treat it either as a commodity in its own right with an intrinsic value in use unaffected by any "liquidity value," or as a pure currency or "veil" behind which the real nature of the transaction as an exchange must be discerned. In this latter case, it is immaterial what the level of prices in terms of this money is, the only thing that matters being the price *ratios*; however, it is necessary in this case to require that individuals finish their trading with the same amount of money with which they started, otherwise the change in the cash balance would be an additional degree of freedom requiring a determining explanation which would be difficult to introduce at this stage in the analysis.

If the y commodity is taken as numéraire, then the resources of an individual may be evaluated in terms of this numéraire: the y intercept of the price line, i.e., OB, is the amount of numéraire that the individual could obtain in exchange for all of his resources; this is termed his "income."

Normally, we consider the indifference curves to be smooth and continuous, as in FIGURE 15. However, it is perfectly conceivable for the indifference curves to have kinks, as in FIGURE 16a, or perhaps to be defined only for discrete values of x, as when x comes in fairly large units, as in FIGURE 16b. In this case, the equilibrium condition becomes that the relative price of x must be no less than the relative marginal utility of an additional unit of x,

[53

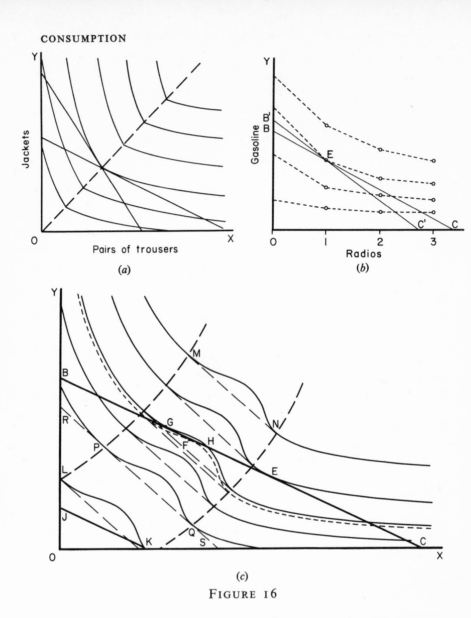

(a)

(b)

(c)

FIGURE 16

but no greater than the marginal utility of the last unit of *x* which brought the individual to the point *E*. Or we can preserve the original formulation by inserting phantom indifference lines between the discrete points, and by substituting microscopic curves for the sharp corners, thus considering that the marginal rate of substitution passes rapidly but continuously through the entire range of values between the upper limit and the lower limit in a small neighborhood of the point *E* instead of jumping discontinuously at the point

54]

E; by this artifice, the equality between the marginal rate of substitution and the price ratio is retained in such cases also. In one way or another such cases can thus be brought within the scope of the analysis. In most cases, however, no new principles are developed by examining such minor discontinuities in detail, and for the sake of simplicity they will as a general rule be disregarded.

FIGURE 16c further illustrates the reason for being concerned only with cases where the indifference curves are convex toward the origin. If there were a set of indifference curves with a concavity, or "cove" as indicated by the portions of the indifference curves between the lines PM and QN, then along a price line such as BC there could be three points, E, F, and G, where BC is tangent to an indifference curve and the price ratio is equal to the marginal rate of substitution. Point E is obviously the point of maximum satisfaction which will be chosen by the consumer if the entire line BC is open to him. Point F is a point of unstable rather than stable equilibrium, in that if the consumer moves away from F in either direction along the line BC he will be better off; it is a point of equilibrium at all only in the very restricted sense that small movements will produce improvements of a still smaller order of magnitude, and in the sense that in the immediate neighborhood of the point there is no indication in which direction the consumer should move in order to improve his position, so that if the consumer is as stupid as Buridan's ass,[4] he might remain immobilized by the opposing attractions of movement in both directions. Point G is a point of local equilibrium, or of what might be termed a micro-stable equilibrium in the sense that small movements away from G will make the consumer worse off, and that it is only if he is able to move beyond H that he will be better off.

Thus if we are considering the behavior of the consumer in a market where he can buy or sell any amount at the given price, all of the equilibrium points within the area $MNQP$ will be either unstable or merely micro-stable; the true points of equilibrium which would be selected by a rational consumer would all lie outside this area in the region in which the indifference curves are convex to the origin. So if indifference curves are to be used to predict behavior in such a market, it will make no difference if the dotted portions of the curves are replaced by the straight lines MN, PQ, etc., which would eliminate the concavity. Or looking at it the other way, if the only evidence that we have concerning the indifference curves consists of observations of consumer behavior in various market situations where the prices are fixed beyond the influence of individual consumers, then no points will be observed within the area $MNQP$, and there will be no evidence by which it can be decided objectively whether the indifference curves are straight lines in this region, or are the dotted curves, or are some other curves either more or less

---

4. The simile of this unfortunate animal starving to death for want of a capacity to choose between two bundles of hay lying in opposite directions is traditionally but almost certainly erroneously ascribed to Jean Buridan, fourteenth-century French Scholastic.

[55

deeply concave than the ones shown. It is thus only under very special circumstances that one can be concerned with indifference curves that are not convex to the origin, at least for economic goods. For example, one might conceivably obtain an equilibrium point within the area $MNPQ$ if the opportunity path of the consumer were curved rather than straight, as might occur, for example, if, as under monopsony, the price is not fixed but depends on the amount the consumer attempts to buy or sell. But such a case is outside the present realm of discourse.

Here again, however, a special caution is required in applying propositions developed in terms of points in the interior of the quadrant to cases where the equilibrium point lies on one of the axes. If, for example, in FIGURE 16c, the consumer's budget line is JK, the point of maximum satisfaction will be K, which could be considered to lie on a concave portion of the indifference curve KL. It is still true that no information is secured that demonstrates the existence of a concavity in curve KL, and the equilibrium point is at the edge of, and not within, the putative concavity, just as, in the interior case, for a budget line RS equilibrium could be observed either at P or at Q on an edge of the concavity. Perhaps it is also worthwhile observing that in a realistic case of an indifference map drawn up in terms of a fairly large number of strictly defined commodities it will be the interior case that is the exception and the case where the quantity of one or more commodities is zero that will be the rule: few if any consumers consume some of every commodity, even when "commodity" is defined fairly broadly.

Income Changes and Engel Curves

WE NOW COME to examine how the behavior of the consumer will vary as we vary the conditions under which he acts. First we examine his behavior as his resources are increased or diminished while market prices remain the same. In FIGURE 17, for example, we can start again at S_3 (corresponding to the point S of FIGURE 15), representing, say, 20 pounds of meat and 30 yards of cloth, and at a price of 0.3 yards of cloth per pound of meat the equilibrium, as before, is at E_3. Similarly, if we started off from point S_4 with more cloth but the same amount of meat, a price line at the same price through the new starting point can be drawn. This new price line, B_4C_4 will have the same slope as the old one, since the price is the same, and on it a new equilibrium will be reached at E_4. Adding or subtracting various amounts of cloth from the original starting point, the new equilibrium points trace out the curve $E_1, E_2, \ldots, E_6$. This curve can be descriptively termed an income-consumption curve, as it traces the changes in consumption arising from changes in income. It is also occasionally termed "standard-of-life line," but is most frequently referred to as an Engel curve, after Christian Lorenz Ernest Engel, a German statistician (1821–1896) who worked extensively in the field of consumer

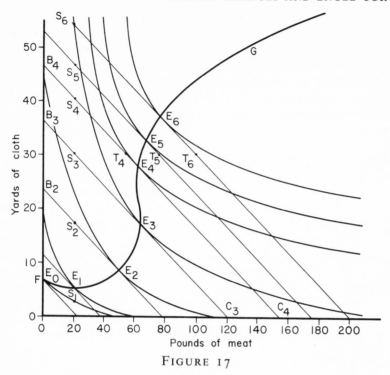

FIGURE 17

budgets. Engel curves are not usually thought of as being quite as sinuous as that shown in FIGURE 17, but the one shown is not at all inconceivable.

For any one price ratio there is only one Engel curve: one could have varied the initial resources of the consumer of FIGURE 17 by adding more meat to his initial resources and so have obtained the starting points T_4, T_5, T_6, and so on, or by eliminating the original meat supply, as at B_2; the equilibrium points would lie on the same Engel curve. Whatever the initial resources, the equilibrium will always lie along the curve FG as long as the price remains at 0.3 yards per pound. Different price ratios, however, will in general produce different Engel curves. In FIGURE 18 we have an indifference map with a number of Engel curves drawn in. In general, through any given point there will be a single Engel curve that can be drawn. Indeed, the indifference map can be covered with Engel curves in the same way as it is covered with indifference curves, and if we know all the Engel curves and the price ratios to which they correspond we can construct the indifference curves.

The above may have to be suitably modified where the indifference curves are not smooth and convex: in FIGURE 16a we can think of Engel curves coinciding with one another for various ranges of prices along the line of the kinks in the indifference curves. Where there is a concavity, as in FIGURE 16c,

[57

the area *MNQP* is probably best thought of as an area without Engel curves: the equilibrium points either pass around the side of the area or jump across it as income is increased.

Usually, if the total resources or income of an individual are increased while prices remain the same, the consumption of a given commodity will increase, at least for a commodity that is defined in broad enough terms. If this is the case for both x and y, in the two-commodity case, then the Engel curve will have a positive slope, and x and y are called "normal" goods.

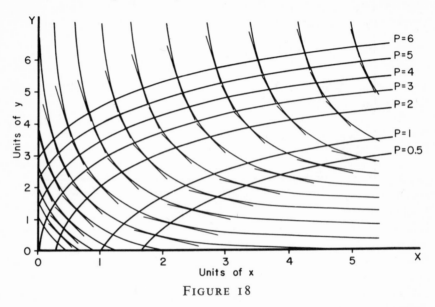

FIGURE 18

However, it is possible that with an increase in income an individual might choose to consume less of a particular good, in which case this good is termed "inferior." In the indifference map, an inferior good reveals itself in a negatively sloping Engel curve: if the equilibrium point moves toward the y axis with increasing income, x is an inferior good, as, for example, between E_3 and E_4 in FIGURE 17. If the equilibrium point moves toward the x axis as income increases, as it does in FIGURE 17 between E_0 and E_1, then y is an inferior good. It is thus possible for both of two commodities in a two-commodity system to be inferior goods, though not at the same point on the indifference map. Or it is possible for one of two commodities to be inferior throughout the indifference map, as is the case for margarine in FIGURE 9. In a system of more than two commodities, it is possible for all but one of the commodities to be an inferior good at a given point, though of course this would be extremely unlikely with any large number of commodities.

In general, any good that is so closely defined as to cause the next higher

58]

grade of the same general class of commodity to be considered a separate good will be an inferior good over the range of incomes above the income level to which the good in question is best suited. Thus in the preference region where a consumer would tend to drive a Buick, Fords would be an inferior good, while at income levels ranging up to where he would tend to drive a Ford, bus rides may be an inferior good. But it is to be doubted whether the broad category "automobiles," or the still broader category "transportation" would be an inferior good over any substantial portion of the indifference map. In general, it seems that the broader the definition of the commodity, the less likely is it to be found to be inferior.

Changes in Price: Demand and Supply

WE NOW COME to study the effect on the consumer of changes in price. If the initial resources of the consumer are represented by S in FIGURE 19a, and the initial price line by SC_1, then a reduction in price will produce a new price line with a lower slope, but still passing through S, such as SC_2. Changing the price amounts to rotating the price line about S as a pivot, whereas increasing income moved the price line parallel to itself. In FIGURE 19a the original equilibrium point was at E, and with the new price line the equilibrium point moves to F. As the price is successively decreased, the equilibrium point traces out the path $EFGHJ$. On the other hand, if the price is increased, the price line rotates in a clockwise direction about S as a pivot and the equilibrium point moves in the reverse direction from E toward S. When the price has risen to the point where the price line is tangent to the indifference curve at S, then the equilibrium point is at S and the consumer has no incentive to trade. If the price rises a little further, the individual depicted by this indifference map would become a seller of x, even though he has very little of it to start with, and the equilibrium point moves from S toward T.

The curve $TSEFGHJ$ may be given the descriptive title of "outlay-consumption curve," for referred to the point N as its origin, the abscissa NR represents the total consumption of x at the point E on the curve, while the ordinate RE represents the outlay of y paid out to secure SR of x, which added to the original amount NS held by the consumer at the outset provides the total consumption NR. Referred to S as an origin, it could perhaps be termed the "outlay-purchase curve," in that the abscissa SR is the amount purchased and the ordinate RE is the total outlay. It is also sometimes termed the "bargaining locus." However, the briefer though somewhat more cryptic designation of "offer curve" given currency by Edgeworth and Bowley appears sufficiently uniformly applied to justify its use.

The offer curve will ordinarily be tangent to an indifference curve at the starting point, S, and will lie wholly inside this indifference curve. The offer

[59

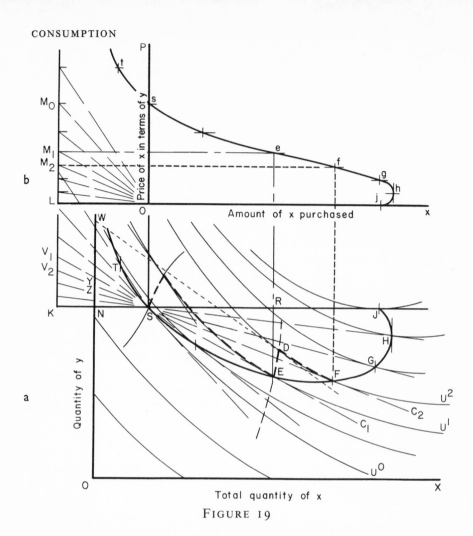

FIGURE 19

curve contains the same information as the more familiar "demand" curve or "price-consumption" curve; in fact, given one curve the other may be derived, either graphically or numerically. Numerically, one can simply read from the offer curve the respective total outlays and amounts purchased at the successive points E, F, G, etc., divide the outlay by the amount purchased in each case to get the corresponding price, and then plot the amount purchased against the price. The following geometrical construction, however, may help to fix more firmly in mind the relationship between the two curves. If we set the origin of our demand curve vertically above S at o in FIGURE 19b, and lay off to the left of o some convenient distance oL (which may be equal to some number of units k of commodity x on the scale of FIGURE 19a), and then draw lines through o parallel to the various price lines, the intercepts of these lines on the ordinate from L, i.e., LM_0, LM_1, LM_2, etc., will correspond to the amount of y on the scale of FIGURE 19a necessary to purchase the amount k of x at the various prices, and will hence be proportional to the prices so that these ordinates can be used as a scale of price. Thus the point f on the demand curve corresponding to the point F on the offer curve is found vertically above F and at a height equal to that of the intercept M_2, and similarly for the other points.

Unlike indifference and Engel curves, there are numerous offer curves that can be drawn through each point on an indifference map; in fact, each starting point generates a separate and distinct offer curve. For example, all starting points that might be selected along the line YC_1 will give offer curves that pass through the point E, but these curves will all differ at other points. To simplify further analysis of the possible reactions of consumers to changes in prices, it is convenient to break down the effect of a price change into two components: an "income effect" producing a movement along an Engel curve, and a "substitution effect" involving a movement along an indifference curve. A reduction in price indeed has two aspects: it makes the consumer better off, by enabling him to reach a higher indifference curve; and it induces a change in the pattern of his consumption, by influencing him to use relatively more of the commodity that has become relatively cheaper and less of others that are, accordingly, relatively more expensive.

In FIGURE 19a, for example, one can think of the shift from E to F in response to a reduction in price from p_1 to p_2, corresponding to a change in the budget line from SC_1 to SC_2, in two stages: in the first stage the budget line moves parallel to itself from SE to WD and the equilibrium point moves along an Engel curve from E to D; in the second stage the consumer moves from D to F along the indifference curve U^2, the price declines from p_1 to p_2, the price line slides along the indifference curve U^2, remaining tangent to it, moving from WD to SF, and income declines again from oW to oZ, thus canceling the increase in income which took place during the first stage, when income increased from oZ to oW with the price constant at p_1. In the second stage the individual is made to substitute x for y in a way that keeps him on the same level of satisfaction.

The importance of this breakdown lies in the fact that we can immediately say that the "substitution effect" of a reduction in the price of x in terms of y will always be in the direction of increasing the consumption of x at the expense of that of y. Thus if the substitution effect is the dominant factor, we can immediately state that a reduction in the price of x will lead to an increase in its consumption, which is the usual assumption as to the shape of the demand curve. But if the "income effect" is large, it must also be considered. However, if x is a "normal" good, i.e., not an "inferior" good, an increase in income will also lead to an increase in the consumption of x, and thus both the income component and the substitution component of a

[61

decrease in price will involve an increase in the consumption of x so that the normal demand-curve pattern will be confirmed.

This is not necessarily true in the case of an inferior good, for which an increase in income means a decrease in consumption along the Engel curve. Even here, however, if the income effect is relatively small, the decrease in consumption due to the income effect is likely to be overcome by the substitution effect and the combined net effect will be a normal demand relationship. Only where x is an inferior good and the income effect is at the same

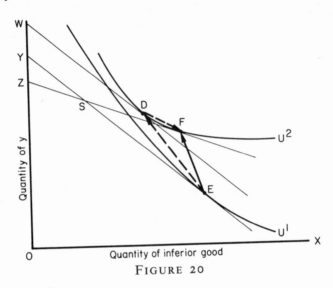

FIGURE 20

time relatively large will the negative income effect predominate and lead to a reduction in consumption as price is decreased. This is illustrated in FIGURE 20, where the income effect, equivalent to increasing income from oY to oW, moves the equilibrium point along the backward sloping Engel curve from E to D, whereas the substitution effect is relatively small, resulting in a movement only from D to F, so that F remains to the left of E and indicates a smaller consumption of x, even though the price has been reduced. A similar situation exists in FIGURE 19a between H and J; in the demand curve in FIGURE 19b, there is a correspondingly positive or "perverse" slope from h to j.

A perverse demand curve thus requires both that the commodity be an inferior good and that the amount purchased by the consumer be substantial so as to give rise to the required large income effect. This phenomenon, which has come to be known as Giffen's paradox, was given currency by Alfred Marshall,[5] who cited bread as a possible example, being both a large part of

5. *Principles of Economics* (New York: Macmillan), 8th edition, p. 132.

the budget of the poor, so that a price change would involve a large income effect, and an inferior good that would be replaced by more appetizing food-stuffs as purchasing power increases. Marshall attributed the origination of the paradox to Robert Giffen, but a statement of the paradox has not been located among Giffen's voluminous writings, and it is possible that Giffen made the suggestion orally if at all.[6] Actually, it is doubtful whether any case of this paradox has ever been substantiated in practice, at least for an entire market. This paradox should in no way be confused with cases which arise in

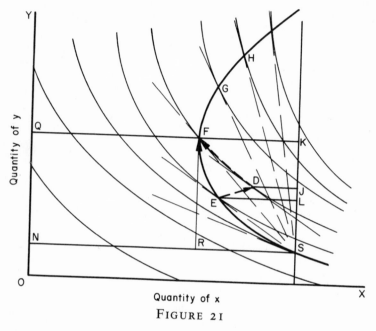

Quantity of x

FIGURE 21

dynamic situations where a price increase is taken as indicating a likelihood of further price increases to come with the result that demand may be tem-porarily increased because of these anticipations. Nor has it anything to do with the cases that arise through the ignorance of the consumer or through snob appeal where a high price is itself taken either as evidence of quality or as a factor in the satisfaction derived by the consumer from the object. None of these elements are admissible within the framework of the present theoretical structure.

The supply curve may be derived and analyzed in a similar manner; how-ever, the results arrived at are significantly different. In FIGURE 21, for example, we have an indifference map similar to that of FIGURE 19a; however, since this consumer is to be a supplier of x, we start him off at S with a

6. See Readings and References, 2.122.

relatively large amount of x and relatively little y (to be sure, in FIGURE 19a the consumer was a supplier of x along the curve TS, but this was such a small part of the whole diagram that there was hardly room to explore the possibilities in full). Again, we can draw price lines radiating from S and trace out the offer curve $SEFGH$. At F, the amount of x being supplied is SR, i.e., the total amount that the consumer started with as his original endowment, less the amount QF that he decides to keep for his own consumption; the amount of y that he obtains in exchange for SR of x is RF.

As for the case of demand, we can decompose the effect EF of a change in the price into an income effect ED along an Engel curve and a substitution effect DF along an indifference curve; in this case, however, the pattern is different. The substitution effect, DF, is still in line with the usual assumptions about supply curves: increasing the price from p_1 at D to p_2 at F while keeping the consumer on the same level of satisfaction increases the amount supplied from DJ to FK. But here, in the case of a normal good, the income effect of an increase in the price of the x being sold will be along the Engel curve from E to D, involving an increase in the amount of x kept and hence a decrease from EL to DJ in the amount supplied. In FIGURE 21, the substitution effect at first outweighs the income effect as we move away from S along the offer curve, but beyond F the income effect begins to outweigh the substitution effect and a further increase in price brings forth a diminished supply.

The relation between the offer curve and the supply curve is similar to that between the offer curve and the demand curve, but to show this more conveniently it is necessary to turn FIGURE 21 around through 180 degrees so as to produce the lower part of FIGURE 22. If we take the point S as the origin for the supply curve, we can again lay off an arbitrary length SL to the left to determine a scale for the supply curve, project the price lines beyond S until they intersect the ordinate erected from L, and use the intercepts as the price scale against which to plot the points s, e, f, g, h, etc., vertically above the corresponding points S, E, F, G, H, on the offer curve. The result is the supply curve giving the relation between the price and the amount supplied, shown in the curve $sefgh$. From s to f, supply increases as the price increases, but further increases in price above f result in reductions in the supply forthcoming.

Thus while the perverse demand curve may be considered something of a rarity, perverse supply curves are much more probable. A perverse demand curve requires an inferior good that is at the same time a substantial part of the total budget. Now while inferior goods are not at all rare, one normally expects the bulk of any budget to be made up of goods that are not inferior at the point of equilibrium. Moreover, we observe that the broader and more comprehensive the definition of the commodity the less likely it is to be inferior, so that to a degree the requirements of being a large part of the

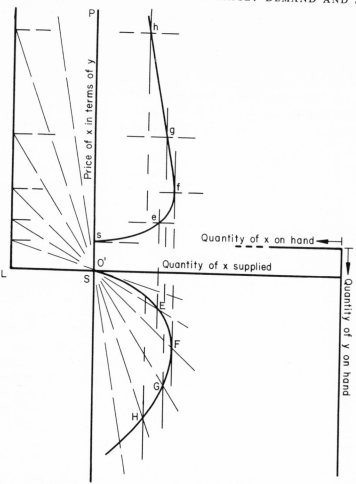

FIGURE 22

budget and of being inferior are mutually antagonistic; commodities are usually inferior because their function is to be replaced by a superior substitute at higher levels of income, which tends to indicate a relatively high substitution effect that would be likely to overcome any negative income effect that might exist. As consumers most individuals are concerned with a great variety of substantially different commodities, no one of which accounts for a preponderant part of the budget. This becomes increasingly so as higher standards of living reduce the relative importance of food. When all these considerations are taken into account, it is hardly surprising that no convincing actual example of Giffen's paradox has been forthcoming, particularly as statistical materials covering communities with a low standard of living in which the phenomenon would be most likely to occur are very scanty.

On the other hand, for the supply curve not only do we not have to look for inferior goods, but the items supplied by most individuals each tend to provide a relatively large part of their income. Thus in the usual case one can find not only a normal income effect, but a fairly large income effect, even with respect to fairly strictly defined commodities. Thus the supply curve for labor in general, or for the labor supplied by any given individual or group, has often been supposed to be of the form shown in FIGURE 22, though for a particular type of labor or for the supply of labor available to a particular group of employers, the supply curve may be of the steadily increasing form owing to the possibility of attracting labor from other occupations and other employers. Similarly, the (long-run) supply for farm produce in general may be of the same shape, though for particular types of produce the supply curve may be upward-sloping throughout, since farmers can to a considerable extent shift their production from one product to another. Another supply curve that may have such a shape is the supply curve for savings in terms of interest rates; this, however, is a special case requiring the consideration of factors not included in an analysis based on indifference curves.

These conclusions have fairly far-reaching implications for economic theory. If in addition to finding that demand curves were almost universally negatively sloping, it could have been maintained that supply curves were almost universally positively sloping, then the intersection of demand and supply curves could have been pointed to with confidence as a point of stable equilibrium. With perverse supply curves not only not ruled out but shown to be quite plausible in an important class of situations, the problem of the stability of an equilibrium in the market will need much closer investigation.

Consumer's Surplus

WHEN A PRICE is reduced from an original value to a new lower value, or when a new commodity previously unavailable is made available at a price (the latter case can be subsumed under the former merely by making the initial price so high that none of the commodity was bought), the consumer derives a benefit. If making this change involves some cost on the part of a government, or other community agency, as in building a bridge or in making some item available at a price which does not cover the entire costs of the operation, it becomes of considerable interest to find some measure of the benefit derived by the consumer from the change, so that the over-all desirability of the change can be properly appraised.

The first attack on this problem from a theoretical point of view was made in 1844 by Jules Dupuit, who was interested in determining whether or not the construction of a bridge or railroad would be worthwhile from the point

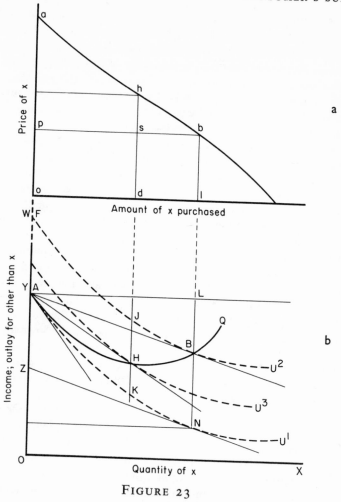

FIGURE 23

of view of the community as a whole. In FIGURE 23a the curve *ahb* represents the ordinary demand curve, defined as the curve showing the amount that consumers will buy during a given period if the price is fixed at various levels. If the actual price is fixed at *op*, or $2, then a consumer is able to purchase all of the 100 units that he elects to purchase for $2 each, or *ds*, whereas he would have been willing to pay *dh*, or $3 each for 70 units. Dupuit supposed that if at a price of $3 the consumer purchases 70 units, but would not have purchased the seventieth unit at any price above $3, then the value of this seventieth unit to the consumer can be estimated at $3. The difference between what he would have been willing to pay for this unit and what he actually does pay, that is *sh* or $1, is the consumer's surplus derived from the purchase

[67

and consumption of this unit, and similarly for the other successive units. Adding the surplus derived from all the units consumed gives the area *psbha* between the demand curve, the *y* axis, and the horizontal line representing the price as the total consumer's surplus derived from the purchase of *ol* at the price of *op*.

Marshall, in defining consumer's surplus as the "excess of the price which he [the consumer] would be willing to pay rather than go without it, over that which he actually does pay," follows the same line of reasoning, except that Marshall in addition makes the important stipulation that for the area *pba* to measure the consumer's surplus exactly, it is necessary to stipulate that the marginal utility of money to the consumer must remain unchanged as the price of *x* falls from *oa* to *op* during the tracing out of the demand curve. For if this is not so, then when the price is *oa*, the consumer will be evaluating the satisfaction derived from the first unit of the commodity in terms of dollars of one marginal utility, and when the price is *dh* the satisfaction derived from the seventieth unit will be evaluated in terms of dollars of another marginal utility, so that combining *pa* with *sh* would be combining dollar amounts that have different contents in terms of satisfaction, and the area *pba* could be given no precise meaning. It is not always clear whether Marshall was assuming that within the range under consideration the variation of the marginal utility of money might sometimes be taken to be so small as to be negligible, or whether he was requiring the demand curve to be constructed by varying other prices, as the price of the good in question is varied, in such a way as actually to keep the marginal utility of money constant. This latter concept is a particularly difficult one to handle, since presumably when there are many "other" prices to vary, there would be many different ways in which they could be varied so as to achieve a constant marginal utility of money, though perhaps it would be appropriate to stipulate that all such prices should be varied in proportion. More serious is the fact that in the absence of a cardinal measure of utility, there would be no operational test of whether the goal of a constant marginal utility of money had actually been attained.

Indifference-curve analysis permits a more direct representation of the significance of consumer's surplus where a constant marginal utility of money can be assumed to hold to a sufficiently close degree of approximation over the range of situations under consideration. Such an analysis will also apply to any case where income effects are absent, even though the marginal utility of money is not known to be constant. In addition, where significant income effects are present, indifference-curve analysis shows the relation between various alternative measurements of consumer's surplus that have been proposed and permits a more precise evaluation of the significance of consumer's surplus in various contexts.

FIGURE 23b shows the indifference diagram corresponding to FIGURE 23a when income effects are absent; a fortiori, the same diagram will represent the case of constant marginal utility of money. Initially, the price is higher than oa, which in turn is the slope of the indifference curve at A. As the price is lowered below oa, the consumer moves along the offer curve $AHBQ$, arriving at B on indifference curve U^2 when the price is op and the price line is ABP; his total outlay is the area $olbp$, which is equal to LB on the indifference diagram. In general, vertical distances, corresponding to amounts of y, on the indifference diagram translate into areas on the demand-curve diagram, and vice versa.

Suppose, however, that instead of giving him the opportunity to buy all he wants at various fixed prices, we sell the consumer the successive units of x separately, each at the maximum price he is willing to pay for it, thus making him move along the indifference curve AKN instead of along the offer curve $AHBQ$; by reason of the assumed absence of income effects, by the time the price is lowered to op the consumer will have bought the same total quantity as before, but he will have paid more, arriving at the point N instead of B. Now at an intermediate point K on the indifference curve U^1 the maximum price which the consumer will pay for another unit is the slope of the indifference curve at K. This, in turn, because of the postulated absence of income effects, will be the same as the slope of the indifference curve U^3 at the point H on the offer curve AHB vertically above K, and this slope, in turn, is equal to the price dh indicated by the demand curve. Adding the various prices payable for the various units under this scheme gives as the area $oabl$ as the total price to be paid for ol of x. Subtracting the amount payable if the price were uniformly op, represented by $opbl$ and LB, respectively, we find that the area pba measuring the consumer's surplus according to Dupuit and Marshall is equal to BN on the indifference map, which may be described as the amount of Y that could be taken away from the consumer after he has established the new equilibrium at B, and still leave him at the level of welfare U^1 represented by the indifference curve AKN from which he started at A. In this case, BN is equal to AZ, which may be described as the amount by which the original income can be reduced and still permit the consumer to reach the original level of welfare U^1 by buying X at the new reduced price. BN is also equal to YW, which may be described as the amount by which the consumer's income would have to be increased, if the price of the new commodity were not reduced, in order to bring him to the same level of welfare U^2 that he could attain with his present income if the price is lowered. Thus with an absence of income effects there is no ambiguity in the notion of consumer's surplus: all of the significant measurements of consumer's surplus turn out to be identical.

Where significant income effects are involved, however, the analysis is slightly more complicated; such a case is illustrated in FIGURE 24. It is assumed here that commodity x is a normal good (i.e., not inferior), as

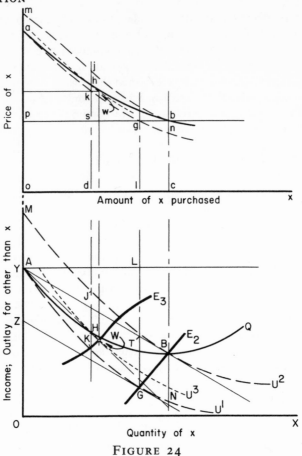

FIGURE 24

indicated by the direction of the Engel curve E_2. In this case, there are three distinct measures of consumer's surplus that may be derived from the indifference map—none of which, however, coincide with the area under the demand curve, which thus becomes a fourth. One may take, for example, the "quantity-compensating variation," BN, which is, as before, the amount of money that can be taken from the individual after he has reached the new equilibrium B, and still leave him as well off as he was originally, i.e., leave him on his original indifference curve U^1, under the assumption that the consumer will not then be allowed to change his consumption of x from the amount established at B. A second measure is the "price-compensating variation" (sometimes referred to simply as the "compensating variation"), YZ, which is the amount of income that can be taken away from the individual and still permit him at the new price to attain the original indifference curve U^1 at the point G, by a suitable purchase of x. A third measure is the "equivalent variation," YM, which is the amount required to be added to income to reach the new level of welfare U^2 if no x can be bought.

To compare these measures with the area under the demand curve, we again proceed by selling the consumer successive units at the maximum price that he is willing to pay for each. This time, we find that as we proceed along the indifference curve $AKGN$, at K the consumer is willing to pay only something less for an additional unit than he would at H, since the marginal rate of substitution remains constant from K to W along the Engel curve E_3, while W is to the right of H by reason of the assumed positive slope of the Engel curves, so that the marginal rate of substitution of y for x increases as we go from W to H along the indifference curve U^3. To represent this process of selling successive units at the maximum possible price on the demand-curve diagram, we may draw a "marginal indifference curve," $akgn$, in which the ordinate of any point k, i.e., dk, corresponds to the marginal rate of substitution of y for x at the corresponding point K along the indifference curve $AKGN$. The marginal indifference curve $akgn$ thus lies below the demand curve ahb. If the price is successively lowered in this way to op, the amount consumed will be only pg, instead of pb. The total amount paid will be $oagl$, which corresponds to LG. However, if the amount pg had been bought at the constant price p, the cost would have been $opgl$, which corresponds to LT. Thus the difference between the cost at a fixed price and the cost at the variable price will be the area pag, corresponding to the amount of income TG, which in turn is equal to the price-compensating variation YZ.

If, instead of stopping when the price reached op, we continue to sell the consumer successive units at still lower prices until he has bought pb units, the last at a price nc, we can show in a similar fashion that the quantity-compensating variation BN is equal to area $oanc$ less area $opbc$, or in other words to area pag diminished by the area of the small triangle gnb. And by first selling the consumer bp units of x at a price op, bringing him to point B, and then buying back from the consumer successive units at the lowest price for which he is willing to surrender each successive unit, we may derive another marginal indifference curve bjm, corresponding to the indifference curve BJM. It is easy to show that with a normal good bjm will lie entirely above the demand curve, and that the area pbm represents the equivalent variation YM.

Thus we see that the equivalent variation is in this case greater than the consumer's surplus as measured by the demand curve, which is itself greater than the compensating variation, which in turn is greater than the quantity-compensating variation.

A similar analysis can be applied to the slightly more complicated case where we have merely a reduction in the price of a commodity already consumed by the consumer, rather than the introduction of a new commodity or the reduction of its price from a level formerly prohibitive. This case is

[71

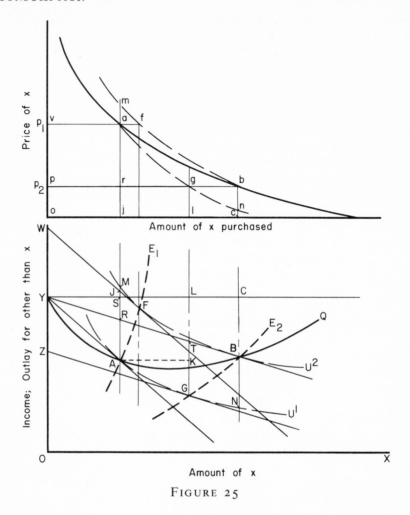

FIGURE 25

illustrated in FIGURE 25. The only important difference is that instead of one equivalent variation *YM*, there is the "price-equivalent variation" *YW* and the "quantity-equivalent variation" *AM*. The change in the consumer's surplus from situation *A* to situation *B* as measured by the demand curve is the area *vabp*, which lies between the equivalent variation *vfbp* and the compensating variation *vagp*.

The rather less important case where the good in question is inferior rather than a normal good can be examined in a similar fashion; in this case, some of the inequalities between the various measures of consumer's surplus are reversed in sign. Also we can have the case of the loss of consumer's surplus from an increase in price, instead of the increase from a fall in price: the only

72]

difference here is that what is called an equivalent variation for a fall in price becomes the compensating variation for a rise in price, and conversely.

Actually, it is the compensating variation *YZ* (in the case of a price increase, the compensating variation becomes *YW*) that is usually of greatest significance for practical problems. The typical problem to which the concept of consumer's surplus is quantitatively important is one where it is proposed to introduce a new service or to reduce its price, with a resulting deficit from operations that will have to be assessed on consumers in some manner. For example, consider the simple case of a community in which differences in consumers' tastes are negligible, so that we can represent their common preferences by a single indifference map, such as that in FIGURE 26, in which the new commodity or service appears on the *x* axis and all previously

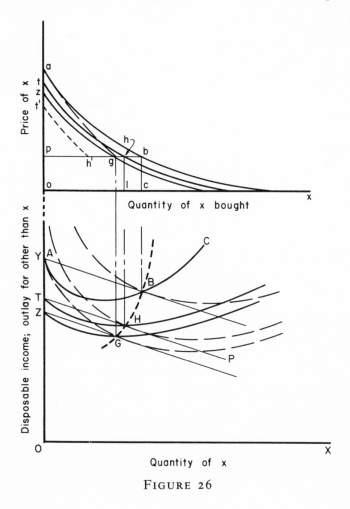

FIGURE 26

existing commodities or services are shown on the y axis as a numéraire. Suppose further that resources are evenly distributed among individuals so that the initial state of each individual before the introduction of the new service can be represented by the point A. Now let us suppose that the introduction of the new service entails a fixed cost equal to AT per capita, and variable costs per unit of x produced are represented by the slope of the line TP. The resources of the community will then be capable of supplying each individual with the combination represented by A, or with any of the combinations along the line TP. If the service is provided, the most advantageous quantity to provide will be indicated by the point H where the line TP is tangent to an indifference curve.

The point H would indeed be reached if each individual were assessed a tax equal to AT and then were offered the opportunity to purchase as much of the service x as he wishes at a price corresponding to the slope of the line TP, i.e., to the "marginal cost" of the service. Whether it is desirable to do this rather than to remain at A depends on whether H is on a higher indifference curve than A, which in turn will depend on whether the tax AT is smaller or larger than the compensating variation YZ. It is interesting to note that as the diagram is drawn, H is in fact on a higher indifference curve than A, and the project is thus a desirable one, even though the offer curve AB lies entirely above the line of feasible operations TP, so that there is no uniform price at which the service could be sold so as to yield sufficient revenue to cover the entire costs of the service: in this case the service could not possibly be financed from sales revenues at a uniform price without the imposition of a tax.

While the exact value of the compensating variation YZ cannot be derived directly from the usual types of demand curve, nevertheless if we are willing to assume that demand curves under varying conditions can be estimated, an unequivocal decision can be reached in most cases. To begin with, if we estimate the demand curve as it would be if no tax were imposed, shown as ab in FIGURE 26, and the consumer's surplus pba as defined by this curve is less than the required tax or subsidy, then we know that the compensating variation pga is still smaller than this and the project is not warranted (still presuming the case of the normal good).

On the other hand, if the demand curve can be estimated as it would be after the imposition of the tax, as at zg, then if the project is unwarranted the tax would have to exceed the compensating variation. But if the tax thus exceeds the compensating variation, then the new demand curve must lie wholly below the marginal indifference curve through A over the relevant range, as shown at $t'h'$, and the consumer's surplus indicated by the new demand curve must be less than the compensating variation and hence less than the required tax. Therefore, if the surplus indicated by this new demand curve is greater than the required tax, the project must be a desirable one. It is only in those cases where the shift in the demand curve caused by the imposition of the tax changes the indicated surplus from an amount exceeding the tax to an amount less than the tax that this method will prove inconclusive.

Actually, of course, the margin of error always present in any estimate of a demand curve will normally be many times the amount by which the demand curve would be shifted by the required tax, so that for most practical purposes this theoretical degree of refinement is superfluous. But it is only by going through the theoretical analysis that one can determine the factors determining the closeness of the approximation involved in taking the area under the demand curve as a measure of consumer's surplus, so as to obtain the necessary degree of confidence in the use of such a measure.

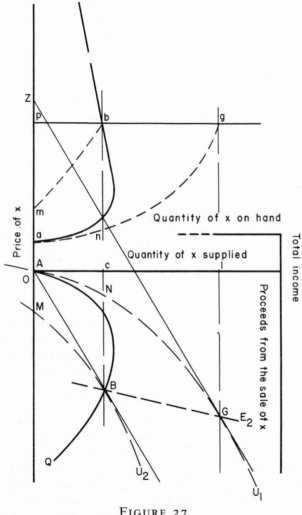

FIGURE 27

Where a trader, instead of being a buyer of the commodity x that changes in price, has a large stock of x and becomes a seller as a result of a price increase, an exactly comparable analysis may be made of the "seller's surplus." This surplus frequently gives rise to "rent," either as an explicit payment or as an imputed element of income, as will be seen in the analysis of production. This situation is illustrated in FIGURE 27; the working out of the details is left to the reader.

Index Numbers

ONE CAN also apply the indifference-curve analysis of individual choice to the theory of index numbers. If an individual is observed in two different situations, each situation being defined in terms of a set of prices and a set of commodities consumed, the value of the commodities consumed at the corresponding prices being the total "income," then one use of an index of prices is to "deflate" these incomes so as to yield a "real income," which is a number intended to reflect the physical magnitude of the corresponding basket of goods consumed. It is obviously desirable that insofar as possible whenever two such computations yield the same "real income," the level of utility of the consumer should be the same, and conversely. Accordingly, the "true" index of the cost of living is defined as the ratio of the money income necessary at a given current set of prices to enable the consumer to reach a specified level of satisfaction, to the money income necessary at a specified set of "base-period" prices to enable the consumer to reach the same level of satisfaction. This true cost-of-living index is defined only relative to a given person at a given level of real income. Obviously, it is possible for the cost-of-living index for a given period in terms of a given base period to be quite different for high levels of income from what it is for low levels of income even for the same individual, inasmuch as the important commodities and their relative prices may differ.

Thus in FIGURE 28, if $Q_1{}^1$ is the consumption pattern (or "basket," or "combination") of x and y chosen by an individual at the set of prices P_1 represented by the line AF, then of course AF is tangent to the indifference curve U^1 at $Q_1{}^1$, and the money income needed to reach this level of satisfaction is oA. This income can also be written $p_{1x}x_1 + p_{1y}y_1$, or more generally $\Sigma_i p_{1i} q_{1i}$; for brevity, where no confusion is likely to result, this income can be designated by A, or by $\Sigma p_1 q_1$.

If the prices in the base period (o) are represented by the slope of the line P_0, then in order to achieve the same real level of satisfaction in the base period, it would have been necessary to have had an income oB (or simply B) resulting in the budget line BG, parallel to P_0, and the equilibrium point $Q_0{}^1$ (where the superscript indicates that the basket of goods designated produces the level of satisfaction corresponding to the indifference curve U^1, and the subscript indicates that the basket designated is one which might be chosen when prices are P_0, i.e., that it lies along the Engel curve E_0). The index for period 1 in terms of period 0 as a base is then oA/oB.

In general, to find the true index of the cost of living at time t_1 in terms of t_0 as a base period, using the indifference curve U^r as a criterion, we first find the point on U^r where the marginal rates of substitution are proportional to the prices P_1, and where therefore the consumer might be in equilibrium at the prices P_1; this point can be designated $Q_1{}^r$. We then evaluate this basket at

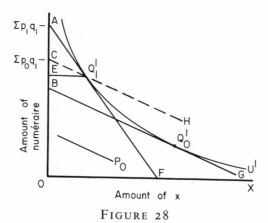

FIGURE 28

the prices P_1, getting the necessary income $_1R_1{}^r = \Sigma p_1 q_1{}^r$. For the two-commodity case, this evaluation can be represented graphically by extending the price line from the basket in question to the numéraire axis; the intercept on the numéraire axis will be the value of the basket in terms of the numéraire. For example, in FIGURE 28, $Q_1{}^1$ consists of oE units of y and $EQ_1{}^1$ units of x. The cost of the $EQ_1{}^1$ units of x is obtained by multiplying them by the price of x in terms of y, indicated by the slope of the price line AF, so that the cost of the x is equal to EA. As the cost of the oE units of y is simply oE itself, the price of the numéraire commodity in terms of itself being by definition 1, the total cost of $qQ_1{}^1$ is

$$p_{1x}q_{1x} + p_{1y}q_{1y} = EA + oE = oA = \Sigma p_1 q_1$$

Similarly, we find the point on U^r where the marginal rates of substitution are proportional to the prices P_0, designated $Q_0{}^r$, and evaluate this basket at the prices P_0 to get the necessary income in this case $_0R_0{}^r = \Sigma p_0 q_0{}^r$. The true index of period 1 in terms of period 0 at the level of income r is then

$$I_{01}{}^r = \frac{_1R_1{}^r}{_0R_0{}^r}$$

[77

Unfortunately, the data usually available do not specify the exact shape of the indifference curve U^r or U^1, nor do they in most cases permit us to determine the basket $Q_0{}^r$ or $Q_0{}^1$, so that the corresponding true index cannot be determined. However, if we ascertain the income required to purchase the basket $Q_1{}^1$ at the prices P_0, we get the income $_0R_1{}^1 = \Sigma p_0 q_1{}^1$, which can be represented in the two-commodity case by oC, determined by drawing the price line through $Q_1{}^1$ having a slope representing the prices P_0, and extending it to the y axis at C. Now C must necessarily be higher than B, as can be seen directly from the diagram, and also more generally by considering that for C to be lower than B would mean that at prices P_0, $Q_1{}^1$ could be obtained for less than $Q_0{}^1$, contrary to the assumption that $Q_0{}^1$ is the cheapest way of reaching the satisfaction level U^1 at the prices P_0. Thus A/C must be less than A/B. But A/C is merely a simple aggregative price index using as weights the amounts of the various commodities being consumed at time I, or in other words the ratio of the cost of $Q_1{}^1$ at prices P_1 to its cost at prices P_0. This index is often termed the Paasche index; its formula is

$$P_{01} = \frac{\Sigma p_1 q_1}{\Sigma p_0 q_1} = \frac{_1R_1{}^1}{_0R_1{}^1}$$

We see immediately that the Paasche index is never greater than the true index of the cost of living *at the current real income level*, and thus furnishes a lower bound for this true index.

The above argument, and the ones that follow, are quite general, and apply not merely to the two-commodity case, which is all there is room for in a plane diagram, but to cases with any number of commodities. The three-commodity case can be visualized by replacing U^1 by an indifference surface and the lines AF and BG by budget planes tangent to this surface, using the intercept of these planes on the y axis as the evaluation of the baskets through which they pass.

Actually, of course, one is more likely to have information on the consumption patterns of individuals for a base period some time in the past than for the current period, since budget investigations take considerable time to carry out. Both for this reason and because it is inconvenient to change the weights in an index each year, most simple index numbers actually constructed come closer to being of the form

$$L_{01} = \frac{\Sigma p_1 q_0}{\Sigma p_0 q_0} = \frac{_1R_0{}^0}{_0R_0{}^0}$$

This is known as Laspeyre's formula, representing the ratio of the cost of the old basket at the new prices to the cost of the old basket at the old prices. By reasoning similar to the above, it is found that Laspeyre's index is never smaller than the true index of the cost of living *at the base period level of real income*. But as we have seen that there is no necessary relation between the true index at one level of income and that at another level, this tells us nothing new about the true index at the current income level. It is sometimes stated that the true index of the cost of living must lie between the Laspeyre and the Paasche indexes, but this holds only if it be assumed that the true index is the same for the two levels of real income. In many cases it can reasonably be presumed that this difference is extremely small, but the difference nevertheless exists, at least in principle. If, however, the true index is assumed to vary continuously as we move up and down the scale of real income (as would be

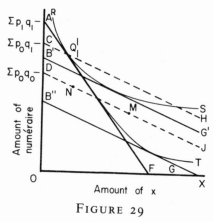

FIGURE 29

the case in the absence of flat spots or discontinuities in the utility function), then there will exist some range of income between the base-period level and the current level, for which the true index will lie between the Laspeyre and the Paasche indexes.

If we confine our attention strictly to the true index at a given level, say that of the current situation at Q_1^1, then adding information concerning the base-period basket Q_0^0 may give us no positive additional information at all about the true index at the level 1. If Q_0^0 lies above the period 1 budget line AF, as at M in FIGURE 29 (i.e., if Q_0^0 would cost more at the new prices than would Q_1^1), then still, for all we know, the indifference curve U^1 may have the shape RS with a sharp curve near Q_1^1 so that the true index can still be found as close as we please to A/C. Or on the other hand there is nothing to prevent the indifference curve U^1 from stretching down close to but just above AF, as shown in the curve RT, which gives the true index a value A/B''. And there is nothing to prevent the line $B'G'$ from being lowered as far as we like, except that if we rule out negative quantities of goods, it would not pass below the x intercept of the original budget line at F. This limitation, however, has merely the effect of asserting that the true index will not rise by more than did the component price that has risen most.

However, if Q_0^0 lies below AF, as at N in FIGURE 29, then we know that

Q_1^1 is preferred to Q_0^0 (otherwise Q_0^0 rather than Q_1^1 would have been bought in period 1, since it was available at a lower cost). Therefore in period 0 it must take more than the income $_0R_0^0 = \Sigma p_0 q_0^0$ to provide the U^1 level of satisfaction, and we can state that the true index must be less than A/D.

It may happen that one has information for the base period not merely for one equilibrium basket, but for an entire portion of the Engel curve, as, for example, when a study has been made of the variation of consumption patterns with income, and the assumption is made that on the average the

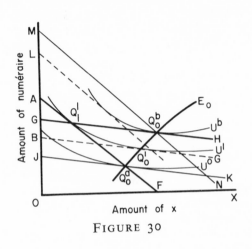

FIGURE 30

basic preference patterns of individuals at various levels of income are the same (though since remote portions of the indifference map are of little relevance to a given individual, and various income classes may be thought to have clear ideas concerning their preferences only for the region in the immediate neighborhood of the situation they are currently experiencing, the remoter parts of the indifference map may have to be thought of as a sort of latent pattern to be developed if and when it becomes relevant to their field of opportunities). The information then consists of a single pattern for time 1, i.e., Q_1^1, and the Engel curve E_0, in FIGURE 30, together with the two sets of prices. It will then be possible to pick out on the Engel curve E_0 a point Q_0^a representing a basket which costs the same as Q_1^1 at prices P_1 (i.e., $_1R_1^1 = _1R_0^a$), and another point Q_0^b representing a basket costing the same as Q_1^1 at prices P_0 (i.e., $_0R_1^1 = _0R_0^b$). The Paasche index based on the basket Q_1^1 and the Laspeyre index based on the basket Q_0^a will then furnish lower and upper limits for the true index at the U^1 level of real income, while the Paasche index, again based on Q_1^1, and the Laspeyre index based this time on Q_0^b will furnish lower and upper limits, respectively, for the true index at the U^b level of real income.

80]

In practice, prices often tend to change in a fairly parallel fashion, so that the differences among the Paasche, the Laspeyre, and the true indexes are fairly slight. Another factor making for small differences among these indexes is that shifts of consumption among commodities whose prices do change substantially are often themselves slight. Indeed, when prices and consumption patterns do change drastically, there is often implied a change in other circumstances that robs of much of its significance the concept of a true index based on an assumed unchanged pattern of tastes. If one wishes to convert pounds into rupees according to a cost-of-living index, for example, whose tastes are to be the criterion, the Indian's or the Briton's? And what meaning is to be given to the cost of securing in England the basket of commodities that is normally consumed at a given level of income in India?

Granted the constancy and validity of a particular set of tastes, however, the margin of uncertainty inherent in the above type of analysis can be reduced or eliminated if it is possible to assume various additional restrictions on the shape of the indifference map. One drastic but appealing restriction of this sort is "expenditure proportionality," which is the assumption that at any given set of prices expenditure on each commodity is proportional to income, so that the Engel curves are all straight lines passing through the origin. In this case, the true index is the same for all income levels and lies between the Paasche and Laspeyre indexes. If a further drastic assumption of "universal-unit elasticity" is made, implying that total expenditure for each commodity remains the same, regardless of price, then the true index can be computed knowing only the prices and quantities at the two extreme points being compared.

Another approach is to assume that prices change gradually over time, and that for each small change in the price pattern the corresponding Engel curve can be ascertained. For the two-commodity case an analysis on these lines is trivial, for if we can cover the portion of the map lying between two Engel curves with a continuous series of intermediate Engel curves, each with its relevant set of prices stipulated, we can derive the indifference curves for such a part of the indifference map and thus ascertain the true index directly. Even for n commodities, however, if prices change continuously through time, the corresponding Engel curve will trace out, over time, a two-dimensional surface in this n-dimensional space, the points in which will be determined by the two parameters income and time. The intersections of the indifference loci with this two-dimensional surface will be curves on this surface, and these curves can be traced out from a knowledge of the Engel curves and the prices to which they correspond, since at each point in this surface the set of prices associated with the Engel curve through this point will be in effect an instruction as to the direction in which one must proceed in order to remain on the same indifference locus. With such curves, for any given point on the initial Engel curve it will be possible to ascertain what point

[81

on the final Engel curve lies on the same indifference locus as the selected initial point, and thus the true index can be determined.

In practice, what this procedure amounts to is the construction of successive indexes between successive periods, using, say, Fisher's ideal formula between each pair of adjacent periods, and adjusting the budget levels used, if necessary, so that for each stage they correspond to the same real income as indicated by the indexes; and then multiplying the successive indexes to get the index between the initial and final states. As the number of steps is increased and the differences in prices and quantities between one stage and the next become smaller and smaller, the possible margin of error between the computed index and the true index can be made as small as desired, subject of course to inaccuracies in the data. This is the justification, such as it is, for the use of linked relatives in the construction of index numbers.

Difficulties analogous to those arising in the construction of cost-of-living indexes occur more or less generally in all index-number construction, including price and quantity indexes that are used to combine more or less closely related commodity groups into single over-all commodities for the purposes of analysis. As we have seen previously, if within a group prices always move in strict proportion, then there is no loss of rigor (and no index-number problem!). But if this condition is not met, difficulties arise in addition to those met with in the construction of cost-of-living indexes. With cost-of-living indexes, one can consider the surrounding circumstances and tastes as relatively constant, and above all it is possible conceptually to have a single ultimate criterion to appeal to in the shape of the indifference map. Group indexes, however, can be affected by changes in the consumption of other types of commodities, some of which may be merely internal to other commodity groups, which will involve changes in the tastes and circumstances relative to the commodity group being considered. For example, certain types of food will be competitive with, and others complementary to, adequate kitchen facilities: having a large kitchen, a kitchenette, a hot plate, or no facilities at all will substantially affect the type of food bought, though expenditure on kitchen facilities may be buried in "housing" expenditure to an extent that would conceal this relationship entirely. And again in constructing an index for a given commodity group, one might apply one set of standards derived from indifference maps in obtaining a measure intended to indicate the ability of the aggregate to satisfy wants, and another set of standards derived from cost functions and production relationships in obtaining a measure intended to indicate the difficulty of producing the output: under competitive conditions with price equated with both marginal cost and marginal utility there might be a fairly close correspondence between the two measures, but where taxes, monopoly elements, and other disturbances enter the picture one may have to choose between a multiplicity of measures and an all-purpose measure that corresponds precisely to no one concept. The "index-number problem" is, however, but one aspect of the complex set of problems that goes by the name of "the problem of aggregation."

Mathematical Appendix

NOTE: The purpose of these mathematical appendixes is not to give a complete mathematical treatment of the subject, but rather to indicate briefly the manner in which the apparatus of mathematics can be used in the further elucidation of the principles brought out in the text, and to give the reader an opportunity to explore a short distance into the vast areas that are opened up by the use of mathematics. For a fuller treatment the reader should consult such primarily mathematical treatments as are to be found, for example, in J. M. Henderson and R. E. Quandt, *Microeconomic Theory*, and R. G. D. Allen, *Mathematical Economics*.

Commodity space. We will suppose that there are altogether r distinct commodities and services. A commodity combination, sometimes referred to as a "basket" or "bundle" or "situation," is specified by r parameters giving the quantities of the various commodities contained in the "basket." If we designate a given basket by $\mathbf{q}$, we can designate the amounts of the ith commodity contained in $\mathbf{q}$ by q_i. A more specific designation for the basket $\mathbf{q}$ is

$$\mathbf{q} = \{q_1, q_2, \ldots, q_i, \ldots, q_r\} \qquad 2.1$$

Such a basket $\mathbf{q}$ has the mathematical properties of a *vector*; it is convenient to distinguish vectors by representing them by boldface characters.

If there are only two commodities under consideration, $r = 2$, and we can put $\mathbf{q} = (q_1, q_2) = (x, y)$, where for convenience instead of using the subscripts 1 and 2 to designate the two commodities we can use x and y. This simplification is less feasible in the more general case because of the likelihood of running out of symbols. In the two-commodity case each basket $\mathbf{q}$ can be represented by a point in the x, y plane.

Indifference curves. With two commodities, an indifference curve can be represented by a function

$$y = f(x) \qquad 2.2$$

for example, $y = (1 - x)/(1 + x)$. To maintain symmetry between the manner in which the two commodities are treated in the representation it is often desirable to express this function implicitly:

$$g(x, y) = 0; \qquad (x + 1)(y + 1) - 2 = 0 \qquad 2.3$$

If we wish to represent a whole family of indifference curves, or an indifference map, a parameter, say k, must be introduced that can be varied so as to

[83

produce the different indifference curves. Thus an entire map would be represented by

$$h(x, y, k) = g_k(x, y) = 0; \qquad (x + 1)(y + 1) - k = 0 \qquad 2.4$$

It is apparent that k can be replaced by various functions of k, say by k^3, $1 + 2k$, etc., without changing the map that is generated by this function; all that is changed is the value of k associated with a given indifference curve. The map of FIGURE 3 is produced, for example, by the function

$$(x - a)^2 + (y - b)^2 = k \qquad 2.5$$

where a and b are the coordinates of the satiation point S. It could equally well be represented by the function

$$(x - a)^2 + (y - b)^2 = 2k^3 + k + 1 \qquad 2.6$$

Utility. If the parameter k is chosen in such a way that points on curves having a higher k are always preferred to points on curves having a lower k, then k can be considered an *index* of satisfaction or utility. There are of course many ways in which k can be chosen so as to meet this condition. In fact if $k^* = f(k)$, with

$$[f(k_1) - f(k_2)][k_1 - k_2] > 0 \qquad 2.7$$

for all k_1, k_2 for which $k_1 \neq k_2$; i.e., if $f(k)$ is a monotone increasing function of k, then if k is an index of utility, k^* is also. To say that k is an index of utility does not imply that it is necessarily a *measure* of utility.

If some particular k is deemed, on the basis of some further information, to be not only an index but a *measure* of utility, we can write

$$k = U = G(x, y) \qquad 2.8$$

or in the general case,

$$k = U = f(\mathbf{q}) = f(q_1, q_2, \ldots q_r) \qquad 2.9$$

For economy of symbols, where no confusion is likely to result, U is used both to represent utility itself and to represent the functional relationship between U and $\mathbf{q}$: $U = U(\mathbf{q})$. For example, the utility surfaces depicted in FIGURE 4 are represented, respectively, by the expressions

$$U_a = s - [(a - x)^2 + (b - y)^2]^{1/2}$$

$$U_b = [s^2 - (a - x)^2 - (b - y)^2]^{1/2} \qquad 2.10$$

$$U_c = s - (a - x)^2 - (b - y)^2$$

$$U_d = s - [(a - x)^2 + (b - y)^2]^{1/3} \qquad 2.11$$

where in each case $s = U(a, b)$ is the satiation level of utility reached when $x = a$, and $y = b$.

84]

It is often convenient to frame the discussion in terms of a specific utility function, even though there may be no basis shown for choosing one k rather than another as the measure of utility. When this is done, however, care must be taken to make use of only those properties of the utility function that are independent of the way in which the utility measure is chosen. This means that if a property P holds for a utility function U, it must also hold for any other utility function V which can be expressed as

$$V = F(U) \qquad\qquad 2.12$$

where F is a monotone increasing function. For example, the marginal utility of a commodity x is $\partial U/\partial x$ or of a commodity q_j is $\partial U/\partial q_j$; for brevity we often write $U_x{}'$ or simply U_x for $\partial U/\partial x$, and even U_j for $\partial U/\partial q_j$. If we express marginal utility in terms of an alternative utility function $V = F(U)$, we have

$$V_j = \frac{\partial V}{\partial q_j} = \frac{dV}{dU}\frac{\partial U}{\partial q_j} = F'U_j \qquad\qquad 2.13$$

Thus the marginal utility in terms of V in general differs from the marginal utility in terms of U. However, since F' is necessarily positive for a monotone increasing transformation, the marginal utility in terms of V will have the same sign as the marginal utility in terms of U. The sign, but not the magnitude, of marginal utility is invariant with respect to the choice of a utility function; thus the phenomenon of satiation, which is where $U_x = 0$, is determined independently of the choice of a utility function.

Marginal rate of substitution. If an indifference curve is described by the function $G(x, y) = k$, the marginal rate of substitution is the negative of the slope of this curve:

$$S_{y/x} = -dy/dx \qquad\qquad 2.14$$

This can be evaluated by differentiating $G(x, y) = k$ totally with respect to x, keeping k constant:

$$\frac{dG}{dx} = \frac{\partial G}{\partial x} + \frac{\partial G}{\partial y}\frac{dy}{dx} = 0 \qquad\qquad 2.15$$

whence

$$S_{y/x} = -\frac{dy}{dx} = \frac{\dfrac{\partial G}{\partial x}}{\dfrac{\partial G}{\partial y}} \qquad\qquad 2.16$$

if k is identified with utility, so that we can write

$$U = G(x, y) = U(x, y) \qquad\qquad 2.17$$

then we have

$$S_{y/x} = \frac{U_x}{U_y} \qquad\qquad 2.18$$

[85

i.e., the marginal rate of substitution (of y for x) is equal to the ratio of the marginal utility of x to that of y. It can immediately be verified that this expression for $S_{y/x}$ is actually independent of the choice of the utility function, for if again we put $V = F(U)$, then in terms of V,

$$S_{y/x} = \frac{V_x}{V_y} = \frac{F'U_x}{F'U_y} = \frac{U_x}{U_y} \qquad 2.19$$

This result generalizes immediately to cases of many commodities.

Convexity, independence, and decreasing marginal utility. The property of increasing marginal rate of substitution (of y for x, as y is substituted for x) can be expressed by

$$\frac{d}{dy}(S_{y/x}) = \frac{\partial}{\partial y}(S_{y/x}) + \frac{dx}{dy}\frac{\partial}{\partial x}(S_{y/x}) = \frac{\partial}{\partial y}(S_{y/x}) - \frac{\mathrm{I}}{S_{y/x}}\frac{\partial}{\partial x}(S_{y/x}) > 0 \qquad 2.20$$

Putting $S_{y/x} = U_x/U_y$ from 2.18 into 2.20, and for brevity putting U_{xy} for $\partial^2 U/\partial x \partial y$, we get

$$\frac{U_{xy}U_y - U_{yy}U_x}{U_y{}^2} - \frac{U_y}{U_x}\left(\frac{U_{xx}U_y - U_{yx}U_x}{U_y{}^2}\right) > 0 \qquad 2.21$$

Given that U_x and U_y are both positive, this condition is equivalent to the requirement that

$$-U_x{}^2 U_{yy} - U_y{}^2 U_{xx} + 2U_x U_y U_{xy} > 0 \qquad 2.22$$

It is readily verified that this property is invariant with respect to the choice of the utility function. If 2.22 is not fulfilled, this would indicate a concavity in the indifference curves, such as is indicated in FIGURE 16c.

If the marginal utility of x is not affected by the amount of y present, then

$$\frac{\partial}{\partial y}(U_x) = U_{xy} = 0 \qquad 2.23$$

Since $U_{xy} = U_{yx}$, this independence is symmetrical. It is not, however, invariant with respect to the choice of utility functions since if $V = F(U)$, then

$$V_{xy} = F''U_{xy} + F'U_x U_y \qquad 2.24$$

so that $U_{xy} = 0$ implies $V_{xy} = 0$ only if $F' = 0$, implying that the transformation from U to V must be linear, unless indeed U_x or U_y is zero.

Similarly, the property of decreasing marginal utility, expressed by the conditions $U_{xx} < 0$ and $U_{yy} < 0$ for the two commodities, respectively, is dependent on the choice of the utility function. If, however, the utility function is chosen in such a way as to yield decreasing marginal utility for both x and y, and independence between them, we have $U_{xx} < 0$, $U_{yy} < 0$, and $U_{xy} = 0$, so that condition 2.22 must be satisfied and the indifference curves must be convex.

It is possible to have both increasing marginal rate of substitution and independence and yet have increasing marginal utility for at least one commodity: FIGURE 8a can be considered to represent the function

$$U = -(1 - x)^2 + y^2 \qquad\qquad 2.25$$

which has increasing marginal rate of substitution in the region where U is positive and $x < 1$, but U_{yy} is positive, and independence is indicated by $U_{xy} = 0$. The situation in FIGURE 8b is approximated by the utility function

$$U = 4(x^2 + y^2)^{1/2} - x^2 - y^2 - 3 \qquad\qquad 2.26$$

and it is readily confirmed that in this case as long as $x^2 + y^2 < 2$, U_x and U_y are positive, U_{xx} and U_{yy} are negative, but 2.22 indicates a decreasing marginal rate of substitution. If we insist on using the equation of a torus rather than a rough approximation, this would be

$$U^2 = 4(x^2 + y^2)^{1/2} - x^2 - y^2 - 3 \qquad\qquad 2.27$$

The results are the same as in the previous approximation, but the algebra becomes an excellent illustration of how involved even relatively simple geometrical relations can become when expressed algebraically. It is readily verified that this property is invariant with respect to the choice of the utility function. If this condition is not fulfilled, it would indicate a concavity in the indifference curves.

Of the four expressions given above at 2.10 and 2.11, U_c is distinguished by the property of independence with $U_{xy} = 0$. And if we modify U_a slightly to make it

$$U_e = s - [(a - x)^2 + (b - y)^2 - c^2]^{1/2} \qquad\qquad 2.28$$

we get a utility function in which if we take some $h < c$, and put $x = a - h$, and $y = b - h$, we find U_{xx} and U_{yy} both positive, even though the marginal rate of substitution is increasing.

Complementarity and substitution in a binary system. In defining complementarity in terms of a reference curve of the form $x^b y = k$, we have first to select that reference curve of this form that passes through the point under examination and has the same marginal rate of substitution at that point as the indifference map being measured. We then compare how fast the marginal rate of substitution of the subject indifference curve changes relative to the rate of change of the slope of the reference curve. For the latter we have $y = kx^{-b}$, $-dy/dx = bkx^{-b-1}$, and

$$\frac{d}{dx}\left(-\frac{dy}{dx}\right) = -b(b + 1)kx^{-b-2} = -b(b + 1)yx^{-2} \qquad\qquad 2.29$$

For the rate of change of the marginal rate of substitution of the subject curve, we have

$$\frac{d}{dx}(S_{y/x}) = \frac{d}{dx}\left(\frac{U_x}{U_y}\right) = \frac{\partial}{\partial x}\left(\frac{U_x}{U_y}\right) + \frac{dy}{dx}\frac{\partial}{\partial y}\left(\frac{U_x}{U_y}\right) = \frac{\partial}{\partial x}\left(\frac{U_x}{U_y}\right) - \frac{U_x}{U_y}\frac{\partial}{\partial y}\left(\frac{U_x}{U_y}\right)$$

$$= \frac{1}{U_y^3}[U_y(U_x U_{yx} - U_y U_{xx}) - U_x(U_y U_{xx} - U_x U_{xy})] \qquad 2.30$$

To determine the value of b, we have

$$\frac{U_x}{U_y} = -\frac{dy}{dx} = bkx^{-b-1} \qquad 2.31$$

so that $b = xU_x/yU_y$. Taking the ratio of 2.29 to 2.30 and using this value for b, we obtain for the coefficient of complementarity

$$c = \frac{U_y^2 U_{xx} - 2U_x U_y U_{xy} + U_x^2 U_{yy}}{U_x U_y}\left(\frac{xy}{yU_y + xU_x}\right) \qquad 2.32$$

This is discouragingly elaborate! It is, of course, invariant to changes in the choice of the utility function.

Potential independence. If we make the width of the rectangle of FIGURE 13 become vanishingly small, it is clear that if we keep x fixed, $\partial/\partial x(S_{y/x})$ must be proportional to $S_{y/x}$, as y is varied, if the independence criterion is to be satisfied. The factor of proportionality can of course vary as we vary x, but we can write

$$\frac{1}{S_{y/x}}\frac{\partial}{\partial x}(S_{y/x}) = \frac{U_{xx}}{U_x} - \frac{U_{xy}}{U_y} \qquad 2.33$$

Then if this expression, when evaluated, is independent of y, potential independence exists. A symmetrical test is obtainable by interchanging x and y. Actually, if an algebraic utility function is available, potential independence will usually be evident from inspection, if it exists.

EXERCISES

GENERAL SUGGESTIONS FOR GRAPHICAL EXERCISES: *A transparent ruler and a transparent draftsman's triangle will be useful instruments. Unless a line is actually asked for, it will be desirable to avoid drawing it, if possible; where the intersection of two lines is required, it will usually be sufficient to draw a small bit of each of the two lines in the vicinity of the point where the intersection will take place. The equations of the curves, where given, may be ignored except by those with a knowledge of calculus and considerable facility with algebra who may wish to try their hand at an analytical solution; the analytical solution is considerably more difficult than the graphical one, but may be of interest to mathematicians. Proceed one step at a time: the problems are not as formidable as they may seem at first glance. It may also help to draw curves relating to different individuals in contrasting colors or line characters (dotted, dashed, etc.).*

I

IMAGINE that a group of you living together in a dormitory have decided to have breakfast together in one of your rooms, perhaps with a view to a discussion of the finer points of economic theory. You send one of your number out to get the breakfast for all of you, and he is to spend exactly 65 cents per person, and bring back for each one cup of coffee (or tea) with cream and sugar as desired and one small glass of fruit juice; he is to spend the remainder on varying amounts of scrambled eggs and toast. Prices of toast and eggs in the cafeteria have a habit of fluctuating violently from day to day, from, say, one cent per egg or per slice of toast up to 50 cents each, and being budding economic theorists, you each issue your instructions to the one who is to get breakfast for all of you in the form of an indifference map, which your agent is to follow by spending your 65 cents in such a way as to reach the highest indifference curve possible. The 65 cents, for some unfathomable reason must all be spent, no matter how high or how low the prices, and the eggs and toast must all be eaten, lest the crumbs attract vermin. Lay out axes on which you can represent 0 to 6 slices of toast horizontally and 0 to 10 eggs vertically, and draw your indifference map in the space thus defined.

Assuming that on four different days your agent finds the following situations in the cafeteria, what amounts of eggs and toast do you expect him to bring back for you?

	COST OF COFFEE PLUS FRUIT JUICE, CENTS	PRICE OF EGGS, CENTS PER EGG	PRICE OF TOAST, CENTS PER SLICE	NUMBER OF EGGS	SLICES OF TOAST
Monday	25	15	5	—	—
Tuesday	15	10	2	—	—
Wednesday	20	10	15	—	—
Thursday	30	20	10	—	—

Draw the budget lines on your indifference map, and locate the equilibrium points.

II

IN THE diagram reproduced at the top of page 90, the curves in the lower-right-hand part of the sheet represent the indifference map of an individual between two commodities (say meat, measured vertically, against eggs, measured horizontally).

1. a. Suppose a consumer *A* comes to market with an annual supply of 50 pounds of meat, but no eggs. Mark his "starting point" "*A*."

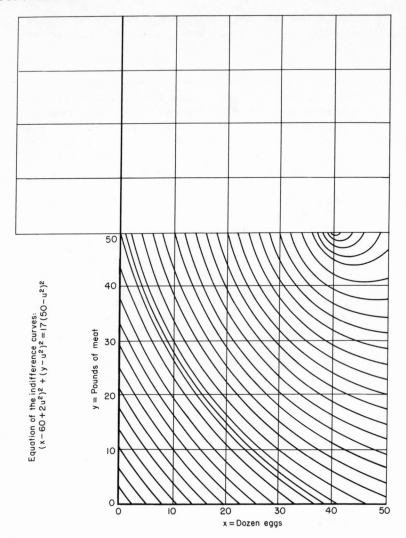

Equation of the indifference curves:
$(x-60+2u^2)^2 + (y-u^2)^2 = 17(50-u^2)^2$

y = Pounds of meat

x = Dozen eggs

b. *A*, on coming to market, finds the current price of eggs is 1.25 pounds of meat per dozen eggs; i.e., five pounds of meat will buy four dozen eggs. Draw the "opportunity curve" ("price line," or "budget line").

c. Mark the point that *A* will select among those open to him at this price, "*E*." *A* will then purchase _____ dozen eggs, at an outlay of _____ pounds of meat, retaining _____ pounds of meat for his own consumption.

2. a. If *B* comes to market with only 30 pounds of meat and finds the price to be 1.25, and *B* has no eggs to start with, draw his opportunity

curve and locate on it the point *F* which he will select if his tastes are the same as those of *A*. *B* would then purchase _____ dozen eggs at an outlay of _____ pounds of meat, retaining _____ pounds of meat for his own consumption.

b. Draw the Engel curve ("income-consumption curve," or "standard-of-life line") for the price of 1.25. Label this curve $P = 1.25$ (Hint: It is not necessary actually to draw further budget lines to get more points on the Engel curve. Other points may be obtained if one edge of a triangle is placed on the initial budget line, and a ruler or another triangle placed against another edge; the triangle may then be made to slide along the ruler so that the first edge is always parallel to the initial budget line. The points of tangency to the successive curves may then be marked and the resulting Engel curve drawn in.)

3. a. Similarly, draw Engel curves for the following prices: $P = 2.0$; $P = 0.5$; $P = 0.25$; $P = 0$.

b. The curve $P = 0$ indicates _____
_____ .

c. Of which commodity is there a surfeit in some region of the part of the indifference map shown? _____. Indicate on the indifference map the region in which surfeit exists (by shading ////).

d. Which commodity is an inferior good in a portion of the sector of the indifference map shown? _____. Indicate by shading (XXXX) the area in which this commodity is inferior.

e. Indicate with *S* the point of complete satiation with both commodities.

4. a. For an individual coming to the market with 50 pounds of meat, what will be the point of equilibrium if the price is 2.0 (Hint: It is not necessary actually to draw the opportunity line: if a ruler is laid in the position of the opportunity line the point of equilibrium can be marked without actually drawing the line, thus avoiding adding confusing lines to the figure.)

b. Similarly, fill in the following table:

PRICE OF EGGS (pounds of meat per dozen eggs)	OUTLAY (pounds of meat spent)	MEAT CONSUMPTION (pounds of meat)	EGG CONSUMPTION (dozen eggs)
2.0	—	—	—
1.5	—	—	—
1.25	—	—	—
1.0	—	—	—
0.5	—	—	—
0.25	—	—	—
0.0	—	—	—

(NOTE: Be sure your answers are consistent with the given price.)

c. Draw A's offer (or "outlay-consumption" curve). (Hint: If a pin or thumbtack is inserted at the point about which the price lines pivot, and a ruler rotated against this pin, the successive points on the curve can be easily marked off.)

5. a. Using the upper-right-hand part of the sheet, and taking the unit horizontal distance laid off at the upper-left as a basis for constructing a price scale, construct A's demand curve for eggs. Label the price axis appropriately.

b. How high would the price of eggs have to be for A to stop consuming eggs entirely? $P = $ _____.

6. a. An individual C with the same tastes as A has initially 50 dozen eggs a month and no meat. Mark his starting point C and draw his offer curve.

b. Draw C's supply curve. (This may be done graphically on the same sheet, if supply is measured leftward from the right-hand side of the graph. Alternatively, prepare a table as in the case of A above, and plot the supply curve on a separate sheet of paper. In either case, label both axes appropriately.)

c. The supply curve has a perverse slope for prices in the range from $P = $ _____ to $P = $ _____; within this range supply _____ as the price is increased.

d. What is the minimum price below which no supply will be forthcoming? $P = $ _____.

e. What might C do if the price were greater than 5.0? (Consider different assumptions leading to different answers.) (*Optional*)

7. a. (*Optional*) An individual D initially has 20 dozen eggs and 35 pounds of meat. Draw his offer curve (in both directions!).

b. D will be a seller of eggs at prices _____, and will be a buyer of eggs at prices _____.

c. Draw D's combined demand-supply curve. Use the same scale units as for the other demand and supply curves. (Supply may be conveniently represented as measured to the left, demand as measured to the right of the vertical axis.) (The curve may be conveniently constructed graphically if D's starting point is taken as the origin, price being measured vertically upward, demand to the right, and supply to the left.) (Alternatively, construct a table similar to that for question 4b and draw the demand-supply curve on a separate sheet.)

8. A consumer starting at A with 50 pounds of meat and no eggs is given the opportunity to buy eggs at a price of 1.25 pounds of meat per dozen eggs.

a. What is the price-compensating variation?

b. What is the quantity-compensating variation?

c. What is the estimate of the consumer's surplus obtained from the demand curve? (Assume the demand curve meets the axis at a price of 4.0. Divide the area to be measured into trapezoids [or small triangles and rectangles] and estimate the area of each separately, adding the results together.)

(In each case, use meat as the numéraire in which the consumer's surplus is to be measured.)

9. In period 1, the price of eggs is 1.25 pounds of meat per dozen eggs, and a consumer is observed consuming 25 pounds of meat and 20 dozen eggs per period. In period 2, the price is 0.5 pounds of meat per dozen eggs, and the same consumer is observed consuming 9 pounds of meat and 43 dozen eggs.

a. In terms of meat as numéraire, what are the Paasche and Laspeyre price indexes for the prices of period 2 in terms of period 1 as a base?

b. What is the true index of the cost of living at the real income level of period 1? What is the true index (for period 2 in terms of period 1 as a base) at the real income level of period 2?

c. What are the indexes of a and b if eggs are taken as a numéraire? How are they related to the meat indexes?

d. What are the indexes of a and b if period 1 is taken as the current year and period 2 is taken as the base year?

III

TURNING the graph on page 94 on its long side, the curves are supposed to represent the indifference map of an individual between two commodities which may be thought of as butter, measured vertically, against margarine, measured on the horizontal axis. (Note the general instructions given with Exercise II.)

1. a. Draw the income-consumption curves ("standard-of-life lines") for $P = 2/3$ (one pound of margarine costs two-thirds of a pound of butter); for $P = 3/8$; for $P = 1/4$.

b. Assuming the result to be typical of the entire indifference map, how do you characterize the pattern (in economic terms)?

2. An individual A with the tastes shown in the map starts out with 50 pounds of butter (per year) and no margarine.

a. Draw A's offer (outlay-consumption) curve. (This must be done with some care if the intended behavior is to be exhibited. Use a pin or thumbtack.)

b. Using the unit laid off at the upper-right as a basis for the price scale, draw A's demand curve for margarine in the space at the top.

c. What will happen if the price is greater than 1.0?

d. What circumstances can you postulate that would provide a reason for the behavior of the consumer indicated at very low prices?

3. An individual B starts out with 50 pounds of butter and 30 pounds of margarine (annually), and the same tastes. Draw the offer and demand curves. (The demand curve may be drawn with the origin at the 30 pounds of margarine on the indifference map so as to keep corresponding points of the offer curve and demand curve in vertical

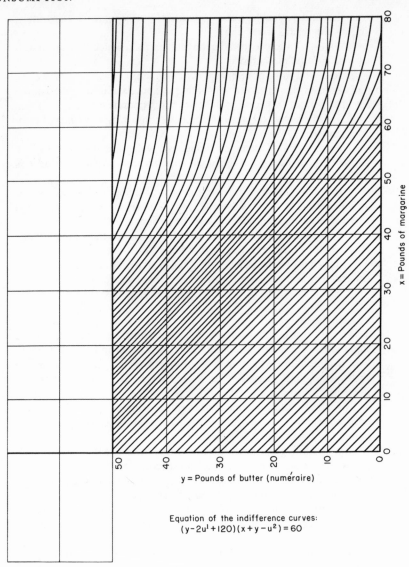

x = Pounds of margarine

y = Pounds of butter (numéraire)

Equation of the indifference curves:
$$(y - 2u^1 + 120)(x + y - u^2) = 60$$

alignment. If this is done the quantity axis of the demand curve must be appropriately labeled.)

4. An individual C starts out with 40 pounds of butter and no margarine.

a. Draw the offer and demand curves. (Preferably, use the same price scale for the demand curve as for 2b.)

b. What happens when the price of margarine rises above $P = 2/3$?

c. What happens when the price of margarine rises above $P = 1.0$?

(Think these last two questions through carefully in terms of the concrete situation that the diagram represents. Extend the demand and offer curves in accordance with your answer.)

5. D starts out with 80 pounds of margarine and no butter.

    a. Draw the offer curve.

    b. What can be said about the supply of an inferior commodity?

IV

AT TIME t_0 with the price of x equal to 1 and the price of y equal also to 1, individuals at all levels of income are found to spend half of their income on x and half on y. At a later time t_1, a certain individual A is still found to spend half of his income of 60 on x and the other half on y, though the price of x has risen to 2, the price of y having remained at 1. What are the limits between which the "true" index of the cost of living must lie for t_1 in terms of t_0 as a base at the level of satisfaction that A enjoys at time 1?

V

AT A TIME when the price of x is 0.5 and the price of y is 1, an individual is observed to consume 5 of x and 20 of y. On another occasion, when the price of x is 2.0, the price of y still being 1, this individual is observed to consume 19 of x and 10 of y. What confidence would you have in an index derived from such data that purported to approximate the "true" cost-of-living index? What hypotheses can you suggest that might account for the observed phenomena?

VI

ASSUME that for a particular household a commodity Q is (a) a necessity and (b) an inferior good.

1. Lay out a graph with dollars of money per year measured on the vertical axis and units of Q per year on the horizontal axis.

2. For any price you choose, and for a range of income extending from bare survival upward, lay out an income-consumption (Engel) curve compatible with assumptions (a) and (b).

3. Lay out a field of indifference curves compatible with this Engel curve, the price to which it corresponds, and with assumptions (a) and (b).

4. For any income level you choose, not too close to bare survival, draw a price-consumption (demand) curve compatible with the indifference map.

5. Could you have followed the above instructions and come out with a demand curve for Q that had a positive slope?

VII

TEST the functions of 2.10, 2.11, 2.25, 2.26, 2.27, and 2.28 for potential independence by the criterion of 2.33.

CHAPTER THREE

Competitive Exchange

The Assumptions of the Perfect Market

THUS FAR we have been discussing the reactions and relationships of consumers, individually or in groups, to one or more given market situations. We come now to examine how the interactions of the various groups in the market determine the market situation.

To keep the analysis tractably simple, we begin with the concept of the perfect frictionless market, in which the basic additional assumption needed, in addition to the general assumptions of the static economy, is that the process of exchange is without cost (or at least that these costs are negligible in magnitude). This in effect means that the price, or the slope of the opportunity path, with which a buyer is confronted is the same as that with which the seller is confronted; i.e., if the buyer of meat gives up three yards of cloth for ten pounds of meat, the seller will receive three yards of cloth for each ten pounds of meat that he surrenders. If there were costs of exchange, as in practice there always are, the seller would perhaps have to give up eleven pounds of meat, or the equivalent, for each three yards of cloth, one pound being lost in some way in the process of exchange.

Not only is the actual physical exchange supposed to be costless, but the process of bringing together buyers and sellers is likewise assumed to be costless, so that in effect there is no obstacle to any mutually advantageous exchange taking place. Each trader is supposed to have complete information concerning all transactions in which he might become interested, or at least information as to the prices at which such transactions take place. This leads to there being only one price in the market at any given time for any particular commodity; two separate transactions between pairs of buyers and sellers undertaken at separate prices, each pair aware of the other transaction, would presumably lead to action by the seller getting the lower price to try to get some of the advantage of the higher price, and conversely for the buyer paying the higher price, which would tend to result in the prices being brought into line with each other.

In a general theory of exchange, it is supposed that the several commodities can be exchanged directly for one another (i.e., by direct barter or exchange without the necessary intervention of money or any other "medium of exchange").Thus there may be exchange rates between each pair of commodities. However, in a frictionless market the various prices must be in such a relation that the amount of one commodity secured in exchange for another must be the same whether the exchange be direct or whether it be carried out in two or more stages through the purchase and resale of intermediate commodities. If this were not so there would be opportunities for profit through "arbitrage," i.e., for a series of exchanges to be carried out in a complete circuit in such a way that the trader would come out with more than he started with of some commodity and at least as much of all others; the effect of such transactions would be to reduce the discrepancies until they vanished. An actual example of this is found in the operation of international exchange in the absence of artificial restrictions: if francs are selling 400 to the dollar, and if dollars are selling three to the pound, then necessarily the exchange rate between francs and sterling must be very closely 1,200 to the pound, plus or minus a small margin representing brokerage costs, for if substantially more than 1,200 francs could be had for a pound, the owner of francs could buy dollars, with the dollars secured buy pounds, and with the pounds so secured buy more francs than he originally sold for dollars; conversely, if a pound is obtainable for substantially less than 1,200 francs, the reverse sequence of exchanges would yield a profit.

Since this relationship must exist between the various exchange ratios, all exchange ratios will be determined once the price of each commodity in terms of any single commodity is given. Accordingly, in order to reduce the amount of confusion in talking about prices, it is customary to select some commodity arbitrarily as a numéraire, in terms of which the prices of all the other commodities are expressed. This choice of a numéraire is purely arbitrary, and has nothing to do with the role of the selected commodity in actual exchange; in fact, there is nothing to prevent the selection of a commodity as numéraire which itself enters only relatively infrequently into exchanges, and perhaps even which is exchanged directly with only one other commodity. Two different investigators might describe a given situation in terms of completely different numéraires, and still come to exactly the same concrete conclusions. The concept of a numéraire should not be confused with other functions of money, for although money is in practice the almost universal numéraire in modern markets (except in some cases where rapid inflation may lead to the use of some other numéraire even though money is required by law to be used as a medium of exchange), this use of money as numéraire is in principle quite separate from its use as a medium of exchange. Indeed, in the perfect market which we are assuming there is no need for money as such: since transactions are costless, there is no advantage in the use of a specific circulating medium to reduce the number of transactions needed to convert the commodities that a trader wishes to supply into those that he wishes to procure, nor does any commodity command a liquidity

[97

premium over any other as being more acceptable or convenient as an intermediate commodity in a chain of exchanges.

A further assumption that will underlie a major part of the analysis is the assumption that the market is competitive. Traditionally, the competitive market has been interpreted as necessarily meaning a large number of buyers and sellers of each commodity, so that no individual buyer or seller could hope by his own independent action to influence significantly the price in the market; each trader would therefore behave as though the price were fixed beyond his control. Actually, what we are after here is merely an assumption that will justify the proposition that each trader will adjust his purchases and sales so that the marginal rates of substitution in terms of his own indifference map will be equal to the corresponding exchange ratios (at least for two commodities figuring in a ratio both of which are consumed in positive amounts; if one of the two commodities is not consumed, the appropriate inequalities must hold). For this purpose, it is not absolutely necessary that the individual traders in each commodity be numerous, if only they believe that they have no influence on the market price and act accordingly, even though in fact they might have a substantial influence. And even if they believe that they have some influence, but nevertheless determine to act as though they do not, from whatever motive, the results will be as developed on the assumption of competition.

On the other hand, merely the presence of numbers is no guarantee of competition, for collusion is always possible, and even in the absence of organized or overt collusion there may be any number of subtle influences at work tending to produce more or less substantial departures from competitive behavior. And obviously a single large trader may exercise an appreciable influence on price even though there may also be numerous small fry in the field. Strictly speaking, competition is an attribute of the behavior of buyers and sellers, rather than of the market itself, though that behavior may be greatly influenced by the characteristics of the market.

It is immediately apparent that administered prices do not normally conform to this concept of competition: one cannot be at once determining the price at which one will sell and assuming that prices are fixed beyond one's control. Perfect competition thus normally requires that each trader follow an "output policy" (or as a buyer, an "input policy") in which the amount to be placed on the market (or purchased) is determined in accordance with the price found to rule in the market, and is sold for whatever it will bring. A "price policy," in which a price is set after considering the state of the market and other factors, with the intention of selling as much as buyers wish to purchase at that price, is not an admissible policy if competition is to be perfect, though under favorable circumstances such procedures can produce results not too far removed from those predicted by perfect competition.

We have seen in the preceding section that the equilibrium of consumers requires that they be at the highest point on what they consider to be their opportunity path, which, if they are behaving competitively, will be a straight budget line with a slope corresponding to the price ruling in the market. Equilibrium of the market in addition requires that the amount that buyers wish to buy at the current prices shall equal the amount that sellers wish to sell, for each commodity, so that there are no surpluses or unsatisfied demands. Fulfilling this condition in addition to the conditions of consumer equilibrium will ordinarily determine uniquely the equilibrium price ratios and the amounts bought and sold by each trader. To see how this comes about, it is convenient to study first some oversimplified cases.

The Two-Group, Two-Commodity Case

IN THE SIMPLEST possible case that is of any interest, we may consider an economy with two commodities, and two groups of traders each consisting of

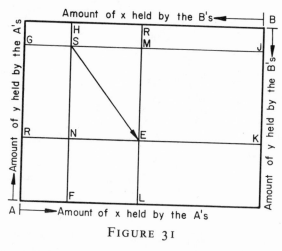

FIGURE 31

a number of individuals of identical tastes and identical initial resources, the number in each group being large enough to permit assuming competition. The two groups differ from one another, however, either in tastes or in initial resources or both, so that mutually advantageous trade between the members of the two groups is possible. Such a case can be illustrated in FIGURE 31, in which the width of the rectangle represents the total supply of one commodity, x, which we may think of as meat, and the height of the rectangle represents the total supply of the other commodity, y, say cloth. Any point within this rectangle will represent some division of this total supply between the A's and the B's; thus the point S represents a situation where the A's have GS of x and FS of y, while the B's have the remaining JS of x and HS of y.

An exchange may be represented on such a diagram by a motion from one point to another: thus going from S to E means that the A's buy from the B's an amount SM of x, and that the A's pay the B's an amount SN of y. The price of x in terms of y is then represented by the slope of the line SE, and the final situation is that the A's have RE of x and LE of y, while the B's have KE of x and QE of y. We assume that since they have the same tastes and the same opportunities, all of the individual members of the A group behave

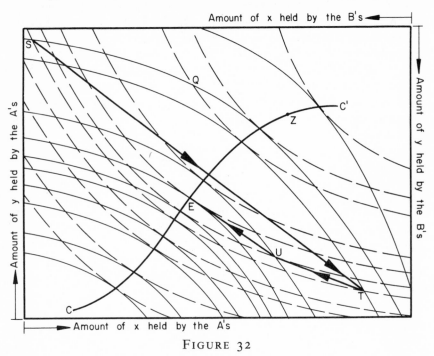

Amount of x held by the B's ◄————┤

Amount of y held by the A's

Amount of y held by the B's

Amount of x held by the A's

FIGURE 32

similarly, and likewise for the members of the B group; we can then consider the diagram as showing the aggregate shares of all the A's and all the B's, or as showing the shares of each individual A and each individual B, provided only that the scales of the diagram are changed in proportion to the number of A's and B's, respectively.

Considering the diagram as representing individual shares, we can super-impose upon the diagram the indifference curves of the individual A's and B's as shown in FIGURE 32 (A's curves being shown by broken lines, B's curves by solid lines). The summit of the B's indifference map is near the origin of that of the A's, where the B's have most of the x and the y and the A's very little; the summit of the indifference map of the A's is in the top right-hand corner near the origin of the B's map.

Through any point S there will in general be two of these indifference curves, one for the A's and one for the B's, and these two curves will enclose a lens-shaped area which is the area of mutually advantageous exchange starting from S. That is, a move from S to any point T inside this area will be a move to a higher indifference curve for both the A's and the B's. The point T in turn will in general define a further somewhat smaller area of mutual advantage so that a further trade from T to, say, U inside this new lens-shaped area will be of advantage to both parties. Eventually, however, a point E is reached where the two indifference curves are tangent to each other, the lens-shaped area enclosed by the two curves has entirely disappeared, and there is no possible further trade that would benefit both parties. It is still possible to trade from E in a way that would benefit one at the expense of the other, but the one injured by such a trade normally has the power to refuse to trade further and at such a point trading ceases. The curve CC' passing through all such points where the indifference curves are tangent is known as the "contract curve."

In general, for any point Q not on the contract curve there will be a number of points on the contract curve that will be preferred to Q by both A and B; on the other hand, for any point on the contract curve it will in general be impossible to find any other point that does not make either A or B worse off. Thus if there is any allocation of resources that is to be considered an optimum it must be located somewhere along the contract curve. For if anyone were to assert that a point such as Q, which is not on the contract curve, represented the best possible allocation of resources, one could immediately point to some point on the contract curve within the two indifference curves passing through Q, such that both A and B would agree that it is preferred to Q; such a point Q could hardly be considered an optimum when there is another attainable point unanimously preferred to it, unless one were to bring into consideration some criterion extraneous to the preferences of the A's and B's.

This is not to say, however, that any point on the contract curve is necessarily to be preferred to a point not on the contract curve. For example, point Z might be held to represent such an extremely unequal distribution of resources as between the A's and the B's that the point U, though not on the contract curve, would be preferred as representing a more satisfactory or equitable distribution as between the A's and the B's. But if one is told that U is to be preferred to Z, then one can say that there exists on the contract curve a point E that is at all events to be preferred to U, and hence in this case also to Z. Without making interpersonal comparisons we can narrow the location of the point that is to be considered optimum to somewhere on the contract curve; determining which point on the contract curve is to be considered the most desirable requires making such interpersonal comparisons, or at least the setting up of some standard as to the proper distribution of income among the various members of the economic community.

Competitive Equilibrium

IN DEALING with a frictionless competitive market, of course, consumers do not make successive purchases at different prices, but rather are faced with a single price at which they can buy or sell as much as they want. To consider the behavior of the A's and the B's in such a market, we can draw their offer curves from the starting point S, as shown in FIGURE 33. The competitive market will be in equilibrium when the price is such that the amount the A's wish to buy is equal to the amount the B's wish to sell. This equilibrium point E is found at the intersection of the two offer curves, the price line SE determining the equilibrium price. Since the point E is on A's offer curve, A's indifference curve at E must be tangent to the price line SE; similarly, B's indifference curve at E must be tangent to the price line SE, if E is on B's offer curve. If the two indifference curves are tangent to SE they must be tangent to each other, and therefore E must be on the contract curve CC'. Thus competition produces a result that lies on the contract curve. It is therefore not possible to move away from the competitive equilibrium in a way that will benefit all parties, or benefit some parties and injure none. This

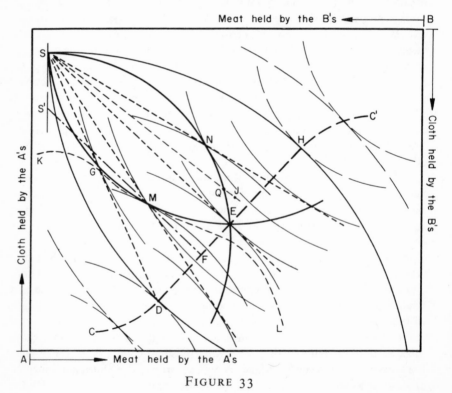

FIGURE 33

is the fundamental justification for the claim that competition produces an optimum allocation of resources.

Simple Monopoly

THE COMPETITIVE result may be compared with other possible situations. For example, let us suppose that the B's get together and organize a joint trading agency in the operations of which we may suppose that they are all to share equally, and that this trading agency is able to fix the price at which it will sell x for y, while the A's accept this price as a datum and buy competitively as indicated by the offer curve. Alternatively, and perhaps with less disturbance to the formal operation of the market, the B agency might decide on the total amount of x to be sold, allowing the bidding of the A's on the market for this quantity to determine the price. We will assume further that the B agency is able to determine, by experiment or otherwise, the position of the offer curve of the A's. By thus determining either the supply or the price, and letting the A's then determine the corresponding price or quantity, the B agency can choose among the points that lie on A's offer curve. Thus the offer curve of the A's becomes the opportunity path for the B's. This is a case where the opportunity path is a curve, in contrast to the straight-line opportunity path that obtains when price is considered fixed. If the B agency sets the price (or the quantity) so as to reach the highest possible point on the indifference map of the individual B's, it will select the point where the offer curve of the A's is tangent to one of the indifference curves of the B's, i.e., at M.

This would be, incidentally, one case where it would be possible to observe the choice by a consumer of a point within a concavity in his indifference map, as would be the case, for example, if one of the indifference curves of the B's had the shape indicated by the curve KL. It is one thing, however, to observe a consumer at a point that may in fact be in a concavity, and quite another to show from a series of observations that it is a concavity. Indeed, while an observation of a competitive equilibrium at E tells us immediately that the slope of the indifference curve at E is equal to that of the price line SE, observation of monopoly at M itself tells us nothing about the shape of the indifference map, unless we happen to know the offer curve of the A's. And indeed, it is not the actual offer curve of the A's that is relevant, but what the B agency considers the offer curve of the A's to be. This great difficulty in ever finding concrete evidence of the existence of such concavities in terms of overt behavior can be considered further ground for disregarding such possibilities in most economic analysis.

The point M arrived at by the monopoly is not in general on the contract curve. This does not necessarily mean that the point M is to be considered inferior to the point E. Indeed, if the B's initially had the smaller share of the total resources, then changing from competition to monopoly on the part of the B's might be approved as representing a method of redressing this originally unequal distribution. But while granting that this monopoly might be considered better than leaving the original competitive situation alone, it is certainly not the best way of redressing this inequality. For there exists a point F on the contract curve that is unequivocally better than M. Rather than permit the B's to organize the monopoly, it would be better to redistribute the initial resources from S to S' by some system of taxes or bounties, and then competition would produce a result on the contract curve in the vicinity of F. Or if a monopoly by the B's is established at M, it would then be to the advantage of the A's for them to make a lump payment of SS' to the B's, if they could do so, in return for assurance that the B's would give up their monopolistic practices; such a procedure might likewise result in F, or at least a point on the contract curve in the neighborhood of F, which would be preferred to M by all concerned.

Discriminatory Monopoly

ANOTHER possibility would be that the B's practice not mere simple monopoly in which they set a single price and allow the A's to take as much or as little as they want at that price, but instead practice discriminatory monopoly in which they sell different amounts under different circumstances at different prices. The most extreme and at the same time the simplest form of such discriminatory monopoly is for the B's to offer each A the opportunity to buy a set amount at a set price on an all-or-nothing, take-it-or-leave-it basis. In this case, the B's will derive the greatest possible advantage by offering the A's a trade that will bring them to point D on the contract curve, just inside the indifference curve of the A's that passes through S. The B's can in effect select for the final result any point inside the area of mutual advantage, but not one beyond this, for in that case the A's, finding themselves better off at S than at the proposed point, will simply refuse to trade at all. If the B's could enforce on the A's a trade that was to the net disadvantage of the A's, then the situation would be considered no longer one of trade but one of tyranny.

Opportunities for discrimination of this type are comparatively rare, however. To begin with, it is necessary that the A's be unable to resell among themselves, for if reselling were possible, then it would be possible for, say, half of the A's to accept the offer SD, and then share with the remaining half of the A's, thus arriving finally at G rather than at D, which might, as in FIGURE 33, be even less desirable to the B's than the results of simple monopoly at M. Opportunities for such discrimination arise chiefly with respect to personal serivces such as medical care, hairdressing, or transportation, which once performed cannot be transferred. Moreover, while here we have assumed that the tastes of all of the buyers were the same, so that the same offer would extract the maximum advantage from each, in practice there would be variations among the buyers as to tastes and resources, so that a separate appraisal of the situation and a separate offer would be required for each of the buyers if the point D were to be attained; this would be extremely difficult to achieve. Thus while a theoretically perfect degree of discriminatory monopoly would produce a result on the contract curve, in practice a result close to the contract curve may be considered quite unlikely.

Types of Equilibrium

WHILE E, M, and D are all in a sense points of equilibrium, the nature of that equilibrium is quite different in the competitive case from what it is in the monopoly cases. The equilibrium at E is reached more or less automatically through the market mechanism. Each individual concerned reacts only to a price that is determined in the market and that is an overt fact of common knowledge, in combination with his own preference schedule concerning which he himself is the final judge. In the case pictured in FIGURE 33 the equilibrium at E is a stable one, as can be seen from the similar case shown in FIGURE 34, in which the offer curves of the A's and the B's are shown in relation to the corresponding demand and supply curves. If the price should happen to be greater than the equilibrium price for some reason, as represented by the price line SLK, or the ordinate oq, then the amount the A's wish to buy, as indicated by the offer curve, will be SU (or ql as indicated by the demand curve); the amount the B's wish to sell as indicated by the offer curve of the B's will be SW ($= qk$). In this situation, some B's who wish to sell will be unable to find buyers, and their presence in the market unsuccessfully seeking buyers will drive the market price down toward op, and the price line toward SE. Similarly, if for any reason the market price were below the equilibrium price, the presence of unsatisfied buyers would tend to push the price up and restore the equilibrium situation.

But it should not be assumed that any intersection of the offer curves represents necessarily a point of stable equilibrium. There is in fact nothing to prevent the offer curves from intersecting several times, as in FIGURE 35. In such cases there will be a corresponding number of intersections of the demand and supply curves. The intersections will represent alternately stable and unstable equilibria. In FIGURE 35, the points E, F, and G represent stable equilibria, while U and V represent unstable equilibria. As long as the price remains at the point U or V, supply and demand are equal and there is nothing to produce an immediate change. But any slight movement away from these points caused by any random disturbance will bring into play forces tending to produce further motion in the same direction, away from

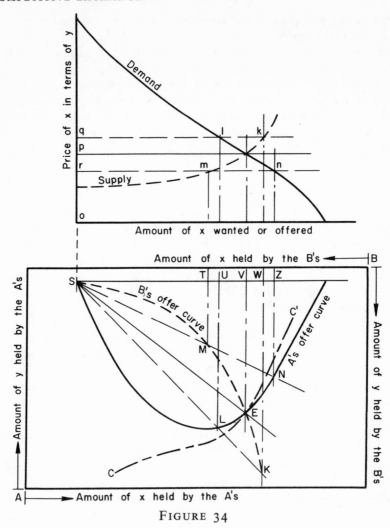

FIGURE 34

U or *V*, and this shift will continue until one of the points of stable equilibrium is reached. Thus if the price should rise above either *u* or *v*, demand would exceed supply and the presence of unsatisfied buyers would push prices up still further until the market finds another equilibrium at *f* or *g*, and conversely for a fall in price. The point *F* may be termed a point of microstable equilibrium in that if disturbances are kept sufficiently small, the market pressures resulting from the relation between demand and supply will tend to bring the price back to the equilibrium at *F*. But if there is a disturbance sufficiently large to carry the price below *u* or above *v*, the price will tend to continue on to *e* or *g*, respectively, and the situation *f* will not be regained.

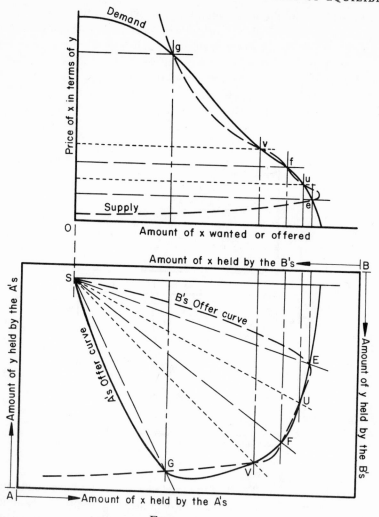

FIGURE 35

Similarly, point *e* is stable against downward variations in price of any magnitude, but merely micro-stable against upward fluctuations in price, and likewise, *mutatis mutandis*, for point *g*.

Another possibility is illustrated in FIGURE 36, in which we have neutral equilibrium over the range between the points *NN'*. At any point in this range, buyers and sellers are doing all the trading they wish to do at the going price, and there are no unsatisfied buyers or sellers tending to push the price up or down; if a change in the price within this range is brought about by some external or accidental force, there is nothing in the system as stipulated that

[107

would tend to restore the initial situation. Just where in the range NN' the situation will stand at any given moment will depend on chance or on outside factors such as bargaining power, historical accident, institutional factors, or other similar influences. Indeed, the moment we abandon the assumption of strictly competitive behavior on the part of the traders, the situation may be thought of as violently unstable, since any small reduction in demand or supply would tend to drive the price down to N' or up to N, and thus each

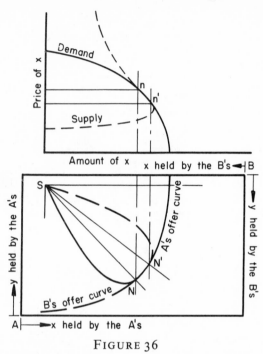

FIGURE 36

trader, even if only a small part of the total market, would have an incentive to withhold a part of his trade in the hope of influencing the price substantially in his favor. If all traders behave in this way, however, the effects may partially cancel out, and the results become difficult to determine.

In strictest terms, the occurrence of such cases of neutral equilibrium is of course infinitely unlikely a priori, since it requires the coincidence of two curves that are determined independently. However, if we extend this case to cover instances where the two offer curves are merely so close together that the market forces are insufficient to overcome frictions and inertias of various descriptions, this case may be of significant frequency, though probably still relatively rare.

Often the cases of multiple equilibria are dismissed as curiosa unlikely to be encountered in practice, but it is not at all clear that this is justified. Indeed, it is possible to show a priori that given the total supply of x and y and the tastes of the A's and the B's, it will in general be possible to find starting points for which there will be multiple competitive equilibria. For the indifference maps and the aggregate supply determine the contract curve. At any point E on the contract curve, one can draw the common tangent to the two indifference curves through that point, and every starting point on such a tangent will have an equilibrium point at E. Now if we take any two points on the contract curve, and draw the tangents to the indifference curves at these two

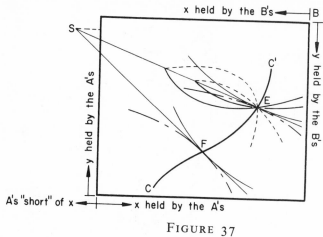

FIGURE 37

points, it is a priori unlikely that these two tangents will be exactly parallel, and still more unlikely that all such tangents at all the points on the contract curve are parallel. If the tangents at some two points E and F are not parallel, they meet at some point S, and if S is used as a starting point, then both E and F will be points of equilibrium, as illustrated in FIGURE 37. To be sure, the starting point so determined may lie outside the rectangle of positive resource distributions, but this may be interpreted in terms of having the A's or the B's or both start out owing the other some of commodity x or y; i.e., they may be considered as having entered into a "short" contract. This, to be sure, is a somewhat artificial situation; but on the other hand it would be rather presumptuous to assert that no two of all of the tangents at the contract curve intersected within the rectangle.

It is possible indeed to construct cases where no stable equilibrium exists at all. If we consider a case where the A's start out with less than the minimum requirement of a necessity x, while the B's similarly start with less than the minimum essential amount of y, so that neither could survive without trade, then we could conceivably have the situation depicted in FIGURE 38, where U is a point of unstable equilibrium, and where in the usual sense there are no other intersections of offer curves. If the price should rise above u, demand

[109

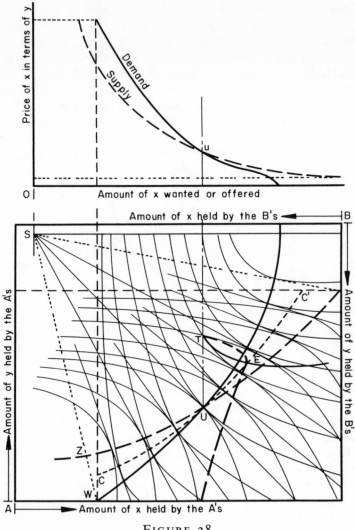

FIGURE 38

would exceed supply and drive the price still further up until the A's must offer all of their y (or perhaps all of their y above the minimum necessary amount) in order to get enough x to subsist, as at W. But at this price the amount the B's are willing to supply is still not enough to support all the A's, there is still no equilibrium, and the price tends to go still higher. At such a higher price, the A's are unable to get enough x to survive. If a sufficient number of the A's die off, emigrate, or otherwise remove themselves from the picture, a solution of sorts may be found at Z relative to the indifference map of the B's, where the price is determined by the line SW, and the trade SZ is divided among a sufficiently smaller number of A's so that the share of each in SZ is equal to the amount SW divided among the former larger number, and the reduced number of A's is able to eke out a subsistence. This example might be considered a modern version of the "iron law of wages."

The tendency to exploitation in such a situation can be perfectly symmetrical: if, "come the revolution," the A's manage to push the price below u, it will then be the B's turn to cling to the margin of subsistence while the A's enjoy the bulk of the available resources. Indeed, precisely this reversal might be considered implicit in the diagram if, by chance fluctuation, the offer curve of the reduced number of A's gets pulled entirely inside the offer curve of the B's in the neighborhood of Z, as might happen if the A's, for example, suffer an epidemic that reduces their number below the number that can be supported at the subsistence level.

One can also read into this analysis a suggestion that specialization may be an important factor in producing instability. If, instead of starting out at S with the A's specialized in producing y and the B's specialized in producing x, they started at T where the A's produce enough x to satisfy at least their own minimum requirements and the B's likewise are the original producers of enough y for their own minimum needs, then the two offer curves intersect in the normal way at E and there is a stable equilibrium. If, then, seduced by the doctrine of comparative advantage, the two groups specialize, moving the starting point in the direction of S while at the same time expanding total output and shifting the indifference curves of the B's relative to those of the A's (a feature that cannot be clearly shown on the diagram, as the diagram is based on a fixed total output), an equilibrium such as U might be reached that is indeed unequivocally preferred by both groups to the original point E. But if the equilibrium at U breaks down, one or the other group may come to regret the trend to specialization, particularly if the shift has been irreversible so that it is not possible to return to the original situation at T. If the specialization process is reversible, then of course the exploited group would be able to some extent to protect themselves against the more extreme results by shifting their production back toward diversification.

At this point it should be mentioned that for a demand curve to lie to the right of a supply curve at prices lower than the equilibrium price (as at g in FIGURE 35) does not always indicate a stable equilibrium, nor the reverse (as at v in FIGURE 35) an unstable one; each case has to be examined in terms of the nature of the market being represented by the curves and the precise meaning attached to the demand and supply curves themselves. For example, in FIGURE 39 the relative position of the demand and supply curves is apparently similar to that at the points u and v in FIGURE 35, and might, accordingly, be thought to indicate an unstable equilibrium. But consider the case where the supply curve S, in FIGURE 39, rather than representing the

[III

response of sellers to a market price assumed to be fixed, instead represents a declining long-run average-cost curve in a competitive industry in which there are external economies of scale, so that it represents the level to which the price that will be charged will settle, given the total amount that can be sold. Here, if price exceeds the equilibrium price, then demand exceeds supply; this may push the price up, temporarily, to be sure, and in the short run there may be an equilibrium determined by the intersection of the short-run supply curve S' with the demand curve D; but eventually new firms enter the industry, or old firms expand their capacity and drive the price down again, and the external economies permit the price to be reduced below its original level,

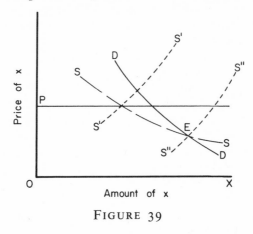

FIGURE 39

until finally the long-term equilibrium is reached at E. This will be explained more fully in Chapter 6. Conversely, if the positions of the demand curve and the long-run average-cost curve are interchanged, the intersection would be a point of unstable equilibrium, and not of stable equilibrium as is the case with the similar-appearing point g in FIGURE 35.

This is but one of the pitfalls that lurk in the way of a determination whether a given equilbirium is stable or otherwise. Indeed, this question cannot be fully answered without a lengthy investigation of the processes by which an adjustment of a disequilibrium resulting from a disturbance takes place, and such investigations are often not complete without fairly extended excursions into the realm of dynamics. The problem moreover becomes much more complicated when the analysis is extended to more than two commodities: a single price fluctuating in the neighborhood of the equilibrium is very likely to pass through the equilibrium point in its movements; a system of two or more prices, however, can easily keep swinging in circles around the equilibrium point without ever reaching a situation where all prices are at their equilibrium levels at the same time, so that disturbances continue. And a system may well be stable with respect to disturbances in one price, or one parameter, at a time, but be unstable with respect to combined disturbances in two or more parameters. Great caution is therefore necessary in interpreting the results of static analysis, and particularly of analysis limited to two dimensions at a time.

The nature of the monopoly equilibrium is quite different from that of the competitive one, and it too bears examination. The competitive equilibrium is brought about by the actions of individuals based on their own preferences on the one hand and the market prices on the other; the market price is an objective fact concerning which they are not likely to remain ignorant. The

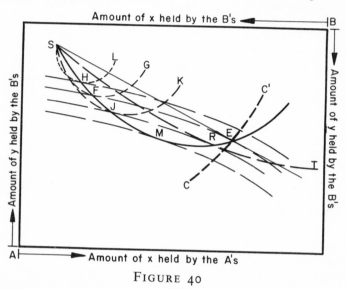

FIGURE 40

monopoly equilibrium, on the other hand, is the result of the monopolist's considering his own preferences in relation to *what he believes to be* the offer curve (or demand curve) of the buyers. Now there is no reason to suppose that a monopolist will necessarily have a correct impression of this offer curve. All that his current experience tells him unequivocally is that a given point at which he is operating is on the offer curve of the buyers, and he may be completely wrong about the direction or slope of the offer curve at that point, without this error giving rise to any apparent inconsistency. The price actually set by the monopolist may therefore be not that which actually produces the greatest satisfaction to him of the points on the actual offer curve, but merely a point on the actual offer curve that produces a greater satisfaction to the B's than any other point on the curve that the B's *believe to be* the offer curve. For example, if in FIGURE 40 the curve $SJMRE$ represents the actual offer curve of the A's, then the equilibrium point is M if we assume that the monopolist estimates this offer curve correctly. However, it would be perfectly possible for the monopolist to set a price that would result in position J, and to be satisfied to remain there because he believes that the offer curve is SJK rather than $SJMRE$. Or the monopolist might be satisfied with setting a price that results in R, under the impression that the offer curve is SRT rather than $SJMRE$. At J, both the A's and the B's are worse off than they would be at M; at R the B's are worse off but the A's are better off than at M. In effect, an error by the B's that carries the equilibrium point toward S from M injures both parties; an error from M in the direction of E will benefit the A's at the expense of the B's. It is thus in the interests of the A's to propagandize the B's to the effect that their offer curve is like SRT rather than SJK, i.e., that their demand is elastic. In any case, the result will still be off the contract curve: the only assumed offer curve that would lead to the B's selecting the point E would be a straight line SE, implying that the demand is perfectly elastic. But no monopolist acting as such would assume a perfectly elastic demand, or at least if he did, he would be acting, *pro tanto*, in a perfectly competitive manner.

To be sure, the monopolist might experiment with different prices so as to actually trace out a portion of the offer curve. However, such experimentation takes time, if only because consumption does not respond instantaneously to price changes (or at least the reaction to a temporary price change may be different from that to a more permanent change, owing to anticipatory buying and the like). Further, if we conceive of other monopolists making similar experiments in fields that impinge on his, additional sources of uncertainty are introduced. And of course in the real world the over-all situation is continually changing, so that there seems to be no way of assuring that the monopolist's estimate of the offer curve will ever approach the correct one, even allowing an extremely long period for the process of adjustment to work itself out without the injection of further exogenous disturbances.

A somewhat similar condition surrounds the equilibrium at D that the discriminating monopolist is conceived to be attempting to approach. All that the monopolist will know for sure is that the offer is or is not accepted and is therefore inside or outside the area of mutual advantage determined by the starting point S. And since the various methods of discrimination and the various possible combinations of rates involve a large number of parameters each one of which may be varied, instead of only a single price, the possibility of exploring substantial proportions of the likely possibilities is even more remote. The likelihood of approaching the point D with any great degree of precision must be considered even more remote than that of arriving at the point M.

The case where the A's as buyers of x organize a monopsony while the B's act competitively is of course exactly symmetrical, the differences being solely those of terminology.

Bilateral Monopoly

THE SUPERIMPOSED indifference-curve diagram of FIGURE 33 can also be used to study the case of bilateral monopoly in which there are only two parties involved; in fact, this appears to be the problem to which this diagram was first applied when it was developed by Edgeworth. But there is on the whole very little that can be said with certainty about the outcome of such a case, other than that any trade must proceed to a point within the area of mutual advantage. Early economists supposed that if the bargaining process lasted long enough one could assume that one would reach a final contract located on the contract curve (hence its name), somewhere between D and H, the exact point depending on the relative bargaining abilities and strategic strength of the two parties. This would seem, however, to assume that having made one deal, from, say, S to T in FIGURE 32, the way would still be open for a further trade from T to U, which being of advantage to both parties would necessarily be made. Possibly this could be justified on the basis of a latent assumption that the particular occasion is unique, and that neither party has in the back of his mind the effect of his current action on the type of trade made on the next occasion. Indeed, one party might refuse to agree to a trade from T to U on the ground that to do so might prejudice his opportunity to get an initial trade as favorable as ST in the next succeeding period. Or negotiations may be stalled through each party holding out in the hope of compelling the other to accept a more favorable settlement: the parties may remain in this way at S for more or less protracted periods of time, as is observed in the case of strikes.

To be sure, if at least one party is supposed to know the indifference map of the other, as might happen if negotiations are conducted in an open and cooperative spirit, or if the nature of the needs and requirements of one of the parties is fairly obvious to the other (as when the nature of a manufacturer's operations is fairly well understood by labor-union leaders), then it would be apparent to at least one of the bargaining parties that a move, from T to U in FIGURE 32, for example, would be advantageous to both, and thus one could expect in such cases a result close to the contract curve. In cases where the bargaining parties are very similar in nature, there will be an agreement to split the benefits derived from the trade more or less equally between the parties, thus landing fairly close to the contract curve about half way between H and D; such a point may in many cases be close to E, the competitive equilibrium, but need not be. Contracts for the interchange of power between interconnected electric-power systems are often of this type, for example.

However one's ability to conceal the nature of one's indifference map from the opposite party, or even to mislead him as to its shape, is often one of the important elements in bargaining power. If neither knows the indifference

[115

map of the other, then neither knows where the contract curve is, and it is possible for trading to stop at T with each party believing that the contract curve has been reached, or at least with each being uncertain, and perhaps of opposite opinions, as to the direction in which the area of further mutual advantage lies. And the nature of the bargaining process may be such as to preclude their mutually enlightening each other. There is here a basic unsolved problem of prescriptive economics: Is it possible to devise a set of bargaining procedures that in the light of this analysis would be most likely to lead to an approach to the contract curve without prejudice to the interests of either party?

The contracts resulting from bilateral monopoly very often take the form of the establishment of a price with one or the other party free to determine the scale of the transaction, rather than take the form of a specification of the quantities to be traded. Thus labor contracts frequently specify the wage rate, with the employer free to hire as much labor at that rate as he wishes (or, in some cases, as much as he can find). In such cases, the locus of possible final contracts that suggests itself consists of the two segments of the offer curves ME and NE in FIGURE 33. As bargaining power is normally exercised by buying or selling less than one would under competitive conditions rather than more, the portions of the offer curves beyond the contract curve (as seen from S) seem to represent unlikely results, as do the portions of the offer curves short of the monopoly and monopsony points.

Even where the contract is to specify both amount and price, there appears to be some indication that each party will feel that in the bargaining process the price will be influenced in his favor by his offering to buy or sell less; accordingly, if one party were to consider a possible contract J in the region between the offer curves and the contract curve, he would in general be better off at the point Q on his offer curve involving the same price, and since pushing for Q would not be likely to move the price against him, not much consideration would be given to J as a possible contract. Such hazy considerations lead to a notion that the area between the offer curves, and especially the area just inside the portion MEN, is perhaps somewhat more likely to contain the final contract than other areas in the entire zone of mutual benefit. But such notions are highly speculative.

Other attempts have been made to derive rational results in this situation on the basis of game theory; however, most of the analysis of game theory requires the assignment of cardinal utility values to the indifference curves, and is generally too abstruse to be considered here; accordingly, it is deferred to the section on imperfect competition generally.

Other Uses of the Bargaining Diagram

THIS TYPE of indifference-map analysis is sometimes applied to problems of international trade. If we are willing to assume that two nations are composed of identically situated individuals with identical tastes, the analysis in terms of the groups of A's and B's applies directly; the only difficulty is that the introduction of such things as transportation costs, tariffs, and the like tends to make the diagram somewhat more complicated and difficult to use than it is where used to represent simple trade in a perfect market. To apply the analysis to cases where tastes and resources vary among the members of a nation, it is necessary to find a way of defining something that can be described as the indifference map for the nation or community as a whole. If one can assume that within each nation the distribution of goods is optimalized through a perfectly competitive market, and that redistributive devices can be employed to maintain any specified distribution of incomes among individuals, then *relative to a given distribution of income* a community indifference curve can be defined as the locus of those minimal combinations of goods and services that if optimally distributed would suffice to keep all members of the community on the same indifference curve as they found themselves in the initial state. The fact that changes in the international trade situation will almost inevitably produce changes in the internal distribution of income within a country and hence change the community indifference map vitiates the exactness of this tool of analysis to a greater or less extent; nevertheless, in some contexts it can be used as an approximate instrument, provided that its limitations are kept firmly in mind.

Another method of constructing a community indifference map is merely to infer such a map from observed or presumed amounts supplied and demanded in the aggregate at various prices, assuming a competitive aggregate behavior. But while transitivity of choice is not too unreasonable an assumption for an individual conceived to have a consistent set of preferences, transitivity is much more difficult an assumption to justify in the case of a community made up of individuals with conflicting interests; nor is it clear what welfare implications could legitimately be drawn from such a map without fairly drastic assumptions as to constancy of income distribution and the like. Used with care, however, such indifference maps provide a useful first-order approximate analysis in many situations.

The process of exchange can also be appraised in terms of maximizing the combined consumers' and sellers' surplus. If the indifference maps of both parties are such as to admit of the assumption of a constant marginal utility of money or of the numéraire commodity, then the contract curve becomes a vertical straight line parallel to the money axis, and any point on the contract curve will maximize the sum of the consumers' and the sellers' surplus. This maximum sum will vary according to the starting point (it will obviously be zero if the starting point is itself on the contract curve), but for any given starting point all points on the contract curve would yield the same sum, equal to the distance between the two points at which the indifference curves through the starting point intersect the contract curve. If, however, the indifference maps do not admit of such an assumption, then there is relatively little that can be said in this direction, other than the rather trivial proposition that some point on the contract curve will yield a higher sum of the equivalent variations (from any given starting point) than any other point lying between the two indifference curves passing through the given point on the contract curve. The sum of the surpluses will indeed vary, in general, as we move along the contract curve, but there would appear to be very little virtue in selecting a point on the contract curve that maximizes one variety or another of the consumers' and the producers' surplus.

General Equilibrium of Exchange

ALL OF THE ABOVE has to do with an extremely simplified economy of only two goods and two types of traders; nevertheless, the results are quite interesting and give considerable insight into the workings of more complicated systems. However, to extend the same type of analysis to more complicated systems involving more commodities or more persons immediately goes beyond the capacity of mere two-dimensional diagrams. To be sure, one can conceive of a corresponding diagram for a three-commodity two-party system, in which a point located within a three-dimensional rectangular prism would represent the division of the three commodities between the two parties; the contract curve is still a one-dimensional curve running from one corner diagonally to the opposite corner; indifference curves become indifference surfaces, and offer curves become offer surfaces. Some new methods of analysis have to be applied by reason of the fact that the offer curves meet in a curve rather than a point so that the equilibrium point cannot be determined merely from the intersection of the offer surfaces, and a trade from one point to another on the diagram can in general be accomplished under more than one set of prices. But very little that is essentially new is added by going into these details. And if we go to the case of three parties and two commodities, four dimensions are immediately required for a complete representation.

Actually, very little can be done with the more complicated cases without introducing a certain amount of mathematical notation, and once this is introduced, it causes very little additional difficulty to proceed at once to the general case of simple competitive exchange of R commodities among N individuals. In such a more general case, it is not possible to say very much in a simple fashion about the patterns that might develop; about all that can be done is to show that a system in which all the elements are interrelated may still have a definite equilibrium state, and to ascertain just how much information is in principle necessary in order for the equilibrium state to be determinate.

In examining the general case of competitive exchange, we take as given the indifference maps or preference systems of the individual traders and the amounts of the various commodities with which each trader comes to market. For the simplest case where at the equilibrium point each trader consumes some positive amount of each commodity, we can then consider that equilibrium requires (1) that for each trader the marginal rate of substitution between any two goods for the point on his indifference map corresponding to his final consumption of goods must be equal to their ratio of exchange in the market; (2) that the purchasing power represented by the goods which each trader brings to the market must be just exhausted by the final consumption of each trader (i.e., each trader takes away from the market as much as he can); and (3) that the total amount of each commodity taken away from the market by all traders must equal the total amount brought to the market: demand must equal supply. It turns out that these conditions are just sufficient in general to determine a solution, and that on the other hand a solution can in general be found that fulfills all these conditions.

Let us put q_x^a for the amount of commodity x consumed by individual a,

$$S_{y/x}^a = S_{y/x}^a(q_x^a, q_y^a, q_z^a, \ldots q_r^a)$$

for the marginal rate of substitution of y for x for individual a, which is assumed to depend only on the amounts of the various commodities consumed by a;

$$U_x^a = U_x^a(q_x^a, q_y^a, q_z^a, \ldots q_r^a)$$

for the marginal utility of x to individual a according to an unspecified utility index, assumed likewise to depend only on the amounts of the various commodities consumed by a; and $p_{x/y}$ for the price of x in terms of y. Then for each individual the first condition gives us a series of relations such as $S_{y/x}^a = p_{x/y}$. Since we know that whatever index is arbitrarily selected as a measure of utility, we must have $S_{y/x}^a = U_x^a/U_y^a$, and since $p_{x/y} = p_x/p_y$ regardless of what money or numéraire the prices p_x, p_y, etc., are expressed in, we can write $p_x/p_y = U_x^a/U_y^a$, or turning this proportion the other way we can write $U_x^a/p_x = U_y^a/p_y$. Combining this with similar relations between other commodities we can combine all the marginal conditions for the individual a in the following set of relations

$$\frac{U_x^a}{p_x} = \frac{U_y^a}{p_y} = \frac{U_z^a}{p_z} = \frac{U_w^a}{p_w} = \ldots = \frac{U_r^a}{p_r} \tag{1}$$

which is to say that for each individual a, the marginal utility of a dollar's worth of each commodity must be the same as for any other commodity. If there are R commodities, there will be in effect $R - 1$ independent equations of this kind for each individual, for if we count the equation between x and y, for example, and also that between y and z, it is not possible to consider an equation between x and z as an additional independent equation, for it gives us no new information not contained in the previous two, since it can be derived from them.

If there are thus $R - 1$ of these equations for each individual, there will be altogether $(R - 1)N$ of these equations for all the N individuals.

Let us further put $Q_x{}^a$ for the amount of x bought by individual a—i.e., the excess of the amount $q_x{}^a$ consumed over the amount $r_x{}^a$ he started out with. If a happens to be a supplier rather than a purchaser of x, we can express the amount supplied as a negative purchase. Thus if a started out with 25 pounds of x, and consumes ten pounds, we would have $Q_x{}^a = -15$ pounds. The second or "budget" condition for consumer a then becomes

$$Q_x{}^a \cdot p_x + Q_y{}^a \cdot p_y + Q_z{}^a \cdot p_z + \ldots + Q_r{}^a \cdot p_r = 0 \qquad (2)$$

That is, the sum of the value of the goods bought less the value of the goods sold must be zero. There will then be one of these budget equations for each consumer, or N budget equations altogether.

Finally, the third, or "market-clearing," condition may be expressed as follows:

$$Q_x{}^a \cdot p_x + Q_x{}^b \cdot p_x + Q_x{}^c \cdot p_x + \ldots + Q_x{}^n \cdot p_x = 0 \qquad (3)$$

That is, the sum of the values of the purchases of x by the various consumers less the value of the sales of x by the various sellers must be equal to zero. This equation is sometimes written without the common factor p_x in each term, but it simplifies the exposition slightly to leave it in. There will be one of these market-clearing equations for each commodity, or altogether R equations. However, the equations (2) and (3) are all not independent, for if we are given the equations (2) and all but one of the equations (3), the last equation of the set (3) can be derived from the others; indeed, if we add together all of the equations (2) and then subtract from this total all but one of the equations (3), the remaining equation (3) is obtained as a residue. This is equivalent to saying that if each consumer balances his budget and if all but one of the markets are cleared, it is not possible for the last market not to clear. Or if all markets clear, and if all consumers but one balance their budgets, the last consumer must necessarily balance his budget: There is no one to whom he can be lending or from whom he can be borrowing. Thus of the N equations (2) and the R equations (3), one must be left out out as adding no new information, so that of these two types of equations together we have only $N + R - 1$ equations. Together with the $N(R - 1)$ equations of type (1), this makes $NR + R - 1$ equations.

From these equations we are to determine the amounts of each of the R commodities bought or sold by each of the N individuals (which together with the given amounts they had to start with, will tell us how much they consume of each commodity), and the prices. There are $R - 1$ and not R prices to be determined, for the price of whatever commodity is taken as numéraire is thereby fixed at 1; alternatively, we can consider that it is price ratios and not the absolute prices that are important; indeed, if the numéraire is not itself a commodity, then the whole set of prices could be multiplied by any arbitrary factor without affecting the equilibrium. With the NR individual quantities to be determined, this makes $NR + R - 1$ quantities to be determined altogether by the $NR + R - 1$ equations.

The fact that we find a number of determining equations equal to the number of unknowns to be determined is an indication that the equilibrium sought is sufficiently but not excessively determined; that is, we have specified a sufficient number of conditions to determine a solution that in general will be unique, while on the other hand we do not have so many conditions to satisfy that it is not possible in general to find a solution that satisfies them all.

If the equations were less than the number of unknowns, this would mean that in general the information given is insufficient to determine the equilibrium position completely; there would generally be an infinite number of "solutions" that would satisfy the conditions laid down, and more information would be needed to determine which of the possible solutions would be the one actually arrived at in any particular instance. It is possible, in certain rare critical cases, for a unique solution to be specified by a number of equations less than the number of unknowns, but such a result is unlikely. For example, if we wish to find the coordinates of a point in space (three unknowns), specified as lying on the surfaces of both of two spheres (i.e., at specified distances from two points: two equations), all points on the circle formed by the intersection of the two spheres will be solutions; however, if the spheres happen to be tangent, the point of tangency will be the only solution. In this tangency case, the specified conditions will be very closely fulfilled even if the point moves about over a considerable range in the neighborhood of the point of tangency; one is led by this physical analogy to feel that in such rare cases where the solution happens to be fully determined by a number of conditions less than the number of unknowns, the solution may be somewhat less rigidly or exactly determined than where the number of constraints equals the number of degrees of freedom.

It is also possible for two or more of the conditions to be completely incompatible so that there is no solution at all, as when the two spheres in the above example are completely separate. In this case, there is no "real" solution (though in some cases a solution may be found if "imaginary" numbers involving $\sqrt{-1} = i$ are introduced and provided with some sort of interpretation).

On the other hand, if there are more equations than unknowns it will in general be impossible to satisfy all the conditions at once and one or more of them will have to be abandoned, unless of course the solution determined from a set of equations equal to the unknowns should happen to fulfill the remaining conditions. If this should happen, it would either be by sheer coincidence or because there existed an undetected relation between some of the equations whereby the fulfillment of a certain number of the conditions automatically required the fulfillment of some of the others. Thus if we happen to specify that a point in three-dimensional space shall be at specified distances from four other points, we shall in general encounter a contradiction. But it may happen that the point determined by three of the conditions does actually lie at the specified distance from the fourth point, and this may turn out to be so by reason of some property of the method by which the four specified distances were obtained. In the case of the general equilibrium equations, we saw, for instance, that one of the market-clearing equations was superfluous because it was already implied in some of the other equations of the system. If we had not observed this fact, we would have come out with more equations than unknowns and might have overhastily concluded that the solution was overdetermined and that one of the specified conditions would have to give way. Or if in addition we had failed to observe that our system would be equally well solved by any set of prices proportionate to those of any given solution, so that the general level of prices is indeterminate, we might have attempted to solve for R prices instead of $R - 1$ prices, and come out with an assertion that the conditions prescribe something that is not in fact determined by the conditions. Thus the operation of counting unknowns and equations is something to be done with considerable care.

Moreover, as we have seen, equality between the number of equations and the number of unknowns by no means guarantees a unique solution. Systems having several discrete solutions are not inherently unlikely, as was seen in FIGURE 35, for example. It is even possible, though here the possibility may be set down as inherently unlikely, for systems of equations to have an infinite number of solutions, along, say, a continuous segment of a curve, as in FIGURE 36, even though there is equality between the number of unknowns and the number of equations. It is also possible to produce systems with equations equal to unknowns that have no solutions, as in FIGURE 38, though here it is often possible to reinterpret matters so that a solution exists.

Another matter to consider in connection with a general equilibrium system is that the above system of equations was set up on the assumption that at the equilibrium point each trader would consume some positive amount of each commodity. Obviously, unless the commodities in the system are extremely broadly defined, for each trader there will in general be many commodities that are not consumed at all, in which case, as we saw on page 53, the equality between the marginal rate of substitution and the ratio of exchange may not hold, and the equations (1), sometimes called the Gossen equations, may have to be modified. To do this, it is convenient to introduce a new parameter for each individual, corresponding to the common ratios of (1), which may be called the "marginal utility of money" λ^a. Instead of the $R - 1$ equations (1), for each individual, we will now have, for each of the R commodities, the following conditions to be met, for each individual:

either $$U_x{}^a = p_x \lambda^a \quad \text{and} \quad q_x{}^a > 0$$

or $$U_x{}^a \leq p_x \lambda^a \quad \text{and} \quad q_x{}^a = 0$$

(1')

We thus have always at least one equation, but in some cases it is the equality between the marginal utility of a dollar's worth of the commodity and the marginal utility of money, and in other cases it is the statement that none of the commodity is consumed. We thus have R equations for each trader, as compared with the $R - 1$ that we had previously, but of course we have introduced the new variable λ^a, so that the equality between equations and unknowns is undisturbed. We have, however, introduced a new type of condition, the inequality, but these are restrictions and not constraints; they may cut down the range within which the solution must lie, but they do not reduce the number of degrees of freedom in general. How to assure oneself that these inequality conditions can be met is actually a rather difficult problem, which cannot be fully dealt with here.

It should perhaps be further noted that in the above analysis the marginal utility of money is not the same thing as the marginal utility of the numéraire commodity as a commodity, and may differ from it if none of the numéraire commodity is actually consumed. The marginal utility of gold to a given individual, in terms of the possible direct uses he has for it, may be quite small relative to the marginal utility of the things he might purchase with the gold, if he had any left over.

The problem of determining whether a model has an equilibrium point and if so whether it is unique is thus not a simple one, and a complete treatment calls for rather high-powered mathematical analysis. For ordinary purposes, the matter may be summed up by saying that if the number of equations equals the number of unknowns, a certain presumption is created that the result is uniquely determined, while if the number of equations is greater than the number of unknowns, there is a certain presumption that no solution will satisfy all the conditions, and if the number of equations is less than the number of unknowns, there is a certain presumption that the solution is indeterminate. These, however, are mere presumptions, rebuttable through showing that the equations stand in certain special relations to one another. Accordingly, a comparison of the number of unknowns and the number of equations is useful chiefly as a preliminary check to see whether or not the number of conditions specified is sufficient, or whether more conditions must be sought, or whether some of them should be abandoned.

It is also important to remember that such a system of equations or relationships does not necessarily tell us whether or not the system will tend to approach the indicated solution or equilibrium if originally it starts from

[123

a situation in which the equilibrium conditions are not met, rather than engage in a series of movements that never reach an equilibrium. Nor does it even tell us, after an equilibrium has been previously reached, whether or not the system will tend to return to this equilibrium position if disturbed. To determine such matters we must add equations of motion that tell us how the system will react if it does not happen to be in equilibrium; a precise study of such behavior properly belongs to the study of dynamics. Nevertheless, if we are to make useful distinctions between equilibria that are stable and those that are unstable, it is appropriate, even as a part of a static analysis, to investigate the rudiments of the dynamics of the system, as was intimated on page 112.

Mathematical Appendix

TO MAXIMIZE a utility function $U(q_1, q_2, \ldots q_n)$ subject to the budgetary constraint

$$B = r - \sum_i p_i q_i = 0 \qquad\qquad 3.1$$

r being the limit on total expenditure and B the unspent margin, the more elegant and symmetric procedure is to form the function

$$V(q_1, q_2, \ldots q_n, \lambda) = U + \lambda B \qquad\qquad 3.2$$

and determine $\mathbf{q}^*$, λ^* in such a way that

$$V(\mathbf{q}, \lambda^*) \leq V(\mathbf{q}^*, \lambda^*) = V^* \qquad\qquad 3.3$$

and
$$V(\mathbf{q}^*, \lambda) \leq V^* \qquad\qquad 3.4$$

for all $\mathbf{q}$ and all λ. Clearly condition 3.4 requires $\partial V/\partial\lambda = 0$, i.e., $B = 0$, so that $V^* = U(\mathbf{q}^*) = U^*$. Then if there were a $\mathbf{q}^+$ for which $B(\mathbf{q}^+) = 0$, and $U(\mathbf{q}^+) > U^*$, we would have

$$V(\mathbf{q}^+, \lambda^*) = U(\mathbf{q}^+) + \lambda^* 0 > U^* = V^* \qquad\qquad 3.5$$

contradicting 3.3, so that if 3.3 and 3.4 are satisfied, the resulting $\mathbf{q}^*$ must be the maximizing set of quantities within the budgetary constraint.

Relation 3.3 then requires us to put

$$\frac{\partial V}{\partial q_i} = 0 \qquad\qquad 3.6$$

or $U_i - \lambda p_i = 0$. Together with $B = 0$, this gives $n + 1$ equations to be solved for the $n + 1$ unknowns $q_1, q_2, \ldots q_n, \lambda$. The equations 3.6 can be written $U_i/p_i = \lambda$; the left-hand side of this equation can be interpreted as the marginal utility of the amount of q_i that can be purchased for one unit of money; λ can thus be considered the "marginal utility of money." The procedure can be thought of in terms of assuming that any budgetary surplus B can be spent at a price of unity on some extraneous commodity that has a constant marginal utility of λ (or if B is negative, the deficit must be made good by selling some good or service with a constant marginal disutility of λ). V is then the combined utility inclusive of that derived from this extraneous commodity, and in the maximization process λ is adjusted so that $B = 0$ and the dealings in this extraneous commodity vanish.

If the consumer is not required to spend all his income, the budgetary constraint becomes $B \geq 0$; since we must also exclude any negative marginal utility of money, in this case, we have $\lambda \geq 0$. 3.4 then requires either

$$B = 0 \quad \text{and} \quad \lambda \geq 0 \qquad\qquad 3.8$$

or
$$B > 0 \quad \text{and} \quad \lambda = 0 \qquad\qquad 3.9$$

If in addition we insist that for some of all of the q_i, negative values must be excluded, 3.3 then requires, instead of 3.6, the following alternatives:

either
$$\frac{\partial V}{\partial q_i} = U_i - \lambda p_i = 0 \quad \text{and} \quad q_i \geq 0 \qquad\qquad 3.10$$

or
$$\frac{\partial V}{\partial q_i} = U_i - p_i < 0 \quad \text{and} \quad q_i = 0 \qquad\qquad 3.11$$

for each i for which negative values of q_i are excluded, with 3.6 remaining in effect for the remaining values of i. Thus the marginal utility of a commodity is equal to the marginal utility of its money price when some is bought, but may be less than this when none is bought. If we have $\lambda = 0$, the point of satiation has been reached; if $B = 0$ satiation has just barely been reached, but if $B > 0$, this indicates that some of the available budget remains unused and there is money to burn. In this case we have $U_i = 0$ for all commodities i actually consumed, and $U_j \leq 0$ for all other commodities j. There is an obvious extension for the case where some of the q_i can take on only negative values, representing commodities sold rather than purchased, or services rendered.

The above conditions, while necessary to a maximum of utility, are not sufficient: They may be satisfied at a minimum or a saddle point: for example, the indifference curves might be concave to the origin at the point in question. For two commodities, it is sufficient that we satisfy the convexity conditions of 2.22; this can be written in determinant form:

$$\begin{vmatrix} 0 & U_x & U_y \\ U_x & -U_{xx} & -U_{xy} \\ U_y & -U_{xy} & -U_{yy} \end{vmatrix} < 0$$

It is sufficient if this is negative; it is necessary that it not be positive. If it is zero, we have a special case in which further and rather difficult investigation is necessary if we are to determine whether we have a true maximum. Fortunately, this case is unlikely to arise in practice; it represents the case where there is a high order of contact between the budget line and the indifference curves.

The algebra involved in deriving the conditions for more than two commodities is fairly involved, but the results can be summarized as follows.

Let T be the set of commodity dimensions i for which q_i is positive at the point of equilibrium under investigation, and let S be any subset of T. (Actually, T may be extended to include those dimensions j for which by coincidence the marginal utility equals the marginal utility of its price, even though $q_j = 0$.) Define

$$D_S = \begin{vmatrix} 0 & \mathbf{U}_S' \\ \mathbf{U}_S & -\mathbf{U}_{SS} \end{vmatrix} \qquad 3.10$$

where $\mathbf{U}_S$ is a column vector of the marginal utilities of the commodities in S, $\mathbf{U}_S'$ is the corresponding row vector, and $\mathbf{U}_{SS}$ is the matrix of the second derivatives of U with respect to the commodities in S. Then it is necessary, for a maximum of U to exist subject to the budget constraint, that D_S never be positive for any set $S \subseteq T$. It is sufficient for the existence of at least a local maximum if the first order conditions, $U_i = \lambda p_i$, are satisfied and in addition D_S is negative for each of some sequence of sets S, starting with some two-element set and adding one commodity at a time until T is reached. If the necessary conditions are met but none of the sets of sufficient conditions are met, which will occur when one of the $D_S = 0$, the question of whether a true maximum exists locally at the point in question can only be resolved by more involved and quite difficult investigations, usually involving third- and possibly higher-order derivatives. If S has only one element, then

$$D_S = \begin{vmatrix} 0 & U_1 \\ U_1 & -U_{11} \end{vmatrix} = -U_1{}^2$$

and the test is met trivially.

Engel curves. In what follows discussion will be limited to the set of commodities T for which $U_i = \lambda p_i$ holds at the equilibrium point, including chiefly those commodities where q_i is positive at the equilibrium point. q and λ constitute $n + 1$ unknowns to be determined by the $n + 1$ equations

$$U_i = \lambda p_i \qquad (i = 1, 2, \ldots n) \qquad 3.5$$

$$\sum_i p_i q_i = r \qquad 3.1$$

as functions of the $n + 1$ parameters $\mathbf{p}$ and r. It is natural to think of these equations as being solved so as to give $\mathbf{q}$ and λ explicitly as function of $\mathbf{p}$ and

r; if we then hold $\mathbf{p}$ constant and vary r, $\mathbf{q}$ will trace out an Engel curve. For small changes in r, the "income effect" is then $(\partial q/\partial r)_p$, the p outside the parenthesis being added to make explicit which are the variables that are being held constant during the partial differentiation. In order to investigate this effect, we carry out the partial differentiation of 3.1 and 3.5 with respect to r, keeping $\mathbf{p}$ constant, we get, from 3.1

$$\sum_j p_j \left(\frac{\partial q_j}{\partial r}\right) = 1 \qquad\qquad 3.14a$$

and from 3.5,

$$p_i\left(\frac{\partial \lambda}{\partial r}\right) - \sum_j U_{ij}\left(\frac{\partial q_j}{\partial r}\right) = 0 \qquad (i = 1, 2, \dots n) \qquad 3.14b$$

Substituting for p_i and p_j from 3.5, we get

$$\sum_j U_j \left(\frac{\partial q_j}{\partial r}\right) = \lambda \qquad\qquad 3.15a$$

and

$$U_i\left(\frac{1}{\lambda}\right)\left(\frac{\partial \lambda}{\partial r}\right) - \sum_j U_{ij}\left(\frac{\partial q_j}{\partial r}\right) = 0 \qquad (i = 1, 2, \dots n) \qquad 3.15b$$

Regarding the variables $(1/\lambda)$, $(\partial\lambda/\partial r)$, and $(\partial q_j/\partial r)$ as the $n + 1$ unknowns to be determined by these equations, we note that the determinant of the co-efficients of these variables on the left side of these equations is precisely the D_S of 3.10 above, with $S = T$. Put $D_{T;i,j}$ for the cofactor of the ith row and jth column in the expansion of the determinant D_T. Then, using Cramer's rule for the solution of these equations, we have

$$\frac{1}{\lambda}\frac{\partial\lambda}{\partial r} = \frac{D_{T;0,0}}{D_T}\lambda \quad \text{and} \quad \frac{\partial q_j}{\partial r} = \frac{D_{T;0,j}}{D_T}\lambda \qquad\qquad 3.16$$

The only thing that can be said a priori about the signs of these effects is that if the p_j are all positive, not all of the $(\partial q_j/\partial r)$ can be negative, which indeed follows from 3.14a. 3.16 will determine whether any particular good is "inferior" at a given point.

Offer curves. To examine the effect of a variation in a given price, with income and all other prices constant (this is the "Walrasian" type of demand curve, as distinguished from what is sometimes termed the "Marshallian" type of demand curve) we differentiate 3.1 and 3.5 with respect to p_k, and after making the substitutions for p_i from 3.5 as in the previous case, the results become

$$\sum_j U_j \left(\frac{\partial q_j}{\partial p_k}\right) = -\lambda q_k \qquad\qquad 3.17a$$

$$U_i \frac{1}{\lambda}\frac{\partial\lambda}{\partial p_k} - \sum_j U_{ij}\frac{\partial q_j}{\partial p_k} = -\lambda\delta_{ik} \qquad (i = 1, 2, \dots n) \qquad 3.17b$$

[127

where δ_{ik} is the Kronecker δ, defined to have the value I for $i = k$ and o otherwise. Solving again by Cramer's rule, we have

$$\frac{1}{\lambda}\frac{\partial \lambda}{\partial p_k} = \frac{1}{D_T}[-\lambda q_k D_{T;0,0} - \lambda D_{T;k,0}] \qquad \text{3.18a}$$

$$\frac{\partial q_j}{\partial p_k} = \frac{1}{D_T}[-\lambda q_k D_{T;0,j} - \lambda D_{T;k,j}] \qquad \text{3.18b}$$

Comparing 3.18b with 3.16b, we see that 3.18b can be written

$$\frac{\partial q_j}{\partial p_k} = -q_k \frac{\partial q_j}{\partial r} - \lambda \frac{D_{T;k,j}}{D_T} \qquad \text{3.19}$$

The first term on the right can thus be called the "income effect" and the second term the "substitution effect." The direction of the income effect is obviously opposite to that of the price change in p_k if q_k is positive, whenever j is a normal good, which by definition means that $(\partial q_j/\partial r)$ is positive, and in the same direction when j is an inferior good; these comments are, however, reversible if q_k is negative, which might be the case, for example, if commodity k is one being sold rather than purchased by the individual in question.

The last term of 3.19 can be called the "substitution effect," for which we can use the symbol

$$S_{kj} = -\lambda\left(\frac{D_{T;k,j}}{D_T}\right) \qquad \text{3.20}$$

Since D_T is a symmetric determinant,

$$D_{T;k,j} = D_{T;j,k} \qquad \text{3.21}$$

so that $S_{kj} = S_{jk}$. The substitution effect is thus symmetrical: the substitution effect of a drop in the price of a commodity x on the consumption of y is equal to the effect of a drop in the price of commodity y on the consumption of x, both effects having the dimension

$$\frac{\text{(units of } x) \text{ (units of } y)}{\text{(units of numéraire)}}$$

The income effect, however, is not symmetrical; indeed, we may have $(\partial q_j/\partial r)$ positive while $(\partial q_k/\partial r)$ is negative. In general, therefore, $(\partial q_j/\partial p_k) \neq (\partial q_k/\partial p_j)$.

If $j = k$, so that q_j and p_k are referring to the same commodity, we have $D_{T;k,j} = D_{T;j,j} = D_V$ where $V = T - (j)$; from 3.11 we know that neither D_T nor D_V can be positive if utility is being maximized, hence S_{jj} cannot be positive; i.e., the substitution effect of an increase in a price on its own commodity is never positive.

More generally, since replacing the jth column of D_T by a duplicate of its first column gives a zero determinant, we have $\sum_k U_k D_{T;k,j} = 0$, so that

$\sum\limits_{k} U_k S_{kj} = 0$. Since the U_k are all non-negative, this means that at least some of the S_{kj} must be sufficiently positive to offset the negative term S_{jj}. If then we define complementarity between two distinct commodities as meaning that S_{kj} is negative—i.e., increasing the price of one, income effects aside, tends to decrease the consumption of the other, and, conversely, that substitution between two commodities means S_{kj} is positive—then complementarity between distinct commodities must on the whole be outweighed by substitutability, at least when the marginal utilities are used as weights. In particular, if there are only two commodities, S_{12} cannot be negative: a rise in the price of one of the two commodities cannot produce a decrease in the consumption of the other, except via the income effect.

The effects of price and income changes on utility can be obtained by the summation of the effects mediated by the various changes in quantities:

and

$$\frac{\partial U}{\partial r} = \sum_{j} U_j \frac{\partial q_j}{\partial r} = \lambda \qquad \text{(from 3.15a)} \qquad\qquad 3.24a$$

$$\frac{\partial U}{\partial p_k} = \sum_{j} U_j \frac{\partial q_j}{\partial p_k} = -\lambda q_k \qquad \text{(from 3.17a)} \qquad\qquad 3.24b$$

3.24a can be considered further justification for calling λ the marginal utility of money or, perhaps better, income.

It is instructive to consider a simultaneous variation of p_k and r in such a way as to keep U constant, all prices other than p_k being kept constant. To avoid ambiguity, we adopt a notation in which the variables being kept constant during a differentiation are indicated by subscripts outside parentheses enclosing the derivative. We then have

$$\left(\frac{\partial U}{\partial p_k}\right)_{p_j} = \left(\frac{\partial U}{\partial p_k}\right)_{p_j,\,r} + \frac{\partial U}{\partial r}\left(\frac{\partial r}{\partial p_k}\right)_{U,\,p_j} = 0, \qquad\qquad 3.25$$

which becomes, using 3.24:

$$-\lambda q_k + \lambda\left(\frac{\partial r}{\partial p_k}\right)_{U,\,p_j} = 0, \qquad \text{whence} \quad \left(\frac{\partial r}{\partial p_k}\right)_{U,\,p_j} = q_k \qquad\qquad 3.26$$

Another way of looking at this question is to think of all the variables U, λ, r, $\mathbf{p}$, and $\mathbf{q}$ as varying simultaneously in a unique way as functions of some, parameter t, not necessarily identified with "time" in a calendar sense. Considering the relation between U and $(r, \mathbf{p})$ as given by 3.1 and 3.5 we have

$$\frac{dU}{dt} = \frac{\partial U}{\partial r}\frac{dr}{dt} + \sum_{i}\frac{\partial U}{\partial p_i}\frac{dp_i}{dt} = \lambda\frac{dr}{dt} - \lambda\sum_{i} q_i\frac{dp_i}{dt} \qquad\qquad 3.27$$

[129

If we now require that the variation in the variables be such that $(dU/dt) = 0$, and $(dp_i/dt) = 0$ for all $i \neq k$, we have

$$0 = \lambda \frac{dr}{dt} - \lambda q_k \frac{dp_k}{dt}, \quad \text{or} \quad \frac{\left(\dfrac{dr}{dt}\right)}{\left(\dfrac{dp_k}{dt}\right)} = q_k \qquad 3.28$$

The effects of such a combined variation of p_k and r on the quantities q_j is then given by

$$\left(\frac{\partial q_j}{\partial p_k}\right)_{U, p_{i \neq k}} = \left(\frac{\partial q_j}{\partial p_k}\right)_{r, p_{i \neq k}} + \left(\frac{\partial q_j}{\partial r}\right)_p \left(\frac{\partial r}{\partial p_k}\right)_{U, p_{i \neq k}} \qquad 3.29$$

$$= -\lambda \frac{q_k D_{T;0,j} + D_{T;k,j}}{D_T} + \lambda \frac{D_{T;0,j}}{D_T} q_k \qquad 3.30$$

$$= -\lambda \frac{D_{T;k,j}}{D_T} = S_{kj} \qquad 3.31$$

where 3.30 is obtained by putting 3.16b and 3.18b in 3.29. The substitution term S_{kj} is thus simply the net effect on q_j of a change in p_k combined with a "compensating" change in r just sufficient to permit the consumer to maintain the same level of U.

In the same way, for the effect on the marginal utility of money of a compensated price change we have

$$\frac{1}{\lambda} \left(\frac{\partial \lambda}{\partial p_k}\right)_{U, p_{i \neq k}} = -\frac{\partial q_k}{\partial r} \qquad 3.32$$

making use of 3.16a and 3.18a; the effect is thus opposite in sign to the income effect, and is zero when the income effect is zero.

EXERCISES

I

IN THE graph reproduced on page 131, any point in the lower-right-hand rectangle represents the division of the total supply of two commodities (say 4,000 bushels of wheat, y, and 50,000 pounds of cotton, x) between two groups A and B of 100 individual consumers each. The dashed curves represent the indifference curves of the A's, assuming that all the A's have the same tastes and that the amounts of the various commodities in the possession of the A group is equally distributed among the members of the A group. (The curves may be considered the individual indifference maps of the individual A's if the scales are divided by the number of A's in the group.) Similarly, the solid curves represent the indifference curves of B.

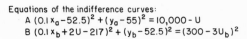

Equations of the indifference curves:
$$A \ (0.1 x_a - 52.5)^2 + (y_a - 55)^2 = 10{,}000 - U$$
$$B \ (0.1 x_b + 2U - 217)^2 + (y_b - 52.5)^2 = (300 - 3U_b)^2$$

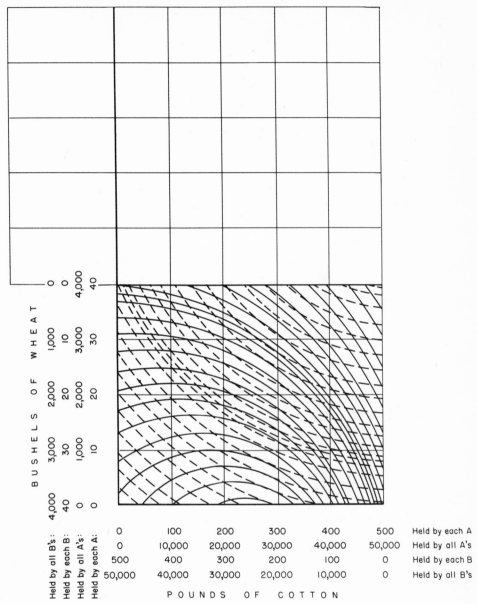

				0	100	200	300	400	500	Held by each A
Held by all B's:	Held by each B:	Held by all A's:	Held by each A:	0	10,000	20,000	30,000	40,000	50,000	Held by all A's
				500	400	300	200	100	0	Held by each B
				50,000	40,000	30,000	20,000	10,000	0	Held by all B's

POUNDS OF COTTON

BUSHELS OF WHEAT

1. Draw the contract curve (the locus of points such that there is no further exchange that is desirable simultaneously to both A's and B's). Mark the curve *UUU*.

2. Suppose that initially the 100 A's hold the entire supply of commodity y (equally divided among them), say 40 bushels of wheat each, while 100 B's hold similarly the entire supply of x, say 500 pounds of cotton each.

    a. Locate the initial point and mark it S.

    b. Designate by *MMMMM* the boundary of the area of mutual benefit dependent on S, within which both the A's and the B's will be better off than at S.

    c. Draw the offer curves of the A's and the B's (these can be considered either individual or aggregate curves, depending on the scale to which they are read).

    d. Draw the demand curve of the A's and the supply curve of the B's. (These may be conveniently drawn in the space left at the top right of the page, using the unit price laid off at the top left.)

    e. If both the A's and the B's behave competitively, what will be the results? Mark the point C, and enter the results in the table at the end of these instructions.

    f. If the B's organize a simple monopoly market and set a price at which the A's may buy as much as they please and the A's act competitively, what will be the results if the B's succeed in selecting the price most favorable to them? Mark the point M_b and enter the results in the table.

    g. If the B's organize a monopoly and are able to specify both the price and the quantity that the A's are to be permitted to buy (and the A's cannot resell among themselves), what would be the result that would be approached if the B's succeed in exploiting their position to the fullest possible extent? (It is assumed, of course, that the A's can always refuse an offer that makes them worse off than they were initially.) Mark the point D_b and enter the result in the table.

    h. If the A's organize a simple monopsony and set the price but not the quantity, and the B's behave competitively, mark the point M_a, and enter the result in the table.

    i. If the A's organize a discriminating monopsony and set both the price and the quantity they will agree to purchase, which transaction the B's may only accept or reject individually without resale among themselves, enter the result which the A's will try to approach in the table. Mark the point D_a.

3. Suppose that initially both cotton and wheat were divided equally among A's and B's.

    a. Designate the starting point E.

    b. Indicate by *mmm* the area of mutually advantageous trades that might be made from E as a starting point.

    c. Under conditions of competition, what would be the result of starting from E? Enter the results in the table and designate the point F.

d. What is the locus of starting points that would yield the point F under conditions of competitive trading? Designate the locus GG.

e. From the starting point of # 2, how much wheat would have to be taken from the A's and given to the B's (before they come to the market, for example, by an income tax), to provide that the subsequent competitive trading would end at F? _____ bushels each.

4. Compare (a) the income tax with (b) collective bargaining as methods of equalizing the distribution of income.

	Price of cotton (in bushels of wheat per pound of cotton)	Amounts traded		Final share of each A		Final share of each B	
		Wheat, bushels	*Cotton, pounds*	*Wheat, bushels*	*Cotton, pounds*	*Wheat, bushels*	*Cotton, pounds*
2e. Competition	———	———	———	———	———	———	———
f. Simple monopoly by B	———	———	———	———	———	———	———
g. Discriminatory monopoly by B	———	———	———	———	———	———	———
h. Simple monopsony by A	———	———	———	———	———	———	———
i. Discriminatory monopsony by A	———	———	———	———	———	———	———
3c. Competition (from initial equal distribution)	———	———	———	———	———	———	———

II

A POINT in the rectangle at the bottom of the graph (p. 134) represents the division of the total supply of 6,000 yards of fabric and 70,000 feet of lumber between 100 A's and 100 B's. The solid curves represent the indifference curves of the A's, who are assumed to share their portion of the commodities equally among themselves and to have identical tastes; similarly, the dashed curves represent the indifference curves of the B's.

1. Observe the indifference curves from both directions. What is the relation between the tastes of the A's and the B's?

2. Initially, the A's have all the fabric and the B's all the lumber.

a. Draw the offer curves of A and B.

b. Draw A's demand curve and B's supply curve in the space above the indifference curves. (Note: For lack of space a unit scale for prices was not provided; the price can, however, be transferred readily with a pair of dividers using a convenient arbitrary distance as the unit and measuring for each price line the vertical distance corresponding to this unit horizontal distance.)

[133

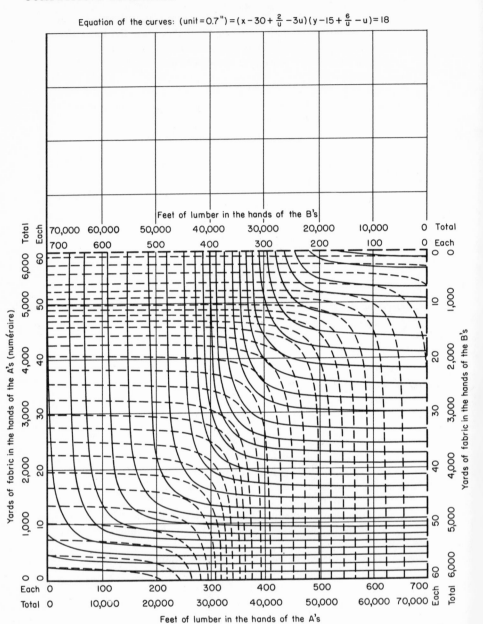

Equation of the curves: $(\text{unit}=0.7") = (x-30+\frac{2}{u}-3u)(y-15+\frac{6}{u}-u)=18$

Feet of lumber in the hands of the B's

Yards of fabric in the hands of the A's (numéraire)

Yards of fabric in the hands of the B's

Feet of lumber in the hands of the A's

c. Under competitive conditions, what are the points of equilibrium? Which of these are points of stable equilibrium? Mark them C_s. Which are points of unstable equilibrium? Mark them C_u.

d. Draw the contract curve. How is this related to the points of equilibrium?

3. Initially, both the fabric and the lumber are equally divided between the A's and the B's.

a. Locate the starting point. Mark it E.

b. What will happen when the A's and the B's come to market?

c. What are the necessary conditions for economic trade?

(Refer also to Exercise I, 3c.)

GENERAL NOTE: The indifference curves may be conceived to refer to a case where fabric and lumber are to be used by the consumer for the manufacture of furniture for his own use, and that the proportion of these materials used in a given type of furniture is fairly fixed (hence the fairly marked complementarity shown by the curves). As income increases (or, more properly, as the consumption of furniture increases), consumers insist on styles of furniture requiring more fabric and relatively less wood, with the result that the income-consumption curves bend upward.

CHAPTER FOUR

Production

The Nature of Production

THUS FAR we have been considering an economy in which the total amount of each commodity and of each resource was fixed, and the sole economic question concerned the way in which this fixed total would be distributed among the various individuals or economic units, as effected through the process of exchange. We now come to consider the impact on the theoretical structure of the fact that it is possible to take certain of the initially given resources and goods and use them up in the production of other goods and services.

Generally, we can define "production" as any process whereby certain available commodities and services, known as "factors of production," are converted into certain other commodities and services, known as "products." Production is of advantage to the individuals in a community in that through production resources may be converted into products that are more desired by the individuals than the original factors.

Production can be conceived to be carried on under various institutional arrangements. At one extreme, production may be carried out by a politically controlled agency under more or less arbitrary rules, with the cooperation of the various factors of production being to varying extent enforced by the exercise of the police power of the state. At the other extreme, production may be carried on by completely independent autonomous units with factors secured only through free contract and exchange, i.e., under the so-called free-enterprise system. It is this latter type of production that is assumed in most of economic theory; indeed, since the assumptions connected with this type of production are ordinarily simpler and more tractable than those related to other types of productive organization, it is profitable to study this type as a preliminary even though one's primary interest may be ultimately in other types: basic principles that are brought into the open and forcibly brought to the attention of the theorist in a free-enterprise system may then be applied to other systems, whereas the reverse approach, though possible, would be considerably more difficult both conceptually and analytically (though perhaps assertions of this sort are somewhat biased by reason of long familiarity with one particular system and method).

Many types of productive organization between these two extremes are of course possible. Completely authoritarian production and distribution is perhaps somewhat rare in the modern world, though prison production may approximate it. Authoritarian production is indeed not entirely restricted to governments, for we have instances of private individuals or organizations exercising fairly complete control over a wide range of activities, as in plantations, company towns, and the like. Nor is the acquisition of factors other than by free exchange and contract a sole prerogative of the state: on the fringe of illegality are such practices as shanghaiing, peonage, squatting, and the like; at a more respectable level, there is the staking of mineral claims. In many other phases of the exploitation of natural resources, the factors of production are acquired more nearly by discovery or seizure than by production or free exchange. On the other hand, governments often carry on production on more or less free-market terms, buying factors in a free market and selling the resulting product in a market, though in most cases many of these markets will be more or less monopolized.

Moreover, in nearly all modern societies there are instances of almost every type of productive organization. At one extreme, the state may order specific resources to be used in specific ways regardless of the desires of the owner, as in the case of prison labor, or require specific services to be performed for specific individuals regardless of their desires, as in education; while in the most authoritarian community (where "everything that is not compulsory is forbidden"), there is usually some field overlooked by the omnipotence of the state where individuals will step in on their own initiative, whether as tolerated exceptions to the general rule or as a clandestine activity operating through a black market. And, finally, we find production carried on by various hybrid forms of organization such as cooperative associations, religious orders, philanthropic organizations, committees, associations, and the like.

For purposes of economic theory, the pure type of individualistic production unit is known as the "firm," and the activities of this firm in carrying out the production process are under the general direction of an individual or group known as the "entrepreneur." In general, this entrepreneur is considered to be motivated by a desire to obtain as large a "profit" as possible, profit being the excess of the proceeds from the sale of the product over the amounts paid for the use of the necessary factors.

Factors of Production

THE FACTORS of production used by a firm in the production of its products are treated, conceptually, in the same way as the commodities of the pure exchange economy, and indeed the same dilemma immediately arises of whether to define the factors of production in broad or narrow terms. Narrow definitions imply carrying on the analysis in terms of a very large number of factors, with a corresponding complexity that may be hard to

[137

grasp; broad definitions on the other hand pose the problem of obtaining a satisfactory measure of the physical quantity of something composed of heterogeneous units, with the introduction of the uncertainties attendant upon the use of index numbers.

For some purposes it is convenient to speak of extremely broad categories of factors of production, classified on the basis of very general characteristics. Classical economists spoke of three basic categories of original factors of production: namely, land, labor, and capital. From the point of view of the individual firm, there must be added another broad category, that of intermediate products of other firms. From the point of view of the over-all production process of the economy as a whole, however, any such intermediate product can in its turn be considered as representing land, labor, capital and other intermediate products that went into its production, and by carrying this process back through all the preceding stages of production, all factors can be apportioned in some way to these three basic categories.

For these "original" factors, the total supply is supposed, for the purposes of short-run static theory, to be fixed. However, the amounts of these factors actually engaged in production may fall short of the total supply, for one reason or another. Some factors may remain unused because the use of additional amounts would not enable the product to be increased: ordinarily, in this case, such factors are no longer economic goods but "free" goods, although under dynamic conditions factors temporarily idle may command a price reflecting possible future use. Or some of the total supply of the factors may be devoted to supplying direct consumption satisfactions as when potential labor time is consumed by the individual in the form of leisure. Sometimes factors may be unused because of the malfunctioning of the economy, but ordinarily this is supposed to be excluded under the conditions of static competitive equilibrium, which ordinarily would require that the presence of unused quantities of a factor would tend to drive the price down until either the factor is fully used or it becomes a free good. Or factors may be held out of production through monopolistic restraint.

The classical division of original factors between land, labor, and capital was intended to reflect basic differences in their economic characteristics. Strictly speaking, of course, one should talk about the services or use of land and capital as corresponding in dimensions to labor. That is, so many manhours of labor are combined not with so much land, but with so much land in a given time period, or so many "acre-years" of land.

Land is singled out as a factor because, with minor exceptions, it cannot be created or destroyed. The term "land," in this sense, is applied only to those elements of real estate which possess this property, i.e., to the "original and indestructible powers of the soil" to which may be added, for some purposes, site value, or the value due to location plus extension in space plus ability to support structures, plus benefits from meteorological phenomena. Thus land is in principle distinguished from improvements that can be added or allowed to deteriorate.

Labor, consisting of the services of individuals, is distinguished by the fact that the extent and manner of its use is a direct source of satisfaction or dissatisfaction to individuals, these being in turn a part of the ultimate goals of the economy. The degree and manner of use of other factors is of no such direct concern, though humane considerations are often given some weight in the utilization of the services of animals; this seldom goes much further, however, than merely the avoidance of purposeless cruelty.

One may note that an economy of a totalitarian sort, in which the welfare or desires of individuals, or of some of them, have no part in the ultimate goals of society, is at least conceivable, in which case labor would be on the same footing as the services of domestic animals. Indeed, the more brutal forms of chattel slavery approached such a condition. It is important to distinguish, however, between chattel slavery, in which the interests of the slave were given no consideration whatever in law, in public policy, and unfortunately often in the church (as in many English-speaking slave-holding communities), and other forms of status slavery as it existed at times in classical Greece and Rome and to a degree in Spain and Latin America, under which slavery was more nearly a temporary misfortune than an ineradicable and insuperable barrier to being considered a part of the community, and in which both the church and the state took interest in the possibility of amelioration in the status of at least some individual slaves.

Capital as a factor of production may be defined fairly inclusively as all stored-up provision for the production of future goods, derived from past effort or abstinence. Capital so defined is a category of physical goods or possibly configurations, and should be distinguished from the term "capital" used to denote a quantity of funds, or credit, or the ability to command goods in the market. Various subcategories of capital can be usefully distinguished, if only to make the content of the term clearer. The central idea in the concept of capital is that of an aggregate of tools or instruments used in production: buildings, machinery, permanent improvements to land, and the like. In addition to this, we have as a necessary adjunct of production a certain amount of inventory, goods in process, and the like. Both of these types of assets are unequivocally capital, whether viewed from an individual point of view or from the point of view of the over-all resources of the economy.

In addition to these physical assets, certain intangibles must also be considered. The term "good will" often reflects in large measure the capitalization of a monopoly income of some sort; however, there is a definite value in the organizational momentum of a concern actually in operation, with a suitable staff collected, trained, and accustomed to working together. Further, in a world where markets are less than perfect, there is a value to having trade connections established and information concerning the product and the location of the firm more or less widely disseminated. These elements of a firm's productive potential cannot be duplicated or replaced without the expenditure of substantial quantities of real resources; even from a social point of view an economic system in full operation will be able to produce more in the future than could an economy possessing the same physical assets in a state of more or less disorganized disuse, no matter how intelligently and industriously the task of bringing the system to a higher level of operation is performed.

From the social point of view, the current state of the population is also a form of capital: A community with a well-trained population with a large proportion of individuals at the beginning of their productive careers has a better outlook for future production than one that is poorly trained, or that has a larger number of infants and aged. Indeed, it is possible to "invest" in the improvement of the "human assets" by increasing training, and very often this is one of the most profitable of investments. The effect of migration on the human capital of the regions of origin and destination is also a matter to be considered very seriously. There is a certain tendency to overlook this form of capital, in part because in the absence of slavery human capital is ordinarily inalienable, at least directly; in effect, it satisfies only imperfectly, if at all, the "transferability" postulate stipulated in the specification of the scope of economic theory on page 3. And as its capital value is not reflected quite so directly in a price tag as is the case with a piece of machinery, analysts understandably shy away from the task of evaluation that would be necessary if it were to be explicitly included in an analysis.

All of the above types of capital are exhaustible in the sense that the use of some of any particular type of capital for one purpose detracts from the amount of it available for other purposes. Capital embodied in technological information and the results of research on the other hand is often inexhaustible in the sense that its use in one instance in no way interferes with its use in another, and may indeed facilitate its use, as when experience with one application proves of value in another. Indeed, it may be somewhat anomalous to include this in capital at all. However, knowledge is to a considerable extent the result of previous investment in research, and is capable of being added to by further research; moreover, in the form of patent rights and the like the results of research do become the basis for exchangeable values. It has even been asserted that technological knowledge, together with the training of individuals, is more important to the future production of an economy than its physical capital, witness the rapid reconstruction of war-devastated industrial economies.

Not all items that have value to individuals, however, can be considered productive capital from the point of view of the community as a whole. Rights to future incomes, expressed either as bonds or other securities, are not in themselves part of the capital of the community. In some cases they represent a more or less direct interest in actual physical capital, as do ordinarily the securities of corporations engaged in competitive enterprise. But this is not necessarily so—for example, in the case of most government bonds. And in some cases assets valuable to the individual owner may represent an actual impairment of the productive capacity of the community, as in the case of values arising from monopoly privileges or positions.

In the more recent economic analysis of production, the tendency has been to put rather less emphasis than formerly on the three-fold division of factors between land, labor, and capital, and to develop new classifications of factors. On the one hand, the distinction between land and capital has tended to disappear and land is increasingly treated as merely a form of capital. From the point of view of the individual firm, of course, land is merely a factor that must be acquired or paid for in the same way as the buildings erected on it; on the other hand, the chief difference from the individual point of view is that the land is seldom considered to depreciate in value through use, whereas buildings and other similar capital items are thought of as eventually wearing out and having to be replaced or subjected to extensive repairs. But there are other improvements that do not wear out or need repairs: the grading of railroad rights of way, the drainage of swamps, and so on. In many instances, a line is drawn between depreciating and nondepreciating assets, a classification that corresponds only very roughly with the classical one.

Another consideration that weighs heavily against the retention of the classical distinction is the fact that the supply of land is by no means a rigidly fixed quantity: deserts can be irrigated; ponds, lakes, and swamps drained; reservoirs created; polders reclaimed from the sea; and even the climate of a region affected by the extensive cutting or growing of timber. Nor does there seem to be any use in drawing a hard and fast line between the original state of the land and man-made improvements; few powers of the soil are indestructible, and it is often impossible to tell which powers were the original ones: conceivably a given area might have been originally forest that has been cleared for cultivation; another area originally prairie that has been developed into a shelter belt or woodlot. Or areas may have been shifted from one state to another several times, with the original state of the land lost in antiquity. The fertility of the soil may itself be alternatively built up by careful cultivation and proper treatment, or exhausted through continued cropping and erosion. In such cases, it may be impossible to say how much of the present value of the land is due to the original state of the property and how much is man-made. In any case, for the purposes of economic analysis bygones are forever bygones and the problem is what to do with what exists rather than to mull over what might have been.

The original separation of land as a special type of factor different from other forms of capital may be in part due to the obstacles, partly legal and partly traditional, in the way of complete alienation of land that were still present in the eighteenth and early nineteenth centuries as a legacy from feudal times. Under such circumstances, it would be more natural to speak and think about land in terms of a rental than it would in the case of other types of capital assets, and of landlords as a distinct class with interests differing from those of owners of other types of property.

On the other hand, the entrepreneurial functions that in classical economics were assumed to be carried on as a natural and even a necessary concomitant of the furnishing of the capital of the firm, have been broken up and new managerial factors of production have made their appearance. Originally, the entrepreneur of an enterprise was more or less identified with the person who furnished the capital, thus combining in one person the several functions of providing capital, taking risks, managing and supervising operations, making decisions, and generally conducting the operations of the firm. We still have instances of this sort: the small business operated by a single proprietor and, more commonly, the independent farmer. But the gradual development of the modern corporation has made the entrepreneur of classical economic theory a somewhat unreal figure in a large part of the typical modern industrial economy, and the functions formerly concentrated in the entrepreneur have been to a considerable extent separated from each other and distributed in varying combinations among large numbers of individuals. Thus management, in the sense of the immediate supervision of operations and the making of day-to-day decisions as to the factors to be used, the manner of their use, the prices at which to buy and sell, is often completely separated from the ownership of capital and to a considerable extent from the bearing of risk. Management thus comes to be regarded as more nearly a special type of labor than an adjunct to the furnishing of capital.

The bearing of risk, as distinct from the mere supplying of capital, has in part been taken over by insurance companies, and the remainder has in some cases been combined with a minimal part of the function of the supplying of capital and handed over to the common stockholders, the remainder of the capital being supplied by preferred stockholders, bondholders, banks, and other creditors together with a much smaller portion of the risk-bearing element. It appears difficult to dissociate entirely the risk-bearing element from the capital-supplying element; however, where the practice of holding stocks on margin is prevalent, it is possible to have a great deal of risk-bearing associated with very little of the capital-furnishing; on the other hand, where a firm is well established, the capital represented by its bonds is furnished with very little of the risk-bearing element.

Indeed, the essence of entrepreneurship itself, comprising the functions of making the over-all decisions as to what shall be produced, what processes shall be employed, and what general policies shall be pursued, while nominally in the hands of the stockholders collectively, is usually exercised by directors who, while nominally representing the interests of the voting stockholders, are often more intimately associated with and influenced by the management which they nominally control. Corporate directors often appear to be influenced by considerations other than the financial advantage of the stockholders, so that an assumption that corporations are run for the profit of the stockholders would often be somewhat unrealistic. Just where in the modern corporation the decisions are made that in classical theory were supposed to be made by the entrepreneur is often somewhat of a mystery. In some cases, indeed, the real entrepreneur may be someone who is often out of the picture by the time the actual operations are well under way: namely, the promoter who provides the initial impulse and gets together the various elements of the corporation, and takes his profit in terms of a share in the new corporation, which he may sell out, to be able to apply his capital to a new feat of entrepreneurship, as soon as the market for the shares has become well established.

Nevertheless, in spite of the vagueness surrounding the locus of the entrepreneurial function in modern economic life, for purposes of economic analysis it is convenient to postulate an individual, or possibly a cohesive group, who makes the basic decisions as to the policy the firm will follow, and at the same time supplies at least some of the capital, bears at least some of the risks, and devotes at least some of his time to the management of the firm. Indeed, if we follow out the process of specialization to the limit and postulate some sort of "control" that is completely dissociated from the supplying of capital, risk-bearing, and operation, assuming that all of these factors are supplied in some way from a perfectly competitive factor market, there will be really nothing left to give character to the firm or to determine what form of production or other activity it will engage in. Here is one of those instances where if we refine our theoretical concepts to the limit, the structure we are erecting may collapse for lack of substance, and there may be nothing left to theorize about.

Thus the characteristics of a particular firm are established by a more or less unique association between the entrepreneur and certain specific factors of production that he is in a special position to exploit better than other entrepreneurs. For example, an entrepreneur ordinarily stands in a special relationship to his own managerial or other skills: it may be difficult for him to hire himself out as a manager or other minor executive to another firm, because of the lack of knowledge of others concerning his abilities; or he might not work so effectively for others as for himself owing to the necessary differences in incentives; or he may simply get a certain additional satisfaction out of being his own boss and making the entrepreneurial decisions. Or the potential entrepreneur may have (or think he has) relatively superior knowledge concerning some asset and the uses to which it might be put, or he may be linked to it in some other way. For example, a farmer may know more about the best way to farm a certain piece of land than others who might be interested in it; if he owns it he can therefore get more out of it by farming it

[143

himself than he could by renting it to others, while if he does not own it he can get more by renting it and working it than he could by working elsewhere; or he is established there and reluctant to move, and hence willing to accept possibly a lower return for his resources by staying than he might be able to get by moving. Or an entrepreneur may have at his disposal a certain amount of capital resources that he might lend to others who might be considered to be able to do as well as he could himself, on the average, with the capital; however, the lender might well consider the net return from the loan to be less owing to the risk of default, or because of the extra expense involved in assuring himself that the prospects of the borrower are good, thus duplicating the expense that the borrower has already put forth. Or again he may have friends who have confidence in his ability and integrity who are willing to lend funds for a certain project of which he has special knowledge. In some way or other, a firm gets its start from special association of resources with an individual who wants for one reason or another to engage in the function of entrepreneurship.

Given this basic nucleus of resources that gives the firm its characteristics, the entrepreneur may then obtain additional labor, capital, management, risk-bearing, land, or other resources in such amounts as he feels are to his advantage, considering the terms on which he can hire, lease, borrow, or otherwise secure them. Under strictly competitive assumptions, such additional resources would be obtainable, in any quantity desired by the entrepreneur, at constant prices. It is important to note, however, as a factor tending to limit the size of the operations of an individual firm, that in many cases one or more of the essential types of resource will be available, after a certain point is reached, only at increased cost or subject to certain other disadvantages. Most frequently this will be capital: sources of capital less closely associated with the entrepreneur may require a higher rate of interest, or a dilution of the equity of the entrepreneur, or compliance with irksome restrictions as to the particular form the physical capital is to take, or partial surrender of control. In general, some factor of this sort is needed to place a limit on the scale of operations of the firm, wherever this is not done by the internal "diseconomies of scale" of the production process in which the firm engages, otherwise a firm might well expand, in the absence of such constraints, until it forms such a large part of one or more of the markets for the factors or products in which it deals that it can no longer realistically ignore the effects of its own actions on prices, so that the competitive analysis can no longer apply.

Conceptually, the firm, like the economic man, is free from relations with other entities aside from those consisting of the purchase and sale of goods in the market at prices over which no single firm has an appreciable influence. Actually, of course, relations between firms are not always confined to this impersonal dealing at arm's length, and we find trade associations, trusts, combinations, and cartels being formed of individual firms, and in some instances taking on some of the attributes of firms. On the other hand, some very large corporations conduct the operations of their various departments and divisions very much as though they were independent firms, even to the point of encouraging the various departments to purchase in the open market rather than from other departments if they can obtain a price lower than the one that for accounting purposes is reckoned to reflect the cost of an item to a supplying department. Thus for some purposes the unit that corresponds most closely to the theoretical concept of the firm is larger than the legal business entity, be it corporation, partnership, or other, and for some purposes it may be much smaller than the entire corporation. Such entities might perhaps be distinguished by calling them "quasi-firms," although an adequate theoretical counterpart of such situations appears rather too difficult to specify or manipulate.

Profit Maximization

THE ACTIVITIES of the firm are conceived to be carried out with the goal of maximizing the "profit" of the entrepreneur. The "pure profit" that the theorist assumes is to be maximized differs, however, from what is loosely termed profit in everyday language, in that it means only the excess of the net revenue of the firm over what could be earned by the factors owned by the firm if the firm were broken up and the factors leased, rented, loaned, or hired out to others in the open market. Very often a firm will show on its books an undifferentiated "profit," which is what remains after deducting from receipts only the amounts actually paid for the use of factors not owned by the firm. For example, a farmer may receive $25,000 for his crops, and after deducting $10,000 for the actual outlays for seed, fertilizer, hired help, and other similar items, record the remaining $15,000 as farm profit (and indeed this is where such an item would appear in most statistics). If, however, the farmer and the working members of his family could have earned $5,000 by taking jobs elsewhere of equal difficulty, and if he could have rented the land to someone else for $1,000, and if the $10,000 that was tied up during the year in seed, fertilizers, and wage payments could have been invested and earned $400 in interest, then all of these items would have to be deducted in order to get the "pure profit" of $8,600. And if instead of $25,000, the farmer had received only $15,000 for his crops, his profit as reported would be $5,000, but the "pure profit" would have been a loss of $1,400.

These amounts that represent not actual outlays but rather what could have been obtained from using in some other way the resources belonging to the firm are termed "opportunity costs" in that they represent opportunities forgone in order to carry on the activity of the firm. The principal types of opportunity costs are wages of management or imputed wages, imputed rent,

[145

and imputed interest. It is the "pure profit" after deducting these opportunity costs that is supposed to be maximized, although since in many cases these opportunity costs will remain substantially constant over a wide range of entrepreneurial action, maximizing a "profit" inclusive of these opportunity costs may produce the same behavior as maximizing a "pure profit." While ownership of all kinds of resources can produce a gross profit, the sources of pure profit are somewhat limited, as will be seen; among them are windfalls, other unforeseen eventualities, and monopolistic restraints.

One might, to be sure, apply the theory of consumer behavior to the entrepreneur and conceive of him as maximizing his satisfaction, thought of as a joint function of profit, managerial effort, sense of security, and perhaps other factors. Such an approach would be unduly vague, however, in view of the unknown nature of the function and the difficulty of measuring such qualitative factors, and for the sake of simplicity we may as a first approximation assume that profit maximization is the sole, or at least the dominant, goal; at least this will give us a reasonably tractable assumption to start with. If further refinement is deemed necessary it may become possible to treat the disutility of labor or the other factors in the preference function of the entrepreneur as a kind of opportunity cost.

Nevertheless, it should be recognized that a theory built exclusively on the maximization of profits will be ignoring several very real restraints on the entrepreneur. In some cases he may have some sense of social responsibility which will tend to curb actions that he conceives to be against the public interest, even though such actions might be indicated by purely profit-making considerations. Or various social pressures may be brought to bear. Moreover, pervading a large part of the business community is a persistent remnant of the medieval just-price notion to the effect that to secure more than a reasonable or normal profit is either unethical or, in some vague way, unwise. To be sure, this notion of a reasonable profit may be quite high, but there is nevertheless a point where some entrepreneurs at least take counsel of moderation. This tendency to moderation in the seeking of profits can also be further motivated by a kind of fear of nemesis, felt either merely in a vague and general sense or perhaps in the more specific form of possible government investigation, regulation, or antitrust action, or in the form of entry of additional competitors, or demands by unions; there may in some cases also be a desire to remain on amicable terms with customers who may at the same time be suppliers, or vice versa.

On the other hand, it is possible to treat households and individuals as firms engaged in maximizing utility instead of profit, and indeed there are many formal similarities between the two types of analysis. The chief difference is that the production process through which the firm carries on its profit-maximizing activity is directly observable in detail, and the characteristics so observed may be the basis for additional propositions and analysis, whereas the process whereby consumption goods are turned into "utility" is hidden in the psychology of the consumer, and hypotheses concerning the details of this process must be much more subjective, introspective, and speculative. Profit itself is something that comes much closer to being measurable in an objective sense than does utility. Another basic difference is that the scale of consumption is much more strictly limited by the capacities and budget of the individual or household, there being only very limited tendencies for households to grow in size by amalgamation with other households; in the firm the limitations as to scale are much more subtle and tenuous.

To some extent, the difference between the household and the firm is one of degree and emphasis rather than of an absolute nature: households do, to a certain extent, engage in "productive consumption"; i.e., the purchase of suitable equipment, clothing, food, and even training is in part designed to enhance earnings rather than to provide an immediate satisfaction. But even so the motives are often mixed, and in few households are such outlays governed to any major extent by the type of economic calculation that is considered typical of the entrepreneur. The distinction between consumption and production theory is thus a practically valid one, though not as clear-cut as one might expect at first glance.

Consumption theory has preceded production theory in this presentation for two reasons. First, because consumption theory is somewhat simpler, as the inner workings of the process of consumer choice, with present techniques, are beyond detailed analysis, so that the analysis is less cumbered with awkward details. Second, and more important, it is possible, as we have seen, to construct fairly complete and sensible models that involve only consumption but not production, as was done in the pure exchange economy, whereas a model that involves only production without implicitly assuming something about the nature of consumption as the goal to be served by the production process would necessarily be somewhat incomplete. Unfortunately, as matters now stand students often appear to have a somewhat greater previous familiarity with production concepts than they do with the more abstract concepts of consumption theory, so that even though production theory is more complex, it occasionally furnishes a less unfamiliar entry into the field of economic theory. Thus far the route followed has been the logically rather than the pedagogically indicated one, though for those who wish to do so, there should be little difficulty in starting with production and taking up consumption theory afterward.

The Production Function

GIVEN a firm, i.e., given an entity whose individuality is determined by the relationship of an entrepreneur to certain factors of production, the nature of this relationship and possibly the predilections and skills of the entrepreneur will determine the general nature of the production process to be undertaken: i.e., the product or products to be produced and the factor or factors to be used. To solve the economic problem of how much of each product to produce and how much of each factor to use, we postulate that the entrepreneur has certain technological knowledge concerning the relationship between the various possible combinations of inputs and the various possible outputs. This technological information is thought of as embodied in what is known as a "production function." Specifically, for any given combination of amounts of inputs, and any given combination of the amounts of all but one of the outputs, the production function is supposed to tell the entrepreneur what is the maximum amount of the remaining output that can be produced. Or, conversely, given any combination of amounts of all the various outputs, and of all but one of the various inputs, the production function will give the minimum amount of the remaining input required to produce the given outputs. Of course, the specified inputs and outputs may be such, in a particular instance, that no amount of the residual input would permit the stipulated outputs to be obtained, or that even if none of the residual output is produced, the stipulated outputs cannot be produced, in which case the production function would so indicate. But such cases are of course immediately rejected; we will be interested in only those cases in which the stipulated outputs can be obtained with the stipulated inputs and the production function does actually specify an amount of the residual output or input (which may, in the limiting case, be zero).

The problem of determining what arrangement or relationship between given quantities of factors will produce the required quantities of the given outputs and the maximum possible quantity of the remaining output is, in terms of the theory of the firm, at least, considered to be one of technology rather than of economics. It is a problem that the entrepreneur as such is supposed in principle to be able to leave to his technician or engineer. Of course, in many cases the function of the entrepreneur and the technician will be lodged in the same individual, but for theoretical purposes we split the individual up according to function. Only when a question arises of the possible desirability of producing more of one output and less of another, or more of an output with the use of more factors, or vice versa, or the same output with more of some factors and less of others, and so on, must economic decisions be made.

To be sure, in a large and complicated firm that carries on several productive processes, possibly in several stages or as alternative parallel operations, the engineer may well turn to the economist for assistance in working out the relations between the various processes in order to be able to answer correctly the question put to him by the entrepreneur; in effect, in such cases, the firm is often best treated as a miniature economic system in itself. But for the purposes of investigating the relations of the firm as a whole with the rest of the economy, we assume that these intra-firm problems have been solved, or, alternatively, that for the time being we are dealing only with firms that are so small that these intra-firm problems are trivial, or at least are readily handled as engineering or technological problems.

In the most general case, of course, there would be m factors of production and n products. This, however, is too complicated a case to use in developing the analysis, although the analysis must eventually be extended to cover it. At the other extreme, the conversion of a single factor into a single product is more or less trivial. The only important case is the rendering of personal services that require no equipment; in this case it appears to be of little importance whether the service be measured in terms of units of service performed or in terms of man-hours of labor, at least as long as the technique of performance remains unchanged, and in such cases it is perhaps simpler to consider this as merely a transfer of the service rather than as actual production.

The two-factor, one-product case provides sufficient scope for the illustration of most of the fundamental principles, and at the same time is simple enough to be represented fairly completely with the graphical methods available, and, accordingly, we will investigate this case fairly completely. Extension of the principles to processes involving more than two factors will then require an extrapolation that should not be too difficult to make even though in such cases graphical illustration will be less feasible. Indeed, general economic discussion is often couched in terms that imply a type of production involving m factors and only one product, or somewhat less frequently as involving n products but only a single more or less generalized input; while in general this causes no trouble, it should always be remembered that the more typical case is that of many factors and many products, at least if the inputs and outputs are at all narrowly defined.

If there are to be only two factors, it is almost inevitable that they be land and labor, in that it is hard to imagine any production process being carried on entirely without human intervention (although some plants come fairly close to complete automaticity), or to imagine a production process that requires no space in which to operate. We may consider, accordingly, the case of land and labor being used in various combinations to produce some crop, say wheat. The complete production function for this simple case may be represented by a surface in three dimensions, as in FIGURE 41, in which the right-hand axis X denotes the number of man-days (of a given grade of labor) used per year, the left-hand axis Y denotes the number of acres (of a given grade of land) to which this labor is applied, and the vertical axis Z represents the annual output of wheat in bushels. Given the inputs in terms of man-days of labor and acre-years of land, the height of the production surface above the point in the oXY plane that corresponds to these inputs will give the resulting output of wheat to be expected. (We will abstract from variations in yield due to the vagaries of the weather and other extraneous circumstances; for example, we may consider only the average output to be expected over a long period of years.)

To examine more closely the shape that this production surface may be expected to have, we may for the time being consider what happens if we take some fixed amount of land, say oA, and apply varying amounts of labor to this land. This amounts to cutting the production surface with a plane through A perpendicular to the oAY axis, and considering only points in this plane.

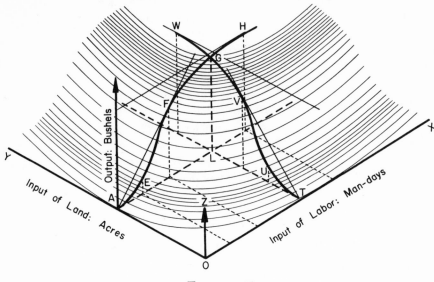

FIGURE 41

The intersection of this plane with the production surface results in the curve $AEFGH$, which we can reproduce in FIGURE 42a; this curve traces the relation between the total output of wheat and the total input of labor, for this fixed amount of land.

If in the relation of FIGURE 42a we regard the input of labor as the independent or controlled variable and the output of wheat as the dependent or consequent variable, we may derive from the total-output curve two other curves that will help to bring out the characteristics of the production function; these are the average-product and the marginal-product curves shown in FIGURE 42b. The average product, for any given input of labor, is obtained by dividing the total product in bushels by the labor input in man-days. This average product can be plotted vertically against the labor input measured horizontally to give the curve $akfj$. Similarly, the marginal-product curve is determined by taking the increment of output that results from a small increment of labor, and dividing it by the increment of labor, and then plotting

150]

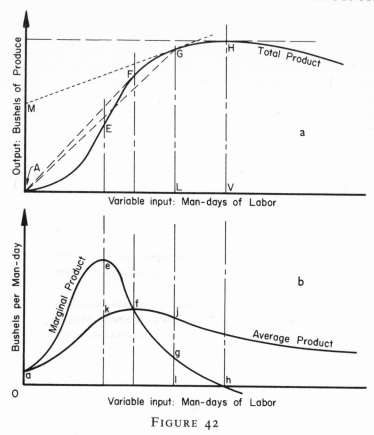

FIGURE 42

this resulting marginal product vertically against the labor input plotted horizontally, to give the curve *aefgh*. Thus the ordinate *lj* of the average-product curve corresponds to the slope of the line *AG* from the origin to the point *G* on the total-product curve, while the corresponding point *g* on the marginal-product curve has an ordinate *lg* which corresponds to the slope of the line *GM* which is drawn tangent to the total-product curve at *G*.

The curves shown in FIGURE 42 illustrate most of the features to be found in such curves in general, although the over-all proportions may vary widely, and in some cases certain of the features presented in this example may not be present at all, or if present occur so far beyond the realm of actual experience as to be mere hypothesis. From *A* to *E* the total-product curve is concave upward, indicating that successive increments of labor produce increasingly large increments of product as shown by the rise in the marginal-product curve from *a* to *e*. Over this range average product is ordinarily also rising, as shown from *a* to *k*. Beyond *E*, the total-product curve is concave downward,

[151

and successive increments of labor produce decreasing increments of product, as shown by the decline of the marginal-product curve *efgh*. However, the average product continues to rise to point *F*, as indicated by the segment *kf* of the average-product curve. At *F*, marginal and average product are equal, as indicated by the fact that the tangent at *F* and the line *AF* coincide. From *F* to *H*, both the average product and the marginal product are falling, the marginal product being less than the average product. Here the possibilities for increasing the yield by further cultivation are being exhausted. Finally, in the region beyond *H* the total-product curve turns downward, and the marginal product is negative. Here the point has been reached where further application of labor will actually reduce the crop through excessive trampling of the soil, overcultivation, the withdrawal of land from production for housing and recreation, or for other reasons.

Increasing and Diminishing Returns

FOR PURPOSES of analysis we divide the diagram into three regions, as follows. The region from *A* to *F*, where the average-product curve is rising, is called the region of increasing returns. The range from *F* to *H* is termed the region of diminishing returns, and finally the region beyond *H* is the region of negative returns. It is obvious that it would be only through gross error that a firm would operate in the region of negative returns, and, accordingly, for most purposes it is ignored. Moreover, the point *H* usually comes at such extremely large values of the variable input that it is usually completely beyond the range of a diagram drawn to a scale such that the normal range of operations occupies a prominent place. Accordingly, it is often convenient to consider simply two regions: the region of diminishing returns then includes everything to the right of *F*. Nevertheless, for some analytical purposes it is useful to note the theoretical possibility of negative returns.

It is important to note that increasing and diminishing returns are defined with reference to average productivity and not marginal productivity. The reason for this will be apparent in due course; it is necessary to avoid the temptation to think of increasing and diminishing returns in terms of increasing and diminishing marginal product.

Other forms of total-product curve are of course possible. FIGURE 43, for example, shows a case where a certain minimum amount of labor is required before any product at all is forthcoming. The region of increasing returns is here preceded by a region of "zero returns," but again we do not expect to observe any operation in such a region, and for analytical purposes, if such a region exists, it can be considered as included in the region of increasing returns. In FIGURE 44 we have an instance where the region of increasing returns has disappeared completely, and diminishing returns are encountered from the very start. In FIGURE 45 we have a case where some product is

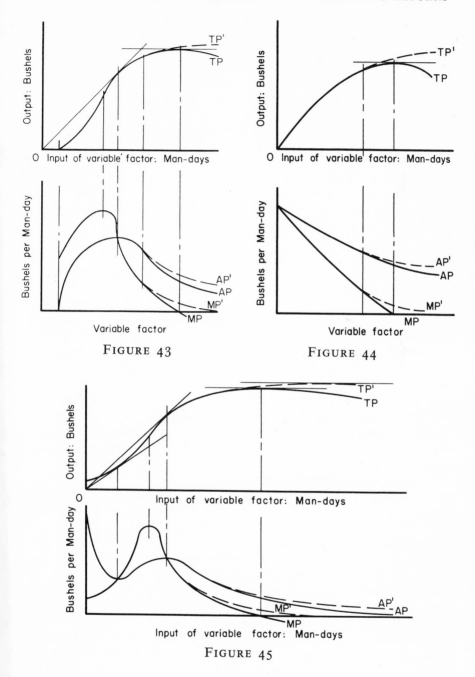

FIGURE 43

FIGURE 44

FIGURE 45

obtainable without the application of any labor at all, and there is therefore at the very beginning a region where the average product is decreasing. However, for many purposes it is desirable to restrict the concept of diminishing returns to regions where both the marginal and the average product are decreasing, and it will usually be convenient to include this region with the region of increasing returns proper, though in some cases special treatment will be necessary. It would be possible, of course, though unlikely, to have a production function with two or more distinct regions of diminishing returns, even under this more restricted definition, but this would ordinarily involve a "lumpiness" of the production process, a complication we prefer to avoid for the time being. To permit the representation of the production function by a relatively smooth surface, we will assume here that such lumpiness as exists is small relative to the scale at which we are operating. Another possibility is that the total-product curve has no negative-return regions, at least within any readily imaginable range of inputs, so that instead of eventually reaching a maximum and then falling off, the total-product curve continues to rise indefinitely, as indicated by the broken-line curves in FIGURES 43, 44, and 45. This does not necessarily mean that the total product is unlimited: the total product may approach an upper bound asymptotically, as in FIGURE 45.

The significant feature that is common to all of these total-product curves is that they have a more or less extended range over which diminishing returns prevail. It will be shown presently that for a stable competitive equilibrium to exist, it is necessary that diminishing returns prevail at the point of equilibrium. The much misunderstood "law of diminishing returns" can be considered in effect a postulate that this prerequisite to the existence of a competitive equilibrium will always be satisfied somewhere.

In its more restricted formulation, the law of diminishing returns simply states that the application of successive amounts of labor and capital to a given amount of land will, after a certain point has been reached, result in a reduced average product per unit of labor or capital. In such terms the law on the one hand is very plausible, but on the other hand is a truism or tautology, for were one to point to an instance where increments of capital or labor increased the average product per unit of capital or labor, the "law" would still not be disproved, for this would merely show that the "point of diminishing returns" had not yet been reached. Whether or not the point of diminishing returns would "eventually" be reached, in any given case, there may be no way of knowing, short of actually reaching the point.

More significance can be attached to the "law of diminishing returns" if it is taken to mean that, as a general rule, agricultural production is subject to diminishing returns over the range of proportions of inputs to land actually observed. One can then speak of agriculture and certain other processes as being carried out under conditions of increasing returns, or rather loosely as "subject to a law of diminishing returns." In this sense diminishing returns is a generalization about agricultural production to which it would be possible to point out contradictory instances. If such instances are actually found, then the law would be considered disproved, or at least would be demoted to a general rule subject to exceptions. If no imaginable set of observations would serve to contradict a proposed "law," then of course the law tells us nothing new and is essentially tautological.

On the other hand, the law of diminishing returns has been generalized to cases where the factor remaining fixed is not land, but virtually any factor of production. As thus generalized, the law of diminishing returns postulates that as the amount of one factor of production is increased, the other factors being unchanged in amount, eventually a point is reached where the ratio of the amount of product to the amount of the variable factor diminishes. In this formulation, the significance of the law turns on how broadly or narrowly the factors of production are defined. If the variable factor is an extremely narrowly defined factor, the law operates severely, but is not very consequential: it is hardly news to be assured, for example, that the doubling of the number of janitors in a plant will increase the total output of the plant to much less than twice the original output. If any sort of composite factor is admissible as the variable factor, the law may become logically absurd: if we combine into one composite-variable factor all the factors of production except for some small trivial factor, then if the omitted item is in fact sufficiently trivial, and if the variable composite can in fact be duplicated exactly, then on the general principle that the complete replication of an experiment should produce identical results, a doubling of the composite-variable factor would always at least double the output, to the contradiction of the supposed law. It is therefore necessary to specify, in the formulation of the law, that among the factors omitted from the composite-variable factor there must be at least one factor sufficiently important to make the law work. If for convenience we call such a factor a "limitational factor," then about all that such a "law" actually does is to define the term "limitational factor."

Of course, even with the broadest possible definition of the variable factor, it eventually becomes impossible to duplicate exactly all of its various components and an exact duplication of the production process becomes impossible. If nothing else, all production requires at least some space in which it is to be carried out, so that either the variable factor cannot be increased without changing its nature, or land is excluded from the variable composite and becomes a fixed factor. If, as it seems likely, land in these circumstances eventually becomes a limitational factor for all production, then the law of diminishing returns is upheld at least in principle.

Carried to this extreme, however, the law of diminishing returns is largely irrelevant to the discussion of actual economic systems. What we are interested in is in general whether the point of diminishing returns is reached at a sufficiently small input of the variable factor so that both in the market for the variable input or its components and in the market for the various outputs, the volume of trading of the particular firm is small enough in relation to the total volume of trading in each factor or product so that it is reasonable to assume that competitive conditions can be realized or at least approximated in practice. If so, we can proceed with our analysis on the assumption that competitive conditions exist, i.e., that firms act without regard for any effect which their actions might have upon the market price of the commodities and services in which they deal. If not, then analysis based on the assumption of competitive conditions is unrealistic and possibly meaningless, and other methods of analysis become necessary. At this point, increasing and decreasing returns become classifications that indicate the lines which the analysis of a particular case should follow. For the time being, we will confine our attention to cases where diminishing returns do set in before the sales or purchases of any one firm become a substantial fraction of the total volume of trading in the respective markets.

Competitive Equilibrium of the Firm—Labor Variable

LET US, ACCORDINGLY, consider an entrepreneur who has available to him a given amount of land, and who hires labor to work the land and sells the resulting product, both the hiring of the labor and the selling of the produce being done in competitive markets in which the entrepreneur makes no attempt to influence the price. Given the prices at which the produce can be sold, we can construct a curve, as shown in FIGURE 46a, showing the market value of the total product that will be produced with different labor inputs. This curve is exactly similar to the curve in FIGURE 42a with the exception that the vertical axis now represents the value of the product in dollars (or numéraire) rather than its physical quantity. Since the price is a constant the curves will have the same shape (except for a possible stretching or compression in the vertical direction), and indeed the same curve can be made to serve both concepts by merely adding an alternative scale to the vertical axis.

From this curve, which may be termed the total-revenue curve, we may derive curves showing the value of the average product and the value of the marginal product per man-day of labor, as given in FIGURE 46b; these curves correspond to the curves in FIGURE 42b, the only difference being that the vertical axis is now scaled in terms of dollars per man-day instead of bushels of produce per man-day. (A careful distinction must be made between the terms "value of the marginal product" and "marginal revenue-product"; while under competitive conditions these two are usually the same, this is not the case where the price of the produce depends upon the amount produced, as under conditions of imperfect competition, to be discussed later. The term "marginal value-product" is ambiguous and is to be avoided.)

Now if labor can be hired at some fixed wage, the cost of labor will be

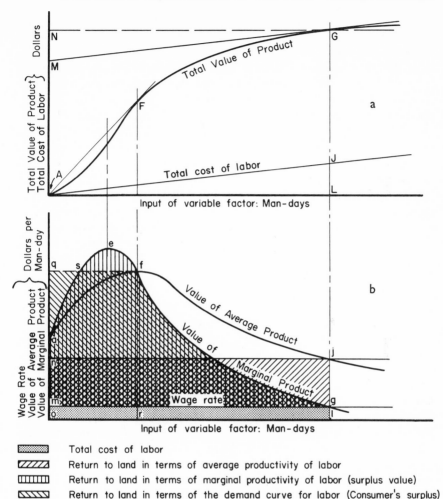

FIGURE 46

proportional to the amount of labor used, and we can represent the total cost of labor by a straight line on FIGURE 46a, such as *AJ*, where *LJ* represents the total cost of hiring *AL* units of labor. The difference between the total value of the product *LG* and the cost of labor *LJ* will be the gross profit that the entrepreneur receives, out of which he will pay the rent on the land he is using, the remainder of this gross profit representing net profit. If the rent is fixed, then maximizing the net profit will be equivalent to maximizing *JG*. Obviously, *JG* will be at a maximum where the tangent *MG* to the total-revenue curve is parallel to the cost of labor line *AJ*. The slope of *AJ* is equal to the wage rate,

[157

and the slope of *MG* is the value of the marginal product, so that the entrepreneur chooses to operate at the point at which the wage rate is equal to the value of the marginal product. The total product *AN* is divided between the wage earner, who gets *MN*, and the entrepreneur and landlord, who get *AM*.

The same result can be arrived at in terms of FIGURE 46b. If the wage rate is *om*, then to the left of *l* the value of the marginal product added by hiring another man-day of labor will be greater than the wage *om* that must be paid, and, accordingly, it will be profitable thus to increase the amount of labor used. Beyond *l* the reverse is true, and thus *l* is established as the most profitable mode of operation. The total-wage bill is the product of the wage rate *om* and the amount of labor used *ol*, i.e., the rectangle *omgl*. The total revenue is the product of the value of the average product *lj* times the amount of labor used, *ol*, i.e., the rectangle *onjl*. The difference between the two rectangles, or the rectangle *mnjg*, thus represents the gross profit.

Another representation of the gross profit may be obtained by considering that the value of the total product is the sum of the values of the increments of product successively added by all the successive units of labor, i.e., the area under the marginal-product curve, *oaefgl*. Subtracting the wage bill *omgl* gives as the gross profit the area *maefg*. This may be regarded as a quasi-Marxist representation of the profit, in that the profit is created by the "surplus value" of the product of the earlier units of labor over the wage paid, which is equal only to the smaller product of the "last" unit of labor.

If now the market-wage rate changes, while the price of the produce remains the same, the equilibrium point *g* will move along the value-of-marginal-product curve *fg*. This curve, accordingly, indicates the relationship between the wage rate and the amount of labor that will be hired. It is, in effect, the demand curve of the entrepreneur for labor. However, if the wage rate should rise above *oq*, which is the maximum value of the *average* value-product, there would of course be nothing available for profit; in FIGURE 46a, the wage-cost line at such a wage rate would lie wholly above the total-revenue curve. In this situation, unless there were some special reason compelling the entrepreneur to stay in operation even at a loss, he will abandon the enterprise completely, and cease to hire labor. Thus the demand curve does not follow the marginal-value-product curve past *f* to *e*, but rather jumps from *f* to *q*, and for wage rates above *oq* it coincides with the axis. It is convenient, however, to consider the demand curve as including the horizontal segment *fq*, even though no actual operation along this segment would be observed: the actual amount of labor demanded at a wage rate of *oq* would be either zero or *qf*, not any intermediate amount.[1] If we adopt this convention, then we can speak of the gross profit as being the area between the demand curve and the wage rate,

---

1. Inclusion of the segment *fq* as part of the demand curve is especially apt when the demands of several identical firms are being aggregated: a point along *fq* would represent a situation in which some firms were at *f* while others were at *q*.

i.e., *qfgm*. For since at an output of *qf* the total value of the product can be represented either by the rectangle determined by the average-cost curve, i.e., *orfq*, or by the area under the marginal-cost curve *oaefr*, these two areas are equal, and the one can be substituted for the other. If we take the area under the marginal-cost curve out to *l*, *oaefgl*, and make this substitution, we get the area under the demand curve, *oqfgl*, which is thus seen to represent the total revenue-product. Subtracting the wage bill *omgl* gives *qfgm* as another measure of the gross profit.

Now this area *qfgm* corresponds exactly to the area that was considered to measure consumer's surplus in the case of the demand curve of an individual consumer purchasing the commodity in question for his own immediate consumption. The only difference is that here the commodity is a factor of production being purchased for the sake of producing a product that can be sold at a profit, and the "consumer's" surplus emerges in more tangible form as an actual gross profit, to be shared, in a manner as yet unspecified, between the entrepreneur and the landlord.

Competitive Equilibrium—Cost Aspect

THE SAME result can be arrived at in a slightly different way if we reverse the respective roles of the variable input and the output, and consider the output as the independent or controlled variable and the variable input, labor, as the dependent or affected variable. To do this we simply interchange the axes of FIGURE 42a to get FIGURE 47a. In effect, this is the result of flipping FIGURE 42a over on its back, about a line making an angle of 45 degrees with the axes. Since, however, in treating the output as the independent variable we are implicitly asking, "How much labor is required to produce a given output?" (rather than, "How much output will a given input of labor produce?"), and the answer we want is obviously the lowest value possible, the portion of the curve above *H*, if the curve does indeed turn back on itself in the manner indicated, is irrelevant and can be ignored, since the answers given by this part of the curve for given outputs are always higher than the answers given by the lower part of the curve. *H* indeed indicates the maximum amount of product that can be secured from the given amount of the fixed factor, regardless of how much of the variable factor is applied, and the curve above *H* of course represents negative returns. However, the conclusions to be reached will in no way be affected if we were to assume that there is no region of negative returns, and that the total-cost curve instead of turning back on itself at *H* continues to rise indefinitely to the right, as indicated by the dashed curve. This could be either by the curve approaching some vertical asymptote as a limit, indicating an upper bound beyond which production cannot be pushed, or, if the fixed factor is relatively unimportant to the production process, by the curve extending indefinitely to the right as well as upward.

[159

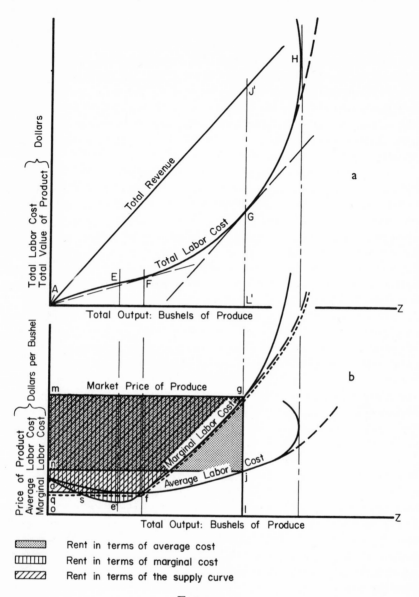

FIGURE 47

If we take the market-wage rate as fixed, we can immediately rescale the vertical axis in terms of the money cost of the various amounts of labor, rather than in man-days. This makes the curve *AEFGH* a total-labor-cost curve (or total-variable-cost curve), showing the total cost of the labor required for the various outputs. From this total-cost curve we can derive the average-cost and marginal-cost curves shown in FIGURE 47b. As the cost referred to is the cost of the variable factor only, in this case labor, the average cost thus derived is referred to more specifically as an average-variable-cost curve to distinguish it from an average-total-cost curve in which fixed costs, such as rent paid for the land, would be included; as the marginal-cost curve is the same whether or not any fixed cost is included in the total-cost curve, it does not need to be distinguished in this way.

It will be noted that except for multiplication by a constant factor, representing a ratio of fixed prices, the average cost and marginal cost are the reciprocals, respectively, of the average product and marginal product for corresponding rates of operation. Thus when the average product is rising, as output increases, the average cost is falling, and vice versa, and similarly for marginal product and marginal cost. However, it should immediately be noted that one curve is *not* derived from the other simply by changing the vertical scale into its own reciprocal, for the horizontal scale is different in the two cases. In FIGURES 42 and 46 the horizontal scale shows the scale of operation as indicated by the input of labor, whereas in FIGURE 47, the horizontal scale likewise indicates the scale of operation, but in this case scale of operation is measured by output. Thus if we start in both cases with the same production function and the same relation between total input of the variable factor and total output, the point *f* in FIGURE 47 would be relatively nearer to *g* than it would be in FIGURES 42 and 46. (However, in the diagrams as drawn, the curves were somewhat modified in order to keep the various points and areas clearly distinguishable, and this particular relationship was not maintained.)

If now we consider that the market price of the produce is fixed, say at *om*, in FIGURE 47b, we can indicate the total revenue to be obtained from the different outputs by the straight line *AJ'* with a slope equal to this price. The total revenue from the output *AL'* will be *L'J'*; deducting the variable cost *L'G* leaves the profit *GJ'*, and if this is to be a maximum, the entrepreneur must choose to operate at the point where the total-cost curve is parallel to the total-revenue line *AJ'*. Or the same thing can be shown in FIGURE 47b, by which it can be seen that where the market price of the product, *om*, is greater than the marginal cost, it will pay to produce another unit, since revenue will be increased by more than the cost will be; conversely, when the marginal cost is greater than the price, profit will be increased by reducing output. The equilibrium position is therefore at *g* where the marginal cost is equal to the market price. The total revenue is then given by multiplying the output *ol* by

[161

the market price, *om*, obtaining the rectangle *omgl*. The total cost of the variable factor, labor, can be shown by multiplying the average variable cost, *lj*, by the total output, *ol*, obtaining the rectangle *onjl*; the amount left as gross profit, including the return to the fixed factor, is *nmgj*. Or the total cost of the labor may be measured by the area under the marginal-cost curve, i.e., as the sum of the marginal costs of the successive units of output; this is the area *oasefgl*, and in this case the gross profit is represented by the area *masefg*.

Again, if the market price of the product is now made to vary (with the entrepreneur still assuming that prices will not be affected by his own actions), the equilibrium point *g* will move along the marginal-cost curve *fg*, and as the point *g* traces out the relation between the price of the product and the amount produced by this particular entrepreneur, we see that this locus *fg* is in fact the supply curve of this entrepreneur for his product, assuming meanwhile that the wage rate remains constant. The supply curve does not follow the marginal-cost curve to the left of *f*, however, for if the price goes below *f*, the entrepreneur will, if he can, shut down completely and supply nothing rather than continue an operation in which his revenues are less than his variable costs and he is operating at a loss even before allowing any return on the fixed factors. We may thus regard the supply curve as tracing out the path *oqsfg*, provided we note that no operation at any point between *q* and *f* will actually be observed and that output will jump discontinuously from nothing to *qf* as the price passes the value *oq*. Given this as a supply curve, the gross profit can be expressed as the area between the supply curve and the price line, i.e., as the area *mqsfg*. It will be noted that the areas *aqs* and *sef* must be equal, as indeed is also true of the corresponding areas in FIGURE 46.

The Equivalence of the Two Approaches

IT IS EASY to see that for a given wage rate and a given price for the produce, the same result will be obtained whether we regard the entrepreneur as balancing marginal cost against the price of the product, or as balancing the value of the marginal product against the wage rate. In the one case, we have

$$\text{(wage rate)} \frac{\text{(increment of labor required)}}{\text{(increment of product resulting)}} = \text{(price of product)}$$

and in the other

$$\text{(price of product)} \frac{\text{(increment of product resulting)}}{\text{(increment of labor input)}} = \text{(wage rate)}$$

These equations are simply two ways of expressing essentially the same relationship. Thus in both cases the output will be the same, the total revenue the same, as also the amount of labor used and the total wage bill, and hence the gross profit. And as long as the entrepreneur owns the land (or at least if there are no rental transactions of comparable land for purposes of comparison), there is little point in inquiring how the gross profit is divided between pure profit and an imputed rent.

However, if we consider the entrepreneur as not owning the piece of land that he uses, but renting it from a landlord, the gross profit will be divided between rent and net profit, and to obtain a complete picture we must find out how this division is determined. To retain a strictly two-factor case and at the same time provide some income for the entrepreneur, we may consider that he devotes a specific amount of time to the management of the farm, and that he pays himself a wage for this labor, which is combined with the hired labor and the total treated as a composite "labor" factor. If this particular entrepreneur is of merely average skill, so that there are other entrepreneurs able to make an equally large gross profit from the use of the land, there may be competition among these entrepreneurs for the use of the land. If the amount set aside as wages of management represents a satisfactory compensation for the time and effort put in (or at least if it is as much as the entrepreneurs could secure with a similar amount of time and effort as employees or in some other occupation), then competitive bidding among these entrepreneurs for this piece of land will force the rent up until it is equal to the entire gross profit.

The net profit to the entrepreneur in this case is zero; his compensation consists entirely of "wages of management," which are comparable to what could be secured in any other line of endeavor. Moreover, for the entrepreneur who owns the land in addition to functioning as manager, the gross profit will be divided between wages of management and imputed rent on his land, and there will be nothing left over in the form of pure profit. The refinement of the concept of profit has in effect caused it to vanish, at least at the equilibrium point. If of course an entrepreneur fails to make the best possible use of his land (or at least if he fails to do as well as the normally efficient entrepreneur could be expected to do), he will suffer a loss, in the net economic sense of the term. Even though he may still be earning a gross profit, in this case it is less than he could secure in a perfect market for his land and his labor by leasing and hiring out to others. So that though pure profit has been defined out of existence in the competitive case, pure loss is there, at least potentially. It is a case, as in the Red Queen's domain, of having to run as fast as you can in order to stay in the same place.

To be sure, an entrepreneur who is more skillful than most may be able to secure a better gross return, but even here, if we wish, we can again define away the profit by imputing to the entrepreneur a higher "wages of management" commensurate with his higher skill. Indeed, if the skill of the entrepreneur is a general one and implies that he could command higher wages than other entrepreneurs if he were to seek employment elsewhere, such an imputation is called for as an opportunity cost. It is only where the ability of the entrepreneur is specific to this particular operation so that he could not realize an equally high income elsewhere that the option exists to call it a pure profit. And in such a case bargaining between such an entrepreneur and the owner of the piece of land or other factor with respect to which the entrepreneur has the special ability would no longer be carried on under conditions of perfect competition, but rather of bilateral monopoly, so that such a profit could be ascribed to departure from perfect competition.

But one can rapidly reach the stage of diminishing returns in the pursuit of terminological refinement; more importantly, one should develop a clear picture of the objective relations that develop under given assumptions from given initial conditions.

Inclusion of Fixed Costs

THE PAYMENT of a fixed rent can be incorporated into the cost diagrams as shown in FIGURE 48, which is similar to FIGURE 47. If AJ represents the total revenue, and AFG is the variable cost, the gross profit at equilibrium will be JG, which will become the rent to be paid on the property. If this fixed rent JG is added to the variable cost AFG, the result is the total-cost curve TJ. Comparing this with the total-revenue line AJ, it is seen that the pure or net profit is zero at J, and is negative everywhere else.

If the fixed cost AT is divided by various volumes of output, the result can be plotted as the average-fixed-cost curve, which has the shape of a rectangular hyperbola. (A rectangular hyperbola has the formula $xy = k$, or $y = k/x$; one variable varies inversely as the other. All rectangles inscribed between a point on such a curve and the axes have the same area. Such a curve is sometimes described as having a constant elasticity of -1.) Adding this average fixed cost to the average-variable-cost curve afj gives the average-total-cost curve, which has its minimum value at g, the point where the marginal cost is equal to the market price. The rent AT is equal to the area $mgfea$ between the marginal-cost curve and the market price. In addition, because the rent is also equal to the area $mgfq$ between the supply curve and the market price, the consumers' surplus, which is the complementary area between the demand curve and the market price is by analogy often termed "consumers' rent."

Symmetry as Among Factors of Production

TRADITIONALLY, the analysis of production with one factor fixed is normally carried through in terms of applying varying amounts of labor to a fixed amount of land, as is natural considering that for the economy as a whole the total supply of land is more or less fixed, whereas the supply of agricultural labor is more variable, whether through population growth or through shifts into

164]

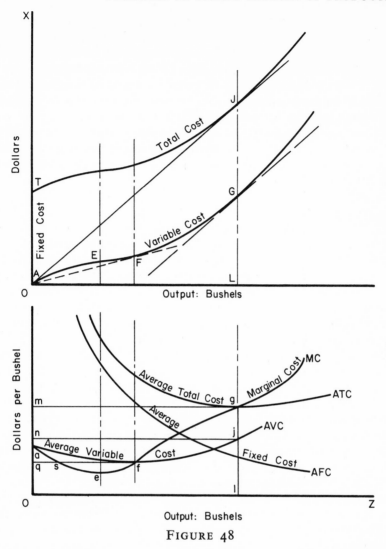

FIGURE 48

industry. But from the point of view of an individual firm, at least, the amount of land used can also be varied, and there is nothing to prevent considering the case of an entrepreneur with a given amount of labor at his disposal, who is considering how much land he should rent in order to obtain the maximum return. Indeed, a strict case of this sort is almost easier to imagine than the former one, as here the entrepreneur is also the laborer and there is no need to distinguish sharply between wages imputed to management and wages actually paid to hired labor. Specifically, this is the case of the farmer who has at his

[165

disposal a certain amount of his own labor and of that of members of his family, and who needs to rent the land he is to farm.

In this case we can return to the production function used in the previous analysis, shown in FIGURE 41, and instead of taking a cross section perpendicular to the oY axis, with the amount of land constant, we now take a cross section perpendicular to the oX axis, with the amount of labor constant, getting a total-product curve $TUVGW$. This curve will ordinarily have somewhat the same characteristics as the labor-input vs. total-output curve $AEFGH$, but may also have one of the shapes illustrated in FIGURES 43, 44, or 45. The type of curve shown in FIGURE 42a, however, can be used to illustrate the significant relationships.

Using this curve as the relation between total output and the variable input, we can go through exactly the same formal analysis as was carried through on pages 150–64, reversing the roles of land and labor. Thus instead of considering land as the fixed factor and labor the variable one, labor is now the fixed factor and land the variable factor. For a given price of the produce, instead of balancing the marginal product of labor against the price of labor, we now balance the value of the marginal product of land against the going rent for land. Or instead of balancing the price of the product against the marginal cost in terms of labor, we balance it against the marginal cost in terms of the additional land required to produce the increment of output with a fixed input of labor. Instead of paying for the labor used at a given wage rate and considering the surplus product as the return to the landlord, we now pay for the land used at a given rental per acre, and the surplus of the marginal products of the intra-marginal units of land, above this given rental, is the compensation to the entrepreneur for the use of his fixed amount of labor. And, finally, instead of thinking of the excess of the market price over the marginal labor cost of the intra-marginal units of output as the return to land, or rent, we now consider the excess of the market price over the marginal land cost of the intra-marginal units of output as the return or compensation to labor. The diagrammatic representation of all this is exactly as shown in FIGURES 46, 47, and 48, except that the shape of the curves is somewhat altered as required by the difference between the shape of the basic curves $AEFGH$ and $TUVGW$, and references to land and labor are interchanged.

Consistency of Alternative Imputations

IF WE THUS analyze a given productive operation alternatively on the basis of taking different factors as the fixed factor, we obtain what on the surface appear to be different rules for apportioning the proceeds from the sale of the product among the various factors of production that contributed to the process. For example, we may consider on the one hand a landlord with oA

of land at his disposal (FIGURE 41) and suppose that the going wage rate and the market price of produce are just such as to lead him to use oT units of labor so that he operates at the point G on the production surface. And on the other hand we may consider a farmer with oT of labor available, and suppose that the going rental of land, in relation to the same market price of produce, is such that he finds it most advantageous to rent oA acres of land and thus also produce at G on the production surface. Technologically, the two operations, using as they do the same amounts of the two factors, should be exactly similar and yield the same total product, LG. In the first case, the amount of this product that goes to labor is equal to the marginal product of labor at the point G on the production surfaces, multiplied by the amount of labor used, and the landlord gets whatever is left over. In the second case, the rent paid to the landlord is equal to the marginal product of land at the point G times the acreage used, the remainder of the product going as compensation to labor.

It may not at first be obvious why these two methods of "imputation," i.e., of dividing the product between the various factors that contribute to its production, should give the same result. Conceivably, the owner of the factor who is also in the role of entrepreneur might in some way be able to "exploit" the other factor and so obtain more than would be imputed to it on the basis of its own marginal productivity. Indeed, it is quite tempting at this point to try to seek out some "residual claimant" whose share in the total product will be the balance remaining after other factors of production have been rewarded according to their respective marginal productivities. It might seem that the share of the residual claimant could be either more or less than its own marginal productivity would indicate, though presumably in most cases more, if anything, since it would be odd to find an entrepreneur getting less as a return to the factors he owns than he could get by simply hiring them out; indeed, in this case the inclusion of opportunity costs in his total costs would leave him with a net loss. On the other hand, there may also be something odd in the notion that the owner of a factor would accept less for its services than he could obtain by hiring the appropriate complementary factors and becoming an entrepreneur, as long as entrepreneurship remains a simple role and there are no barriers to its assumption. And again one might also be led to raise questions if one found that the proportions in which the factors were combined in producing a given product differed according to whether the entrepreneur making the decision as to this proportion happened to be the owner of one type of factor rather than the other.

However, it is possible to reconcile these different methods of imputation, showing that they all lead to the same results and that, accordingly, these troublesome questions do not arise if the production function in the neighborhood of the equilibrium point shows "constant returns to scale," and that, moreover, in a complete competitive equilibrium production will in fact be

[167

carried out at a point on the production function that has this property. The condition of constant returns to scale is satisfied if a simultaneous increase in *all* of the various factors by the same small percentage increases the product in the same proportion. Thus if *A* acres and *M* man-days of labor produce *Q* bushels of produce, and *kA* acres of land and *kM* man-days of labor produce *kQ* bushels of produce, for all values of *k* sufficiently close to 1.0, then at this point the production function can be said to have constant returns to scale.

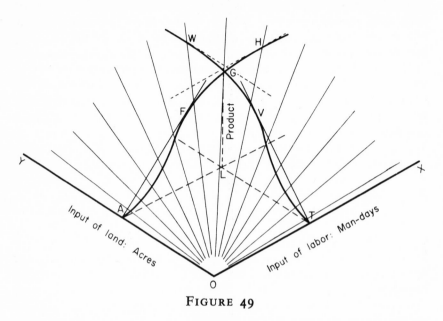

FIGURE 49

In the special case where this relationship holds for all values of *A*, *M*, *Q*, and *k*, we say further that the production function is "homogeneous of degree one," or simply "homogeneous." In this case the production function can be represented by a fan or "cone" of straight lines radiating from the origin, as illustrated in FIGURE 49.

Now on the general principle that if one repeats the same experiment a second time, using the same materials and the same methods, one should get the same result, one would actually expect a production function to be approximately homogeneous, except where some special influence operates to make the second experiment necessarily different from the first. Thus if one landlord has twice as many acres of land as another, and hires twice as much labor to work on it, one would expect to get approximately twice as much produce, at least if the land and the labor are in fact all of the same quality. Actually, the spreading of the entrepreneurial efforts of the landlord over more land may affect the result adversely, and thus be an influence in the direction of "decreasing returns to scale," whereas the possibilities of speciali-zation and reorganization of the work to provide a more detailed division of labor might affect the result favorably, leading to "increasing returns to scale."

If for the moment we ignore these influences or assume that they exactly offset each other so that we do have a case of constant returns to scale, then we can show that the same imputation is obtained whichever factor of pro-duction is considered the residual claimant. For suppose that at some initial point on the production surface the application of M units of labor to A acres of land produces a product Q. Now suppose that we add kA units of land, keeping the amount of labor fixed at M, and as a result get some increase in the total product to $Q + x$. Then if to this second combination we add an amount of labor kM, the assumption of constant returns to scale tells us that from the resulting inputs of $(1 + k)M$ of labor and $(1 + k)A$ of land we should get an output of $(1 + k)Q$. These three results can be shown in tabular form as follows:

	AMOUNT OF LABOR USED	AMOUNT OF LAND USED	TOTAL PRODUCT
1	M	A	Q
2	M	$A + kA$	$Q + x$
3	$M(1 + k)$	$A(1 + k)$	$Q(1 + k)$

Comparing 1 and 2, we see that the addition of kA units of land produced an additional product of x, so that the marginal productivity of land is thus $x/(kA)$. If each of the A acres of land is paid for according to this marginal productivity, the total rent paid will be x/k. Again, comparing 2 and 3, we see that the product added by increasing the labor input by kM is $(kQ - x)$, and the marginal productivity of labor is therefore $(kQ - x)/(kM)$. If each of the M units of labor is paid at a wage rate corresponding to this marginal produc-tivity, the total wage bill will be $(kQ - x)/k$, or $Q - (x/k)$. If now we add the total rent to the total wages, we get $Q - (x/k) + (x/k) = Q$, so that the result of giving to each factor a reward according to its own marginal product is just to exhaust the total product. (Of course, the marginal product at the point 1 will not be exactly the same as the incremental product between the points 1 and 2 the points 2 and 3, but since we can make k as small as we please, we can bring these three points as close together as we please and thus make this difference as small as we please, so that this difference will not interfere with the validity of the demonstration as long as the production surface is smooth at the point in question and the marginal productivities do not jump discontinuously. The proposition still holds true where the produc-tion function is not smooth, but in this case marginal productivities must be given a special interpretation in order for the proposition to hold, as will be seen later.)

The same proposition can be shown geometrically, as in FIGURE 50. If we consider a production function which is smooth and thus has well-defined marginal productivities at a point G, then we can construct the unique plane that is tangent to the surface at the point G. Such a plane contains all the lines that are tangent to the surface, including Go, which is part of the surface itself, MG, the tangent to the curve $AEFG$, and GR, the tangent to the curve $TUVG$. Now Mo and GR are parallel, being the intersections of a plane with two parallel planes, as are SR and MA, both being vertical lines, so that the

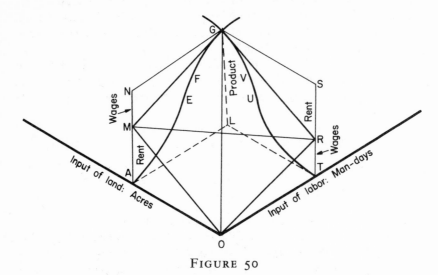

FIGURE 50

angles oMA and GRS are equal, and since the lines GS and Ao are equal in length, and oAM and RSG are right angles, triangles oAM and GRS are congruent and SR and MA are equal. But we saw in FIGURE 46a that MA is nothing but the amount left over for return to the landlord after labor had been paid at a wage rate equal to its marginal productivity; by an exactly similar construction SR can be readily shown to be the amount needed to pay the rent at a rate equal to the marginal productivity of land. Thus the amount available for rent is the same whether computed as a residuum or on the basis of the marginal productivity of the land.

Competition and Returns to Scale

EVEN THOUGH the production function for a particular process may not be homogeneous throughout, it is often possible to find points on such a production function where for sufficiently small deviations the homogeneity conditions are satisfied and where, accordingly, all factors may be rewarded according to their respective marginal productivities without leaving either a surplus or a deficit. Indeed, it will be shown that it is only at such points that production can take place under conditions of perfect competition. Such points will be characterized by the fact that a line from the origin to such points will be tangent to the production surface at that point. Not all production functions will have such points within any normal range of operations, but, for example, in the two-factor case, where such points exist they will tend to lie on some such curve as *SGK* in FIGURE 51. *SGK* can be thought of as the

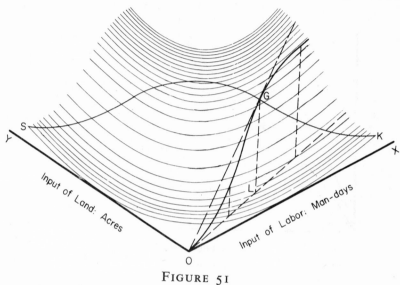

FIGURE 51

locus of points on the "sky line" of the production surface or "hill" as "seen" from the origin; it separates the points that are "visible" from o from those that are hidden from o by being "over the shoulder" of the surface.

This sky line will then be the locus of constant returns to scale; points short of this line would in general be characterized by increasing returns to scale, and points beyond it by decreasing returns to scale.

To show the tendency, under competitive conditions, for production to take place at a point on this sky line, it is desirable to consider simultaneous variation in the inputs of all factors. To do this conveniently, we use a representation of the production surface by means of a contour map consisting of iso-product curves, as in FIGURE 52. Here the two axes represent the amount of product, and the iso-product curves each represent the various combinations of the two factors that would be required to produce a given amount of product. Such a diagram is analogous to an indifference map such as that in FIGURE 2, with factors of production instead of consumer goods and product instead of utility. There is an important difference, however, in that while in

[171

FIGURE 2 utility is a matter of rank only and is not directly measured, here the product is actually a directly measurable quantity, and the spacing between the curves can be given significance by drawing them at equal intervals of total product and labeling each curve with the appropriate total-product level. Marginal products can then be estimated from the spacing of the curves, whereas no judgment as to marginal utility could be inferred directly from the indifference map.

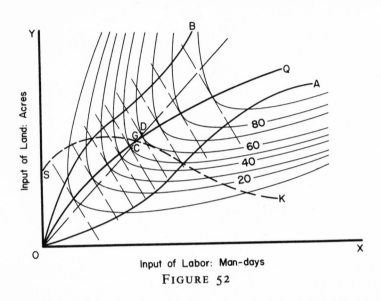

FIGURE 52

Pursuing the analogy to consumer equilibrium further, we may suppose that a given entrepreneur has a given sum of money that he can use for the purchase of factors of production at prices fixed by the market; the possible combinations of factors that he can buy will then be given by a "constant-outlay" line, exactly similar to a consumer's budget line or price line. Of these possible combinations of factors, the entrepreneur will obviously choose that one which gives the largest output; this will normally be the combination indicated by the point where the constant-outlay line is tangent to an iso-product curve. (As in the case of consumer equilibrium, cases will arise, particularly where there are more than two factors, where some factors are not used at all and the tangency is of a more limited sort.) If now we vary the amount the entrepreneur decides to spend, while keeping the market prices of the factors of production constant, this moves the constant-outlay line parallel to itself, and the successive points of tangency with the product contours trace out a "scale line" that corresponds to the Engel curve in consumer analysis. For each ratio of factor prices there will be one such line, and it is

172]

easy to see that given any set of factor prices in the market, the point selected by the entrepreneur must lie on the corresponding scale line.

In the case of the production function that is homogeneous throughout, illustrated in FIGURE 53, the scale lines are all straight lines radiating from the origin; thus as might be expected the proportion between the two factors is always the same for a given price ratio. Two of these scale lines, oA and oB, pass through the points on the product contours that are, respectively, horizontal and vertical. Between these two lines lies the region of decreasing

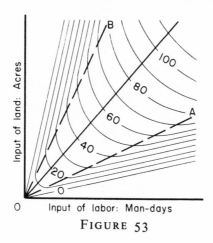

FIGURE 53

returns to both land and labor. The line oA is the line along which the marginal product of labor is zero and the average product of land is a maximum; an entrepreneur would operate along this line if labor were free. Similarly, if land were free, an entrepreneur would operate along the line oB, where the average product of labor is a maximum and the marginal product of land is zero. When payment is required for both land and labor the entrepreneur will operate between these lines and will not ordinarily operate outside them. Between the line oB and the land axis there are increasing returns to labor, but negative returns to land, and conversely in the area between oA and the labor axis. Operation will not ordinarily take place in these regions, as more product could be secured by getting rid of part of one of the factors, or leaving it out of the productive process. Indeed, if we have constant returns to scale, increasing returns to one factor necessarily implies negative returns to some other factor.

Returning to the more general case of variable returns to scale, the total outlay represented by each constant-outlay line will be proportional to the distance from the origin to the line. If we set up a plane perpendicular to the constant-outlay lines corresponding to a given set of factor prices, and then project the corresponding scale line from its meandering course over the

[173

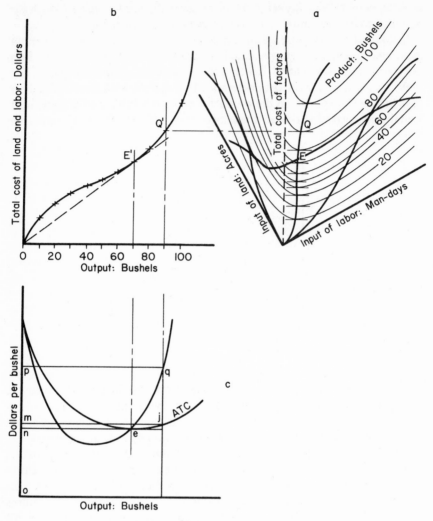

FIGURE 54

production surface onto this plane, we get a curve, as shown in FIGURE 54b that, if given a suitable scale, can be considered the relation between output and total cost for the various points along the scale line. In effect, this curve is the profile of the production surface as seen from the direction of the constant-outlay lines. From this total-cost curve we can immediately derive average- and marginal-cost curves as shown in FIGURE 54c, and if the price of the produce is *op*, the amount produced will be determined by the output for which the marginal cost is equal to *op*; the amount produced will thus be

174]

pq, and production will take place at the point *Q* on the total-cost curve and on the scale line.

If these prices persist, then this entrepreneur will be able to make a profit *qjmp* over and above his outlays for land and labor. If we assume that the effort the entrepreneur devotes to the enterprise is included in the labor factor and that he considers this wage an adequate compensation, this will be a pure profit. But if there are other entrepreneurs equally capable, who are also able to use land and labor to get the same results, i.e., who have the same production function, then this profit will induce these others to engage in this particular type of production. The effect of the entry of other entrepreneurs into the markets for the factors and for the product will be to drive the prices of labor and land up and the price of produce down, thus lowering the product price *op* relative to the marginal-cost curve. This process will continue, as long as there is free entry and there are more potential entrepreneurs with access to the same production function, until final equilibrium is reached at a point such as *e*, where average cost is at a minimum, marginal cost, average cost, and price are all equal, and there is no profit over and above a normal "wages of management." The corresponding point *E* on the production surface is a point at the intersection of the appropriate scale line with the sky line where constant returns to scale prevail, and where, accordingly, all factors of production can be rewarded according to their respective marginal products without leaving any residue. Of course, if during the adjustment process the relative prices of the factors shift, this will in general cause a shift in the scale line and corresponding changes in the shape as well as in the level of the marginal- and average-cost curves; the ultimate equilibrium, however, must still have the properties of the point *e*.

In practice, of course, a number of considerations may intervene to prevent this complete competitive equilibrium from being reached in this simple fashion. If, for example, the particular entrepreneur *A* is more skillful in conducting this particular productive process than any other entrepreneur *B* that might be attracted to this process by the profit prospects, this will mean in effect that the production function of the new entrepreneur *B* is different from that of *A*, and *B* may not be able to achieve as low an average cost. The entry of new entrepreneurs *B* will then cease when the price has been reduced to their minimum average cost, which may be greater than *A*'s minimum, and, accordingly, *A* will be able to retain a profit over and above his "wages of management," and this profit will vary with the degree to which his skill is superior. Of course, if this skill is a generalized one by which *A* could achieve superior results in any field, or even merely in a moderately wide range of fields, then the possible profits from the use of these skills elsewhere would be reckoned an opportunity cost and included in the wages of management. But it is still possible that *A*'s superior skill is specific to this particular operation, in which case the profit will be greater than this opportunity cost.

[175

However, one can even in this case still speak of the marginal product of A's managerial services as the amount of product that would be lost if they were withdrawn, and in general in a competitive situation the profit accruing to A would correspond to this marginal product, so that one can still speak of factors being rewarded according to their marginal productivity.

Similar considerations may apply to land or labor or any of the other factors of production: a potential competitor may not be able to secure land or labor that is quite as well adapted to this particular process. In such cases, profit will ordinarily be imputed to and paid for the use of this specially qualified land or labor, and thus again the profit emerges as a species of special rent which can under competitive conditions be considered as compensation according to marginal productivity.

It may be noted that although for simplicity the analysis has been conducted in terms of factors of uniform quality, the achievement of the competitive result by no means depends upon there being a large number of suppliers of any particular grade of a factor. Every parcel of land may indeed be *sui generis*, but each landlord may nevertheless be faced with a market in which there is a definite rent that can be obtained for the land, and it is useless to ask for more, to take less, or to withhold part of the land from the market in the hope of pushing its price up. In such a case, the competitive conditions will be realized, in spite of the fact that each landlord is in a sense a monopolist, in that his land is unique. The same is true of labor or any other variegated factor. If, however, there are two or more complementary factors of production that are specially qualified, not merely for a particular productive process, but for a particular operation by a particular firm, or perhaps by any firm in conjunction only with each other, then the imputation of their joint contributions to the surplus product may become a matter of uncertainty and bargaining. Cases of this sort do fall outside the scope of the analysis of perfect competition.

Firms may also be kept from entering a particular field by institutional barriers of one sort or another, in which case the profit becomes a monopoly profit. Or they may hesitate to enter the field because of the risk of loss, in which case the profit of those in the field becomes a premium for risk-bearing. Or conceivably the output *ne* for which the costs of an individual firm are a minimum might be such a large fraction of the total market that a point is reached where the addition of one more firm would drive the price below *on* and thus result in losses for all concerned, so that even though existing firms are producing an output *mj* at a price of *om*, this situation can continue without the entry of any further new firms which would drive the price down. Ordinarily, however, if the output *ne* is a sufficiently large part of the total output for this to be the case, then the number of firms will usually be small enough so that each firm's actions will in fact have an appreciable influence on the price of the produce, and if the firms take account of this influence, the conditions of perfect competition will be violated. Such cases must then be analyzed as instances of imperfect competition.

A competitive equilibrium can also be achieved when there are constant returns to scale, but in this case the average-cost curve will be horizontal, and while the total output and the total amounts of the factors used by all firms will be determinate, as will the prices of factors and products, the number of firms and the allocation of the total production among them will be indeterminate. A completely specified competitive equilibrium thus requires that production functions be characterized by increasing returns to scale for small outputs and decreasing returns for large outputs, separated by some such boundary as *SGK* in FIGURE 51, along which there is constant returns to scale. Moreover, it is necessary that the output at the point *G*, at the intersection of this boundary *SGK* with the scale line appropriate to the actual market prices of the factors, should be small enough so that the share of the firm in the markets for the factors and products should be small enough so that the firm can reasonably act without considering the effects of its actions on market prices. It behooves us therefore to examine somewhat carefully the factors that determine the position of this margin between increasing and diminishing returns to scale.

Economies and Diseconomies of Scale

IT IS immediately apparent that economies and diseconomies of scale are likely to be less striking on the whole than the phenomena of increasing and diminishing returns that occur when the amount of one or more significantly important factors is kept constant. Indeed, on the general principle of constancy of natural laws one would expect to be able to obtain the same results by duplicating any given productive set-up, as long as factors of the same characteristics are available or, conversely, if the factors of production are perfectly divisible, to split up a process into two equal parts and get half as much product in each.

However, factors are not in general perfectly divisible, so that ordinarily a reduction in the scale of the process eventually comes to the point where it is not possible to use a smaller amount of some factor without changing the character of the factor or the manner of its application. When such a point occurs, we have "imperfect divisibility" or, more briefly, "indivisibility." But the use of the term "indivisibility" should not be interpreted as necessarily implying a discontinuity in the production function. For example, while the change from a single-track railroad to a double-track line might be considered a discontinuous jump, it is also possible to consider intermediate stages where varying fractions of the total line are double-tracked. With this caution, the terms "indivisibility" and "economy of scale" can be taken as substantially synonymous.

[177

The most pervasive source of indivisibility is of course the human element. Employing less than one individual (i.e., using part-time labor) usually involves rather substantial increases in costs as compared with what they will usually be if an individual's full-time services can be utilized. And the advantages of division of labor and specialization as outlined by Adam Smith lead to substantial economies through the use of several individuals in specialized tasks rather than a smaller number of Jacks-of-all-trades. Certain types of machines are similarly indivisible, or at least smaller models have different and less advantageous characteristics. This may or may not again trace back to the human element: Many machines are of the size they are because they are made by and must be operated by human beings; however, many of the economies of scale are inherent in the machines themselves, and technological trends seem to be headed in the direction of developing processes with ever larger minimum scales of operation, as with continuous rolling mills or nuclear reactions. For any given process, however, after a given size is reached, increasing the size of individual units brings new problems that put a limit to the advantages of increased size. Thus a small plane may take off from a pasture; a plane constructed by merely multiplying each dimension by 3 (and hence areas by 9 and volumes and weights by 27) would probably not even fly, and even if modified sufficiently to fly (and to be flown by pilots of normal stature) would require hard runways and other auxiliary changes.

But even after the individual machines in a plant have reached the optimum size, further expansion of plant size is possible by increasing the number of units operating in parallel; moreover, there will still be possibilities for economies where the optimum size for different machines operating in sequence involves different quantities of the product. The optimum plant size would in theory have to be such as to permit optimum-sized machines of various types to be used together in sequence without waste, i.e., without one type of machine being partly idle because the optimum size of some associated type of machine is insufficient to keep the first type busy. In effect, the optimum size of a plant on this basis would have to have a product equal to a least common multiple of the products of the optimum size of the component units. Where it is possible to design each machine for a particular use, this is probably not too serious, since there is usually a fairly substantial range of size where characteristics are not substantially different from those of the theoretically optimum size, and a plant designed with an output equal to the largest optimum output for any of the component processes will probably come very close to the theoretical minimum cost.

In practice, however, machinery and equipment is manufactured in a number of discrete sizes, so that at best there will be a certain amount of unusable capacity in many of the component processes, which in general will tend to decrease as the number of component units becomes substantial. More important, probably, is the advantage of having in a plant several of even the largest units for the sake of avoiding a complete shutdown of the entire plant in case of breakdown or for necessary periodic overhauls or repairs. Another somewhat similar factor making for increasing returns to scale is the fact that a larger plant can protect itself from the effects of various unforeseeable fluctuations in rates of operation, delivery of supplies, orders, and the like with a less than proportionately larger inventory of materials, supplies, and product at various stages of manufacture; indeed, in some statistical models the inventory required to give a constant level of protection is found to vary as the square root of the volume of business.

In contrast with these rather definite factors making for decreasing costs, the factors making for increasing costs within the firm are much more tenuous. Indeed, while it would in general not be possible to copy a given operation on a diminished scale, it would seem possible to replicate any given operation fairly closely as long as the supply of factors holds out. And if it is not possible to secure duplicate supplies of the appropriate factors without materially increasing the price (or in the case of unique factors such as land, without disturbing the relationship between rent and marginal productivity for the various parcels), then the conditions of competition are already violated in these factor markets, in that the firm is already so large that the entrepreneur will find it difficult to ignore his influence on the prices of the factors.

However, if a doubling of output is attempted by running two or more duplicate establishments under a single management, the character of this management must to some extent change and we can look to this change as one source of increasing costs. As long as the entrepreneur does all the work himself, there is no need to waste time giving orders; and even if he hires assistants, the greater the share of the work done by himself, the less time is wasted in the mere coordination of activities. As the operation becomes larger, the hired labor is less immediately and effectively supervised. Eventually, supervision requires the hiring of assistant managers or foremen, and at this point additional communication between the entrepreneur proper and his staff on very general matters is required; moreover, the incentives for assistants to exercise their best judgment will inevitably be somewhat less immediate and effective than the incentives that would operate on the entrepreneur himself, and coordination of differences of judgment between assistants and the entrepreneur is more difficult.

This is not to say that there may not be substantial advantages to large-scale management, through specialization as to information and skills, the stimulation brought about from consultation, and advantages summed up in the adage that two heads are better than one. But it is at least possible that at some stage in the growth of the firm and the elaboration of the managerial structure these advantages become outweighed by the increased volume of paper work and communication, the dilution of incentives, the increase in auditing to insure proper performance at the various levels, and work to interrelate the various parts. Another and in many cases much more important factor is that in many cultures there is a value attached to the independence associated with the role of entrepreneurship that leads individuals to be satisfied with a lower return for their efforts as independent operators than they could secure as employees in a similar managerial capacity. As a result, managerial labor may be available to small firms at a rate of compensation much lower on the whole than the same degree of skill is paid for by larger firms. Another factor in this result is the requirement that is apparently fairly generally felt that there should be a certain minimum ratio or differential between the salaries of persons at successive steps of a hierarchy, and this in turn may tend to push the compensation to the upper tiers of a hierarchy beyond what would be required by a perfectly competitive market.

Thus it is at least admissible to suppose that at some point, as the size of a firm increases, the possibilities for further economies of scale on the technological side diminish to the point that they are outweighed by these diseconomies of large-scale management. A point of diminishing returns to scale may be reached in this way, and if this point is reached while the firm is still but a small part of any of the markets in which it deals, the competitive equilibrium may be established.

However, these diseconomies of scale in the field of management are at best not nearly so striking as the technological economies of scale, particularly as we pass from medium- to large-sized firms. While these diseconomies may be fairly substantial as we pass from the one-man business to the small establishment in which the entrepreneur is in close and direct contact with all of his employees, and as we pass from such a scale to the next in which this direct contact is largely lost or at least greatly impaired, and perhaps even somewhat beyond this, it appears on the whole likely that once the stage has been reached where a fairly elaborate managerial hierarchy is required, further expansion produces few if any diseconomies of this sort. Indeed, modern accounting techniques, increased facility of communication, and other developments in the modern technique of management seem to have operated in the direction of decreasing very markedly the managerial diseconomies of scale. Thus once a firm has become fairly large, it does not seem that these managerial diseconomies alone would seriously impede its further expansion.

Indeed, it is quite possible to regard the competitive market itself as a sort of super-management device for organizing the entire economy. Large firms in fact often establish within themselves an internal system of accounting and directives that to some extent imitate the operation of a free market. The component units of a firm may be given considerable autonomy as to their operations, and may even on occasion purchase required supplies outside the firm rather than from within if the market price found to rule outside is lower than the price established within the firm for internal accounting purposes. With the competitive system as a model to copy, it would indeed be rash to assume that integration by management of the various parts of a large firm would necessarily be less efficient than the integration of the operations of independent units that is brought about through the operations of a competitive market.

Capital Rationing

ANOTHER possible diseconomy of scale lies in the supply of capital. Nearly all forms of organized production, and especially those carried out on a fairly large scale, require substantial amounts of capital. While fixed factors of production can often be rented or leased, ordinarily this involves additional cost and is less satisfactory than outright ownership of at least a substantial equity in the fixed capital by the entrepreneur. Thus a farmer who owns his own land has an incentive to maintain its fertility that a tenant farmer lacks, as it is virtually impossible to allow in the terms of a lease for changes in fertility, or to ascertain at the termination of the lease precisely what changes in fertility have occurred. Even where the farmer sells his land at the end of a term of operation no longer than the tenant's lease, the terms of sale are likely to reflect to a considerable extent the underlying increases in value resulting from careful husbandry. Even were an attempt made to allow for such values in a lease, the result may be less satisfactory, as there is a significant difference between an appraisal, even by a neutral arbitrator, that is to be compulsorily binding on the parties, and mutual bargaining between buyers and sellers who are free to decline to deal.

Similar considerations apply in even greater force to other types of capital assets, particularly if they must be specially adapted or designed for a particular production process and thus may have relatively little value outside of their use in a particular process, as is the case with special tools and dies. In addition, factors must ordinarily be paid for before the product is sold, entailing a certain amount of working capital, although this may in some cases be reduced by the use of credit extended by suppliers.

Now while the capital used by a single entrepreneur is usually only a very small part of the total supply, and should, in a theoretically perfect capital market, be available to him in unlimited amounts at a constant set of terms, actually the terms on which capital is available will vary rather sharply with the amount invested in the business. A small initial amount of capital may consist of the entrepreneur's own savings, and the cost of such capital may be merely the opportunity cost measured by the return he might have obtained by investing this capital in securities or other passive investments. At somewhat greater cost he can borrow on various kinds of security, possibly life insurance, a mortgage on his house, or a straight extension of credit by a bank secured by inventory or other assets of the business. Additional funds may perhaps be borrowed from immediate acquaintances who have direct knowledge of the competence and honesty of the borrower, but such loans will often involve some substantial costs of solicitation and of investigation of the proposed project by the lender in addition to the actual payment of interest, which may also be somewhat higher than required by the earlier sources. Securing of further capital may involve admitting the investors to a voice in the management, and ultimately additional capital may be obtainable only at the expense of substantial loss of the control of the firm by the original entrepreneur and his ceasing in effect to function as such. Floating an issue of stock to the public at large is likely to involve fairly heavy underwriting expenses as well as dilute the equity of the original entrepreneur. And a stage may be reached where capital is not available on any terms within reason.

In general, it seems that this "capital-rationing" phenomenon with its sharply increasing cost of capital is likely to have a somewhat more decisive effect upon the size of the firm, at least in the short run, than would the increasing costs of management. At least, it seems plausible to believe that the effects of capital rationing continue to have a restraining effect on expansion for firms that have already passed the stage at which the increasing cost of management are substantial. Even here, however, once a firm has reached the size represented roughly by the ability to get its shares listed on some fairly active exchange, it seems likely that the costs of securing capital tend to decline rather to increase. It appears to be on the whole easier to sell shares in a large company that has become fairly widely known than in a small closely held firm. Thus again, once a certain hump has been surmounted, there seems to be very little hindrance to the growth in size of a firm until a point is reached where further expansion is limited by the aggregate demand for the product. Even at this point further expansion often occurs through an increase in the number of different products produced by the firm.

Diseconomies of Rapid Growth

THUS IN STATIC terms, it is probably necessary to think of analysis of a system of perfect competition as applying with reasonable accuracy to only those industries where the technological economies of scale are exhausted at a fairly small size of firm, where increasing costs of management or of capital procurement are such as to inhibit further expansion. If this were all, competitive theory would apply to only a relatively minor part of the economic system. Fortunately, there are in the real world other factors that limit the growth of firms. Particularly, if for the moment we abandon the static assumptions, one can think of costs as being adversely affected by too rapid a rate of growth of the firm. Thus in a new industry in which several new firms are developing, there might be a tendency for a dynamic equilibrium to be established by reason of the fact that any one firm could not grow at more than a certain rate without having its costs increase, which would limit the size it could attain at any given time, and thus in some cases provide room for other firms to compete and grow alongside of it. Then even when the market becomes saturated and the rate of growth slows down, there would be several firms in the field with a substantial vested interest in their capital investment, and while the situation may eventually become more or less unstable, it is at least possible for a certain precarious stability to be maintained with several firms in the field, provided that the long-run average-cost curve for each firm is sufficiently close to horizontal.

This restraint on rapid growth probably comes into play more strongly on the side of the supply of capital than on the side of operating costs. To be sure, a too-rapid growth can mean the use of inadequately trained personnel, internal maladjustments not ironed out, and excessive costs, and perhaps poor design of hastily erected capital equipment and structures. The real restraint on growth, however, is likely to be the supply of capital. Capital can usually be secured for a new firm if it is secured gradually as the firm grows, so that marginal investors will have evidence of the profitability of the venture in the results of the initial small-scale operations before they commit themselves in substantial amounts. Moreover, a large part of the capital secured by firms is in the form of reinvested profits, whether as undistributed profits of corporations or as reinvestment or ploughing back of profits by individual proprietors. The profits thus reinvested of course may consist not only of pure profits in the economist's sense, but of profits in the wider everyday sense inclusive of imputed returns to factors contributed by proprietors or stockholders. Also, if we can for the moment deviate further from the assumption of the perfectly competitive market and admit a degree of monopoly profit into the picture, there is a conflict between the objective of securing higher profits so as to be able to expand, on the one hand, and of keeping prices low so as to enlarge sales, on the other. One can perhaps imagine a firm setting prices at a level that will result in the expansion of sales at a rate that can be just taken care of by the expansion of capacity that can be financed by the profits that can be conveniently retained out of those produced by the selected price.

Other institutional factors of course affect the size of firms and may indeed be the dominant influence in determining their size where the effects of increasing or decreasing returns are too small to have much influence. A desire on the part of the management to extend the reach of its economic imperium may be a fairly potent force for expansion, and may even overcome a considerable degree of increasing cost, especially where the stockholders whose profits are at stake are unable to control the corporation effectively by reason of a wide dispersal of stock ownership. Also, the mores of the business community are often such that expansion is taken to be the prime

[183

index of skill and success in management, and growth and size confer great prestige.

On the other hand, the expansion of an enterprise may be limited by a desire on the part of the management to avoid the loss of the personal touch, or by fear of adverse public sentiment, or by antitrust action, actual or threatened, or even by a devotion to the preservation of the benefits of competition above and beyond the call of self-interest. The net result of the interplay of such motives cannot, of course, be determined in terms of economic theory alone.

Extension of Production Theory to Other Cases— Many Factors and Products

THUS FAR, for simplicity, the analysis of the firm under perfect competition has been developed under the assumption that the production function was a continuous smooth surface, and was for the case of two factors and a single product. The extension to cases involving several factors and several products follows in a more or less routine fashion, as long as the smoothness assumption is maintained. It is of course no longer possible to represent the production function as a surface in three dimensions, and if it is to be thought of at all in geometrical terms, it must be as a function in a hyperspace of the required number of dimensions. It thus becomes necessary to treat the problem analytically with algebraic symbols rather than by means of geometrical diagrams. The terms "average product" and "average cost" may lose their meaning, in that it is not always possible to allocate the total cost among products unequivocally, but marginal product and marginal cost retain their significance. For the continuous one-product case, it will still be true that at the point of equilibrium the market price of the product must equal its marginal cost, and that this marginal cost will be the same whether this is computed in terms of an expansion along the scale line with all factors increasing simultaneously, or is computed on the basis of obtaining the increment in product by increasing any one factor by itself. And in a purely formal sense, it is always possible to select one product as the main product, treating all other "by-products" as negative inputs or negative factors of production, and so reduce the problem to the one-product–many-factor case for analytical purposes. A "net total cost" can then be obtained by deducting the proceeds from the sale of the by-products from the total cost of the factors, and average-product and average-cost figures can be obtained on this basis that are at least unambiguously defined, even though they may not be highly significant.

The obverse of the many-factor–one-product case is of course the one-factor–many-product case. If the single factor is required to be a well-defined homogeneous entity, then this category may well be an empty box. If we

184]

admit for the single factor a composite bundle of some sort, or perhaps merely measure the total input in terms of its money value at constant prices, we can get in this case another useful tool of analysis, the "transformation curve." In FIGURE 55 the axes measure the amounts of the various outputs to be secured, and each transformation curve connects the points representing the possible output combinations that can be secured from a given level of input. For example, the curve ABC would indicate that for the given inputs of land and labor to which it corresponds, one could obtain either oA of beef, or

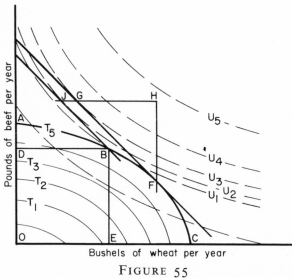

FIGURE 55

oC of wheat, or a combination of oE of wheat and oD of beef. The curves are generally concave to the origin, indicating a decreasing "marginal rate of transformation;" i.e., as one gives up successive units of output of wheat, one is able to secure smaller and smaller increments in the output of beef in exchange, and vice versa. This in general reflects the notion that for a farm that is not completely homogeneous, there will be acreage that is relatively well adapted to the raising of cattle and poorly fitted to the raising of wheat, and vice versa. If both the wheat- and beef-producing operations are at strictly constant returns to scale the curve would be a straight line. While in principle it is possible for such curves to be convex to the origin, actually one would never observe operation at such a point under competitive conditions (unless the point were on one of the axes), since there would always be, at fixed prices for the products, another point yielding a higher total value for the product of the same inputs.

Equilibrium for an isolated individual having such a transformation curve for his productive process or processes can be found by superposing his

[185

indifference map on the transformation-curve diagram, and equilibrium will normally be found at a point such as *B* where the transformation curve is tangent to an indifference curve and the marginal rate of transformation is thus equal to the marginal rate of substitution in consumption. If on the other hand such an individual obtains access to a market in which beef and wheat can be exchanged at a fixed rate indicated by the slope of the line *GF*, then equilibrium will be found by shifting production to the point on the transformation curve (also sometimes called the "production-possibility curve") which will yield the maximum total value of product at these market prices, which will be at the point *F* where the marginal rate of transformation corresponds to the market rate of exchange. Having produced the combination *F*, he will then trade in the market by giving up *GH* of wheat in exchange for *FH* of beef, thus bringing him to the point *G*, on the highest indifference curve he can reach, where the marginal rate of substitution corresponds to the market rate of exchange. This point *G* is on a higher indifference curve than the point *J*, which would have been attainable if the consumer had started trading from the original production combination *B* without shifting it in response to the market conditions.

Extending the analysis to the case of many factors also brings into prominence the possibility that for some sets of factor prices some of the factors may remain entirely unused in a given production process. In such cases, at equilibrium the price of each factor will equal the respective values of the marginal products for those factors that are actually used; the value of the marginal product of unused factors may be less than the price of such factors. Similarly, while for any product that is actually produced, the marginal cost at the equilibrium point must be equal to its market price, it may be that some of the products that might be produced from a given production process actually are not produced at equilibrium, in which case the marginal cost of producing such products by this particular process may be greater than their market price.

Corners and Breaks in the Production Function

MORE TROUBLESOME is the failure of many production functions to approximate reasonably closely a smooth continuous surface. For example, in many production processes factors must be employed in fairly well-defined proportions, and any amount of one or the other factor in excess of the proper proportion is substantially wasted. Chemical reactions are often of this character. Or if the factors are very specifically defined as the particular parts that make up a machine, or the specific ingredients in a recipe, their proportions may not be alterable without, in the strict sense at least, changing the quality or specifications of the final product. Or possibly various products must be produced in rather definite proportions, as in the production of wool,

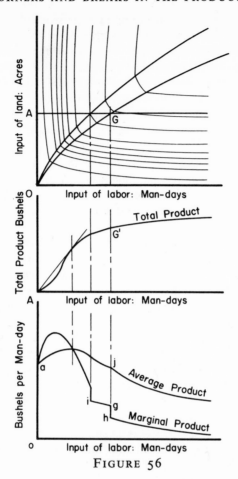

FIGURE 56

hides, and mutton from a given breed of sheep. If proportions are rigidly fixed in this way, it may suffice, for the theory of production, to treat such factors or products as single composite factors or products, so that the analysis may actually be simplified in such cases by reducing the number of variables to be considered.

More difficult, but not essentially different, is the case where while the proportions are not absolutely fixed, there may be a normal proportion that can be departed from only with comparative difficulty. This may be represented by a sharp corner or crease in the production function as illustrated by FIGURE 56. If a cross section is taken with only one factor variable, the resulting total- and average-product curves will have a corresponding corner, while the marginal-product curve will have a jump or discontinuity at that point, reflecting the fact that the marginal product of the variable factor will

[187

be substantially higher as the critical point is approached from below than it will be when the critical point is approached from above. The equilibrium conditions will be satisfied as long as the price of the factor lies below the "from below" value of the marginal product, and above the value of the marginal product "from above," so that in this case the price of the variable factor can vary in this case over a considerable range, i.e., *gh*, without affecting the point at which production will take place. Outside this range, however, the equilibrium point moves away from the "crease" and the continuous-case analysis applies.

There may be, of course, several such creases on a single production surface, indicating several possible modes of operation that are each fairly well defined and become the optimum modes at different ranges of the price structure, as, for example, when one can have either one-man or two-man operation of streetcars or buses.

Another complication arises when the amount of a factor cannot be varied continuously, but must be increased in more or less discrete units. A process may be such as to call for a machine of a fairly specific size and capacity, and the total output of a firm may be variable only in terms of a specific number of such machines, and if their capacity is large compared with the total output under consideration, the production function, instead of being continuous in the direction of this factor, consists in effect of a series of cross sections at discrete intervals. Or, more frequently but less significantly, equipment may be available only in a series of standard sizes. With specialized personnel, it is often awkward or even impossible to increase a specific type of labor input by a fraction of a person: one can have either two or three laborers (or book-keepers) but not two and a half, although there may be cases where part-time labor can be used effectively, or where an employee can be used part time in a number of different jobs within the firm, though usually in each case with some loss of efficiency. In this case, the total-product curve for such a factor consists not of a complete curve but only of a series of discrete points. Nevertheless, in analyzing such a case under conditions of perfect competition it will usually be sufficient to carry through the analysis as though the points were connected by straight lines, with the corresponding marginal-product curve becoming a series of horizontal segments, i.e., a "step-function," as shown in FIGURE 57. Again, the amount of the factor used will remain constant over substantial ranges in its price, jumping to the next higher available level when the price falls below a critical figure.

For example, in FIGURE 57 the equilibrium can be determined by taking the current price of the quantized input (here machinery, measured by its cost at some standard set of prices) and dividing by the given market price of the output; if the quotient, as measured along the vertical axis of the lower half of FIGURE 57, falls between the limits *od* and *oc*, then production will take place with the use of *cg* units of machinery, at *G* on the production surface.

188]

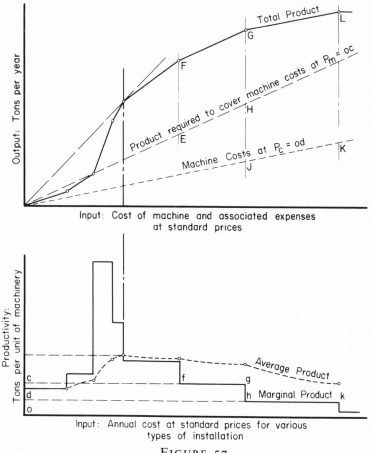

FIGURE 57

If the price of machinery rises above the level yielding a quotient of *oc*, then the use of machinery will be suddenly curtailed from *og* to *of*. If the price of machinery is such as to yield a quotient of exactly *oc*, the result will be indeterminate; profits will be at the same maximum level with *of* or *og* of machinery, as indicated by the fact that *EF = HG* in the upper part of the diagram. The demand curve for machinery thus becomes a step function, and the elasticity of this demand is either zero or infinite for any small change in the price.

Actually, as long as factors of production are defined in fairly broad terms, variations within the factor category will take place, and in any case the production surface is not known with absolute accuracy but only approximately, so that such sharp corners and discontinuities tend to be blurred. Moreover, even within strictly defined categories, some margin of variation is

[189

usually possible. While the proportions of the reagents for a chemical reaction, for example, may in principle be quite exactly known, as in the proportion of alkali and fat in the manufacture of soap, in the actual production process there may be an excess of one factor or the other allowable, and the degree of care used in salvaging excess amounts, recycling, minimizing losses and wastes of various kinds, and the like, will in principle be subject to variation with changes in relative prices. The amount of cloth needed for a suit, for example, may vary with the care exercised in laying out and cutting the patterns, and similarly with leather for shoes. Thus the proportions of the raw factors employed may not be absolutely fixed, and the production function instead of having a sharp crease has merely a ridge with a very small radius of curvature; marginal-product curves instead of being discontinuous merely have some very steep sections, and the analysis of the continuous case can be applied. But meticulous analysis of such fine structure problems will usually involve difficulties out of proportion to the light that such analysis has to shed on the conduct of a particular operation, and is generally not important to the understanding of the over-all operation of the economic system as a whole.

Short-run and Long-run Equilibrium

A MORE SIGNIFICANT modification of the purely static analysis is the separation of "short-run" and "long-run" adjustments. In the context of static analysis, these terms refer only indirectly to periods of time. A "short-run equilibrium" is often best conceived of not as something that actually occurs within any specified period of time, but rather as the result that would be reached after an indefinite period of adjustment if certain specified factors of production which actually can be changed or shifted relatively slowly are not allowed to change at all, while other factors which can be shifted relatively rapidly are allowed to shift and sufficient time is allowed for the shift to become complete and a stable state, subject to the specified restrictions, to be reached. A true "short-run equilibrium" is in effect an internally inconsistent construct that will be approached reasonably closely if the distinction between the variable and the fixed factors is sharp enough and the period required to work out the adjustment of the variable factors is short enough for the dynamic effects of this adjustment to disappear before there has been sufficient time for a material change to have taken place in the fixed factors, and if the rate of change in the fixed factors is sufficiently slow so that the dynamic effects of this change will be negligible.

There can be of course several types of short run depending on the criterion used to separate the fixed from the variable factors. For example, in terms of a railroad, one could think of a very short run in which nothing is done to accommodate changes in traffic and trains are merely run emptier or more crowded; or a short run in which cars can be added to trains or extra sections

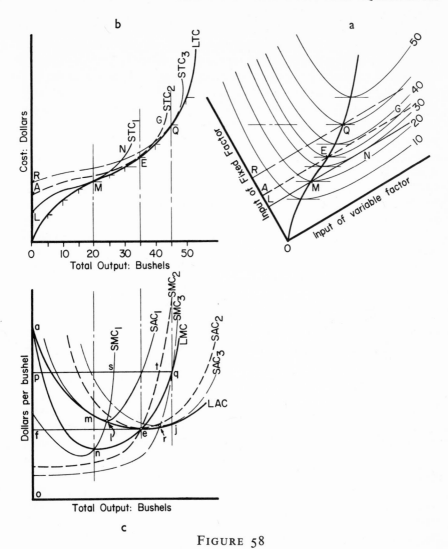

FIGURE 58

operated; or a longer run in which train schedules are revised and perhaps additional equipment secured; a somewhat longer run in which tracks can be added or signaling equipment improved; or the very long run in which entirely new lines may be built.

If we consider all the "variable" factors together as one composite factor, and all the fixed factors together as the other factor, we can represent the long-run and short-run equilibrium in an adaptation of FIGURE 54 as shown in FIGURE 58, in which FIGURE 58a shows the iso-product contours with the

[191

axis o*LAR* representing the fixed factor and the other axis the variable factor. The diagram is so oriented that the constant-outlay lines for the ruling price ratio between the fixed and variable factors will be horizontal, as in FIGURE 54; the long-run "scale line" for this price ratio, which contains the possible points of equilibrium in the long run, when all factors can be adjusted, is o*MEQ*, and the projection of this upon the cost plane in FIGURE 58b is the "long-run total-cost curve," also labeled o*MEQ*. If the amount of the fixed factor is held constant at o*L*, for example, the entrepreneur will be restricted to the line *LM* in his choice of modes of operation, and this, projected on the plane of FIGURE 58b becomes the "short run total-cost curve" *LMN*, with the amount o*L* representing the fixed costs of the fixed factor. Similarly, *AE* is the short-run total-cost curve when the amount of the fixed factor is o*A*, and *RQ* is the short-run total-cost curve when the amount of the fixed factor is o*R*.

Each of these short-run total-cost curves lies above the long-run total-cost curves except at one point where it is tangent (though in special cases this point of tangency could spread out over a finite range). This reflects the fact that the short-run total cost must be greater than or at least equal to the long-run total cost for a given level of output, since the long-run curve represents the better adjustment that the entrepreneur can make when he is free to vary the fixed factor.

From each of these short-run total-cost curves can be derived corresponding short-run average-cost and short-run marginal-cost curves, shown in FIGURE 58c. The relation between the short-run and the long-run average-cost curves is similar to that for the corresponding total curves; i.e., each of the short-run curves lies above the long-run curve, being tangent to the long-run curve at some point; in fact, the long-run curve *amej* is the "envelope" of the short-run curves, i.e., the boundary of the area covered by the short-run curves. It should be noted that in general the point at which the short-run curve is tangent to the long-run curve differs from the minimum point of the short-run average-cost curve (except for the particular short-run curve that has its point of tangency at *e*, the minimum point of the long-run average-cost curve). The point of tangency indicates the output for which the given plant is the optimum plant, i.e., for which the total cost is less (for the same output) than would be obtainable with any other plant. But in general there will be some other output for which the average cost for the given plant will be lower, though the given plant will not be an optimum plant for producing this output. Thus, for example, the curve SAC_1 corresponds to a plant of a size that will be optimal for producing an output indicated by the point *m*, whereas the point *l* indicates the minimum total average cost attainable with this plant at a somewhat higher output. At this output this plant is not optimal, for as indicated by the long-run average-cost curve, a slightly larger plant could be expected to produce this output at a still lower average cost.

192]

The relation of the short-run marginal-cost curves to the long-run marginal-cost curve is quite different. Each short-run marginal-cost curve intersects the long-run marginal-cost curve at an output equal to that where the corresponding short-run average-cost curve is tangent to the long-run average-cost curve. For smaller outputs, the short-run marginal-cost curves generally lie below the long-run marginal-cost curves, and for larger outputs they generally lie above it. Thus the long-run curve is not in this case an envelope of the short-run curves. Each short-run marginal-cost curve passes through the minimum point on the corresponding short-run average-cost curve.

Now if the market price of the product is op, and the entrepreneur finds himself with a plant oL, he will for the time being produce at the point where the corresponding short-run marginal-cost curve SMC_1 intersects this price level; i.e., he will produce an output ps. Or, similarly, if he had at the moment a plant oA, he would produce an output pt. These would be points of short-run equilibrium in the two cases. But in neither case is the plant he has at the moment the most economical plant for the output he is producing; moreover, if he adjusts the size of his plant so as to reduce total costs, the most profitable output will also shift. If, indeed, the prices of factors and products were to remain unchanged over a long enough period so that the entrepreneur has whatever time is needed to expand his plant as far as he wants, then this long-run equilibrium will occur when plant has been expanded to oR, which is the plant best adapted to the production of the output pq determined by the point where the long-run marginal cost is equal to the price. The output pq will then be produced at the lowest possible total (and also average) cost, and profits will be maximized.

If this price structure is maintained in the market, and if for some reason it is not possible for other firms to enter the market with a similar production function, then this will be a final long-run equilibrium. Such a case could occur, for example, if production involves, in addition to the fixed plant on the axis oR and the variable factors represented on the other axis, some further factor that is in some way specialized and unique to this particular process or firm, such as, for example, a mineral deposit of specially favorable characteristics. In such a case, the profit, represented by the area $pqef$, will appear in the form of rental or royalty payments accruing to the owner of the mineral deposit.

However, if all of the factors of production required for this particular process are freely available in quantities that are large relative to the amounts that could be absorbed in this particular industry, and if other entrepreneurs are equally skilled and able to reproduce the results indicated by the production function of FIGURE 58a, then, as we observed previously, there will be an opportunity for new entrepreneurs to make a profit, as long as the price of the product remains above of, by entering the industry, constructing plants of the size oA, and operating them at the output fe with an average total cost of of. This entry of additional firms will thus continue until the price is brought

[193

down to the level *of*, after which there will be no further opportunity for profit and the industry will be in long-run equilibrium both as to the expansion of firms and the entry of new firms. In this situation, all the firms are operating at the point *e* where the long-run average cost, long-run marginal cost, short-run average cost, and short-run marginal cost are all equal to the market price. Production is being carried out in firms of optimum size (i.e., having the lowest possible average cost), and there are just enough firms in the industry to supply the demand that comes forth at a price equal to this minimum cost.

In the interim, however, before the long-run adjustment can take place, either in the number of firms or in the aggregate amount of fixed plant installed, firms in the industry will tend to operate at a net profit if the aggregate amount of the fixed factor installed is less than the long-run equilibrium amount, or at a loss if the aggregate amount of the fixed factor installed is in excess of this. In the short run, the fixed factor plays much the same role in the determination of an equilibrium as does land in longer run analysis, in that in the short run the amount of the fixed factor cannot be increased or decreased. Accordingly, the profit or loss will tend to be imputed to this fixed factor: the amount payable for its use will in the short run depend only on its marginal productivity at the moment, and will be independent of the cost of providing more of the fixed factor in the long run.

Because of the close analogy between the rent of land in the long run and the rent of fixed factors generally in the short run, this short-run return to fixed factors has been termed by Marshall "quasi-rent." If this quasi-rent is greater than the usual rate of return or interest on the cost of producing additional amounts of the fixed factor, due consideration being given to the rate at which it is likely to wear out or become obsolete, there will be an incentive for entrepreneurs to borrow, use the proceeds to produce more of the fixed factor and lease it to others, or use it themselves in a way that will yield to them a net return equal to this quasi-rent, and thus secure as a net profit the difference between this quasi-rent and the interest (and amortization) charges on the loan. On the other hand, if the amount of the fixed factor in existence is so great that the quasi-rent corresponding to its marginal productivity is less than such capital charges, then those who have produced quantities of the fixed factor in the past (i.e., constructed buildings, erected plants, etc.) will be unable to obtain a return for their use sufficient to cover the capital charges on their cost, and will thus suffer a net loss. Under these conditions, no more of the fixed factor will be produced until enough of the existing supply has worn out or been scrapped to bring the total supply down to where the quasi-rent will again cover the capital charges on the cost of producing more of it. When this has happened, production of the fixed factor of production will be resumed at a rate expected to be just sufficient to keep supply and demand for the products balanced at a price which will result in a quasi-rent just equal to the normal rate of return on the cost of production of the fixed factor. To the extent that further developments deviate from those anticipated by the producers of the fixed factors, quasi-rents will again deviate from the normal level. Further analysis of this situation, however, properly belongs with the analysis of risk and uncertainty.

Ratchet Effects

THERE IS LIKELY to be a certain asymmetry, however, between long-run adjustments in the upward as compared with the downward direction. New plant or other fixed factors can usually be produced in a fairly short period in almost any desired quantity, provided that the industry for which the plant is required is a small part of the total market for such construction. Thus adjustment in the upward direction may be fairly prompt; quite rapid expansion may occur even though quasi-rents may be only slightly above the normal return on costs. But if the fixed factor is fairly specialized and incapable of being used in other industries, adjustment in the downward direction may be considerably slower, for ordinarily if such a fixed asset is scrapped or otherwise taken out of service, the entrepreneur will as a rule be able thereby to save only a part of the fixed costs associated with it. It is only if the quasi-rent falls substantially short of the normal return that it will pay to scrap the fixed factor before it is worn out. For more moderate deficiencies in the quasi-rent, reduction in the amount of the fixed factor in use must await the general wearing out of units.

In effect, it is convenient to divide the cost of the fixed factor into "avoidable fixed costs" and "sunk costs," the former being the amount of the charges on the fixed factor that the entrepreneur can save or salvage by scrapping it, the remainder being charges that go on regardless of what is done to the fixed factor. The avoidable costs will consist of interest or normal profit on the salvage or scrap value of the fixed factor, plus whatever current expense for maintenance or overhead is associated with the use of the fixed factor.

This situation can be described somewhat roughly in terms of FIGURE 59, in which the curve ATC is the (short-run) average-total-cost curve of the typical firm for a level of fixed plant that gives the lowest minimum average cost; ACC is the average-"current"-cost curve, from which the sunk costs have been excluded, and AVC is the average-variable-cost curve, excluding both sunk and avoidable costs. MC is the marginal-cost curve corresponding to all three of these average-cost curves. The horizontal axis is alternatively scaled to represent both the output of the typical firm, and also the output of the entire industry, so as to permit the conversion of the appropriate parts of the cost curves into supply curves for the industry as well as for the firm. Various possible demand curves for the industry are indicated as $D_1 \ldots D_7$.

If the initial demand curve is D_6, there is long- and short-run equilibrium

[195

at *e*, with zero net profit. If the demand then declines to D_5, there will be a short-run equilibrium at *f* along the marginal-cost curve, with firms suffering losses, but with no firm finding it advantageous to shut down entirely or scrap existing plant. Only if demand were to drop below D_4 would there be any immediate scrapping of plant (or allowing plants to remain idle). For example, if demand drops to D_3, and all plants remain in operation, the price will initially tend to fall to the level of *h*, but at this price it will be more profitable for plants to shut down, and a sufficient number of them will be shut down

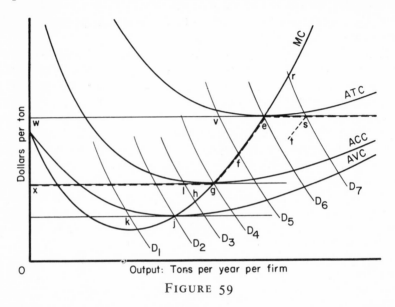

FIGURE 59

to curtail supply to *xl*, raising the price to *ox*, at which price it will just pay some of the plants to remain in operation at a level of output *xg*. However, if avoiding the avoidable costs involves taking some irreversible step such as scrapping a plant or allowing it to deteriorate seriously for lack of proper maintenance, and if there is some prospect that demand may recover so that the plant can be profitably used later on, then the plants can be kept in operation even if the price falls below *ox*, and operation can go to *h* rather than to *l*, all plants remaining in operation. Thus if the drop in demand is deemed temporary, the price can fall as low as *j* without the scrapping or shutting down of plants. If the demand falls below D_2, however, plants will be shut down even if it is still felt desirable to keep them in reserve and spend the required sums on their maintenance, and if the demand curve were D_1, for example, some plants would be shut down and others operated at the output indicated by *j*, with the price of the product just covering the variable costs associated with current production: the output for the industry as a whole would be indicated by k. Eventually, as plant wears out and is not replaced, and the industry emerges from its state of overexpansion, the cost structure will contract to the left, in terms of the industry, and the long-run equilibrium will be established at the intersection of the demand curve with the long-run minimum-total-cost level *wves* (assuming that the industry operates under conditions of long-run constant costs). This may occur either through firms leaving the industry (as would have to happen if the long-run average-cost curve for the typical firm had a well-defined minimum) or may occur through contraction in the size of individual firms if there is a substantial range over which the long-run average cost of the firm remains at the minimum level (see below, pp. 222–23).

If on the other hand demand should expand to D_7, the immediate result would be operation at the point r with a net profit realized. But if this demand is thought to be reasonably permanent, an immediate expansion of fixed plant will take place, either through entry of new firms or (where long-run average-cost curves are flat-bottomed) possibly through the expansion of existing firms, and equilibrium will be established at s after only a relatively short period of adjustment. If, however, contrary to expectations, after the equilibrium has been established at s the demand curve then again falls back toward D_6, the equilibrium would not immediately move back to e, but rather would move down along the new marginal-cost curve produced by the expansion of the fixed plant, toward t, for example, and would stay at t for a relatively long period of time, returning to e only after the additional plant or an equivalent amount has had time to wear out.

In effect, thus, the "medium-short-run" supply curve of the industry is *xlges*, with the location of the "step" *ge* shifting according to the amount of fixed plant currently installed. One can think of *ge* as being fairly readily shifted to the right, particularly in response to demand shifts that appear permanent, but capable of contracting back to the left only fairly slowly.

Even this, however, is a rather strenuous oversimplification, for it in effect assumes that complete units of fixed plant wear out all at once like the deacon's one-horse shay, and that there comes a time when one can make substantially a fresh start and decide upon the type of plant to be built without being affected by decisions made in the past. Actually, of course, plants wear out only piecemeal; one is likely never to have the opportunity, even in the very long run, of making a completely fresh start. Actual decisions to be made are more likely to consist of a series of decisions on the appropriate character of some relatively minor outlay that is needed to keep the old plant running. A plant may have been located at A rather than at B at some time in the distant past, and it may be apparent that were one building the plant afresh today, it would be better to build it at B rather than at A; it may even be apparent that in the light of present knowledge it would have been better to have built the plant at B in the first place. Nevertheless, even though each

[197

individual piece of the plant at A may be replaced several times over, there may never be a time when it would be profitable to transfer operations from the plant at A to a new plant at B, for at any particular time when such a move might be made, there might always be some parts of the plant at A with considerable remaining serviceability which would be sacrificed if the move were made. It may be, for example, quite obvious that in Australia it would have been better to have built the railroads to a uniform gauge, and that if built now from scratch they would be so built; changing the gauge now or at any time in the foreseeable future may well be so costly that the savings in operating costs and gains in convenience to the traveling public will never provide a profitable return on the necessary outlay, nor is it possible in this case to change the gauge piecemeal as individual sections of rail are renewed. Thus the "long run" is to some extent an unrealizable abstraction, no less than the "short run," and the Irishman's knife, which lasted 50 years though the blade was replaced twice and the handle three times, is perhaps a better symbol of economic realities than "The Deacon's Masterpiece," however useful the latter may be as a theoretical construct.

Another observation to be made concerning this analysis is that while losses may persist over fairly long periods of time while the excess of the fixed factor is being liquidated, profits substantially in excess of the normal rate will persist only for the relatively short periods of time required to construct additional plant. To the extent that entrepreneurs are aware of this tendency, therefore, one would expect to find in the normal rate of profit on investments in fixed assets a fairly substantial premium to compensate for this tendency for losses below the normal level of profit to continue for longer than the corresponding profits above this level. Moreover, one can expect the size of this premium to vary with the durability of the investment and with the degree to which it is specialized, i.e., with its "illiquidity," a concept to which we will return later.

Plant Flexibility

ANOTHER oversimplification in the above analysis lies in the fact that in specifying an optimum plant for a given output we have tacitly assumed that output would be constant, or at least that the plant could be designed as though price relationships would remain constant over time. Actually, this is hardly to be expected in most cases, and even within the framework of static theory, seasonal fluctuations in demand are quite admissible. While seasonal variation could be handled formally by considering the commodity in winter as a different product from the same commodity produced in summer, analysis in terms of fluctuation of demand and price for the same commodity is also of interest.

The flexibility consideration is usually introduced by an observation that if the average output that is expected is oA, it does not suffice to choose that design of plant which will produce the output oA at the minimum average cost, illustrated in FIGURE 60 as the curve AC_s, the average-cost curve of a highly specialized and mechanized plant, since, it is argued, under fluctuating demand conditions such a plant might never be operated at the average output oA, but always either at the peak period output oB or the slack period output oC. The flexible plant with the average-cost curve indicated by AC_f

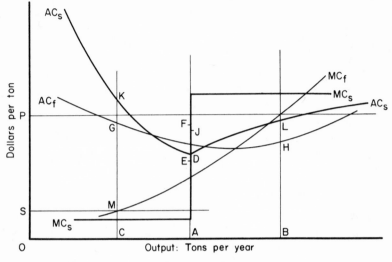

FIGURE 60

may well be preferable, having lower costs for the range of outputs contemplated as a whole, even though for any given output it would be possible to design a plant that would have a lower cost than is provided by the flexible plant.

This argument is somewhat faulty, however, as applied to conditions of perfect competition, since it implies that the manner in which the output of the two plants would fluctuate would be similar, whereas in general under competitive conditions they would differ considerably. The argument as given applies to conditions of imperfect competition where prices may be rigid and the demand to be supplied by the individual firm is determinate. Under competition, however, each firm can decide for itself how its output is to fluctuate over time in response to the given pattern of price fluctuations, and though the conclusion remains valid, it must be supported by a slightly different form of analysis.

Let us suppose, as an extreme example, that the specialized plant has costs characterized by a substantial fixed cost, plus a marginal cost that remains constant at a low level up to single-shift capacity operation, at which point

[199

the marginal cost jumps to a substantially higher level by reason of premium pay for overtime or second-shift operation, whereas the less mechanized type of plant has lower fixed cost even with its higher "capacity," and can expand output substantially without going to overtime or second-shift operation. If, under competitive conditions, the price during the peak season is oP, and during the slack season oS, the specialized plant may nevertheless keep its output constant at its minimum-cost point oA, so that the average cost is consistently AD. However, the average price received, over good periods and bad, may work out only to $AE = p \cdot OP + s \cdot OS$, where p and s are the fractions of the year constituting the peak and slack seasons, respectively, and thus this plant may lose money.

On the other hand, the flexible plant will, as indicated by its marginal-cost curve, produce an output oC during the slack season and oB during the peak season, thus selling relatively more of its product at the higher price, and getting a better average price for its product than did the specialized plant. If the average cost CG for the slack period and BH for the peak period works out at an over-all average of, say, oJ, the flexible plant may still obtain a net profit if the average price realized is, say, oF, while the specialized plant is losing money.

Thus the advantage of the flexible plant under strictly competitive conditions is not so much that it will have a lower over-all average cost, but that the average price obtained for its product will be higher, and may be sufficiently higher to overcome the disadvantage of the higher average cost.

One consequence of this is that considerable difficulty is created in defining what is meant by the capacity of a plant. If plants were designed with the expectation that they would be operated at a constant output, it would be simple to define capacity as the output indicated by the tangency between the long- and short-run average-cost curves, i.e., the output for which this plant gives the lowest possible cost, of any plant. But where there is no longer a definite and unique output for which the plant was solely designed, nor is there anything that will serve as a unique long-run cost curve for the plant curve to be tangent to, this criterion breaks down. Perhaps the best theoretical definition of capacity would be the minimum point on the short-run average-cost curve; unfortunately, this would imply that for most plants designed for a fluctuating demand output would be above capacity for a substantial part of the time; moreover, the empirical determination of such a point is by no means easy. But except in cases where we find the marginal-cost curve taking a very substantial jump at some point that corresponds roughly to the general notion of capacity, there seems to be no other unequivocal definition available. Consequently, in nearly all cases where plants are designed with a fairly substantial amount of flexibility, arguments based on any precise specification of capacity must be regarded with considerable caution.

Mathematical Appendix

IN ITS most general form a production function is simply a constraint on the possible combinations of inputs and outputs, which can be written

$$F(r_1, r_2, \ldots r_m, q_1, q_2, \ldots q_n) \leq 0, \quad \text{or} \quad F(\mathbf{r}, \mathbf{q}) \leq 0 \qquad 4.1$$

where the r_i are the quantities of factors of production or resources used, and the q_j are the amounts of the various products. Profits are

$$G = \sum_j p_j q_j - \sum_i v_i r_i \qquad 4.2$$

where the p_i are the product prices and the v_i are the factor costs; G is to be maximized subject to the condition 4.1, and also, presumably, to the condition that the r_i and the q_j shall be non-negative. Proceeding as in the appendix to Chapter 3, we put $Z = G + \lambda F$, and either

$$\left(\frac{\partial Z}{\partial r_i}\right) = -v_i + \lambda\left(\frac{\partial F}{\partial r_i}\right) = 0, \quad \text{and} \quad r_i \geq 0 \qquad 4.3$$

or

$$\left(\frac{\partial Z}{\partial r_i}\right) = -v_i + \lambda\left(\frac{\partial F}{\partial r_i}\right) \leq 0, \quad \text{and} \quad r_i = 0 \quad (i = 1, 2, \ldots m)$$

and either

$$\left(\frac{\partial Z}{\partial q_j}\right) = p_j + \lambda\left(\frac{\partial F}{\partial q_j}\right) = 0, \quad \text{and} \quad q_j \geq 0 \qquad 4.4$$

or

$$\left(\frac{\partial Z}{\partial q_j}\right) = p_j + \lambda\left(\frac{\partial F}{\partial q_j}\right) \leq 0, \quad \text{and} \quad q_j = 0 \quad (j = 1, 2, \ldots n)$$

as necessary conditions for maximum profit, given perfectly elastic demand and supply of factors and products. The expressions $-\lambda(\partial F/\partial q_j)$ and $\lambda(\partial F/\partial r_i)$ represent marginal cost and marginal productivity, respectively, the factor λ serving to give these expressions the dimension "numéraire per unit of product" or "of factor," respectively.

Suppose conditions 4.3 and 4.4 to be satisfied at some point $\mathbf{P}_e = (\mathbf{r}^*, \mathbf{q}^*)$. Suppose that in the neighborhood of $\mathbf{P}_e$, we have

$$F(\mathbf{r}^*, \mathbf{q}^*) = F(k\mathbf{r}^*, k\mathbf{q}^*) \qquad 4.5$$

where k is close to 1. Then

$$\left(\frac{dF}{dk}\right) = 0 = \sum_i r_i^*\left(\frac{\partial F}{\partial r_i}\right) + \sum_j q_j^*\left(\frac{\partial F}{\partial q_j}\right) \qquad 4.6$$

Combining this with 4.3, 4.4, and putting the results in 4.2, we find that if 4.5 is satisfied, $G^* = 0$. A production function such that 4.5 is satisfied everywhere is said to be "homogeneous" and to characterize constant returns to scale. A production function in which the condition 4.5 is satisfied only locally is said to have a point of homogeneity.

EXERCISES

I

NOTE: *The figures in this exercise are not to be considered as realistic. It is necessary to foreshorten the proportions if the various potential relationships are to be brought out clearly on one graph. The same relationships would hold, however, if the figures were stretched out to a more realistic pattern. The figures are also given far more accurately than it would ever be possible to determine them in practice, which is necessary if marginal products and costs are to be computed with consistency from the data for increments small enough to approach the conceptual marginal increment.*

SUPPOSE that the following table shows the relationship between the input of labor applied to a 440-acre tract of a given type of land during each year and the annual yield of produce obtained:

Labor input: man-days per year	Yield: bushels per year	Labor input: man-days per year	Yield: bushels per year	Labor input: man-days per year	Yield: bushels per year
0	0.00	400 A	8,056.03	999	9,999.9988
1 A	5.09	499	8,992.98	1,000 A	10,000.00
50 A	474.93	500 A	9,000.00	1,001	9,999.9988
51	489.04	501	9,006.98	1,100 A	9,990.23
100 A	1,382.98	600 A	9,520.95	1,200 A	9,967.11
101	1,404.94	601	9,524.68	1,300	9,936.89
200 A	3,962.26	700 A	9,793.58	1,500	9,868.42
201	3,989.31	701	9,795.47	2,000	9,708.88
280 A	5,967.64	800 A	9,928.06	3,000	9,483.87
290 A	6,186.55	801	9,928.94	5,000	9,267.73
300 A	6,397.06	900 A	9,985.59	10,000	9,085.78
301	6,417.64	901	9,985.91	20,000	8,989.08

(The algebraic relation is

$$z = \frac{160x^2 + 10x}{18x^2 - 3x + 2}$$

where x is input in thousands of man-days and z is output in thousands of bushels.)

PART I. *PRODUCTIVITY*

1. Draw a curve *a* showing the total output resulting from various inputs. (On an 8 1/2 × 11″ sheet of graph paper with the long way vertical: the horizontal scale can be 1″ = 200 man-days, the vertical scale 1″ = 2,000 bushels. Ignore for the time being the data for inputs of over 1,200 man-days.)

2. Draw a curve *b* showing the average product per man-day at various inputs. (Use a separate sheet of paper, and the same horizontal scale. The vertical scale can be 2" = five bushels per man-day. It will be sufficient to plot the points designated "*A*.") Determine the point at which the average product is a maximum.

3. Draw a curve *c* (on the same graph as *b*) showing the marginal product per man-day at various inputs. Compute marginal products based on increments of input of one man-day, and also based on increments of 100 man-days, and show that when appropriately plotted both sets of points fall along a common curve.

Increasing returns prevail between inputs of _____ and _____ man-days; diminishing returns prevail between inputs of _____ and _____ man-days; negative returns prevail between inputs of _____ and _____ man-days.

4. If the produce can be sold in unlimited quantities at $2 a bushel, construct curves showing the value of the total product *d*, average product *e*, and marginal product *f* at various inputs. (Previous curves may be used by inserting substitute scales.)

If labor costs $14 per man-day regardless of the amount employed, how much labor will the landlord employ? What will be the total wage bill, the average product, the total product, the gross proceeds from the sale of the product, and the return obtained by the landlord?

Fill in the following table [approximate figures, read from the graphs, should be sufficient for columns (ii) and (iv)].

Cost of labor per man-day	Labor used man-days	Wage bill	Average product bushels per man-day	Total product bushels	Gross receipts	Return to landlord
(i)	(ii)	(iii)	(iv)	(v)	(vi)	(vii)
0						
2						
5						
10						
14						
20						
30						
40						
50						

Indicate the demand curve for labor *g*.

5. For a labor cost of $5 per man-day, indicate in two ways in relation to curve *d* the division of the gross receipts between wages

WW and return to the landlord *RR*. Indicate the area representing total wages in relation to curve *f*.

Indicate three alternative areas representing the return to the landlord: (i) in relation to the marginal- and average-productivity curves; (ii) in relation to the marginal-productivity curve alone; (iii) in relation to the demand curve for labor.

PART 2. *COST*

6. Draw a curve *h* showing the total amount of labor required to produce various outputs of produce (ignore inputs above 1,000 man-days). (Use the same scales as for curve *a*, but with the axes interchanged, placing the zero of the vertical scale four inches above the bottom of the graph. The curve can be traced, if desired, from curve *a*.)

7. Draw a curve *j* showing the average cost in man-days per bushel corresponding to the various outputs. (A vertical scale of $2'' = 0.1$ man-days per bushel may be used. Place the longer dimension of the paper vertically.)

8. Draw a curve *k* showing the marginal labor cost in man-days per bushel at various outputs. (Marginal cost is obtained by dividing small changes in input by the corresponding small changes in output, plotting the points so obtained near the center of the interval of output.)

Decreasing labor costs prevail for outputs between _____ and _____ bushels. Increasing labor costs prevail for outputs between _____ and _____ bushels.

9. If labor can be hired in any quantity for $14 per man-day, draw curves showing the total variable cost *l*, average variable cost *m*, and marginal cost *n* at various outputs, treating the cost of land, if any, as a fixed cost. (Previous curves may be used by inserting new scales.)

10. If it is known that the produce can be sold in any quantity at $2 per bushel (wages still at $14), how much will be produced? What will be the labor required, the gross proceeds, the total variable cost, the net return to the landlord? Fill in the following table:

Price of produce, per bushel:	Output: bushels per year	Input: man-days per year	Gross receipts	Total variable cost	Return to the landlord
$ .60					
.70					
1.00					
1.50					
2.00					
3.00					
5.00					

Draw the supply curve for produce from this farm, *p*.

11. For a price of $3 per bushel, indicate in relation to curve *h* the wages and net return to the landlord. (Hint: Draw the tangent and extend it to meet the vertical axis.)

12. At $3 per bushel, indicate the area representing total receipts in relation to curve *n*, and show how this area can be divided into wage costs and net return to the landlord in three ways: (i) in relation to the average-cost curve *m*; (ii) in relation to the marginal-cost curve *n*; and (iii) in relation to the supply curve *p*.

PART 3. *CONSTANT RETURNS TO SCALE*

13. A farmer has available 500 man-days of labor during the year. If outputs resulting from various amounts of labor and 440 acres of land are as in Part 1, and there are constant returns to scale, construct a similar table showing the outputs resulting from using this 500 man-days of labor on various amounts of land. (Hint: If 400 man-days on 440 acres produce X, then 500 man-days on 550 acres will produce $1.25X$; if 300 man-days on 440 acres produce Y, then 500 man-days on 733.3 acres will produce $5Y/3$, etc.) It should be sufficient to operate only with the points on the original schedule for even hundreds of man-days; a slide rule should be sufficiently accurate for most purposes, although if marginal cost or product is to be computed from small intervals, a calculator will probably be necessary in order to get consistent results.

14. If produce sells for $2 a bushel, draw a curve *q* showing the value of the total product produced with various acreages and 500 man-days.

15. At $2 per bushel, draw curves showing the value of the average product *r* and the value of the marginal product *s* per acre of land at various acreages.

16. If additional land can be rented for $25 per acre, how much land will be used? What will be the total product? Total rent? Returns on the labor of the farmer? How does this compare with the results in numbers 4 and 10? Indicate the rent and the return to labor in relation to the average and marginal product curves.

17. If land can be rented at $25 per acre, draw curves showing for various outputs, the total land cost *t*, average land cost *u*, and the marginal land cost *v*. If produce sells at $3 per bushel, what will be the amount of land used? Output? Rent? Net return for labor?

18. Fill in the table (top of page 206).

19. Draw the farmer's demand curve for land *w* when the price of produce is expected to remain fixed at $2 per bushel. Show the division of the total product between rent and return to labor in relation to this curve. What becomes of the curve if the farmer is unwilling to farm for less than $3 per man-day (i.e., at this level he would seek industrial employment)?

20. Draw the farmer's supply curve for produce *x* when the rental of land remains fixed at $25 per acre. Show the division of the gross

Land rental per acre	Price of produce per bushel	Acreage used	Bushels of produce	Value of produce	Rent paid	Return to labor
$50	$2	————	————	————	————	————
40	2	————	————	————	————	————
25	2	————	————	————	————	————
10	2	————	————	————	————	————
0	2	————	————	————	————	————
25	1	————	————	————	————	————
25	1.50	————	————	————	————	————
25	2	————	————	————	————	————
25	3	————	————	————	————	————
25	5	————	————	————	————	————
25	10	————	————	————	————	————

proceeds between rent of land and return to labor in relation to this curve.

PART 4. *SUBSTITUTION OF FACTORS*

21. Draw a curve showing, for various acreages of land, the total amount of labor required to produce 5,000 bushels of produce. (Hint: If 500 man-days on 440 acres produce 9,000 bushels, 5,000 bushels can be produced with five-ninths of each of these inputs, i.e., 277.7 man-days and 244.4 acres, etc. Suggested scale: 1″ = 100 man-days, 1″ = 100 acres.)

On this diagram, draw lines marking off the region of diminishing returns to both factors from the regions of increasing returns to labor and increasing returns to land, respectively.

22. If land rents for $2 an acre and labor costs $5 per man-day, in what proportion will land and labor be employed? What will be the price of produce? Fill in the following table:

Rent of land per acre	Wage rate per man-day	Man-days used per acre	Price of produce
$ 2	$ 5	————	————
25	14	————	————
25	0	————	————
0	14	————	————

II

THERE are ten plants of Type A and ten plants of Type B characterized by the following costs:

	TOTAL VARIABLE COSTS	
OUTPUT (tons)	Type A plants	Type B plants
	(dollars per month)	
0	0	0
1	10.1	15.1
19	226.1	321.1
20	240.0	340.0
21	254.1	359.1
49	730.1	975.1
50	750.0	1,000.0
51	770.1	1,025.1

The aggregate demand for the product of this industry is as follows:

PRICE (dollars per ton)	QUANTITY DEMANDED (tons per month)
18	1,150
20	750
22	350

a. Assuming that the demand curve and the supply curves for each plant are all linear, what, under competitive conditions, in the short run, is the equilibrium price, and what are the equilibrium outputs and gross profit of each plant? (Hint: Draw the supply curves for each plant, then the industry supply curve. Use producer's surplus.)

b. A licence fee of $100 per month is imposed on each plant operated. What are then the short-run results?

c. New plants of type A can be constructed and financed for a monthly charge of $60 in addition to the license fee of $100. What are the long-run results?

III

IN THE isolated village of Wheaton, there are 100 farms that are worthless except for the production of wheat. Communication between farms is so difficult that it is impractical to use any part-time or part-year work on any farm: farms can be worked only with a whole number of man-years, with the results shown in columns A and B (table, top of page 208).

The cost of transporting the wheat to the market is the same for all farms, and the uniform annual wage is fixed at $4,032.

a. If the aggregate demand for wheat is 17,352 tons (considered to be, if you wish, completely inelastic), what will be the price of wheat and the rent of the farms?

b. What will be the price and the rent if demand increases to 17,432 tons?

c. What will be the results if demand shrinks to 8,400 tons?

[207

A	B	C	D	E	F
Man-years used	Tons of wheat produced	$\dfrac{B}{A}$	$\dfrac{\$4{,}032}{C}$	ΔB	$\dfrac{\$4{,}032}{E}$
0	0	—	—		
				– – – 62	65.03
1	62	62	65.03		
				– – – 64	63
2	126	63	64		
				– – – 48	84
3	174	58	69.52		
				– – – 32	126
4	206	51.5	78.3		
				– – – 16	256
5	222	44.4	90.8		

IV

COMMUNICATIONS in Wheaton are so improved that there is no difficulty in using labor on a part-time basis for any fraction of a year desired. More detail in the production function thus becomes relevant as follows:

A	B	C	D	E	F
Man-years used	Tons of wheat produced	$\dfrac{B}{A}$	$\dfrac{\$4{,}032}{C}$	ΔB	$\dfrac{\$2{,}016}{E}$
0	0	—	—		
				– – – 24	84
0.5	24	48	84		
				– – – 38	53.05
1.0	62	62	65.03		
				– – – 34	59.3
1.5	96	64	63		
				– – – 30	67.2
2.0	126	63	64		
				– – – 26	76.98
2.5	152	60.8	66.31		
				– – – 22	91.7
3.0	174	58	69.52		
				– – – 18	112
3.5	192	54.57	73.5		
				– – – 14	144
4.0	206	51.5	78.3		
				– – – 10	201.6
4.5	216	48	84		
				– – – 6	336
5.0	222	44.4	90.8		

What are now the prices and rents when total demand is 17,352, 17,432, and 7,800 tons, respectively?

Explain the difference between the results of III and IV.

CHAPTER FIVE

The General Competitive Equilibrium

The General Optimum Properties of Competitive Production

HAVING examined the detailed operation of the competitive system, we come to the question of appraising the over-all performance of the system. In general, it is possible to show that if all of the various explicit and implicit assumptions that have been made in constructing the model are fulfilled, a competitive economic system produces a result that is an optimum in the sense that it will not be possible to modify the result in any way so as to make some people better off without at the same time making others worse off. This criterion is known as Pareto optimality. It will still be possible to benefit some people at the expense of others, of course, but whether any such shift would be desirable on balance will involve interpersonal comparisons, and a judgment expressed in such a matter will be at a lower level of objectivity than a judgment expressed as to the desirability of a change that would make one person better off without making another person worse off.

To develop this property of the competitive economy, we can trace the process of production and distribution through the successive stages from the supply of factors to the consumption of the products. To begin with, if each supplier of each factor of production, such as labor, behaves competitively— i.e., as he would behave if he were to consult only his own self-interest but could exert no influence on market prices—he will adjust the amount of the factor he supplies so that the marginal utility to him of this factor (i.e., the marginal disutility of labor) is equal to the marginal utility to him of the price received (i.e., the marginal utility of money to him multiplied by the wage rate). If we use the term "marginal social cost" to mean the amount of money required to compensate individuals who are adversely affected by a given step, and if we assume that the only one adversely affected by increasing the aggregate input of a given factor is the supplier of the factor himself, then if the supplier behaves competitively, the market price of the factor will reflect the marginal social cost of the factor.

Similarly, if a firm behaves competitively in purchasing the factor, it will consider that the marginal cost of the factor to it will be equal to its market price and hence to the marginal social cost. It will push its purchase of the factor to the point where the marginal cost to it of the factor is equal to the factor's marginal physical product multiplied by the marginal revenue produced by the sale of an additional unit of product. But if the firm is also selling competitively, the marginal revenue produced by the sale of an additional unit of product is precisely the price of the product, so that the price will be equated to the marginal social cost of the product.

Finally, if the consumer acts competitively in buying, he will consider the price of the commodity to be fixed, and will buy it up to the point where its marginal utility to him is equal to its price multiplied by the marginal utility of money to him. If we use the term "marginal social benefit" to mean the amount of money that would have to be given to people who would be benefited by a given step to compensate them for failure to take the step, then the marginal social benefit derivable from the consumption by a given individual of an additional small unit of a commodity will be equal to its market price. Thus under competition the market price of every commodity becomes equal to its marginal social cost and at the same time equal to the marginal social benefit derived from its consumption.

The introduction of more steps in the productive process extends the number of equations that must be satisfied and lengthens the chain of reasoning, but the final conclusion is the same. Or if we deal with a factor of production having a fixed total supply, such as land, so that the marginal social cost cannot be expressed in terms of the sacrifice of the supplier, we nevertheless can derive a marginal social cost reckoned as an opportunity cost in terms of the marginal social benefits that must be foregone in other directions as a result of the use of the factor in a particular direction; we then have two parallel chains of equations instead of one, and the relationship between market price and marginal social cost and marginal social benefit still holds.

Now if any attempt is made to move from such an equilibrium position, this relation between marginal social cost and marginal social benefit will change adversely if it changes at all. For example, if we consider a change involving the production of an additional amount of some particular commodity and the consumption of a corresponding additional amount of this commodity by some given individual, the marginal social benefit derived from this additional amount will tend to become less than the equilibrium market price, by reason of the law of increasing marginal rate of substitution between the commodity in question and the numéraire (or between the given commodity and other commodities in general), which must apply, otherwise the individual would not have been in stable competitive equilibrium with the market. At the same time, the marginal cost of the product must rise, both because of the law of diminishing returns, which must apply if the firms in the industry are in competitive equilibrium, and because of the law of increasing marginal rate of substitution on the part of the supplier of the factor, which also must apply if the supplier is in competitive equilibrium. Or if a factor such as land is involved, having a fixed total supply, the marginal social cost of its withdrawal from other uses must rise, for similar reasons. Thus the amount of money, i.e., of other goods in general, that the consumer would be willing to give up in return for additional units of the product in question, would not be sufficient to compensate the suppliers of the factors needed for its production, or to compensate other consumers for the loss of the products produced by the required factors that were withdrawn from other uses. This consumer therefore cannot be made better off in this way without making others worse off.

A similar line of argument can be produced for changes consisting of the production and consumption of less of some commodity, or for the redistribution of a given aggregate of outputs among consumers, or for changes involving the production of more of some commodities and less of others. In general, it will not be possible to rearrange matters in any of these ways or in combinations of them so that someone is better off and no one is worse off. At best, in exceptional cases where there exist the appropriate ranges of constant returns to scale and constant marginal rates of substitution, it may be possible to find a rearrangement that leaves everyone just as well off. And of course since the equilibrium point, in the case where all the appropriate relationships are smooth, is somewhat analogous to the summit of a round-topped hill, it may be necessary to depart from the equilibrium point by a fairly wide margin before the impairment becomes substantial.

The above line of reasoning, to be sure, is somewhat oversimplified in that it tacitly assumes that all indifference curves and production contours are smooth at the point of equilibrium, that positive amounts of every factor are used by every firm, and that positive amounts of every product are consumed by each consumer. However, the reasoning can readily be repeated, somewhat more cumbersomely, to cover cases where indifference curves or production contours have corners and where some factors are unused by particular firms and some products are unused by particular consumers. For this more general case, the equilibrium conditions are such that in the factor markets the marginal social cost of the last unit supplied by each supplier does not exceed the market price, and the market price in turn does not exceed the marginal social cost of the next unit that might be supplied by any supplier; in turn, the marginal-revenue product of the next unit that might be used in a production process does not exceed the market price of the factor, and the market price in turn does not exceed the marginal-revenue product of the last unit of the factor used. Where the factor is not supplied by a given individual, the limit expressed in terms of the last unit supplied is of course vacuous, as it is where the factor is not used by a firm. Similar inequalities may replace the equalities in the consumption-good markets. It can easily be seen that

[211

even with these more general relationships, it still remains true that it is impossible to move away from an equilibrium position so as to benefit someone without hurting someone else, and indeed if the movement is in a direction in which the equilibrium point is a corner, the impairment tends to become substantial at much smaller deviations from the equilibrium point than is the case where the equilibrium is at a smooth point.

Of course, there is more than just one allocation of resources that has this Pareto optimum property; indeed, a different original distribution of resources will in general lead, upon the establishment of a regime of perfect competition, to different final equilibrium positions, each of which will have the Pareto property. Each such equilibrium position will in general correspond to a different distribution of real income, thought of in terms of specifying the indifference surfaces attained by each individual. Where several competitive equilibria starting from the same initial distribution of resources are possible, each of them will be a Pareto optimum, but in general they will correspond to different distributions of real income reflected in different price structures. In general, the set of all Pareto optimum allocations for a given population, given tastes, and given aggregate endowment of resources will have $n - 1$ degrees of freedom, n being the number of persons in the population. The situation is an extension of what was said on page 101 concerning results on and off the contract curve.

The Assumptions of the Theorem That Competition Is Optimal

THE ABOVE theorem to the effect that perfect competition produces results that are optimal in the Pareto sense and propositions of a generally similar nature are often used as a justification of the "free-enterprise" system, or of some one of the variants of a laisser faire policy. Before transferring such results from an abstract model to recommendations for practical policy, however, it is essential to examine the various assumptions, both explicit and implicit, in the above model, many of which are far from being satisfied in real economic systems, either actual or proposed.

The first and most explicit of these assumptions is that competitive behavior, i.e., behaving in such a way as to maximize profit or satisfaction without regarding the effect that these actions may have upon prices, prevails generally. It should be noted that competitive behavior, so defined (and it is this definition and not some other definition that is relevant to the theorem), is a matter of mental attitude, and does not necessarily depend on mere numbers. Competition is often defined in terms of the number of buyers and sellers, with the implication that where there are many buyers and sellers the market is necessarily competitive, and that where there are either few buyers or few sellers the market is necessarily less competitive or monopoloid. But while there is a general tendency in this direction, it is possible to have large numbers of buyers or sellers acting more or less independently without producing the competitive result. For example, if each buyer or seller behaves according to some "just-price" notion, or if each reflects in certain ways about the probable influence of his actions on those of others and upon the market price, it is possible for the resulting price to be very far from the competitive price necessary to validate the theorem, and even if the price happened to be the same as that resulting from competition, the amounts traded might differ. On the other hand, even if there are only a few buyers or sellers in the market, or even possibly only a single buyer or seller, if each should choose for whatever reason to act as though the market price were unaffected by his actions (either because he does not know that he is the only buyer or seller, or because he regards himself as a trustee with a duty to approach the competitive norm as closely as possible, or because he believes his one or two competitors to have an extremely elastic supply schedule), then the required condition is satisfied.

It is worth emphasizing again that this definition of competition does not permit any competitor to have a price policy, for if as part of his operations he actively sets a price on his product or announces a price at which he will purchase a commodity he can hardly suppose that the price is established by forces beyond his control. Perfect competition is sometimes defined as a situation where the demand curve facing any one seller is perfectly elastic, so that all of the demand will be supplied by the seller or sellers with the lowest price, sellers with prices infinitesimally higher getting no business. But even this will not do as a description of a determinate situation, for on this basis there is no way of telling how the total sales are divided among those sellers who have the identical lowest price. This division of sales will be determined only if we use some wholly arbitrary rule, or else allow sellers to have an output policy in addition to the price policy. If they have an output policy, then it is simpler for analytical purposes to concentrate on this output policy and think of the price as being determined entirely through some mechanism of the market, which is thought of as being entirely impersonal and automatic, and not by buyers and sellers individually. Indeed, in the perfectly competitive market no seller could set a price higher than his competitors without losing all his sales, nor lower without being swamped with more business than he could handle. His freedom to determine price would be completely circumscribed. Accordingly, we will consider competitive behavior as behavior that accepts market prices as externally determined, and decides upon the amount to be bought or sold accordingly. Any active setting of prices by a buyer or seller then becomes *ipso facto* an indication of a greater or lesser degree of imperfect competition.

Of course, administered prices are the rule rather than the exception in modern economic societies, and, accordingly, the type of perfect competition that has here been specified occurs at most in a minority of cases. This does not necessarily mean that the analysis is completely inapplicable, however, since in many cases it can be taken as a rough first approximation of what actually happens where competition is of the less perfect variety associated with administered prices. But it does mean that in applying the analysis to such cases one should take care to bring into account the differences between perfect competition and competition with administered prices.

A second assumption connected with the competitive market is that the prices are adjusted so as to clear the market, i.e., that the price is adjusted so that aggregate demand and aggregate supply are equal and there is no unsatisfied demand or unused supply. If demand exceeds supply, the market price must increase until demand is choked off and supply stimulated to the point where they are equalized; on the other hand, if supply exceeds demand the price must fall, and if reducing the price cannot equate demand and supply, the price must still drop to zero and the resource must be treated as a free good. In some cases, reducing the price of certain factors of production, particularly labor, may produce a drastic disparity in incomes, but the "optimum" of the theorem takes no account of the distribution of income, and an allocation of resources would be considered to satisfy this optimum property even though half of the population were starving while the other half were enjoying great luxury, inasmuch as remedying this situation would involve benefiting one group at the expense of another, at least in the short run.

The competitive solution also requires for its realization that each firm operate under conditions of increasing costs and diminishing returns, or at the very least that no industry within the competitive system be characterized by decreasing costs due to internal technological economies of scale. Under perfectly competitive conditions decreasing-returns conditions are necessary to put a limit to the size of firms, otherwise there is nothing to keep firms from growing too large relative to the industry for there to be a sufficient number of them in a given market to produce an effective competitive system. In a pinch, constant returns to scale can be accommodated within a completely competitive system if there is some institutional or other limitation on the growth of firms, such as the threat of antitrust action, public opinion, or the like. Or even if firms grow to a size where they do exercise an appreciable influence on the prices in the markets in which they deal, competitive results may be obtainable if the management of such firms, whether through public-spiritedness or because acting under direct governmental supervision or control, or for other reasons, fail to take advantage of its ability to influence prices.

Perfect competition and diminishing costs or increasing returns are mutually incompatible, however, at least in the usual sense of the term. For if average cost is declining, marginal cost is less than average cost. If an entrepreneur under these circumstances were to persist in acting as though the price of the product is fixed, then either the price is above marginal cost, in which case the "competitive" entrepreneur would imagine he could increase his profits (or diminish his losses) by expanding output still further, or if price is not above marginal cost it will be below average cost, and the entrepreneur will be losing money. No equilibrium of the normal type is possible, and the entrepreneur who persists in ignoring the influence of his own actions upon the price will go bankrupt. As we shall see, if in an economy containing such increasing-returns industries an allocation of resources is to be obtained that satisfies the Pareto condition, some form of organization other than self-sustaining profit-motivated private enterprise is needed. In such cases, optimum allocation requires operation at an output such that the resulting market price will be equal to marginal cost, which in turn will result in a deficit to the operating agency that will have to be made up from outside sources.

The third main assumption of the optimum-allocation theorem is that each economic unit affects other units only through its buying and selling on the markets for the various factors, goods, and services. "Neighborhood effects" that are felt directly rather than through the market are assumed to be entirely absent. In effect, each economic unit is regarded as an isolated entity in an impermeable cell, which has contact with other units only through the market.

Actually, of course, economic units affect the welfare of other units directly in many ways other than through their interactions in buying and selling commodities on the market. Many terms have been applied to these neighborhood effects, and not without a considerable degree of confusion and overlapping. The term "neighborhood effect" is itself not above criticism as implying an element of nearness that is not essential to the phenomena being considered, but it is perhaps less likely than most others to be applied indiscriminately to essentially different things. The neighborhood effects may be divided into unpaid costs imposed upon others and unappropriated benefits conferred upon others, in either case usually without the specific consent or expressed desire of the affected parties, and ordinarily without any specific quid pro quo. A procedure or technique developed by one firm and heard about and practiced by another would be an example of an unappropriated benefit where no nearness other than the ability to communicate is implied. Nearness seems to be more essential to the existence of unpaid costs; an example not involving nearness is the fact that the staking of claims by prospectors to minerals in the public domain diminishes thereby the opportunities available to all others, but even here there is in a sense "potential nearness" in that others are not injured unless they might have explored the same area if the claim had not been staked.

Another set of terms often employed to cover the same set of phenomena is "external economies" or "diseconomies," sometimes further qualified as being "of consumption" or "of production." Thus the fact that an increase by one family in the amount of medical attention procured may improve the health expectations of the neighbors would be an example of an "external economy of consumption"; the fact that driving on a congested highway increases the congestion experienced by others may be termed an "external diseconomy of consumption" in the case of the pleasure trip, but an "external diseconomy of production" where the congestion is caused by trucks. In the classical example of external economies of scale in production, the pumping out of one mine lowers the water level in nearby mines and lowers their costs of pumping in turn; a corresponding external diseconomy in production may be illustrated by the competitive drilling and pumping in an oil pool, and indeed in the reduction to private possession of fugacious or unclaimed resources generally: productive activity on the part of one producer makes production more difficult for others. Prospecting, however, is a somewhat ambivalent case: on the one hand, the claim staked out by the successful prospector diminishes by that much the mineral wealth to which the rest of the population may some day lay claim; on the other hand, knowledge of the results of the prospecting gives others that much more information as to where and where not to look.

However, the terms "external economies" and external diseconomies" are often applied to effects that are felt entirely through the market, and it is on the whole more important to distinguish these cases than it is to draw a some-times difficult line between economies of consumption and economies of production. Thus where an industry uses a large part of the total supply of a given factor, the fact that expansion of that industry will raise the price of that factor is sometimes spoken of as an external diseconomy. This kind of "external diseconomy," however, in no way invalidates the competitive theorem, and indeed if there are a large number of firms in such an industry one would expect the Pareto optimum allocation conditions to be fulfilled.

On the other hand, external economies of scale arising entirely through the market do not fit quite so well into a competitive framework. About the only important case where such economies arise and expansion of an industry lowers the price of a factor is where the factor is supplied by an industry characterized by internal economies of scale. Expansion of an industry in a given locality may, for example, so increase traffic on a railroad serving the community that each individual firm is able to secure lower freight rates, because of the decreasing-cost character of the railroad operation. In this case, while the railroad cannot be operated as a multi-firm competitive industry, there is no incompatibility between the attainment of a Pareto optimum and a competitive regime in the industry enjoying the external economies. The problem of securing an optimum allocation of resources lies wholly in dealing with the internal economies of scale of the railroad, and if this is dealt with adequately, the market mechanism itself can be relied upon to produce the proper effect on the shipper industry.

A fourth assumption necessary to the validity of the theorem is that consumers are to be considered the court of final recourse as to the relative satisfactions that they derive from different situations, and that they are capable of predicting accurately the satisfaction which they will derive from the consumption of various contemplated combinations of goods. The acceptance of "consumer sovereignty" as a basis for judging economic systems is fundamentally perhaps as much a matter of ethics, philosophy, and political theory as it is of economics. In discussions of economic theory proper, it is often taken as a postulate for which the primary justification lies outside the realm of economics. In any case, it is a basic value judgment for or against which it would be difficult to adduce objective evidence.

But even though consumer sovereignty be accepted as a basic principle, whether on ethical, philosophical, or other grounds, the assumption that consumers can predict accurately the satisfaction they will derive from various patterns of consumption is open to question on much more objective grounds. Of course, the knowledge of the satisfaction derived from the current consumption pattern would be a good guide to the satisfaction to be experienced tomorrow if, on the basis of static assumptions, it is assumed that the same pattern of consumption is to be followed today that was followed yesterday. However, this carries the static assumption somewhat further than necessary from the point of view of an over-all static state: the general pattern can well be "static" without necessarily implying a static consumption pattern on the part of each individual. Indeed, a necessary part of individual growth and aging would be some degree of change in consumption patterns, with, accordingly, considerable occasion for the prediction of future satisfactions rather than the mere projection of past experience. But more than even this is actually necessary for the validity of the theorem: it is necessary to suppose that each consumer can accurately estimate the satisfaction derivable from various alternative hypothetical patterns of consumption that can be obtained at given prices for a given total outlay, otherwise the consumer might rest content with his current pattern or with a particular choice of future patterns, the results of which he might appraise correctly, in ignorance of the fact that some other available pattern would produce a preferable result.

This assumption of adequate consumer information is in practice contradicted by the actual market behavior of consumers. Certainly much selling expense and most types of advertising are motivated by the assumption that consumers are to some degree at least uncertain concerning the satisfaction that will result from alternative patterns of expenditure. Moreover, consumers often behave in a manner suggesting that their preference scales change through time not only by reason of changing age and other external parameters, but through change in underlying states of information and attitudes. In such cases, there is a problem of deciding whether to compare the desirability of two situations on the basis of the earlier or the later tastes: one

[217

cannot always assume that the later set of tastes is necessarily based on more accurate or complete information. Where such changes in tastes are deemed to have taken place, there is no method of determining by a priori economic analysis which of the two scales of preference is to be taken as the final criterion, or whether indeed some unspecified amalgamation of the two (or more) scales is not needed. Whatever decision is reached on this point will ordinarily be reached on grounds outside the confines of economic analysis.

But even if failure to fulfill this assumption would mean that the result reached might not be so good as some other hypothetical result reached if individuals were wiser in their choice of outlays, the failure may still be compatible with the proposition that the result is better than any other method of distributing consumer expenditures. If we may admit that the consumer is at times mistaken, it may be possible to assert (though probably not to prove in any rigorous sense) that the consumer, after securing whatever expert advice he may feel the need of, can still come closer to the optimum distribution of his resources than any outside person could do acting arbitrarily on his behalf.

But even if some expert could be found who could prescribe a complete consumption pattern for an individual that would in some sense be reliably better than the one the individual would select for himself, many of us would still not be persuaded to give up consumer sovereignty as an operating principle. In the cultural tradition of individualism, there is a value attached to freedom of choice over and above any superiority of results that may be assumed to flow from the exercise of that choice. An individual will in general consider himself better off, and he will be considered to be better off by others, if he is observed to have a certain consumption pattern freely selected by himself from among a number of available alternatives, than if he is observed to have an exactly similar consumption pattern that has been imposed on him through outside forces. Indeed, in some cases this freedom of choice appears to be the dominant element in the satisfaction derived by the consumer.

On the other hand, one of the most important services that the consumer buys is advice about what to consume. Much, if not most, of the service rendered by doctors is of this nature, and there are many other professions devoted to the giving of advice. The consumer must choose in this case how much of what kind of advice to purchase. One can even get advice about the getting of advice, and so on ad infinitum, but a regression of this sort probably leads nowhere. In any case, however, the fact that advice of this kind is sought and paid for is in itself an instance in which it would be logically impossible for consumers to have complete knowledge of the satisfaction to be derived from that which they purchase.

However, while in some circumstances the process of choice may in itself be a substantial source of satisfaction, as for the person to whom "shopping" becomes a pleasurable exercise, in other circumstances choice may be a chore.

Nearly all consumers will in some cases take the first thing at hand rather than spend the time and effort necessary to assure themselves of getting the best value for their money. Thus sooner or later the fact must be faced that consumer choice (and indeed all making of decisions) entails a larger or smaller aleatory element. While specific consideration of such uncertainty must be reserved for later discussion, its existence should not be lost sight of entirely, even in a discussion of a strictly static economy. Too often the "economic man" has been conceived of as an individual with an "irrational passion for dispassionate rationality."

Correlative with the assumption of knowledge on the part of the consumer as to consequences of various consumption patterns is the assumption that the entrepreneur has complete knowledge of the production function of the process in which his firm is engaged, or at least of those regions of the production function that are at all likely to merit economic consideration; he of course must also know the market prices of all the factors and products involved. It is further necessary to assume that adequate consideration is given to the possibility of making use of all possible productive processes, i.e., that for every productive process that comes within striking distance of being economical there shall be at least one entrepreneur who knows the likely regions of the corresponding production function. For each process actually in use there must of course be a sufficient number of entrepreneurs who know its production function to permit the competitive conditions to be realized.

Again, the amount of information that is, in principle, required for the strict application of the theorem is substantially greater and more varied, detailed, and exact than we are likely to find in practice. Nevertheless, it is precisely at this point that a competitive economic system puts in its claim to being not merely as good as any other, but actually superior to most others in the degree to which the ideal adjustment will be approached in practice. For indeed an omniscient central economic planning board, given a knowledge of all of the information available to each consumer and entrepreneur, could, in principle at least, produce a plan that would achieve the Pareto optimum property, and presumably could do this on the basis of any desired pattern of distribution of incomes. But information on this scale cannot be squeezed inside the skull of any single mortal, nor within the skulls of any committee of manageable size, and could this be done the sheer cost of transmitting the information to the central agency and distributing its directives would be prohibitive. A competitive economic system decentralizes the making of decisions and permits the decisions that affect only a specific area directly to be made by those who are particularly familiar with that area, integrating those independently made decisions into a harmonious whole through the mechanism of the market. Only in a competitive economic system, it is argued, can this decentralization be carried through to the optimum extent,

[219

and while of course the results will not be perfect, it can be claimed that they will be more nearly so than they would be where the nature of the economic system requires decisions to be made in a centralized manner on the basis of information that must be abstracted from the complete body of information in order to be of manageable size, and which in the process of abstraction and transmission has necessarily become more or less inaccurate.

However, it is by no means certain that an increase in decentralization will always improve the quality of the information on which decisions are based. At one level, one may say that on the whole the smaller the area concerning which knowledge is required, the better that information can be; one might be willing to suppose that the manager of an independent grocery store would know more about the actual operations of his business than any one person could possibly know about the operations of a chain of stores. But one of the most important types of knowledge, for the making of economic decisions, is a knowledge of the effect of variations in the methods and patterns of operation; in this case, a chain of stores, by keeping standard sets of accounts and by considering the differences in various factors affecting the operation of its various units, and perhaps by experimenting with different methods of operation in single units at a time, can in principle be expected to be able to obtain a better idea of how the results of operation are affected by various differences in circumstances and methods. The owner of an individual store could less easily isolate the effects of various changes in methods of operation from the various other influences that affect his results, and might even find experimentation with alternative methods rather difficult. Thus while there is some reason for saying that the smaller unit is more likely to "know" the operation more intimately, it is far from certain that equal or better knowledge cannot be obtained through some other form of productive organization, up to even a state trust, a consumer cooperative, or a type of organization yet to be devised.

Thus the conditions required for the validity of the theorem that competition produces an optimum result are in fact violated to a greater or lesser degree in a large variety of ways, and the competitive model can serve as only a crude approximation of the actual economic world. Nevertheless, this model serves as a useful framework within which to consider the operation of an economic system in more detail, and in fact is an almost indispensable construct without which it would be difficult to reduce the complexities of modern economic life to any semblance of systematic order. And if this over-all model is suitably modified at the points where immediate attention is being concentrated, it may serve as the basis for a series of workable approximations to particular areas, even though if one were to attempt to consider simultaneously all of the various modifications indicated by substantial differences between the model and the real world the model would become so complex as to be completely unwieldly and unanalyzable.

The Competitive System as a Normative Construct

THE USEFULNESS of the concept of perfect competition is not limited to its use as a skeleton to which to add "flesh" in the form of additional modifications and complexities in the hope of approaching more nearly to reality. The competitive system can also be used as a normative standard to assist in the devising of changes in the actual economic system which will bring the actual system closer to realizing the optimum condition that the hypothetical system has been shown to satisfy. Where the actual economic system fails in some respect to correspond to the assumptions of the hypothetical system, comparison of the two may indicate what changes to make in the actual system in order to improve its operation.

Possibly the prerequisite that is most fundamentally and pervasively unfulfilled in the actual economic system is that of increasing costs or diminishing returns to the firm. The development of modern technology has been such that substantial technological economies of scale are often enjoyed up to increasingly large sizes of productive units. In some cases the output for which the technological economies of scale are substantially exhausted may exceed the entire capacity of the economy to absorb the product, and indeed in such cases there may be no experience to indicate whether or not technological economies of scale would ever be exhausted. In other cases the point at which technological economies of scale are exhausted may occur at an output that is a large fraction of the total demand, so that there is room for at most only a very few firms of a size large enough to enjoy the major technological economies, and this small number of firms may be too few to permit entrepreneurs to consider that each has no influence on the price of his product. Where the transportation costs of the product are substantial, then even though the economy as a whole would absorb the output of several plants of minimum-cost size, it will often be economical to distribute the production among a larger number of plants with slightly higher costs in order to reduce the costs of transportation, and in such cases technological economies of scale will not be exhausted.

More generally, substantial technological economies of scale may continue until a size of firm has been reached such that most of the financial and managerial diseconomies of scale have already been incurred and more than offset by the technological economies; then even though there may be no further economies of scale to be exploited, there may on the other hand be no positive disadvantage to further expansion. A firm large enough to operate one steel mill of the most efficient size, for example, will usually already have had to use an organized capital market for its financing, and will probably have its shares listed on some fairly active exchange; it will probably already have a fairly elaborate managerial hierarchy set up. The diseconomies involved in expanding the firm to include a second similar steel plant are likely to be inconsequential, particularly if the expansion can take place in stages over a fairly long period of time, and these diseconomies will at most be too small to weigh very heavily against expansion if the management has even a moderately strong desire to expand in size and importance. Thus even in the case where the economy could support a fairly large number of firms sufficiently large to enjoy all the substantial economies of scale, and sufficiently numerous to produce a close approach to competitive conditions, there might be, in the absence of interference, a fairly general tendency for firms to be larger than necessary, particularly where business mores yield a high prestige value to growth and expansion. Even though the firms would not necessarily become so large as to incur increasing costs, they might well become so large, and therefore so few, as to no longer be genuinely competitive.

The desire of economic theorists to draw cost curves for illustrative purposes in such a way as to bring out their points most clearly is probably responsible for the failure of such considerations to gain adequate attention. Economists, including the writer, are prone to draw average-cost curves that have a well-defined minimum point, as, for example, in FIGURES 47 and 48, whereas actually everywhere the long-run average-cost curve for a given firm has a minimum point, the curve may be so nearly horizontal over a wide range of outputs that variations above the minimum are almost immaterial over this wide range. Indeed, the inevitable uncertainties present in the ideas of the entrepreneur concerning his production function make it highly unlikely that he would be able to locate the minimum point with any accuracy. This situation may be illustrated by FIGURE 61, in which the average-cost curve drops rapidly at first, but at C nearly all the economies of scale have been exhausted and from there on the curve is nearly horizontal. While a minimum point has been specified at M, ordinarily the curve could probably be drawn with a minimum anywhere between A and B without contradicting any known facts, and over the range from C to D the amount by which average costs exceed the minimum may well be so small that the entrepreneur might well ignore the difference.

The chief result of changing from a tacit assumption of average-cost curves with well-defined minima to a more realistic admission of flat-bottomed average-cost curves is that while in the former case the total output, price, number of firms, and respective sizes of the firms are all determinate, in the flat-bottomed case the price and total output of the industry are determined, but the number of firms and their respective sizes are not determined by the cost characteristics of the industry. Instead, there is a fairly wide range in both number and size, and the actual number and the actual sizes of the various firms may fall at almost any point over this range, as determined by institutional, historical, and other forces not specified in the theoretical structure. To be sure, there may be a specific size and a specific minimum point that would be approached in a completely frictionless economy, but in practice the forces that would tend to cause firms to approach this ideal point may be so slight that they will be overcome by almost any sort of accidental pressure or institutional bias. Thus if the range covered by the flat bottom of the average-cost curve is wide enough, rather minor differences in the institutional environment may spell the difference between an industry made up of a large number of reasonably competitive units and an industry made up of large units too few in number to create a competitive atmosphere.

On the basis of such a model, a case can therefore be made for introducing deliberate modifications of the institutional and legal environment in the direction of favoring smaller units in general. Among these modifications

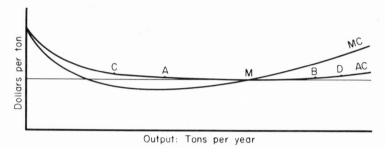

Output: Tons per year

FIGURE 61

might be included taxes moderately progressive as to size, various types of laws against or other hindrances to mergers and consolidations, such as the Sherman and Clayton acts, restrictions on pyramiding of corporations, trading on equity, and other similar means by which entrepreneurs increase the amount of capital subject to their control out of proportion to the increase in their own equity; and possibly a general effort to change the mores and prestige judgments of the business community away from an association of growth and size with social merit.

Whatever means are thus employed to overcome an undue tendency to increase the size of firms, it should be kept in mind that these measures will almost inevitably be applied also in cases where they are not needed and where the diseconomies of scale alone would be sufficient to preserve competition. To the extent that they are applied in such cases and are not needed, they will tend to cause firms to be somewhat smaller than the optimum size, which will result in costs in such industries being on the whole higher than would otherwise be the case. Accordingly, it will in general be necessary to use care in applying restraints on size, lest the restraints be too powerful and the preservation of competition in some fields be bought only at too high a cost in decreased efficiency in other fields.

Indeed, even where firms are too few in number to create a short-run competitive situation, prices may be held at the competitive level for fear of inducing additional firms to enter the industry, or merely because the firms are satisfied with a normal profit. But while in most cases such forces may operate, they will not in themselves be strong enough to bring prices quite down to the competitive level. Where firms voluntarily abstain from extracting what they consider to be an excessive profit, the "normal profit" that they permit themselves may be fairly generously conceived and may exceed by a considerable margin the level of profit that would be enforced by effective competition, even though it may fall short of what might be secured, in the short run, by raising prices to the fullest extent possible. And while there may be in the offing a threat that if prices are too high new firms would enter, new firms may hesitate to enter where the effect of their entry would be to create excess capacity and possibly inaugurate a period of losses for the entire industry. Particularly where the smallest firm that will have available the major economies of scale is fairly large, and where capital investment is fairly heavy and specialized, the threat of entry by new firms may be sufficiently remote so as to exert only moderate restraint on the prices set by the firms already in the industry. Thus one cannot place too much reliance on potential competition as a force tending to bring about competitive conditions, and specific restraints on large firms may still be indicated.

A slightly more serious problem is posed when substantial economies of scale are encountered up to an output representing a major fraction, say one-third or more of the total demand. Here it will not be possible to have a sufficient number of firms in the industry to give effective competition unless firms are so small as to push average cost above the minimum. It will still be possible, as long as the economies of scale are substantially exhausted by the time the output of the firm has become large enough to supply the entire demand for the product (at a price that just covers costs), to have the total output produced at the lowest possible cost, and at the same time obtain sufficient revenues from prices equal to marginal cost to cover the costs of the firm and provide a normal profit. But it will no longer be possible to rely on competition to keep the price down to the marginal-cost level.

In such cases it may be possible to fulfil the requirements of optimum allocation by private operation subject to regulation of the price of the product, or by operation as a public enterprise on a self-liquidating basis. Under regulation, the private firm would be required to supply its product at a price determined by a public authority or regulatory commission, and this price could be determined in such a way as to just cover total costs (including a suitable return on the investment). Thus price would be made approximately equal to average cost, which in turn would approximate marginal cost if the average-cost curve has reached its minimum level. A self-liquidating public authority could likewise be directed to follow a price policy aimed at just covering total costs, which in this case would mean a price fairly close to marginal cost.

Multiple Products

IN PRACTICE, however, even in this relatively tractable case, the setting of prices so as to cover total costs settles the matter only where there is but a single product and a single price to be determined. Where many different products are produced by a single firm or from a single process, mere equating of total costs to total revenues will not suffice to determine several prices. To determine the several prices, it will be necessary to allocate total costs among the various products. Since we have assumed that the firm is operating at a point where the economies of scale have been about exhausted, the production function in the neighborhood of this point will be linearly homogeneous, and we can show here (in the same way as for the imputation to factors of the total product according to their respective marginal productivity) that if each product is charged for at its marginal cost of production, the total revenue will just equal total cost. Marginal cost then becomes the appropriate criterion for the allocation of the total costs among the various products.

Seasonal Fluctuations

EVEN WHEN there is only a single product in the physical sense, there will often be seasonal or other fluctuations in demand or supply that may make it necessary to distinguish between the product in, say, period 1 and the product in period 2. Although physically similar, the products are economically distinct and must be treated as separate products. Usually, such products are at the same time joint products in that almost always there will be elements of fixed plant that will be needed to produce the product at either of the two times but which need not be doubled to produce the same amount of product at both times. For example, a certain proportion of the costs of providing hotel service go on whether or not the rooms are occupied; a room at the peak season and a room in the slack season are two very different commodities, economically speaking, both from the point of view of the user and of the marginal costs of the rooms.

Consider, as an oversimplified example, the case of a hotel for which the various categories of cost vary strictly in proportion to the corresponding parameters of service; i.e., the operation is under conditions of constant returns to scale, at least over the range of magnitudes to be considered. Assume further that costs are of three types: (1) "carrying costs" of $200 per room per year that continue regardless of whether rooms are occupied or not or whether the hotel is open or closed: capital charges on the investment in the hotel would be an example of such a cost; (2) "current overhead costs" of $1 per room per day that continue as long as the hotel is open, regardless of whether the rooms are occupied or not: heating and certain types of maintenance may be types of costs that belong in this category; (3) "direct

[225

costs" of $2 per day for each room actually occupied: laundry and maid service would be examples of this type of cost. Finally, assume that opening the hotel is an "all or nothing" matter, i.e., that it is not possible to save any substantial part of the current overhead by opening only part of the hotel, while constructing and operating two hotels of half the size of that indicated when there is to be only one would bring the scale of operation down to the

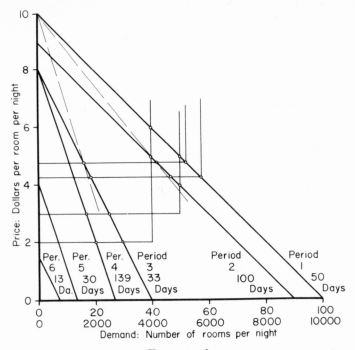

FIGURE 62

range where economies of scale are significant to an extent that the higher cost of the two smaller-scale operations would more than offset the gain from the possiblity of shutting down only one of the two hotels during certain seasons.

On the demand side, suppose that during the peak season of 50 days, as in FIGURE 62, the demand for hotel rooms is given by $100 - 10P$ rooms, P being the price per room; that on 100 other days the demand recedes to $90 - 10P$; for a third period of 33 days demand is $40 - 5P$; for a fourth period of 139 days it is $28 - 3.5P$; for a fifth period of 30 days the demand slacks off to $12 - 3P$, and for the remaining 13 days the demand is only $6 - 4P$. How should one determine the size of hotel to construct, assuming this pattern of demand to be permanent, what rates should be charged during the various seasons, and during what periods should the hotel remain open for business?

Consider the case where the pattern of demand is accurately known in advance to the management, and where there is complete freedom to vary the rates in accordance with these anticipated fluctuations in demand. It is fairly obvious immediately that for such periods as the hotel is open but not full, the marginal cost of having additional guests consists of the $2 per room direct cost, and that if optimum allocation of resources is to be secured, this is the price to be charged during such periods. Also, it is clear that while the hotel is full the price must be such as to just cut the effective demand to the capacity of the hotel, otherwise either the hotel would not be full or there would be unsatisfied demand that would need to be rationed by something other than the price mechanism. In most cases, a nonprice-rationing would mean that some would-be guests are turned away to whom the rooms would have been worth more than to some of those fortunate enough to get a room, and thus the total benefit derived from the occupancy of a given number of rooms would be less than it would be if the price were set high enough so that only the most eager guests (in terms of the price they are willing to pay) would actually occupy the rooms. (We shall see later that in some cases nonprice-rationing, as through queues, may be needed in order to achieve an optimum allocation of resources, but it is ordinarily not desirable where demand is correctly anticipated and the price is flexible, as in this case.)

In a case of this sort, one can find the answer only by considering each of the more likely modes of operation, securing the best possible adjustment for each mode of operation, and comparing the results. However, let us assume, as we will verify in due course, that the optimum mode of operation involves keeping the hotel open for the four periods of highest demand aggregating 300 days during the year, and that the hotel will be full for the two periods of highest demand, or 150 days. For this mode of operation, the optimum number of rooms to be constructed may be determined as follows: Let the number of rooms in the hotel be Q. The price to be charged during the peak 50-day period will then be $P_1 = (100 - Q)/10$ if the demand is to just fill the hotel, and similarly the price to be charged during the second period of 100 days will be $P_2 = (90 - Q)/10$.

Now the benefits derived from the services of an additional room for that part of the year during which adding such a room would increase the services rendered can be measured by the price that the additional guest would just be willing to pay; in period 1, this price is P_1 per day, or $50P_1$ for the entire duration of period 1; similarly, the value of the additional room for period 2 would be P_2 per day, or $100P_2$ for the entire duration of period 2. Since by assumption building another room will not increase occupancy during periods 3, 4, 5, and 6, nothing is to be added on this account and we have as the total of such benefits:

$$B = 50P_1 + 100P_2 = 500 - 5Q + 900 - 10Q = 1,400 - 15Q$$

[227

On the other hand, the marginal cost of adding an additional room and having it occupied for 150 days during the year would be $200 additional carrying charges, plus $300 additional current overhead costs figured at $1 per day for the 300 days during which the hotel will remain open, plus $300 of direct costs figured at $2 per day for the 150 days during which the additional room will be occupied, or a total of $800. If we now determine the number of rooms so that the additional costs resulting from the addition of the last room just balance the benefits added through its use, we can put:

$$1{,}400 - 15Q = 800; \quad \text{whence} \quad Q = 40$$

Thus the hotel will be constructed with 40 rooms. The price for period 1 will be $P_1 = (100 - 40)/10 = 6$, and for period 2 will be $P_2 = (90 - 40)/10 = 5$. For periods 3 and 4, at a price of $2, the demand will be for 30 and 21 rooms, respectively, thus verifying that under these prices the hotel will be full for only 150 days during the year, as assumed. It is fairly obvious that it would not be desirable to have the hotel full for a shorter or longer period, since to have empty rooms during period 2 would imply a marginal cost of $2, and if $P_2 = \$2$, demand in period 2 would be 70 so that the hotel would have to have at least 70 rooms, whereas it is easy to see that a seventieth room would not provide benefits commensurate with the costs involved; conversely, if the hotel is to be full during period 3 at a price of $2 or more, the hotel could be no larger than 30 rooms, whereas the addition of a thirty-first room would clearly produce benefits in excess of the additional cost.

It remains to verify that the hotel should remain open for just 300 days. In period 5, if the hotel were opened and the price set at $2, 6 rooms would indeed be occupied. But there would be current overhead costs of $40 per day involved in keeping the 40-room hotel open rather than in closing it down, in addition to the $2 per day of direct costs. On the other hand, the total daily benefit derived by the six guests would be only $18, composed of the $12 that they pay at $2 per night plus a consumer's surplus of $6 as measured by the area between the demand curve $Q_5 = 24 - 3P_5$ and the line $P = 2$. Thus the cost of keeping the hotel open during this period is clearly greater than the benefits to be derived. This would remain true even if the size of the hotel were adjusted downward slightly, as it would be if it were decided to keep the hotel open during this period, since this would increase the costs involved in adding the marginal room to the hotel, and would thus reduce slightly the size of the hotel at which the benefits and costs of adding another room would be brought into balance. As for period 6, no potential guests are willing to pay even as much as $2, and there is no question of keeping the hotel open.

On the other hand, for period 4 the consumer's surplus is $21(\$8 - \$2)/2 = \$63$ per day; subtracting the $40 per day in current overhead costs incurred in keeping the hotel open during this period leaves a net social gain of $23 per day, so that it is worthwhile to provide the service, even though there is no possible price that could be charged during this period that would permit the hotel to recover directly from these guests both the direct and the current overhead costs involved in keeping the hotel open. The nearest that the hotel can come to covering these costs is to charge $5, at which rate there would be an average of 10.5 guests per day, yielding revenues of $52.50 per day, of which $21 would be required to cover the direct costs, leaving only $31.50 to be applied toward the $40 of overhead. To attempt to collect this amount from these guests by actually charging $5 in this way, however, would reduce the net gain to the community as a whole from the operation of the hotel during this period from $23 per day to $7.25 per day, or by $10.5(\$5 + \$2)/2 - \$21 = \$15.75$ per day, representing the difference between the value of this service to the 10.5 guests per day who would be willing to pay $2 but not $5, and the $21 cost of caring for these marginal 10.5 guests at $2 each.

It should be noted that even this calculation does not absolutely settle the matter of whether the hotel should be open during period 4, for if the hotel were not to be open during this period, the lower current overhead per room per year would have made it worthwhile to construct a somewhat larger hotel to accommodate more guests during the peak period, and a computation based on such a larger hotel with larger daily current overhead might fail to show an advantage in keeping the hotel open during period 4. In this case, however, it is clear that even were the hotel built larger on the assumption that it would not be open in period 4, it would still pay to open the hotel in period 4, in terms of net social benefit. It will be seen from this instance that it would be quite possible to have two or more modes of operation, each of which might appear optimal from the point of view of changing one aspect of the operation at a time, and it would then be necessary to evaluate each mode of operation as a whole in order to determine which one is preferable. Thus even in a simple example, the presence of indivisibilities (in this case, the higher costs of operating two hotels of half the size) leads to some fairly complex analytical problems.

In period 3 the hotel, by charging $4, could cover the current overhead cost of keeping the hotel open, but again, by so doing the number of guests would be cut from 30 to 20, and there would be a loss of net benefits of $10 per day as compared with setting the price at $2. The fact that the overhead could be covered in this way, however, does assure that it is worthwhile to keep the hotel open during this period, at least as long as only a 40-room hotel is considered. Again, planning to open the hotel only during periods 1 and 2 would not justify building so large a hotel that it would not pay to open it during period 3; while in this case the result is fairly obvious by inspection, the possibility does in general need to be considered.

Total revenues obtained by charging $6 in period 1, $5 in period 2, and $2 in periods 3 and 4 will be $39,818, made up of 2,000 units at $6 in period 1, 4,000 units at $5 in period 2, and 990 units in period 3 and 2,919 units

[229

in period 4, at $2. Carrying costs at $200 per room for 40 rooms will be $8,000; current overhead costs for 40 rooms for 300 days at $1 per room per day will be $12,000; direct costs for a total of 9,909 room-nights of actual occupancy at $2 per night will be $19,818, a total of $39,818. Thus at prices designed to produce an optimum allocation of resources, the hotel is just self-supporting, as was to be expected from the fact that the hotel was supposed to be operating at a point of constant returns to scale.

The net surplus or gain to the community as a whole resulting from the operation of the hotel is as follows: Period 1 guests obtain a consumer's surplus ranging from $4 (= $10 − $6) for the guests with the most intense demand to nothing for the guests just barely willing to pay the price charged, or an average of $2 per guest per day, which can be multiplied by 50 days per year and 40 rooms to give a total of $4,000; similarly, for period 2 consumer's surplus is $8,000. For periods 3 and 4 the average consumer's surplus per guest per day is $3, which for 3,909 guest-days comes to $11,727, or a total net surplus for the entire operation of the hotel of $23,727, as the portion of the total benefit reflected in the revenues paid in by the guests just covers the total costs and is thus sufficient to offset benefits that might have been derivable from the use of the resources in other directions.

It is fairly obvious that the price is equal to marginal cost in periods 3 and 4, but one may ask in what sense can it be said that the price of $6 in period 1 and $5 in period 2 represents marginal cost? If we wish to provide a forty-first room for a specific day in period 1, it will be necessary to incur additional carrying charges of $200, additional overhead of $300, and additional direct costs of $2, or a total of $502. On the other hand, if the fortieth room were to remain vacant on a particular night in period 1, the only saving in costs would be $2. One might therefore state that the marginal cost at this point jumps discontinuously from $2 to $502, which would justify any price within this range as a marginal-cost price, provided that at that price the number of rooms actually occupied is exactly 40. This proviso of course, with the given demand schedule, requires that the price be $6. Or one could consider that as a by-product of providing a forty-first room on a particular day we are presented with the opportunity of providing for another guest on other days in periods 1 and 2 at a direct cost of only $2; on 49 of these other days this service will be worth just under $6 (approaching $6 if we could make the increment of capacity infinitely small), and on 100 of the other days this increment of service will be worth just under $5. If we take the difference between the value of these by-product services and the direct costs associated with them, i.e., $49($6 − $2) + 100($5 − $2) = 496, and credit this against the total of $502, the net cost of an additional room comes out at just $6, which is the price set. Or another way of looking at the matter is to say that the marginal social cost of providing a room to one particular guest consists of depriving the next most eager guest of that room, and this cost is to be measured by the price that this next most eager guest would have been willing to pay. Whatever line of approach is used to the fixing of a marginal cost, where, as in this case there are in effect joint products that are produced in rigidly fixed proportions, it is not possible to determine a marginal cost for any one item without considering the demand for and the resulting value of the other co-products.

If we extend the concept of marginal cost in this way to cover such cases, we find that in the case under examination it is possible to have prices equal to marginal costs and still have total revenues equal to total costs. The element of overhead, or capacity costs, does not in itself make it impossible to cover total costs by charging marginal-cost prices; it merely requires that the proper allocation be made on a causal basis. The overhead and carrying charges are not affected by changes in the number of guests accommodated during periods 3 and 4, but only by the number in periods 1 and 2. Accordingly, these costs must be allocated entirely to periods 1 and 2 and the prices established accordingly.

By distinguishing six different levels of demand in the above analysis, we were able to exhibit a number of cases differing in significant respects: peak demand during period 1; off-peak demand that nevertheless makes full use of capacity through appropriate price adjustment, as in period 2; in period 3, demand at a level that could yield enough revenue to cover current overhead costs that might be thought allocable to it as a whole, but where it is better to lower rates below this point to marginal cost; demand at a level where it is not possible to meet the current overhead costs by direct charges to the current users, but where it is still worthwhile to keep the hotel open at marginal cost rates, as in period 4; in period 5, demand at a level where there would be some use of the hotel at marginal-cost rates but where the resulting consumer's surplus would be insufficient to justify the increased overhead involved; and, finally, in period 6 demand at a level where there would be no use at all even if price were lowered to marginal cost. In practice, of course, demand would not vary in such discrete steps, and the solution of the problem of determining the optimum size, mode of operation, and price structure is correspondingly more complex.

It is worthwhile paying some special attention to the role that the current overhead costs during the off-peak periods play in the determination of marginal cost. Since this is still a case of constant returns to scale overall, these costs do get allocated somewhere. But although the most natural procedure would often be thought to be to allocate these costs to the corresponding off-peak users, since these users as a group could be said to cause the incurring of these costs and since they are also the ones to benefit from them, nevertheless the addition of marginal off-peak users does not add to these costs, whereas the addition of marginal peak users will add to these costs by requiring the construction of a larger hotel than otherwise, which will cost more to keep open in the off season. It may be a bit anomalous, but it is nevertheless quite correct that the longer the off-peak season during which it pays to keep the hotel open, while used at less than capacity, the higher will be the marginal cost assignable to the peak users. Even if the hotel were not required to balance its expenses and its revenues, it would not be possible to relieve the peak users of any of this burden of the off-peak current overhead without impairing the net benefit or surplus derivable from the operation.

Accounting practices, however, often run counter to such marginally causal relationships, and may mislead entrepreneurs into setting prices in quite different ways from those indicated by marginal relationships. Also, notions of "just price" and prejudice against "charging what the traffic will bear" may produce a reluctance to vary prices to the extent that would be indicated by the principle of charging at marginal cost. This is particularly true where regulation by a public authority is involved, since necessarily it is much more difficult to police a situation where prices are allowed to fluctuate in accordance with the state of demand than it is where prices are held more nearly constant. There are also mechanical obstacles to varying the price in accordance with shifts in demand: a more complicated price structure requires more record-keeping, makes the accounting more difficult, and may result in such a bewildering array of prices as to confuse the customer rather than guide him to a socially desirable choice. In many cases it is necessary to fix the price some time in advance so that firm contracts or reservations can be made and plans set, and it may not be possible to predict demand or marginal cost in advance with any great accuracy. One of the relative disadvantages of large firms is that it is often difficult for them to delegate to their local agents the same freedom to vary prices in accordance with changes in demand and supply conditions as is enjoyed by the entrepreneur of a small independent firm. The theoretically proper solution of keeping prices strictly in line with marginal cost may not be feasible.

Thus for one reason or another it may be necessary to follow a price policy charging a single price for as long as the hotel stays open at all. Since it will no longer be possible to raise the price in a particular period to ration demand, the possibility arises that during some period queuing or other forms of nonprice rationing may have to be resorted to. But in some cases it may prove desirable to build a hotel large enough to meet the peak demand at the price that is set. This is particularly likely to be the case if the process of turning away would-be guests is costly, or if queuing is especially wasteful, or if there are some guests among those who might be turned away during a peak period to whom inability to secure accommodations is of very great moment, as would be indicated, for example, if the period 1 demand curve were made to curve upward, at the higher price levels, so as to strike the price axis at, say, $100. As this latter case, where there are to be no guests turned away who would be willing to pay the established price, is the easier to analyze, we will treat it first. Given the price, the corresponding size of hotel to be built will be determined by the period 1 demand, and the only remaining problem is to determine what periods the hotel should remain open.

We can first of all see fairly quickly that in this case it will not be worthwhile to keep the hotel open during period 4, since at no price level would the amount that period 4 patrons pay over and above the direct costs of $2, plus their consumer's surplus, equal or exceed the current overhead that keeping the hotel open for them would entail. For example, at a price of $5, the number of guests per day would be 10.5, the margin above the $2 direct costs would be $31.50 and the consumer's surplus $15.75 per day, which together would amount to $47.25, whereas at a price of $5 the required size of the hotel is 50 rooms, which would cost $50 per day in current overhead to keep open. Similarly, at a price of $4 the hotel would have to have 60 rooms, and it would not be worthwhile to keep the hotel open during period 4 even though the consumer's surplus of the 14 guests would amount to $28 per day and the amount they pay in excess of the $2 direct costs would add another $28 to the total of $56. And similarly for other price levels.

On the other hand, such a net benefit does result from keeping the hotel open for period 3, at all prices below $6.80, and it will be found that the appropriate price is actually in this range.

If then the hotel is open for periods 1, 2, and 3, the effect of each reduction in the price by ten cents is to increase patronage by one guest per day in periods 1 and 2, and by an average of 0.5 guests per day in period 3, or a total of 166.5 guest-days. To take care of this increase in service would require enlarging the hotel by one room, with carrying charges therefore increased by $200 and current overhead by $183, since the hotel is to be open for 183 days, while direct costs for the additional 166.5 guest-days would be $333, a total of $716. If this is spread over the 166.5 guest-days, we obtain $4.30 as the value these rooms would have to have if such an increment is to be warranted. If therefore the uniform price is set as $4.30, this will represent an optimum position, since the increment of service induced by the reduction of price from $4.40 to $4.30 was just worthwhile, while that induced by a further reduction in price from $4.30 to $4.20 would not be. The capacity of the hotel will therefore have to be 57 rooms to take care of the period 1 demand, the occupancy for periods 2 and 3 averaging 47 and 18.5 rooms, respectively.

The total number of guest-days will be $50(57) + 100(47) + 33(18.5) = 8,160.5$, yielding a revenue at the price of $4.30 of $35,090.15. When we come to look at costs, however, we find that we have $57($200) = $11,400$ in carrying charges, $57($183) = $10,431$ in current overhead, and $8,160.5($2) = $16,321$ in direct costs, a total cost of $38,052, so that there is a net loss of $2,961.85. The consumer's surplus for the three periods will be $57(50)($2.85) + 47(100)($2.35) + 33($18.5)($1.85) = $20,296.92$, so that the net social gain is

$17,335.07. This is $6,391.93 less than was obtainable when prices could be varied freely.

If it should be deemed necessary to avoid operating at a loss, and to determine the price and corresponding size of hotel in such a way as to just cover total costs, the price (to the nearest ten cents) would have to be $4.70, implying a hotel with only 53 rooms, with 53 occupants in period 1, 43 in period 2, and 16.5 in period 3. Total costs will be 53($200) + 53($183) + 7,494.5($2) = $35,288; total revenues will be 7,494.5($4.70) = $35,224.15, leaving a nominal net loss due to rounding of $63.85, which if necessary could be somewhat more than made up by raising the price by one cent. Consumer's surplus would be

$$53(50)(\$2.65) + 43(100)(\$2.15) + 16.5(33)(\$1.65) = \$17,165.92$$

and adjusting this for the small discrepancy between revenues and costs we have as the net social gain $17,102.07. The requirement that the hotel produce revenues equal to costs (approximately) has thus produced a net deterioration in the allocation of resources of $233.00.

How is it that the optimum price level, given the constraint against seasonal variation in prices, now no longer produces revenues that cover total costs? As far as production is concerned, we still have constant returns to scale, at least if we distinguish between the supplying of rooms at different times of the year and consider a proportional expansion in which the same "product mix" is preserved. The structure of demand, however, is such that as the price is lowered the demand during the off-peak seasons expands relatively more rapidly than does the peak demand, so that the average number of days during the year that the rooms are occupied rises, which of course has the effect of lowering the average cost per room per day.

This phenomenon will occur whenever the elasticity of the demand for off-peak periods is greater than the elasticity of the peak demand, at the same price. If the elasticity of demand at all seasons is the same, then the price that maximizes the net social benefit will also produce revenues equal to total costs. For example, if in the above case we made the demand curves of periods 2 and 3 proportional, at various given prices, to the demand for period 1, at a level such as to give the same effective demand as in the previous examples at a price of $4.70, then we would find that the price of $4.70 in addition to yielding revenues approximately equal to costs also maximizes the net social surplus. The required demand curves are $Q_2 = 81.2 - 8.12P$ and $Q_3 = 34.9 - 3.49P$; if these demand curves are substituted in the problem, the financial results for $P = \$4.70$ remain exactly as before, but now with these demand curves, any change in the price, and in particular lowering the price to $4.30 will lower rather than increase the net social surplus.

Conversely, if the off-peak demand is less elastic than the peak, we would have a situation where the maximum net social surplus is achieved at a price that yields a surplus above costs. For example, if we now let the demand curves of periods 2 and 3 steepen to $Q_2 = 71.2 - 6P$ and $Q_3 = 30.6 - 3P$, we now find that for a ten-cent decrease in price, demand increases by only $50(10)(0.1) + 100(6)(0.1) + 33(3)(0.1) = 119.9$ guest-days. Since the period 1 demand has been kept unchanged, carrying charges and current overhead go up as before by \$200 and \$183, and direct costs go up by $119.9(\$2) = \$239.80$, or a total of \$622.80, which spread over the 119.9 guest-days gives \$5.20 per room per day as the value that must be placed on the additional service if the increment in cost is to be in balance with the increment in benefits. Accordingly, a rate of \$5.20 will be the price that maximizes the net social surplus, and the capacity of the hotel will be 48 rooms, with average occupancy in the three periods of 48, 40, and 15, for a total number of guest-days of $50(48) + 100(40) + 33(15) = 6,895$; costs will be $48(\$200) + 48(\$183) + 6,895(\$2) = \$32,174$; revenues are $6,895(\$5.20) = \$35,854.00$, giving a net profit of \$3,680.00.

If now we compute a consumer's surplus with respect to these new demand curves, noting that the new maximum prices on the demand curves for periods 2 and 3 are now \$11.86 and \$10.20, we get for this surplus $50(48)(\$2.40) + 100(40)(\$3.33) + 33(15)(\$2.50) = \$20,317.50$, and if to this we add the net profit, a total net social surplus of \$23,997.50, is obtained. Of course, since this surplus is computed by reference to a different set of demand curves, it cannot be compared to the surpluses arising in the former cases. However, if we consider lowering the price to \$4.70 again with these demand curves, we will get the same effective demand pattern as before, and the financial results will be a nominal loss due to rounding of \$63.85. If we evaluate the consumer's surplus anew in this case on the basis of the new demand curves we get $50(53)(\$2.65) + 100(43)(\$3.58) + 33(16.5)(\$2.75) = \$23,913.88$, which adjusted for the small loss becomes a net social surplus of \$23,850.03, or less by \$147.47 than is obtained at the price of \$5.20.

Thus price rigidity in the face of fluctuating demand may give rise to either increasing-return or decreasing-return situations, depending on whether the peak demand is less or more elastic than the off-peak demand at the price being considered. On the whole, one is inclined to feel that the increasing-return situation is the more common, for if demand at a given price is smaller in one period than in another, it is generally to be expected that the maximum price that anyone would pay would also vary in the same direction as it would between the two seasons, and this, at least in the case of linear demand curves, would indicate a higher elasticity in the season with the lower demand at the given price. Indeed, if the demand for what is the peak period at the price in question were consistently more elastic than the demand for an off-peak period, this would imply that for a sufficiently high price the demand for the peak period would actually be less than the demand for the off-peak period.

Nevertheless, there are cases where the decreasing-return pattern may be a plausible one, though even here it may be considered rather unlikely. For example, if the peak demand arises largely from recreational or social motives, it may be felt that it is likely to be more elastic at some level of prices than a business demand, which may constitute a base demand. Thus for some rate levels a case of decreasing returns or increasing costs would arise. A case in point is long-distance telephone traffic, where the peak may arise from social calling at Christmas, Mother's Day, and similar occasions, the regular weekday traffic being largely business and not reaching such a high level. But if this were true it would have to be true only at low-rate levels: if a uniform rate were raised substantially, the social traffic would by hypothesis be choked off more rapidly than the business traffic, and eventually it would be the business traffic that furnished the peak. The increasing-return case, however, can persist consistently at all rate levels.

Queuing and Nonprice Rationing

THE ABOVE case assumed that it would be mandatory to install equipment sufficient to take care of the peak demand. In many instances this is substantially the case: in electric power supply, for example, an attempt to carry a load greater than the generating or transmitting capacity of the system leads to damage to the equipment, lowered voltage or frequency or both, with the result that consumers' apparatus functions improperly or at lowered efficiency; to avoid these consequences it is often necessary to resort to "load shedding," partial blackouts, and other fairly drastic measures that have fairly serious consequences. Accordingly, it is usual to maintain a fairly substantial reserve capacity to limit, where possible, such untoward occurrences to those precipitated by a relatively rare and substantial casualty. In other cases, the facilities for turning away customers who cannot be accommodated are somewhat more efficient and the consequences of turning them away not quite so serious. Where hotel space is fairly universally reserved in advance, for example, at least by those for whom failure to find space upon their arrival in the city would be serious, it is possible to "turn customers away" before they commit themselves very far. In the ideal case, the loss a consumer suffers upon being turned away would be limited to the difference between the price he would have been willing to pay, *ab initio*, as reflected in his contribution to the demand curve, and the price actually being charged. In practice, the various methods of nonprice rationing all involve some kind of cost, whether in terms of the time, effort, and communications facilities used in the making of advance reservations or the purchase of tickets ahead of time, or of decreased freedom of action that results where plans must be made far in advance and changed only with difficulty, or of the time and effort expended in queues of various kinds. These constitute an additional price that must be paid for the privilege of purchasing a service or commodity at less than the price that would clear the market.

To return to the example of the hotel, we may consider a case in which it is not deemed imperative to construct the hotel large enough, at the given price, to meet the peak demand. This will be the case, in general, where the peak is sharp or infrequent, since under such circumstances the cost of meeting this peak would be extremely high if computed in terms of the units of additional service to be rendered, and in most cases would be quite out of line with the value of this added service under any but extreme conditions. Given this greater freedom of action, the price to be charged and the size of the hotel to be built can now be determined independently, and in addition of course there will be the question of how long the hotel is to remain open.

As soon as we admit the possibility that effective demand may exceed capacity, it becomes necessary to make some sort of assumption in such cases as to the mechanism by which it is determined which of the customers who desire a given service will actually get it. Even if we make the assumption that there are no costs incurred in the queuing process or in the making of reservations, it still is necessary to ask, in order to estimate the consumer's surplus, whether the successful applicants are predominantly those who are willing to pay the higher prices or those who are predominantly willing to pay only the lower prices and who, accordingly, can be thought of as coming from the lower reaches of the demand curve. Probably the most reasonable simple assumption that can be made here is that the successful applicants will be a random sample of all consumers who would like to obtain the service at the price set. In other words, the average consumer's surplus per consumer (or per unit of service sold, if some consumers take more than one unit) derived by the successful consumers will be the same as the average consumer's surplus per consumer that would have been obtained if the capacity had been sufficient to meet the entire demand at the given price. This is the assumption that will be used in the calculations that follow, although it is not the only assumption that could reasonably be made.

Actually, it might be quite reasonable to suppose that in any queuing process the customers who would be willing to pay most for the service will be likely to make up their minds to use the service longer in advance, if possible, or will be more likely to make whatever effort is required to make advance reservations, so that if the queuing process is itself regarded as costless, the average consumer's surplus may be expected to be somewhat higher than if all could be accommodated. But there is no easy or natural way of specifying just how much higher this would be. At the extreme, one could imagine a perfect speculator's market in the reservations that would permit all persons whose demand price is less than the equilibrium price and who are successful in securing reservations at the official price to sell their reservations to those whose demand price is above the equilibrium price, the equilibrium price being the price that would clear the market. If this retransfer process is considered to be costless, then the total consumer's surplus, including in this term the profits of those who resell their reservations, will be the surplus that would have existed had the price been set at the equilibrium level, plus the spread between the official price and the equilibrium price, applied to the total quantity sold. In such a case, the optimum allocation of the given quantity of service is obtained, even though there is no assurance from this that the quantity of service provided is optimal.

Deviations from the random assumption in the other direction are also possible, of course, but appear to be less likely. There are indeed special situations where deviations in this direction would be plausible. If we assume, for example, that demand for space on a given voyage is made up partly of tourists who make their plans far in advance but who would not be willing to pay very much more than the set price for their space, and partly of businessmen whose travel plans are made on short notice and who would, if necessary, be willing to pay a substantial premium for space, then if demand exceeds the available space and resale is difficult we may find the average consumer's surplus substantially less than it would be if capacity were sufficient to meet the entire demand.

We saw in the previous example that variations in the elasticity of demand for different periods can give rise to either increasing or diminishing returns where it is not possible to vary the price with the season. It might be thought at first that queuing could also give rise to situations where the optimum results can be obtained at a price–capacity–length-of-season combination that would fail to cover total costs, particularly as the benefit obtainable by the marginal customers that are accommodated as a result of an increase in capacity will exceed the price they pay. However, it turns out, surprisingly perhaps, that if we keep elasticity constant for the different seasons, the optimum mode of operation is actually self-supporting, at least in the case where the selection of customers is random and the queuing process is in itself costless. The increasing or diminishing returns that may be found in such cases are attributable to variations in the elasticity of demand and not to the existence of queuing per se.

To show this we need to modify our demand curves to produce a situation where elasticity at given prices remains constant over the various periods. Suppose the period 1 demand to remain at $100 - 10P$, and the demands for periods 2, 3, 4, and 5 to become $80 - 8P$, $30 - 3P$, $15 - 1.5P$, and $10 - P$, respectively. (A period 6 demand curve with equal elasticity and a maximum price below $2 is an impossibility, and for the purposes of this analysis we may consider period 6 to have become absorbed in period 5.) With flexible prices, we can have an optimal self-liquidating operation with prices again at $6, $5, $2, $2, respectively, for periods 1, 2, 3, and 4, with the hotel closed during periods 5 and 6. The consumer's surplus and net social benefit is

$23,840. With a constant-price requirement and capacity required to be equal to the peak effective demand, if the price is set to limit the peak demand to Q, the total occupancy will be $[50 + .8(100) + .3(33)]Q = 140Q$, by reason of the constant elasticity of demand; i.e., the average room will be occupied 140 days during the year, regardless of the size of hotel built. (As before, it is not worthwhile to open the hotel, under these conditions, for period 4.) Since adding one room involves carrying charges and current overhead of $200 + $183 = $383, dividing this by the 140 days per year gives $2.74, which added to the $2 of direct costs gives $4.74 in this case as the optimal and self-liquidating price, with a hotel of 52.6 rooms (i.e., in practice 52 rooms at a price of $4.80, with a slight profit). The consumer's surplus and net social surplus in this case will be $52.6(140)($2.63) = $19,367.32$.

If now we turn to the case where the price must remain constant but it is permissible to turn away peak customers, we may note first of all that for any given price, the optimum size of hotel will always be such as to just satisfy the effective demand for at least one of the periods. For if the hotel were of an intermediate size, the average benefit derived from an additional room and the cost of the additional room remain constant as the size of the hotel is varied from one effective demand level to the next, so that the net social benefit is either rising, falling, or constant over this whole interval, and one of the ends of the interval must give results at least as good as any within the interval. It is also fairly clear immediately that if we assume the hotel is to remain open for at least 183 days during the year (as does prove to be desirable in every case, upon examination), then it should not be built to accommodate the period 1 effective demand, for the added cost of $200 + $183 + 50($2) = $483, spread over the 50 days for which such a room would provide added service, gives a cost per guest-day of $9.66, and the average value of the service to the incremental users would exceed this amount only if the price were to exceed $9.32, since by the random assumption as long as the demand is not fully satisfied the customers are deemed to be drawn at random from those who are willing to pay more than the price; with a linear demand curve the average value of the room to the customer will be about half way between the maximum value, $10, and the price charged, so that with a price of $9.32 the average value to the successful customer will be $9.66. A price as high as this would be justified only if the hotel were smaller than seven rooms, which would obviously produce a net social surplus inferior to other modes of operation.

A similar argument shows that if the hotel were too small to accommodate period 2 effective demand, it would clearly be desirable to enlarge it, since the cost per room works out at $($200 + $183 + 150 \cdot $2)/150 = 4.55, whereas such rooms would on the average be worth $5 per night even though the price were set at zero, and customers were taken at random from the entire demand schedule. Thus the optimal result will have to consist of a price and capacity combination, that just satisfies the effective demand for period 2.

If now we consider adding one room to the hotel, with a simultaneous reduction in price to just fill this capacity in period 2, the added benefits will be as follows: in period 2, 100 additional units of service will be provided, and in period 3 $33(3/8) = 12.4$ additional units; these units will have a value of P, since the previous demand was fully accommodated. In period 1 the additional units of service provided also have a value of P, but for a slightly different reason. Previous to the expansion, 80 per cent of the period 1 demand was accommodated; after the expansion, because of the equal elasticities of the period 1 and period 2 demand curves, the reduction in price indicated by the period 2 demand curve is just such as to increase the effective period 1 demand in the same ratio so that the enlarged hotel will again accommodate 80 per cent of this increased period 1 demand. The successful customers in the new situation are still an 80 per cent sample, but from an enlarged population, and the customers that have been added by the change are to be considered thus an 80 per cent sample of the enlargement of the population from which the samples were drawn. But this enlargement of the population consists entirely of customers whose demand became effective by reason of the reduction in price, so that the value of these added units of service must lie between the old and the new price; for a sufficiently small increment in capacity we can ignore the difference and call the value P.

Thus all the added units of service have the same value P, and the total benefits will thus come to $(50 + 100 + 12.4)P = 162.4P$. The total increment in costs will be $\$200 + \$183 + 162.4(\$2) = \$707.80$. If we set the price to balance the costs and benefits at the margin, we get a price of $\$4.37$, indicating that to accommodate period 2 demand at this price the hotel must be built with 45 rooms. The total number of units sold will be $45(50) + 45(100) + 16.89(33) = 7,307.4$, which at the price of $\$4.37$ will yield revenues of $\$31,933.34$. Costs will amount to $45(\$200) + 45(\$183) + 7,306.4(\$2) = \$31,849.80$, leaving a nominal net profit of $\$83.54$ due to rounding. Consumer's surplus will be $7,307.4(\$10 - \$4.37)(0.5) = \$20,570.33$, and adding the profit to this gives a total social surplus of $\$20,653.87$, which, as could be expected, is less than is obtainable where prices are fully flexible, and more than is obtainable where capacity must be adequate to meet the peak.

If the elasticities of the various demand curves had not been the same, the optimum price-capacity combination would not necessarily yield revenues equal to costs; in the increasing-returns case where the peak demand is less elastic than the demand to which the capacity is being adjusted, not all the added capacity would be used by new effective demand: some of the additional demand that is accommodated would come from the higher reaches of the peak-demand schedule, so that the value of the added service would exceed the market price on the average. For example, if we return to the former set of demand curves with heterogeneous elasticities, and consider an increase by one room in the size of the hotel accompanied by the corresponding price decrease along the period 2 demand curve, only a fraction $(9 - P)/(10 - P)$ of the additional period 1 guests will be drawn from the guests that would not have been willing to pay the former price, and the remaining $1/(1 - P)$ of these guests will be drawn from the entire demand schedule and will place an average value of $(10 + P)/2$ on the securing of the accommodation. Accordingly, we must now write for the total benefit obtained as a result of the added room:

$$\left[100 + 50 \frac{9 - P}{10 - P} + \frac{33}{2} \right] P + \frac{1}{10 - P} 50 \frac{10 + P}{2} = 166.5P + 25$$

Balancing this against the added costs of $\$200 + \$183 + (100 + 50 + 16.5)\$2 = \$716$, we obtain for the optimum price $\$4.15$, implying a capacity of 48.5 rooms. Total occupancy will be $50(48.5) + 100(48.5) + 33(19.25) = 7,910$ guest-nights, yielding revenues, at $\$4.15$, of $\$32,826.50$. Expenses are, however, $48.5(\$200) + 48.5(\$183) + 7,190(\$2) = \$34,395.50$, giving a net loss of $\$1,569$. Consumer's surplus is $50(48.5)(\$2.925) + 100(48.5)(\$2.425) + 33(19.25)(\$1.925) = \$20,077$, so that the net social surplus is $\$18,508$, or just slightly less than is obtainable if the price is made to vary freely, but more· than is obtainable if the hotel must be large enough for the peak demand.

If on the other hand it were necessary to break even, the best that can be done is to construct a hotel of 46.5 rooms, charging $\$4.35$, with total occupancy $50(46.5) + 100(46.5) + 18.25(33) = 7,577$, and revenues of $7,577(\$4.35) = \$32,960$. Expenses are $46.5(\$200) + 46.5(\$183) + 7,577(\$2) = \$32,964$, leaving a nominal $\$4$ loss due to rounding. Consumer's surplus is $50(46.5)(\$2.825) + 100(46.5)(\$2.325) + 33(18.25)(\$1.825) = \$18,478$, and deducting the $\$4$ loss gives $\$18,474$ as the total social surplus, $\$34$ less than when it was not necessary to break even.

These results are further illustrated in FIGURE 63. At the break-even price of $\$4.35$, the total value of the service on period 2 days is given by the area $oCGI$, of which BCG is the consumer's surplus and $oBGI$ the price paid. On period 1 days the value of the service which would have been rendered if the hotel had been made large enough to take all comers at the $\$4.35$ price would be $oDEK$; since we assume the successful applicants to be drawn at random from this potential demand, the value of the service is the fraction BG/BE of this, which can be represented by the area $oDGI = (BG/BE)(oDEK)$. Similarly, the value of the service at the optimal price of $\$4.15$ is $oCHJ$ per day in period 2 and $oDHJ$ per day in period 1; and the difference is $GHJI$ in period 2 but $GDHJI$ in period 1. In the case of equal elasticities, the lines GD and HD coincided, so that only the additional benefit represented by $GHJI$ had to be taken into account, and with constant costs the break-even and the

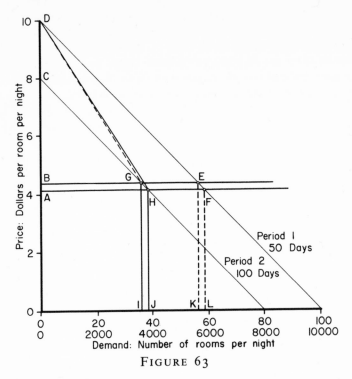

FIGURE 63

optimum prices coincided; here the introduction of the additional benefit factor *GDH* means that the optimum price is below the break-even price.

Seasonal Fluctuations Under Competition

IT IS OF CONSIDERABLE interest to see how the above patterns of pricing developed with the aim of maximizing the net social surplus compare with prices that would be produced by competitive conditions. To permit the free play of competition, let us enlarge the market by a factor of 100, so that we are considering the demand for rooms in a large metropolis or resort area, rather than in a small isolated community. In order to assure the preservation of an adequate degree of competition, let us suppose further that average costs decrease up to a size of 35 rooms, and remain at a constant level thereafter up to a size of, say, 200 rooms, and that for hotels larger than this average costs tend to increase, while within this range of minimum average costs the cost structure is the same as in the small-scale case. All hotels that are built will then be built within this size range.

Under these circumstances, whenever the market price for rooms is less than $3, it will pay a hotel operator to shut down, since the reduction in direct costs and operating overhead will amount to at least $3 per room occupied, even if the hotel is full, and will thus exceed the loss in revenues. On the other hand, whenever the price is higher than $3, each hotel operator who is open will offer all of his rooms, since his marginal cost is $2 as long as the hotel is already open but not full. Or to put it in terms of price policy rather than output policy, a hotel operator with unused rooms will underbid other hotels in an attempt to increase his sales, since perfect competition requires him to assume that his demand curve is perfectly elastic and that even the smallest possible price cut below his competitors will attract at least enough customers to fill his rooms. Whenever the price is above $3, then, competitive price-cutting will proceed until either the price reaches $3 or until all rooms in hotels that are open are filled. If at a price of $3 all rooms are not filled, any operator whose rooms are not all filled will find it profitable to close down, at least temporarily, and sufficient units will be closed down in this way until the remainder are just filled by the effective demand at a price of $3. When demand at $3 exceeds the capacity of the hotels that are open, additional hotels will be opened up as demand increases until all hotels are in operation. Further increase in demand will raise the price above $3 in such a way as to limit demand to the capacity of the existing hotels. If over the course of the year the amounts received during periods of full occupancy over and above the $3 level add up to more than enough to pay the $200 per room carrying charges, more hotels will be built, driving the prices at such period down until these prices over the year just cover the carrying charges. At this point the market will be in long-run equilibrium with prices in the aggregate just covering costs.

The final result is that we have a price of $5 in period 1, $4 in period 2, and $3 in periods 3, 4, and 5. A price of $3 may also be thought to exist in period 6, but at this price there is no demand. Hotels will be built with a capacity of 5,000 rooms, which is the effective demand in periods 1 and 2 at the prices established. The carrying charges per room are met by $2 per room of the period 1 price, for 50 days a year, plus $1 per room of the period 2 price for 100 days per year, a total of $200, as required. The direct costs and the current overhead are together met by the basic $3 charge included in all prices, $1 of this being just sufficient to cover the current overhead costs, since each individual hotel is always either full or closed.

The difference between this pattern of prices and those computed on the marginal-cost basis for the single unit derives from the technological difference between the two situations, namely, that in the large-scale case it was possible to cut the aggregate overhead operating costs in periods of slack demand by closing down a certain number of hotels, whereas in the single-hotel case it was assumed not to be correspondingly possible to save half of the operating overhead at times when the hotel is only half full. We can bring the two cases into more complete comparability by assuming that in the small-scale case the operating overhead varies directly with occupancy and in effect becomes a part of direct costs. Under such cost conditions, pricing at marginal cost in the single-hotel case would result in prices of $5 in period 1, $4 in period 2, and $3 at other times, exactly as in the large-scale competitive case. Sales, revenues, costs, consumer's surplus, and net social surplus would likewise all be proportionally just 1 per cent of the corresponding amounts for the larger case.

Or another way of making the two cases comparable would be to assume that the current overhead expenses are fixed at $300, regardless of how long the hotel stays open. Therefore, in the large-scale case the prices would be $6 in period 1, $5 in period 2, and $2 at other times, the only difference between this and the original case being that now it would be feasible to keep the hotel open in period 5, in the single-hotel case. Thus we can see that the pattern of pricing that was developed from marginal-cost criteria also is the pattern that emerges under conditions of perfect competition, at least where prices are completely flexible.

Quite generally, marginal cost pricing under conditions where there are fixed carrying costs and regular fluctuations in demand will require that where capacity is not fully utilized, prices cover only the direct costs, and that where demand at this price exceeds the capacity, the price is increased so as to just cut down the effective demand to this capacity. Capacity, in turn, in constant-returns-to-scale cases, must in the long run be adjusted to such a level that the total revenues over a complete period of demand variation at the prices determined in the above manner will just be sufficient to meet the total costs.

Competition with Inflexible Prices

OF COURSE, such a pricing pattern can be achieved only where it is possible to adjust prices rapidly enough (or far enough in advance) to keep in step with fluctuations in demand, and where at least the general level of demand is sufficiently predictable to enable capacity to be adjusted so as to satisfy the total-revenue condition. But even in economies that are completely stabilized in the over-all sense, fluctuations will occur in the day-to-day demand that are purely random in nature and cannot be predicted sufficiently far in advance to permit an equilibrium of price, supply, and demand to be reached at each instant. If such fluctuations, even though perfectly random, could be determined in advance and the appropriate adjustments made, there would be no problem that differs essentially from that of regular fluctuations, provided that the frequency distribution remains constant and known. For example, if the demand for hotel rooms in a certain locality averages 40 per day, and each guest determines the days on which he will want rooms independently of the others (i.e., without reference to any common event or season), the demand for rooms on a particular day will have a Poisson distribution, which for large numbers of rooms will approach a normal distribution. If each individual were to decide, say a week or a month in advance, on which days he will want rooms and how much he will be willing, if necessary, to pay for rooms on these days, and if he submitted this information to a marketing agency which would allot reservations in advance on the basis of such bids, then it would be possible for the prices for each day to be adjusted so as to just limit the demand to the supply, except for days when the price is dropped to the level of direct costs. If it is also possible to predict in advance with fair accuracy the number of days in each year on which the demand will be at various levels, even though it may not be known which days these will be, then the proper size of hotel or hotels to build could be determined. In this very special case the problem differs in no essential respect from the case in which the time as well as the duration of the various levels of demand is fully known in advance.

But in practice, of course, individuals make up their minds as to future plans with varying degrees of firmness and at varying lengths of time in advance, and they are not in the habit of disclosing the maximum price that they would be willing to pay for accommodations, so that the above theoretical scheme would break down in practice. Without such a scheme, adjustment of demand and supply through the price mechanism in the face of such random fluctuations may be difficult if not impossible, and other means of adjusting demand and supply must be resorted to. In some cases this is done by having a capacity and a price such that demand will exceed capacity only so infrequently that such contingencies can be treated more or less as emergencies. This type of adjustment is particularly frequent where the major unpredictable fluctuations occur on the supply side, as when unusually dry weather might result in a shortage of water-power, or where a breakdown or other casualty might take a major unit out of service. In such "emergency" situations, attempts may be made to reconcile supply and demand by appeals to self-restraint, or more drastic measures may be taken such as formal rationing, arbitrary regulation, or the cutting off of supply at certain times and places, or various more or less self-instituting adjustments may be allowed to operate, such as queuing, the intervention of speculators, or diminution in the quality, by overcrowding, lowering of voltage or pressure, increased slowness and delay, and the like.

The risk of such emergency shortage will affect both decisions as to how large a capacity should be installed and as to how close to the installed capacity the normal effective demand should be permitted to come through the reduction of price to short-run marginal cost. Indeed the short-run marginal cost in such situations may be considered to include an allowance for increased risk of occurrence of such emergencies, and for the increased severity of such emergencies when they do arise. But since even at the margin a private supplier has reflected to him only a part of the losses that the public suffers in cases of emergency shortage, in the form of loss of potential revenue

[245

and possible loss of good will, an unregulated decision as to aggregate capacity under conditions of perfect competition is likely to result in an inadequate supply from the social point of view, other things being equal.

Where the loss due to such occasional shortage of capacity is moderate, or at least is considered to be short of an emergency, capacity and price may be set at levels that produce a shortage for an appreciable proportion of the time and it may become both possible and desirable to apply analytical methods to the determination of proper levels of capacity and price. This is true in particular where acceptable, moderately close substitutes are available—for example, where a restaurant expects to run out of one or more dishes before the end of the day fairly frequently. In such cases the demand curve for a particular dish, other dishes assumed available at fixed prices, will be quite elastic, and the loss from rationing, i.e., from serving the scarce dishes to the first customers rather than to those who would have been willing to pay the greatest premium over competing prices for it, will be correspondingly small or even negligible. But where the available alternatives are remote or relatively unsatisfactory, the loss from rationing may be substantial. It is necessary to examine in some detail under what circumstances competition will produce optimal results in such cases.

To obtain a completely specified example of competition in such a case, let us return to our hotels, and assume that a group of perfectly competitive hotels at a resort have a peak season of 150 days, and that it is known that on about 100 of these days demand will be at the level previously designated as period 2, and that on the remaining 50 days during the peak season the demand will rise to the level previously designated as period 1. However, we will assume that it is not possible to predict sufficiently far in advance to permit the adjustment of prices which days are to be level 1 days and which days are to be level 2 days, although it is known which days are the peak period of 150 days as a whole, and which are the completely "off-season" days. Further, although the market is imperfect to the extent of not permitting price differentiation between level 1 days and level 2 days, it is otherwise perfect in that all guests make reservations sufficiently far in advance so that the loss resulting from failure to secure a room at the announced price in cases where no further reservations are available is limited to the loss of consumers' surplus as indicated by the contribution of the individual concerned to the demand curve, and does not contain any element of emergency loss such as might occur if a guest were to make plans on the assumption that a room would be available and arrive to meet with disappointment. The process of making reservations is supposed to be sufficiently well organized so as to involve negligible costs, and all hotels are supposed to have exactly similar accommodations so that prospective guests apply first to the hotel or hotels posting the lowest prices, and if refused try hotels in order of successively higher price until they either succeed in obtaining a room or reach a price higher than they are willing to pay. Each hotel can post whatever price it wishes for the busy season of 150 days and for the slack season constituting the rest of the year, and can determine for itself whether or not to stay open during the slack season, but is of course unable to differentiate its price as between level 1 days and level 2 days.

If we assume the simpler cost structure of $3 per room per night of direct costs and $200 per room of overhead and carrying charges, then during the slack season all hotels that remain open will charge $3, and a sufficient number of hotels will open during this season to take care of the demand at this price. Also, a sufficient number of hotels will charge $4.34 during the peak season to meet the level 2 demand at this price: no hotel can charge less than $4.34 during the peak season and meet its costs, even though it is full for the entire 150 days; on the other hand, if there were any unsatisfied customers at this price for level 2 days, there would also be such unsatisfied customers on level 1 days, and it would pay to construct a hotel to serve these customers at any price above $4.33. If we consider the equal elasticity case where the level 2 demand is $(80-8P)100$, this will mean that 4,528 rooms will be priced at $4.34. On level 1 days, however, demand at this price will be for 5,660 rooms, so that 1,132 would-be guests will be turned away from the $4.34 rooms. If we assume that these unsuccessful guests are a random sample of all those willing to pay $4.34, some of these guests will be willing to pay up to $10 for a room, and indeed it will be profitable to construct hotels that are expected to be occupied for only 50 days during the peak season provided that the price obtained is over $7. At the level 1 intensity of demand there will be altogether 3,000 guests willing to pay $7 or more, but as 4,528/5,660 of these, or 2,400, were among those able to secure accommodations at $4.34, there remain only 600 requiring rooms, and so 600 rooms will be priced at $7. Collecting $4 per room on 50 days of the year over and above the direct costs will just permit these hotels to meet their costs.

The result will be an equilibrium: no $7 hotel can gain by raising its price, as they would bear the entire burden of the resulting decrease in aggregate effective demand, and in the limiting case of a very large number of very small hotels, would lose all of their clients; moreover, this would create an opportunity for some new hotel to undercut them and make a profit (or even for one of the $4.34 hotels to do so); nor would it pay to cut the price to any point above $4.34, since on the level 2 days there is no additional demand to be had at any price above $4.34, and if the hotel is to be occupied only on level 1 days no price below $7 will permit breaking even. Dropping the price to $4.34 would merely again permit the hotel to break even even if it could thereby be full for the entire 150 days, and at a price below $4.34 it could not break even even if it were full for the full 150 days. Similarly, none of the low-priced hotels could gain by changing its price. There is no incentive either to leave or enter the industry, but if there is any variation in the number of rooms offered at either price, an incentive to leave or enter will be created.

A little further analysis along the lines of the argument on page 239 will show that this competitive equilibrium is also the mode of operation that maximizes the net social surplus, given the restrictions on price flexibility, but that this would no longer be true if the elasticities of the demand curves differed. It may be a little odd to think of equilibrium as a situation where different prices are charged for the same commodity in the same market; nevertheless, given the restraints on price flexibility, this is the result both of competition and of attempting to achieve an optimum allocation of resources, although the exact prices in the two cases will differ in general where demand elasticities differ. In practice, of course, the phenomenon may be partially concealed by the fact that there are usually some differences between the commodities or services offered at the different prices, and these differences may be given as the pretext for the price differentials. But in many cases the quality differences are not commensurate with the price differences, which are often much greater than would be justified by the quality differences alone; whether this is consciously realized or not, most of the price differential may be attributable not to the quality difference, but to the need for some means of adapting to the fluctuating demand, awkward though it may be.

The above discussion has of course all been in terms of extreme assumptions that result in a greatly oversimplified version of the problem of adjusting prices to fluctuating demand; this has been necessary in order to keep the analysis within the range of applicability of reasonably simple methods. In practice, of course, demand will not jump from one distinct level to another overnight, but will cover a whole range. In the case where the demand curve is considered to vary in a continuous rather than in a stepwise fashion, the problem of attaining optimum allocation of resources becomes a rather difficult problem in the calculus of variations, and at that one which is not solved by the application of the better-known methods, developed as they were to handle problems in mechanics and physics. Thus we see that the precise solution of even relatively simple economic problems is likely to involve mathematical difficulty of a fairly high order, or at least to require the development of new mathematical methods. And even this is before introducing any representation of quality differentials between the rooms in the various hotels.

The above discussion has, however, served to illustrate that when we go from perfect competition to what is sometimes termed "pure competition" in which we still have on the one hand individual suppliers faced with what they consider to be a perfectly elastic demand, but on the other hand imperfection in the pricing and marketing process in which the price does not always represent the marginal utility to the consumer of the last unit consumed, we no longer can be sure that the result obtained is an optimum one, even within the assumed constraints on price adjustments. In the more likely case where the peak demand is less elastic than the off-peak demand, we have in effect economies of greater utilization of a given capacity at lower prices, and an optimum is achieved only at prices that produce a net loss, and to obtain an optimum would, in the long run at least, require a subsidy. However, the net social loss resulting from choosing the best solution compatible with a normal profit or return on investment, rather than the best solution regardless of profit or loss, is not likely to be of a large magnitude in the more typical cases of this sort.

Decreasing-cost Industries

THE MUCH MORE important and pervasive type of situation where competition or regulated self-liquidating enterprise is incapable of producing the optimum allocation of resources is where increasing returns to scale, and especially internal economies within the firm, continue to prevail beyond the point where a single firm is supplying the demands of the entire economy, or of an appropriately delimited market area. In such cases, if price is made equal to marginal cost, there will be a net loss from the operation, since where there are economies of scale and, accordingly, average cost is declining, marginal cost must necessarily be less than average cost. The loss will of course be even greater if the price is below marginal cost. On the other hand, if price is above marginal cost, some demand will be blocked off that would have been willing to pay a price in excess of marginal cost, so that in the absence of special reasons to the contrary there would be a presumption that the social benefits resulting from the production of additional amounts of the commodity or service would exceed the social costs. Accordingly, production of such products and services can, in general, be brought to an optimum level only if some means of subsidizing the operation are available.

The extent to which decreasing costs prevail in modern production has been both exaggerated and minimized. To be sure, what is to be considered a significant degree of economy of scale depends on the context: for purposes of determining the size of firms and the viability of competition and evaluating the tendency to concentration and monopoly, a relatively small advantage accruing to larger scales of operation may turn the trick and be crucial. The difference between a technology tending to produce a fairly competitive organization of industry and one tending to produce a more or less monopolistic organization may be relatively minor. The degree to which the results obtainable on a self-liquidating basis fall short of an optimum, however, depends on the degree to which marginal cost falls short of average cost, and indeed for a given elasticity of demand, the quantitative measure of this relative social loss will vary roughly in proportion to the square of the difference between marginal and average cost. Thus it may well be that in the bulk

[249

of cases that are classifiable in the general category of increasing returns, the advantage of size is just large enough to produce a tendency toward monopoly, but yet not large enough to mean any substantial social loss if the industry is operated on a self-liquidating basis, whether by regulated private enterprise or by publicly owned enterprise. But there still remain several important areas in which economies of scale are sufficiently pronounced to produce substantial differences between long-run marginal and average costs, so that it is necessary at least to consider the loss involved in insisting on a self-liquidating basis of operation and the possibilities of subsidized operation.

The most striking examples of decreasing costs are those related in one way or another to a geographical dispersion of the production process or of the demand, or both. Transportation and public utilities, indeed, are the outstanding examples of decreasing-cost industries. It is obvious that in most cases the cost of providing the right-of-way for various volumes of traffic over a given route varies much less than in proportion to the capacity. Thus a two-track railway line will in general cost somewhat less than twice as much as a single-track line to construct and maintain to the same standards, but will be able to carry much more than twice as much traffic. To be sure, application of modern signaling and despatching methods, such as Centralized Traffic Control, have greatly increased the capacity of both single- and double-track lines, and indeed have made it economical in many cases to scrap extensive mileages of a second main track, with more traffic being handled over a single main track with long sidings than was formerly handled over a complete double-track line; such developments have probably increased the capacity of single-track lines relatively more than that of double-track lines, but substantial economies of scale still remain. Similarly, a four-lane highway may cost about twice as much per mile as a two-lane highway of comparable grade and alignment, and indeed it may sometimes consist substantially of two two-lane highways built parallel to each other; such a highway will usually be able to carry many times more traffic than the comparable two-lane highway before congestion or delays reach any given level. Six-inch pipe will cost less than four times as much as three-inch pipe, since the wall thickness will usually increase less than in proportion to the diameter; it will cost considerably less than twice as much to install, since the ditch will need to be much less than twice as wide; capacity to carry gas, water, or oil will be much more than four times as great, however, since while the area will be four times as great, the resistance to flow will be considerably smaller, permitting larger velocities to be maintained at the same head of pressure. Installation of telephone or telegraph poles may cost much the same whether there are two, ten, fifty, or a thousand circuits, and somewhat similar economies occur in the running of underground cable.

But in addition to such obvious economies, there are others that are sometimes overlooked. Heavier traffic on a railroad or bus line will often mean more frequent or faster service, which if not strictly a "decreasing cost" may at least be considered an "increasing return" in that the product is changed to one of greater value to the consumers. Or if service is not increased, but heavier traffic is accommodated merely by lengthening trains or running more sections, this will usually operate to permit a closer adaptation of the service supplied to the demand, so that, for example, the proportion of empty seats is reduced, with corresponding reduction in average cost per occupied seat. Or in the long run increased traffic may mean, instead of heavier traffic along a given network of routes, the establishment of new routes producing a denser network, so that the amount of travel required to reach a given destination is reduced; for example, instead of having to go from A to C via B, a distance of 450 miles, the same trip can be accomplished by going directly from A to C, a distance of only 400 miles. This may show up in the statistics as a reduction in ton-miles or passenger-miles of service rendered, but the value of the service to the consumer is determined by the points of origin and destination and not by the mileage actually traveled; so that here is another source of long-run diminishing costs or increasing returns. Again, if the more extensive network brings the service nearer to the consumer, the service becomes more valuable: if there are two bus routes rather than one, the average walk to and from the bus is likely to be shorter.

Transportation may also be the factor that limits the market to a degree where the output from a single plant cannot economically be large enough to exhaust all the economies of scale within the plant. This is particularly true for products for which the raw materials are widely distributed in nature, and that are of great bulk or weight in relation to their value. For example, where the demand for hydraulic cement is scattered over a wide area, attempting to concentrate production in plants sufficiently large to exhaust the economies of scale available within the plant would result in long hauls of the product and unduly high transportation costs; smaller plants, even though not achieving the minimum possible cost f.o.b. the plant, will result in a saving in the cost of shipping the product to the consumer. An optimum adjustment in such cases will involve determining the size and location of plants so that the optimal output is produced at minimum total cost, transportation and production costs considered together. If such an optimum adjustment is achieved, plants will be smaller than would give minimum average production cost, and marginal cost at each plant will be less than average cost. There would thus be occasion for subsidy to the production stage, if optimum allocation is to be achieved, in addition to any subsidy that might be provided for with respect to the transportation of the product as such.

The other major class of substantial economies of scale is found in industries whose function is to reproduce and disseminate original or creative works. This will include almost the entire printing and publishing industry, the motion-picture industry, and to a lesser extent the theater. Job printing might be thought of as a decreasing-cost industry, but here the economies of scale are predominantly related to the size of the individual order, and the price schedule can adequately reflect the incremental and marginal costs of the work done for each individual customer and still produce revenues sufficient to cover total costs. Radio and television would also be in this category if they were financed by fees collected from listeners; their financing by advertisers, however, is a symptom of imperfect competition that is difficult to fit within a framework of abstract perfect competition, and in these industries consumer sovereignty is honored at best in a very indirect and biased manner.

Indeed, the most pervasive of all decreasing-cost elements may well be considered to arise in the selling effort required to overcome the inevitable frictions and imperfections in the market. The cost of acquainting a given body of consumers with the properties, real or claimed, of a product is virtually independent of the volume of production. If anything, this cost diminishes as output increases: as the volume of use of a given product increases within a given area a certain amount of word-of-mouth advertising will take place at no cost to the producer; there are also economies of scale in advertising as the potential market area is enlarged, since many advertising media are prohibitively expensive unless the product has a wide distribution. Advertising is of course needed only in imperfect markets, but imperfect information of consumers is a fact that must be dealt with even in Utopia.

In addition to the more important cases of decreasing costs, there are large numbers of products that are so specialized and the market for which is so small that production in a single plant for a nation-wide or even a world-wide market is still on such a small scale as to remain under conditions of decreasing cost. This case is seldom seen in its pure form, as many of the items are patented, which adds an institutional-monopoly element to the natural semi-monopoly element. In some cases the item is manufactured on special order and in part to individual specification, thus blurring the identity of the product and causing some of the economies of scale to become internal to the particular customer, as shows up in extreme form in job printing, while in most cases the product will be only one of a number of products made by the firm. Slug rejectors for vending machines, some types of hospital equipment, specialized machine tools, and apparatus for simultaneous translation at international conferences can be cited as a few of many examples. However, the decreasing-cost elements in such cases are usually either moderate in force, or where they are substantial in relation to the industry itself, are still relatively unimportant in relation to the entire economic system. For the time being we will focus our attention on the more substantial instances of economy of scale.

If for the moment we can overlook the fact that in almost all important cases of decreasing costs the product is of a very complex character, the difference between operating at a self-liquidating price and operating at marginal-cost prices may be illustrated by reference to FIGURE 64. If we can describe the output of the railroads of the United States in terms of a hypothetical uniform composite "ton-mile," and can assume that at an output of 700 billion ton-miles per year total costs of freight service can just be covered by an average revenue of 1.25 cents per ton-mile, this will give us a point on the average-cost curve, shown at *A*. If we further estimate that marginal cost is 68 per cent of average cost, and that this relationship is fairly constant for a substantial range of outputs beyond this level, as appears to be

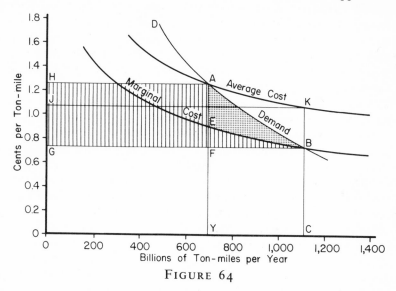

FIGURE 64

not unreasonable for the long run, segments of the average- and marginal-cost curves can be drawn as shown. The relationships will be:

$$A = A_0\left(\frac{x}{x_0}\right)^{e-1}, \qquad M = eA = M_0\left(\frac{x}{x_0}\right)^{e-1}$$

where *A* is average cost, *M* is marginal cost, and *e* is the elasticity of cost with respect to output; the subscript o indicates the point of initial observation. If we further assume a demand curve of unit elasticity, which may be somewhat high if we were considering only the short run, but which would be quite possible if a very long-run point of view is taken in which industries may relocate to a substantial extent if freight rates are changed, and if *A* is also an observed point on the demand curve, the demand curve *DAB* can be drawn. The point *A* will then be the point of self-liquidating operation where revenues cover costs, and the point *B* where the demand curve intersects the marginal-cost curve would represent the operation on a marginal-cost basis, where an optimum allocation of resources would be secured, with average

[253

revenues of 0.7 cents per ton-mile and total output of 1,250 billion ton-miles. The average cost CK would be about 1.03 cents per ton-mile, or a total cost of $12,875 million, which can be represented either by the rectangle oJKC, or by the area o$HAEBC$, obtained by adding to the rectangle oHAY, representing the cost of the original output oY, the marginal costs of the additional units of output from oY to oC, i.e., the area under the marginal-cost curve, $YEBC$. Revenues, represented by oGBC would be $8,750 million, producing a net loss of $4,125 million, represented by the area $HAEBG$, which would have to be made up by a subsidy. The consumers' surplus, however, would be increased by $5,225 million, shown as area $HABG$, leaving a net increase in social surplus of AEB, or $1.1 billion, which would constitute a net addition to the real national product if it could be assumed that the funds for the $4,125 million subsidy could be obtained without producing misallocations of resources elsewhere in the economy.

Of course, railroad freight service is not a homogeneous product, but one that has several parameters, and as we saw even in the relatively simple case of hotel service, wide variations in marginal cost occur even within what seem to be very similar classes of service. A railroad-rate structure based on marginal cost would by no means be a simple one, though perhaps not as complex as the tariffs currently in use. Where, however, subsidy is either out of the question entirely, or is in practice so costly in other directions as to warrant raising rates above marginal-cost levels, still further complexities in the rate structure are often warranted. For even where service is actually fairly homogeneous from the point of view of cost, the market for such services can often be subdivided in various ways and different rates applied in different markets. If, for example, the rate reflecting marginal cost is made available only to one part of the demand, the remainder being required to pay a higher rate, we may find a situation such as that in FIGURE 65. The demand curve JK represents that part of the total demand that is not eligible for the low rate, and must therefore pay the higher rate oS, at which rate an amount SJ of this traffic will actually move. If we add to this the amount of the low-rate traffic that will move at various levels of the lower rate, we get the curve WM showing the total demand for various levels of the lower rate. If the lower rate is to be equal to the marginal cost of the combined demand, it will be set at oV (slightly higher than CB in the previous case), and there will be LK (= MN) of the potential traffic that would be willing to pay more than marginal cost but is ineligible for the marginal-cost rate. The amount by which the net social surplus falls short of that under a uniform marginal-cost price is the area JLK (= MNW) plus the area MNB, representing the effect on marginal cost itself of an increase in output; these two areas may be combined to give BMW.

Now if the price oS is sufficiently higher than the average cost oC of the output equal to the noneligible demand SJ, so that the excess revenue $SQRJ$

is sufficient to cover the amount TLM by which the incremental cost $TUZM$ of the entire balance of the output exceeds the revenues $LMZU$ from the marginal-cost rate, then this combination of rates will be able to cover total costs. And if the ineligible demand curve JK is sufficiently less elastic than the total demand, the net social loss (as compared with setting price at marginal cost) $JLK + MNB = BMW$ may be less than that under a uniform rate, shown in the preceding case as AEB.

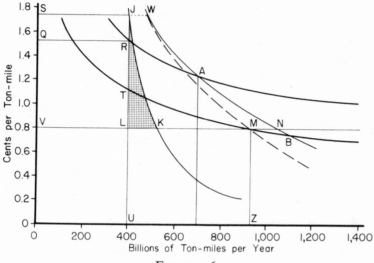

FIGURE 65

Thus with the aid of discriminatory rates of various kinds it may be possible to reduce the gap between self-liquidating operation and subsidized marginal-cost operation, in terms of loss of net social surplus. But it is not possible to close the gap entirely, for there will in general always be some elasticity in the demand that is ineligible for the marginal-cost rate, and hence some exclusion of customers whom it would be economical to serve. Indeed, the best combination of discriminatory rates will ordinarily have its lowest rate slightly above marginal cost, even for the most restricted and most elastic class of customers, since for the first increments of revenue obtained by raising price slightly above marginal cost the net loss produced is vanishingly small. The problem of determining the best possible price or rate structure compatible with covering total cost (or with earning a specified profit or incurring only a specified deficit) is formally quite analogous to that of a discriminating monopolist attempting to maximize profits and will be discussed below on pages 294–97.

But while discrimination can be justified on these grounds, it does not follow that the discriminations actually practiced are so justifiable. Indeed,

[255

discriminatory practices are often based on quite other grounds, such as historical precedent, priority of use, arbitrary accounting rules, or "ability to pay" (which may indeed be another name for inelasticity of demand, but often is not). The railroad-rate structure today bears a substantial imprint of patterns left over from the horse-and-buggy era, with many features that are indefensible economically, but are firmly entrenched behind an impenetrable tangle of administrative procedures and inertia.

On the other hand, price differentials need not be discriminatory. Many such differentials merely reflect differences in the marginal cost of supplying what are essentially different products. Not only are there different grades of service, different locations, and the like, but often what may superficially seem to be identical services turn out on examination to be economically quite different in terms of cost. Estimating marginal cost for each of various types of service is essentially a straightforward technical matter, involving an estimate of the increment in costs that would be associated with a given increment in service under given circumstances. This is in some contrast to the determination of "full cost" or "average cost" for any particular product of a multiple-product decreasing-cost operation. Of necessity such a determination will involve a more or less arbitrary allocation of the joint costs according to some sort of more or less plausible rule. Thus it is possible, in principle at least, to say what the marginal cost of power is at a given time and place, even in a complex interrelated operation such as TVA; or, similarly, what the marginal cost of carrying additional carloads of a specified commodity between two points at a given time would be; it is not possible to determine how much of the total costs should be allocated to these particular products without a considerable degree of arbitrariness.

We have seen that where there are seasonal fluctuations in the demand for a service that cannot readily be stored, delivery of identical items at different times may have to be considered different products from an economic viewpoint. The same concept can be extended to cases where demand conditions vary over the useful life of an item of capital equipment: the cost of the capital equipment is a joint cost of producing the outputs of the various periods. In a constant-cost situation there will in general be some way of allotting the cost of this capital to the output of the various periods, through depreciation or other similar charges, so that the market will be cleared in each period and the total cost thus computed will just be covered by the revenues. However, where there are economies of scale associated with the capital equipment, the distribution of the capital cost over the product of the various periods is correspondingly indeterminate, and there is no inherently correct rule by which to determine, without reference to demand conditions, whether it is better to depreciate rapidly, keeping prices high at first and slowing the expansion of the industry, or whether to depreciate slowly, thus keeping prices low and stimulating an early growth of demand.

More generally, whenever production is being carried on under constant-returns conditions, then the Euler theorem on linear homogeneous functions shows that if all of the various products are priced at marginal cost, the total revenue thus derived will equal total cost. If decreasing costs prevail, then pricing each product at its marginal cost leaves an "intra-marginal residue" of costs not covered by the revenues produced by such prices. By analogy with the contrasting case of increasing costs, such residues are sometimes termed "negative rents," in that they are the exact opposite of the positive economic rents produced when there are increasing costs and revenues at marginal-cost rates exceed the total costs leaving a residue to be imputed as rents to the factors whose imperfect reproducibility led to the increasing costs. There will in general be no way of determining from the character of the production process how this intra-marginal residue should be apportioned among the various products. No one apportionment will have any logical precedence over any other, though some may have a somewhat greater aura of superficial reasonableness.

If we can assume, as has tacitly been done above, that the production function is generally smooth, it may make but a negligible difference how large a unit, within reason, is taken as the basis for computing marginal cost. Strictly speaking, the term "marginal cost" implies that the increment is made vanishingly small; when an increment of substantial size is being considered, this is often distinguished by speaking of incremental cost. But where the production function is uneven—for example, where service or capacity can only be added in fairly large discrete units, as with ocean-passenger service; where demand fluctuates more rapidly than the service or its price can readily be adjusted to meet it, as may happen to transit service when a baseball game is rained out; or where two or more types of service are more or less rigidly tied together so that one cannot be furnished without going a large part of the way toward furnishing another in corresponding amounts, as is true of upper and lower berths in open-section Pullman cars—the value obtained for marginal or incremental cost may depend critically on the size of the unit chosen in making this evaluation. A marginal cost based on an increment consisting of the minimum unit of sale might well fluctuate so erratically that it would be impossible or prohibitively expensive to keep the price equal to marginal cost for every variety of service at every instant. Even if it could be done, a complicated and fluctuating price structure might so confuse customers as to hinder rather than assist them in adjusting their consumption so as to make the best use of the possibilities inherent in a given set of resources and production functions. In such cases a marginal cost computed from a very small increment of a particular variety of product under narrowly defined circumstances may be largely irrelevant. At the time the price is set, the demand that will be evoked by any given price may be uncertain within a considerable range, the range itself depending to a considerable extent on how far in

[257

advance it is necessary to fix the price. The kind of marginal cost that would be relevant for the fixing of rates under such circumstances would be one based on an increment of output of the same order of magnitude as this range of uncertainty in the demand, or perhaps corresponding to the change in effective demand to be expected from the smallest change in price that it is deemed to be worth making. This would mean in general that the more flexible the price policy that can be used, or the shorter the notice required for the putting into effect of price changes, or the greater the detail and the smaller the minimum difference considered permissible in the price structure, the smaller will be the increment of service that can justifiably be used in the computation of the marginal cost from which the price structure is to be derived.

Similarly, where two or more services are produced in a fixed proportion, it will often be wasteful over a wide range of market conditions to produce an increment of one kind of service without also producing the others that are complementary to it. For such a purpose the relevant increment of production would be a composite increment of the entire group of complementary services, and the marginal cost of the entire increment would be apportioned among its components according to the state of the market.

Thus while it is possible that a completely flexible price policy that followed every erratic fluctuation of marginal cost as computed from the smallest possible increments would be too complex and confusing to be useful, a more reasonable interpretation of the principle of marginal-cost pricing based on more substantial increments is quite feasible. Very little practical work has been done, however, upon the application of marginal-cost-pricing principles to concrete situations, and there is a great deal that remains to be done in the field of devising price structures for the purpose of promoting the efficient allocation of resources. Indeed, many parts of this field seem to be still almost virgin territory, even on the theoretical level, while it is hardly too much to say that some of the pricing practices presently indulged in, and even by agencies supposedly set up for the purpose of promoting the general welfare, verge on insanity, when appraised from the point of view of the economizing of resources or the behavior of marginal cost, however logical they may appear in terms of the political and administrative backgrounds of these agencies. Thus tolls are charged on bridges and highways in terms of the history of the individual facility, with little or no relation to congestion and current or future marginal costs, with the result that tolls are high on routes having low marginal cost and little congestion, and are low or absent on older routes having high congestion and high marginal costs. The various classes of fares charged on suburban trains vary almost in exact inverse relationship to the marginal costs of the traffic to which they apply. Freight rates for competing modes of transportation, and especially for competing railroad routes, are often set on the basis of securing for each mode or route a "fair share" of the traffic, regardless of relative marginal costs.

258]

When price rigidities become too extreme, partial amelioration of the situation is often found through the medium of the "speculator." In an ideal competitive case a producer, having decided how much of a service to provide at some future date, but lacking the facilities for varying the price from day to day, might sell his tickets to speculators on the basis of competitive bids, the speculators in turn varying their price as the date of the performance approaches according to their estimates of the state of demand, with speculators expecting to make a profit when demand turns out to be stronger than anticipated, and on the other hand dumping their tickets on the market for what they will bring if at the last minute they have unsold tickets on hand. Such speculators would be performing a socially useful service if they provided a means for raising the price when demand turns out to be strong and lowering it when demand turns out to be weak, on the one hand minimizing the amount of the service that goes unused, and on the other insuring that those who find they badly need the service at the last minute will usually be able to obtain it, even though the price may be high. In other words, utilization will be generally more complete, the service being used on the whole by consumers to whom it is worth more, than would be the case if the service were sold entirely on a first-come-first-served basis at a fixed price.

Of course, in practice matters do not work out this nicely, and particularly where speculators are regulated, ostracized, or forced to operate quasi-clandestinely, the degree to which they improve the allocation of resources will be impaired, while the resources absorbed by their operations will increase to the point where there may be no net gain. But it is important to realize that such speculation often does have a purpose to serve, even though this purpose usually gets buried under the other less savory aspects of their operations.

The Costs of Securing Public Funds

BEFORE leaving the problem of optimum allocation of resources with respect to decreasing-cost industries, it should be noted very emphatically that the above analysis has made the tacit simplifying assumption that the process of obtaining the funds, presumably by taxation, to defray the required subsidies is itself a costless transfer, and that the required increase in tax rates will not in itself have a distorting effect on the allocation of resources. Also, we have ignored any redistributive effects that such subsidy and taxation might have.

The redistributive effects can in principle be dismissed rather simply if we are willing to assume, as seems reasonable, that a redistribution of income within an appropriately defined income stratum can be considered neutral with respect to whatever values are being used as a standard for judgment. For we can estimate the distribution by income classes of the increase in consumer's surplus resulting from adopting a marginal-cost-pricing policy in any given class of projects or industries. If these projects are worthwhile at

[259

all, the tax required to finance this policy will be less than the sum of these consumer's surpluses. By a suitable choice of increments in the income-tax schedule, it will in general be possible to levy the increased tax in such a way that the increment of tax in each income class is less than the aggregate increment in consumer's surplus in that class. As a net result of the two measures, we will thus be able to say that each income class in the aggregate is better off, and that to the extent that any individuals are worse off, there are corresponding individuals in the same income class that are better off by a larger amount measured in money.

In effect, what would be achieved by such a "reorganization" can be thought of as the resultant of two changes: first a change in which every individual is made better off by being required to pay a tax of less than the addition to his individual consumer's surplus, followed by a more or less random redistribution of income among the members of each income class. The first change is unequivocally beneficial, while the second change can be expected to be acceptable as being more or less neutral, or approximately so. The combination of the two should therefore be regarded as beneficial. Indeed, if the class of projects to be shifted to a subsidized marginal-cost basis is made sufficiently broad, so that the number of individual projects is large and their effects widespread, it is not unlikely that the number of persons adversely affected by the reorganization might become vanishingly small, so that possible objections to the redistribution-of-income element in the reorganization would have very scant grounds. Even where on the occasion of the shifting of an individual project to a marginal-cost basis it is not possible to keep the number of those adversely affected down to a negligible figure, this approach can be made applicable by regarding such a measure as an initial step in an indefinite sequence of projects to which the same general policy is to be applied. For many economists, even this would be quite unnecessary to persuade them to consider the change as justified.

The effects of the increase in the tax on the allocation of resources cannot be dismissed so easily. To begin with, the process of collecting taxes is costly and absorbs a certain quantity of resources directly. To be sure, if we assume that the increment of tax is to be obtained by increasing the rates of existing taxes rather than by the imposition of new taxes, much of the cost of collection will be independent of the rates, and the "marginal collection cost" may be considerably less than the "average collection cost." Nevertheless, it would be rash to assume that it is negligible, and there is, moreover, always the possibility that a point will be reached where rates on existing taxes are so high as to require the introduction of new taxes if additional revenue is to be secured.

More important, nearly all taxes (with the possible exceptions of poll taxes, taxes on site values, perhaps some forms of succession taxes, and taxes on monopoly profits) disturb the relationships between alternatives and thus affect decisions at the margin, usually in a direction away from the optimum allocation of resources. Excise taxes, indeed, produce differentials between marginal cost and market price of precisely the type that the subsidy considered above is intended to reduce. Even income taxes, often treated in economic theory as unshiftable, prove in practice to affect decisions as to the use of resources and are thus in part shifted. Of course, many of the points at which income taxes in practice interfere with optimum allocation may be traced to defects in the way the law is drawn up or applied, representing departures from what a universal and uniform income tax should be. But even a Simon-pure income tax agreeing strictly with theoretical concepts would interfere with optimum allocation to an extent that can hardly be ignored.

One of the less striking effects of an income tax is its tendency to distort the choice between consuming in the present and saving for future consumption. This defect can in principle be cured by shifting to a progressive tax on personal consumption expenditures, excluding savings from the tax base and including dissavings. But there still remains the fact that money income from gainful work is subject to an income tax while imputed income from leisure is not taxed, nor does there seem to be any way of including such an intangible item in the income-tax base (though possibly a step in this direction could be taken in obverse fashion by exempting from income tax all earnings from overtime work). Accordingly, an income tax tends to make individuals choose leisure in preference to gainful work to an uneconomical extent, in the sense that individuals will be influenced toward giving up market goods purchasable with the proceeds of the last hours of gainful employment, in return for the privilege of enjoying more leisure, to such an extent that the last hours of leisure secured could, if devoted to production, produce market goods that the individual himself would value more highly than the leisure. This is because at the point of competitive equilibrium the marginal utility of leisure will be less, by the amount of the income tax, than the wage rate which represents the marginal productivity of the corresponding labor time. Spendings taxes, sales taxes, and excises all have this effect in that they impinge only on forms of economic activity involving money exchange, or at least closely similar forms of organized economic activity, and do not bear equally heavily on income in kind and especially on the consumption of one's own services in the form of leisure.

Conceivably, if taxes were levied in the form of a graduated poll tax—the basis for which would be not the income actually earned, but rather the income that an individual would be able to earn by working a standard work week with a standard intensity of application—this difficulty would be circumvented. In practice, however, such a tax would necessarily be based on some external indicia of individual capabilities, at least some of which would be under the control of the individual being taxed, so that the imposition of the

[261

tax would have a tendency to induce the individual to suppress these indicia and thus again disturb the allocation of resources.

Thus even with the best conceivable tax system, there are detriments attached to the raising of additional revenue, over and above the mere transfer aspects. Accordingly, where differences between marginal and average costs are not great, or where the elasticity of demand or supply is small, it may not be worthwhile to go through with the program of lowering prices to marginal cost by means of a subsidy, since in such cases the damage done by increased

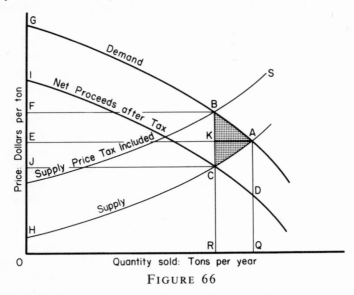

FIGURE 66

tax rates may outweigh the benefits coming from better utilization of the facilities of the particular industry. And even where subsidy is resorted to, it will usually be better to lower prices not quite to the marginal-cost level, thus reducing the amount of subsidy required while impairing the adjustment in the particular industry by only a relatively small amount.

Indeed, we may think of the difference between price and marginal cost in a publicly owned industry as a sort of tax. The final price structure can then be thought of as having been arrived at by first lowering all prices to marginal cost, and then imposing taxes on these prices as well as on the prices prevailing in other industries generally, so as to raise the revenue required to balance the budget or meet whatever standard or over-all fiscal policy is adopted. If we still abstract from distributional aspects, the problem may be considered one of so distributing these taxes as to minimize the damage done to the allocation of resources while still raising the required revenue.

In the simple case of a tax on a single product with a rising supply curve, the net loss produced by the imposition of an excise tax can be measured in terms of FIGURE 66. If the supply curve is *HCA*, which would correspond, in the competitive case, with the marginal-social-cost curve, obtained by adding horizontally the marginal-cost or supply curves of the competing suppliers, and the demand curve is *GBA*, being similarly a marginal-social-value curve, then in the absence of a tax the competitive equilibrium will be indicated by the intersection of these two curves at *A*, with an output o*Q* and a price *QA*. There will be a consumer's surplus *GAE*, and a producer's surplus *HAE*, the latter representing the rent attributable to the excess of the productivity of specialized factors when applied to this industry over their productivity in the next best alternative. The total net social surplus derived from the existence of this industry is then *AHG*; this area can be thought of as representing how much individuals are better off, in the aggregate, because of the existence of this industry, as compared with their state if the particular product had never been developed or its manufacture were prohibited entirely in some way.

Now if a tax per unit of output is imposed equal to *BC*, this can be regarded as an addition to costs, raising the supply curve to *BS*, reducing the equilibrium output to o*R*, with a price, inclusive of tax of *RB*, indicated by the intersection of this new supply curve with the demand curve. Or if the tax is considered to be paid by consumers, the same results can be indicated by lowering the demand curve by the amount of the tax, to *CD*, intersecting the old supply curve at *C*, again indicating an output of o*R*, at a price, net of tax, of *RC*. The total tax revenue will be the rectangle *BCJF*. As far as consumers are concerned, the effect is that the price has been increased to *RB*, or o*F*, and thus the consumers' surplus is reduced to *BFG*. Similarly, the competitive suppliers are concerned directly only with the fact that the net price of their product has been lowered from o*E* to o*J*, and the producers' surplus will now be *HJC*. Adding together the tax revenue and the two surpluses, we get the area *HCBG* as the net social surplus now produced by the operation of the industry; this is less than the previous surplus by the amount *ABC*, and this can be taken to be the net loss resulting from the imposition of the tax.

If the demand and supply curves can be treated as approximately straight lines over the ranges of output under consideration, then the amount of the loss *ABC* can be estimated as $\frac{1}{2}\overline{BC}\cdot\overline{AK} = \frac{1}{2}t\Delta q$, where t is the tax per unit of product Δq is the resulting reduction in sales. Further, the change in output Δq will, for straight-line demand and supply curves, be proportional to the tax rate, so that the net loss will vary approximately as the square of the tax rate, whereas the revenue will vary somewhat less than in proportion to the tax rate. For example, a doubling of the tax rate will less than double the revenue, since the tax base will tend to diminish, but it will approximately quadruple the net social loss. Accordingly, to obtain a given net revenue with a minimum aggregate net social loss, it is in general better to have a large number of small taxes than a few large ones, aside from administrative considerations, which often weigh in the other direction. For example, if there are two industries of similar size with similar supply and demand curves, then instead of putting a tax of $2t$ on industry A and none on B, which would give a net loss of, say, $k(2t)^2 = 4kt^2$, it would be desirable to put a tax of t on both A and B, which would produce at least as much revenue, and the net loss would be only kt^2 for each industry, or altogether $2kt^2$.

This is not to say, however, that the tax system that minimizes interference with the optimum allocation of resources is one that is spread evenly on all

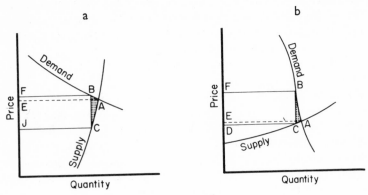

FIGURE 67

products. The relation of the net loss to the revenue varies also according to the elasticity of supply and demand. If, for example, the supply curve is very inelastic, as is illustrated in FIGURE 67a, the ratio of the net loss ABC to the revenue $BCJF$ may be relatively small even for fairly large tax rates, and to a large extent regardless of the elasticity of the demand curve. This is notably the case for land (as distinguished from buildings and other improvements); except for such peripheral operations as irrigation, terracing, drainage, and filling, the supply is substantially fixed, and taxes on land even at high rates have almost no effect on the allocation of resources, aside from the possible income effects produced through changes in the distribution of incomes. In a case such as this, the tax burden falls almost entirely on the seller or lessor of the inelastic resource.

Similarly, if the demand curve is inelastic, the loss may again be relatively small, regardless of the elasticity of the supply curve, as is shown in FIGURE 67b. Thus a tax on sugar (or the much-condemned tax on salt) would be a relatively good tax from the point of view of its effects on the allocation of resources. The demand for cigarettes appears also to be relatively inelastic, and the cigarette tax may thus be a fairly good tax from this point of view, putting aside arguments based on external diseconomies, such as fire hazard, or irksomeness to nonsmokers, or sheer moral disapproval. In cases such as this, the burden of the tax falls almost entirely on the purchaser.

This analysis can be extended directly to cover a "pseudo-tax" applied to increase the price of a decreasing-cost product above its marginal cost: the only difference is that the marginal-cost curve takes the place of the supply curve, and the net social loss becomes an area similar to *BEA* in FIGURE 64. Instead of a positive producers' surplus or rent to be added in in computing an aggregate surplus, there is the "intra-marginal residue" or "negative rent" arising in the operation that is to be deducted from the consumers' surplus. And since the marginal-cost curve may be declining, it will in general be only by reason of the inelasticity of the demand curve that the loss resulting from such a pseudo-tax will be kept small relative to the "pseudo-revenue" obtained thereby. Moreover, where an operating agency is required to just cover its total costs from a large number of different products, either as a regulated private company or as an independent self-liquidating public agency, a similar analysis can be applied to indicate how this may be done with a minimum loss from departure from the optimum allocation of resources.

Care must be taken in such analysis, however, to define the marginal-cost curve properly. The marginal cost that is wanted as a criterion for setting a price which will produce an optimum allocation of resources is a marginal social cost, which normally will correspond to a marginal cost computed on the assumption that the prices of the factors used remain constant. Where the demand of the industry for some particular factor is sufficient to drive its price up as the industry expands, this will give rise to an "external diseconomy" in the factor market; if a total cost were figured for different outputs using correspondingly different levels of factor prices, and a marginal-cost curve were derived from this, it would lie above the marginal social cost, since the additional amount that factors already used by the industry will get as a result of the heavier demand for their services is not a social cost but a transfer of income. Indeed, an industry could be affected with internal economies of scale and external market diseconomies of scale to exactly balancing degrees, so that the average cost at different levels of output is exactly the same, but nevertheless such an industry would still require subsidy if price were to be set at marginal social cost for the sake of preserving the optimum allocation of resources.

We must also take care, in using areas between demand and supply curves as measures of surplus or loss, to confine this use to cases where the underlying assumptions involved in interpreting these areas in this way are reasonably valid. Thus we must come reasonably close to having a constant marginal utility of money, or at least an absence of substantial income effects. That is, the inelasticity of supply or demand upon which is predicated the smallness of a net social loss must be traceable to the smallness of the substitution effect and not to a mere offsetting of a large substitution effect by an equally large

[265

and opposite income effect. For example, even though the supply of labor at a given point may be completely inelastic or even perverse, this does not mean that an income tax will not upset the equilibrium between leisure and remunerative work. It is the marginal indifference curve that accurately reflects consumers' surplus, and this will ordinarily have a substantial elasticity even when the demand curve is inelastic or perverse. Or to put it another way, equilibrium under an income tax may result in the same amount of labor being supplied as without it, the greater need for money offsetting the lower net rate of pay after tax; but this is still considerably different from the equilibrium that would result if the same amount of money had been abstracted in the form of a poll tax, in which case the net marginal rate of pay would not be reduced and the incentive to work would be unimpaired; the optimum allocation of resources would call for an actual increase in the amount of labor offered, in response to the increased need for income as a result of the imposition of the poll tax.

The general conclusion from all this is that given the practical impossibility of preserving at all points the ideal equality between marginal cost, price, and marginal utility, the discrepancies should be fairly well scattered throughout the economy rather than concentrated entirely on a few prices; the discrepancies should be relatively higher where substitution effects are small, as is ordinarily the case where demand or supply curves are inelastic.

EXERCISES

I

PLANS exist for five widely separated bridges, and studies of potential traffic indicate that the demand for passage over *each* will be as follows (independently of what is done concerning any of the other bridges):

RATE OF TOLL	VEHICLES PER DAY
none	1,000
$ .20	800
.50	500
.99	10
1.00	0

the demand curve being linear and the same for each bridge. Bridge *A* can be financed for charges of $600 per day; bridges *B*, *C*, *D*, and *E*, for $330, $310, $160, and $160, respectively, cost being independent of traffic.

Which bridges will be built, what will be the tolls charged, and what will be the addition to the real national income (net social benefit) if:

a. Franchises are awarded to unregulated monopolists.

b. Operation of each bridge is given over to a separate public authority, each such authority being required to cover its own costs from tolls.

c. Bridges are operated by a single authority, which can draw on general revenues (assumed to have no costs of collection) to the extent necessary to produce the maximum net benefit.

d. What will be the result if all of the bridges are placed under a single authority which must cover its costs over-all, but which may take a loss on one bridge to be made up by profits on others, seeking to maximize the net social gain. (Caution: Examine the results when different numbers of bridges are built.) (Hint: Construct a table of total revenue and total utility for different tolls, at intervals of ten cents.) What could such an authority accomplish if it were allotted a subsidy of $360 per day from general funds? How great would be the overhead and other collection costs of providing this subsidy have to become before the subsidy would no longer be worthwhile? Compare this with 1c.

II

THE construction of a bridge at one of two alternative sites is under consideration, one of the sites being considerably cheaper but less attractive to traffic, as indicated by the following table:

ANNUAL COST	ANNUAL TRAFFIC AT TOLLS OF						
	.60	.50	.40	.30	.20	.10	free
		(Thousands of vehicles per year)					
Bridge A $20,000	0	40	80	120	160	200	240
Bridge B $80,000	0	100	200	300	400	500	600

Three modes of procedure are being considered: (a) to sell the franchise for either bridge at the option of the contractor on the basis of the highest bid in terms of a fixed annual payment, the contractor being free to fix whatever toll he pleases; (b) to award the franchise, without payment, to the contractor who will contract for the lowest rate of toll; (c) to operate as a free facility. Compare the three alternatives in terms of welfare economics.

[267

CHAPTER SIX

The New Welfare Economics

I N THE PREVIOUS chapter we have gone merrily on our way assuming that it was legitimate to make comparisons of possible gains to one group of individuals with possible losses to others. Many of the more restrained economists, however, have looked somewhat askance at such practices, and, maintaining that economists *qua* economists should ideally refrain from all such interpersonal comparisons, have sought to place welfare economics on a sounder footing by developing a basis for policy recommendations that would be free of such taint. While very little in the form of additional practical policy recommendations has resulted, the analysis has provided many insights into the nature of economic value judgments.

Initially, it might seem that a strict proscription of all interpersonal comparisons would restrict economists to recommending only those changes that benefit some people without harming others; economics would then be able to make normative pronouncements only very rarely, and then these pronouncements would be fairly trivial. To escape from this dead end, Hicks and Kaldor began by proposing that any reorganization or change in the economic structure should be considered on balance beneficial if, after the reorganization has taken place, there exists a hypothetical set of payments from those who gained from the reorganization to those who lost, such that the making of these payments would leave nobody worse off on balance, and some better off. Note that if the compensation payments are actually made, we are back in the trivial "unanimous consent" case; the point of the proposal is that the reorganization in such a case should be considered desirable even if the corresponding compensation payments are not actually made, and in fact even if, as a practical matter, the compensation could not actually be carried out—for example, because of lack of information as to precisely to whom and from whom the payments are to be made. It would be possible in many cases to state with confidence that the money value of the gains exceeded the money value of the losses, without being able to evaluate the gains or losses for any particular individual.

For this criterion to mean anything, it is necessary to specify that the compensation payments be made in a specified numéraire, or "money," otherwise the criterion becomes meaningless, at least in the pure exchange economy: given an initial situation not on the contract curve, *any* move away from it

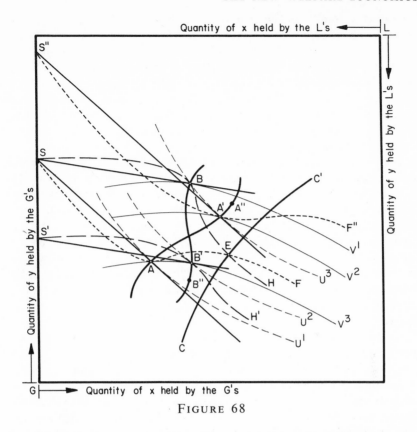

Quantity of x held by the L's

Quantity of y held by the L's

Quantity of y held by the G's

Quantity of x held by the G's

FIGURE 68

would be defined as desirable, since the "compensation payments" could be so defined as to put the economy directly on the contract curve at a point between the initial indifference curves. If the compensation payments can be extended to include contracts for the delivery of goods and services yet to be produced, the same contention can, in principle, be made for a productive economy.

Even if we restrict the compensation payments to a single numéraire, however, this criterion can run into difficulty, where the compensation payments are of such magnitude as to involve substantial changes in the marginal utility of money. This can be shown in the case of the pure exchange economy illustrated in FIGURE 68, where we have two commodities being exchanged between two groups, L (those who will lose in the reorganization to be proposed) and G (those who will gain). Suppose that initially the distribution of resources is as indicated at S, where the L group is organized into a simple monopoly, setting a price p_1 at which the G's buy a quantity of x such as to produce the final distribution as indicated by A. Now suppose that it is

[269

proposed to break up the monopoly of the L's and establish instead a monopoly by the G's, which would lead to a final distribution as indicated at B. To apply the Hicks-Kaldor criterion, we must determine whether there exists any redistribution of the numéraire, meaning by this a shift in the starting point in a vertical direction, which will lead to an equilibrium point within the area enclosed by the indifference curves through A. The redistribution of the numéraire can be indicated by a vertical shift of the starting point S, and as S is thus shifted, the monopsony point B will shift also along some such line as BB', and the test is as to whether the line BB' passes below or above A. In the case indicated, BB' passes below A (i.e., between A and the contract curve CC'), and a point such as B'' can be found on the line BB', which is within the area enclosed by the indifference curves through A, so that therefore the criterion is met and, accordingly, B would on this basis be adjudged an improvement over A. Unfortunately, in this case if we now ask whether a move from B back to A would be desirable, we are forced to answer that this is also an improvement, since from A we can, by retaining the regime of monopoly but changing the initial distribution of resources S, move to a point A'', which is clearly preferable to B. The Hicks-Kaldor criterion in its original form could thus tell us to go from A to B, and then to reverse the move.

It may be noted that this paradox can occur, as in the case depicted in the diagram, even though no price changes are induced by the redistribution (the only price changes being those accompanying the change in regime); on the other hand, the paradox cannot occur if the position to which the move is made is on the contract curve. Nor could it occur in this two-commodity case if there were no "income effect," which would imply that the lines AA'' and BB' would be vertical and hence could not cross, as must happen for the paradox to occur. A comparable condition, in the more general case where the medium of compensation is money rather than a numéraire commodity, would be one in which the consumption by individuals of the commodities whose prices change as a result of the reorganization would remain unchanged as a result of the compensation payments: for example, if railroad fares were lowered to marginal cost by means of taxation, this would itself presumably increase travel, but the hypothetical redistribution of incomes that would be required to make everyone better off as a result of the change would not itself change anyone's riding. Thus while the Hicks-Kaldor criterion breaks down as a completely consistent scheme, it may have a kind of rough applicability in a number of special cases. Even here, however, it has been questioned as tending to conceal the redistribution issue which is at the core of the problem.

To avoid this paradox, Tibor Scitovsky proposed to consider a change beneficial only if the reverse change would not be supported by the Hicks-Kaldor criterion: i.e., while the gainers could (potentially) overcompensate the losers if the change were made, the prospective losers would not be able profitably to bribe the gainers to oppose the change. The relation between this and the Hicks-Kaldor criterion can be seen a bit more clearly by shifting from FIGURE 68 to FIGURE 69, where the two axes represent the utility levels attained by the two groups G and L. The scales on these two axes will be merely indicators of rank and not of magnitude, of course, and we shall have to be careful in our discussion to make use, in this diagram, only of properties that will not be affected by stretching or distorting the scales on these axes. On this diagram, we can again start with simple monopoly by the

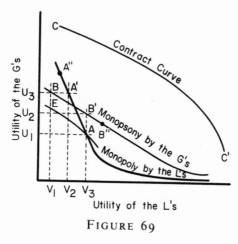

FIGURE 69

L's with the resulting utility levels for the two groups indicated at A; the curve AA'' in this case is a "utility-possibility curve" indicating possible results attainable by redistribution while maintaining the "A" regime of monopoly by the L's. Similarly, B represents the utilities resulting from the shift to a monopsony by the G's, and the curve BB' is the corresponding utility-possibility curve. The Hicks-Kaldor criterion implies that a move from A to B is desirable, since from B the gainers are potentially able to over-compensate the losers by a redistribution resulting in B'', at which point both groups would be better off than at A. But symmetrically, the same argument shows a movement to A from B to be desirable. Scitovsky's double criterion would avoid asserting that movement either from A to B or from B to A is desirable. However, if the utility-possibility curve (which could perhaps better be called a "curve of redistributions") through A, corresponding to a regime of monopoly by the L's were to pass below B rather than above, as is illustrated by the curve AE, then the move from A to B would be indicated by the Scitovsky criterion to be desirable, since there is no redistribution in this case from A which would make all groups better off than at B, whereas B'', potentially attainable from B by redistribution, is better than A.

All this ignores, of course, the possibility that B might be deemed very much worse than A on distributional grounds. Indeed, I. M. D. Little argues that no change can be unequivocally recommended unless, according to some criterion, the distributional aspects of the change are favorable, or at least not unfavorable. Since, however, it is admittedly difficult to set up, even conceptually, a precise notion of what is meant by the distributional aspects of a change being favorable or unfavorable, independently of the changes in regime, such a criterion remains at best vague.

The Arrow Impossibility Theorem

A QUITE different approach to the problem of avoiding interpersonal comparisons in the making of social decisions has been developed by Kenneth Arrow. His approach has been to see how far one can go in developing a rule for social choice where the only information to be considered is the ranking of the various alternatives in the preferences of the various individuals. This approach sidesteps the problem of interpersonal comparisons by making it a matter of indifference to the social decision how intensely a given preference is held, which at the same time makes the social choice proof against attempts by individuals to exaggerate by one means or another their intensity of preference between given alternatives in a strategic attempt to change the social choice to one more to their liking. Arrow's main contribution has been to show formally what many may have previously suspected, that there is in fact no way in which a social-welfare function can be constructed, in general, from information restricted to individual rankings, which will satisfy all of certain quite reasonable requirements.

To illustrate more clearly what is meant by a social-welfare function of the individual rank orders, consider first the case in which there are three social states among which a choice is to be made. There will be altogether 13 ways in which these three states can be ranked by each individual, if we admit ties: six strict rankings, three rankings with a tie for first place, three with a tie for last place, and one three-way tie. If there are p persons in the society to be considered, it would in the most general case be possible for each individual to express any of the 13 possible types of preference as between the three alternatives, and if each individual is free to choose independently of the others, there would be altogether 13^p possible combinations of choices to be fed into the social-welfare function as data. The problem of setting up a social-welfare function is then one of assigning to each of the admissible combinations among these 13^p possible ones (and they may all of them be admissible) a suitable social ranking from among the 13 possible rankings. The difficulty, as shown by Arrow, lies in the fact that if the set of admissible choice combinations is sufficiently wide, it becomes impossible to assign social rankings to each of the admissible combinations of individual rankings without violating one or more of some seemingly essential requirements.

The various requirements that have been suggested for the social-welfare function are of varying degrees of obviousness or essentiality; indeed, since some of them will be seen to be incompatible with others, some of them will have to be weakened or abandoned. We give here first two which seem most firmly established in the sense that no solutions proposed for the social-welfare-function problem appear to have involved their weakening or abandonment.

1. *Honoring of unanimous preferences.* If no member of the community prefers state y to state x, and at least some individuals prefer x to y, it would seem unreasonable for a social-welfare function not to produce a social ranking in which x is chosen over y. The unanimity requirement is that the social-welfare function must honor individual preferences to which there is no dissent. This requirement implies Arrow's "nonimposition" requirement. It bears an obvious relation to the Pareto optimum concept.

2. *Nondictatorship.* An individual is said to be a dictator if the social-welfare function makes the social ranking coincide with the preferences of the dictator regardless of the preferences expressed by the remainder of the community. This is obviously unsatisfactory, and one of the requirements for an acceptable social-welfare function is that it shall not make any member of the community a dictator. This is an essential requirement; i.e., it is necessary to stipulate this as a requirement in addition to all the others, for in general a dictatorial social-welfare function will satisfy all of the other requirements.

These two requirements seem to be fundamental, in the sense that no social-welfare function that violated one of them would be seriously considered. A third requirement which is perhaps slightly less essential is as follows:

3. *Nonperversity.* If we consider a given social-welfare function applied to some initial set of individual orderings, giving us an initial social ranking, and then apply the same social-welfare function to a changed set of individual orderings in which the only change has been that some individuals have moved some particular alternative x upward in their rankings, without changing the relative rankings of the other alternatives, it would be considered highly perverse if the social ranking produced by the social-welfare function in the second case should rank x lower than in the initial social ranking. The nonperversity requirement says in effect that for a social-welfare function to be acceptable, this must never happen.

The Case of Two Persons and Two Alternatives

THESE concepts can be applied to the simplest possible case where there are two persons and two alternatives x and y. Each individual can either prefer

[273

x to y, which we will denote by writing x, or prefer y to x, which will be written as y, or be indifferent between the two, which we shall write i. This gives nine possible ranking combinations which we can write x, x; x, i; i, y; etc., and for each of these nine combinations it is required to assign a value or ranking for the social-welfare function, which social ranking can also be expressed by x, y, or i. The unanimity condition requires us to put $f(x, x) = x$; $f(y, y) = y$; $f(x, i) = x$; $f(i, x) = x$; $f(y, i) = y$; $f(i, y) = y$. In assigning values to the remaining three choice combinations, the nondictatorship condition prohibits us from assigning the values $f(x, y) = x$ and at the same time putting $f(y, x) = y$, for this would make the first individual a dictator. Similarly, we cannot combine $f(x, y) = y$ and $f(y, x) = x$ in constructing the social-welfare function, since then the second individual would be a dictator. Otherwise, we are free to assign any values we choose to the social rankings corresponding to the choice patterns (x, y), (y, x) and (i, i), which leaves us with a total of 21 possible welfare functions that would be permissible under these circumstances.

So far so good, except that if we are considering a social-welfare function as a means of actually determining a decision between alternatives, we need to investigate further the meaning of the value i for the social ranking. It is all right for an individual to indicate that he does not care which of the two alternatives is chosen, but when a choice is to be made, the two alternatives are mutually exclusive; one or the other must be in any given case chosen deliberately or allowed to become the outcome, and since the result i for the social-welfare function does not give explicit instructions, there must be somewhere in the background a procedure to be followed when this value occurs, which procedure will then determine in any given case which of the two alternatives will actually be followed.

There are in general three types of procedures that can be followed when the social-welfare function gives a social ranking in which two or more from among the available alternatives are tied for first place. One is by reference to some arbitrary fixed criterion to break the tie, as by picking the alternative that ranks first in alphabetical order. This would amount to converting every i in the social rankings produced by the function into an x or a y according to this arbitrary precedence criterion. If such an arbitrary criterion is used, it might as well be given effect initially in specifying the social-welfare function itself, which would then give in every case a definite choice for x or y; it would still be possible to construct four different admissible social-welfare functions of this type.

A second method for resolving the case where the social-welfare function yields the value i for the social ranking is to have resort to some random device, or to determine the choice between x and y in a manner dependent upon the occurrence of an event after the act of choosing by the individuals has been completed. Actually, from the point of view of the individuals at the

time of original ranking, the prospect of having to refer to some such subsequent event is a third prospect that could be considered capable of being
compared directly with the certainty of x or the certainty of y, and if this
resort to a random or outside criterion is in fact presented to individuals as
a third choice to be ranked in relation to x and y, then we are in effect considering three alternatives rather than two.

A third method of resolving such cases is to have recourse to the judgment,
opinion, or preference of some arbiter. But again this arbiter can equally well
be considered a third individual whose preferences are in some cases to be
considered in obtaining a social choice; instead of a weak social ordering
from the preferences of two individuals among two alternatives, we would
have a social-welfare function producing a strong social ordering from the
preferences of three individuals.

Where there are three or more persons choosing among two alternatives,
the number of admissible social-welfare functions mounts rapidly. Indeed,
any scheme equivalent to a weighted majority rule, where no individual is
assigned as much as one-half of the total weight, and where the weights used
are such as to preclude ties, is a class of acceptable social-welfare functions.

Three or More Alternatives

WITH THE ADDITION of a third alternative, new possibilities for anomalies
arise. These possible anomalies reflect themselves in new requirements that
an acceptable social-welfare function must fulfill. In general, these are less
fundamental than those previously stated, at least to the extent that each of
them has been taken at various times or by various writers as the one that
should be relaxed in order to resolve the problem of constructing an acceptable
social-welfare function.

4. *Transitivity of social choice.* The social-welfare function should yield a
result in the form of a transitive social ordering of the alternatives. (A transitive ordering, it will be remembered, is one in which whenever x is preferred
to y and y is preferred to z, then x is preferred to z, for any three alternatives
x, y, and z.) This may initially be a weak ordering (i.e., one admitting ties),
but to be entirely satisfactory there must be posited some procedure to be
followed to determine which of the tied courses of action is to be followed.
We have seen above that following an external criterion in such cases is
equivalent to establishing a strong social ordering in the first place; that giving
discretion to some administrative individual is equivalent to putting his
preferences into the social-welfare function in the first place, and that reference
to a random or chance device can be considered in terms of including these
procedures as social states to be submitted to individual consideration in the
first place. Actually, difficulties arise even if weak social orderings are
accepted.

5. *The range of admissible individual preferences.* At the extreme it would be desirable to have a social-welfare function that would work acceptably no matter how freakishly individuals rank the various alternatives. However, the more we restrict the rankings that we will consider admissible—for example, on the basis that we reject some rankings as representing inconsistent or capricious choices, or choices contravening some overriding principle—the more likely we are to be able to set up a consistent social-welfare function. Actually, it is found that relatively modest requirements as to the degree of freedom to be granted in individuals in listing their preferences cause trouble. Arrow merely makes the requirement that there be at least three of the social alternatives under consideration that are related to each other in such a way as to make it reasonable that they be given any of the 13 possible strong and weak orderings by any individual. This is almost, but not quite, enough to make a consistent social-welfare function an impossibility; the exact minimum requirement is fairly complicated, but for the sake of simplifying the proof that follows we will stick to the requirement that any individual may elect any ranking of the alternatives he pleases, without restriction.

6. *Independence of irrelevant alternatives.* If a social choice is to be made between two alternatives x and y, it may happen that the result given by a social-welfare function will depend not only on the relative rankings of x and y in the preference scales of individuals, but possibly on the rankings given to z, w, and other alternatives. These other alternatives may for some purposes be considered entirely irrelevant to the choice between x and y. They may, for example, represent alternatives that are in fact purely hypothetical and not capable of being attained by the community. Or they may represent alternatives that rank so low on the lists of so many individuals that they have in fact no reasonable claim to being considered as acceptable outcomes of the selection process. Or they may represent alternatives that were possibilities at the time individuals listed their preferences, but which are no longer possible at the time the social decision is to be made. That such an extraneous consideration should affect the social choice has been considered anomalous, and, accordingly, one of the requirements that has been imposed upon the social-welfare function is that the social ranking given by the social-welfare function between any two given alternatives shall not depend on the relative ranking given by individuals to other "irrelevant" alternatives. As there is no criterion that can readily be set up in advance to judge which are the "irrelevant" alternatives, for this purpose in effect all of the alternatives other than the two directly under consideration are deemed irrelevant. This in turn means that the social choice between x and y will depend only on the individual preferences given as between x and y, so that a social-welfare function can be thought of as built up from pairwise comparisons of social alternatives.

Decisive Sets

To go further into the study of social-welfare functions, it is convenient to introduce the notion of a decisive set. For a given social-welfare function, a given set of individuals is said to be decisive for x against y if the social-welfare function is such that whenever all persons in the decisive set D prefer x to y, the function places x above y in the social ranking, regardless of preferences of the individuals not in D and regardless of the relative preferences for alternatives other than x and y.

To show that a set D is decisive for x against y, it is sufficient, if the non-perversity and independence conditions hold, to show that the social-welfare function gives x a higher social rank than y in the case where all members of D rank x above y while all persons not in D prefer y to x. This is because all of the other cases required by the definition can be obtained from this one by moving x upward or y downward in the preference scale of individuals not in D, which by the nonperversity rule must cause the social ranking of x to remain above y, or by rearranging the relative rankings of the alternatives other than x and y, which by the independence rule will produce no change in the relative social ranging of x and y.

Further, if a set D is decisive for x against y, and if z is any alternative such that all relative rankings of x, y, and z are admissible, then D is decisive for all decisions as among x, y, and z. To show this, consider the situation where the members of D all have the preference ranking xyz, while those not in D have the ranking yzx. If D is decisive for x over y, then by definition the social-welfare function must, for this set of preferences, place x above y in the social scale. Since everyone in this case prefers y to z, y must be chosen over z in the social scale by the unanimity rule. And if the social choice is to be transitive, x must be preferred to z. But since the members of D are the only ones who prefer x to z, the fact that the social choice agrees with their preference in this instance, in spite of the reverse preference of all others, in turn means that D is decisive for x against z. Conversely, by taking the case where the preferences are zxy for all members of D and yzx for all others, it is shown that if D is decisive for x against y, it is decisive for z against y. By suitably permuting x, y, and z in these demonstrations, the decisiveness of D for any decision among three alternatives is seen to involve decisiveness for all such decisions.

This demonstration can easily be extended to show that decisiveness for any x against any y implies decisiveness for v against u for all v and u such that all relative rankings of x, y, u, and v are admissible. In particular, if there are no restrictions on relative rankings of alternatives by individuals, any one-person set that might be a decisive set for any x against any y would be decisive for all social decisions and hence would be a dictator. Thus under these conditions nondictatorship requires that no one-person set can be decisive for any social decision, given independence, transitivity, and the admissibility of all relative rankings of alternatives, as requirements for the social-welfare function.

The Impossibility Theorem

SUPPOSE there were a social-welfare function that satisfied all of the requirements 1 through 6, and let x, y, and z be a set of alternatives for which all the rankings as specified in requirement 5 (p. 276) are admissible. From all of the sets of individuals that are decisive for social choices among x, y, and z, select a set M such that it has no subsets that are decisive. Sets such as M must exist, since the set containing all the members of the community is certainly decisive, and we can remove members one at a time from this universal set in such a way as to leave a decisive set until a set is reached for which this can no longer be done. Such a "minimal decisive set" M must contain at least two members, otherwise it would be a dictator (at least as among the alternatives x, y, and z, and any other alternatives that are unrestricted as to relative ranking). Let A be some member of M, let B be the set formed by removing A from M, and let C be the set of individuals not in M. C may be empty, as would be the case where the only decisive set is the universal set, but A contains exactly one person and B contains at least one person. Consider the case where the members of B express the preference ranking yzx, A has the preference ranking xyz, and the members of C, if any, have the preference ranking zxy. Now since A and B together make up M, a decisive set, and prefer y to z, y must outrank z in the social scale. Furthermore, the members of B are the only ones that prefer y to x, while B was by construction not a decisive set; accordingly, the social scale must not place y above x. But if x is at least as high as y in the social ranking, and y outranks z, x must be higher than z. On the other hand, A is the only one who prefers x to z, so x must not outrank z in the social scale, otherwise A would be a dictator. Thus x must outrank z and must not outrank z: this contradiction shows that no social-welfare function satisfying all of the requirements 1 to 6 is possible.

However, if any one of the six requirements (except possibly the first) is relaxed, it becomes possible to construct a social-welfare function satisfying the remaining five. For example, waiving the unanimity requirement admits the use of an imposed social-welfare function that always gives the same arbitrary predetermined social ranking regardless of individual preferences. Waiving the nondictatorship requirement admits the use of a social-welfare function that always makes the social ranking agree with that of some designated individual, who is thus the dictator. Waiving transitivity admits of the use of weighted majority voting between successive pairs of alternatives, the weights being such as to make ties impossible while not giving any one person a majority of the weight. This of course gives rise to the Condorcet effect, or "paradox of voting," but otherwise the postulates are satisfied.

Rather more interesting are the various ways in which the range requirement can be relaxed so as to permit a social-welfare function to be constructed. Here the case most discussed in the literature is that of the "single-peaked preferences," where the alternatives can be placed along a one-dimensional continuum in such a way that starting from the alternative ranked at the top by any given individual, his preferences for the remaining alternatives will follow a declining (or nonincreasing) sequence as we proceed in either direction. This is likely to be the case, for example, when the alternatives represent different amounts of expenditure for some object, or a choice between parties ranged in order from radical to conservative. In this case, again, weighted majority rule, with suitable restrictions on the weights, provides a class of acceptable social-welfare functions; the result is the selection of the median alternative. Less well known is the case of "single-troughed preferences," which is obtained simply by reversing all rank orders in the preceding case; it also admits of an Arrow social-welfare function, but in this case the result is fairly trivial, since the top-ranking social choice must be one of the two extreme alternatives at either end, which end being determined, for example, by weighted majority rule.

Single-peaked and single-troughed patterns do not exhaust the possibilities, however, for with four alternatives we can consider the following set of admissible rankings: *wxyz, wxzy, wzxy, wyxz, xyzw, xzyw, yxzw, zxyw.* Majority rule with weights that preclude ties or dictatorship gives us social-welfare functions that satisfy all the postulates but the fifth, or range, postulate. This can be seen by noting that if the total of the weights of the individuals with the first four rankings predominates, then w will get a majority vote when pitted against any of the other three alternatives, otherwise w will lose against each of them. So no intransitivity can involve w. Preferences among x, y, and z are single-peaked, so no intransitivity is possible among them either. On the other hand, this set of rankings cannot be produced by single-peaked or single-troughed preferences: since w appears at the bottom of some of the rankings, it must be located, in the single-peaked case, at one end of the sequence along the underlying continuum; if this were so, then only one ranking with w at the top would be possible, but since there are four such rankings, representation as single-peaked preferences is not possible. A symmetrical argument disposes of the single-troughed possibility.

Another way of approaching a social-welfare function is to impose requirements on the set of possible alternatives. It may be, for example, that the range of admissible rankings is such that although intransitivity does occur, say with a majority-rule function, it occurs only among alternatives that are all necessarily inferior to some dominating alternative, so that if the dominating alternative is actually available, the intransitivity is irrelevant to the social decision to be made. For example, it may be possible to specify all the social states to be considered in terms of a finite number of cardinal parameters—for example, in terms of the amounts of various goods and services distributed to each of the individuals in a society. A social state is then an ordinary vector. Moreover, it is in some contexts reasonable to specify that the available social states form a convex set, i.e., that every social state formed by constructing a weighted average of two available social states is also available. Another not too drastic assumption is that single-peaked preferences obtain among such weighted averages of any two given social states. But even this would not suffice to assure the existence of an otherwise satisfactory function, as can be seen from the example of a set of states consisting of the possible partitioning of a fixed national income among three groups (as in the three-person constant-sum game which will be considered later on) where each group ranks the states according to its own share. Apparently, even more stringent requirements are necessary if a satisfactory social-welfare function is to be assured.

A considerably more promising line of development seems to be the consideration of various relaxations of the independence postulate. This is the postulate which, together with the restriction of the argument of the function to mere rankings, rules out the more usual Benthamesque welfare functions that are obtained by summing individual utilities. Indeed, it does seem rather prodigal to disregard, in deciding between two alternatives, whatever indication regarding the intensity of preferences is furnished by the relative rankings of other alternatives, even though they may not be actually available.

Once this postulate is relaxed, there are many ways in which a social-welfare function can be constructed, many of which adequately fulfill the remaining postulates. The sum of the ranks assigned to each alternative by the various individuals may be taken as indicating the social ranking, as is frequently done in preferential balloting, or perhaps some set of values specified in various ways could be assigned to the ranks, rather than simply the rank numbers. One attractive way of assigning such numbers would be by doing this in such a way that the resulting distribution of values would approximate a normal distribution with unit variance. Or some kind of sequential elimination procedure could be specified, as in various schemes of proportional representation.

All such schemes will of course be open to the objection that the social choice may be affected by changes in the range of alternatives presented to the individuals, even when the selected alternatives are not themselves excluded or included by the change. But this will be true in considerably varying degrees. Where the number of alternatives is small, omission or inclusion of one or two alternatives may be crucial; where the number of alternatives is large, omission or inclusion even of a number of alternatives constituting the same proportion of the total may be much less likely to affect the result. Appropriate selection of the values assigned to the various ranks in the procedure indicated above may help minimize the influence of changes in range, and the particular choice indicated, that which produces a normal distribution, may on some assumptions be the one that does minimize these effects.

There is another objection, however, to such welfare functions, which is that they are vulnerable to strategy, i.e., that individuals may be able to gain by reporting a preference differing from that which they actually hold. Thus if there are two groups roughly equal in numbers, group A ranking the four alternatives in the order $xyzw$, while group B has the preference order $zxwy$, then if both report correctly and the social decision is derived by summing ranks, x becomes the social choice, whereas if the B's, instead of reporting their genuine preferences, report the ranking $zwyx$, then z becomes the social choice and the B's have succeeded in shifting the social choice in the direction of their own preferences. In general, whenever intensity of preference is given effect in the social-welfare function, whether directly or through considering the number of intervening ranks, it will be to the advantage of an individual, or a group, whenever it can be discerned in advance which alternatives are likely to be close rivals for the social decision and which are almost certain to be defeated, to exaggerate his degree of preference for the close rivals, at the expense, if necessary, of understating the degree of preference for or against the "irrelevant" alternatives, whether the irrelevance be produced by technical impossibility or by lack of general appeal of the alternatives. Such strategy could of course lead to counterstrategy, and the process of arriving at a social decision could readily turn into a "game" in the technical sense discussed below on pages 342–67.

It is clear that social-welfare functions that satisfy the independence postulate and are limited to rankings as arguments are also immune to strategy. If some individual prefers x to y, and as a result of reporting this and other preferences correctly the social choice is nevertheless y, there is nothing this individual can do about it (even if joined by others in the same case) since changing his expressed preferences concerning other alternatives can, by the independence postulate, have no effect on the social choice, nor, by the nonperversity postulate, can a change in his expressed preference for x over y. It appears that the converse is also true, and that if a function is to be immune to strategy it must, if it is to be sufficiently general in its range, satisfy the independence criterion though this is not quite so easy to provide a formal proof for. Independence and immunity to strategy are thus at least closely similar requirements, if not actually logically equivalent.

However, the seriousness of one's objection to susceptibility to strategy depends on the circumstances of the case. Where the number of individuals is large with none having any significant weight individually, and where they are unorganized and largely ignorant of each other's preferences and concerning which are the outcomes that are likely candidates, no individual may have the knowledge required to give any other strategy an edge over that of

[281

reporting his preferences honestly. But where individuals are few or well organized or well informed, and the number of likely alternatives is limited, the situation may pass from one analogous to perfect competition to one analogous to oligopoly where the process of arriving at a social choice may become a game of strategy; as we shall see later, in the study of the theory of games, this tends to produce a situation that is difficult to analyze with any degree of precision, and at best the specific outcome in a particular instance tends to become highly uncertain.

Thus whether we base our attempt to avoid interpersonal comparisons in the making of social decisions on potentialities for the payment of compensation, as in the Hicks-Kaldor–Scitovsky approach, or whether we attempt to consider merely the rankings of the different prospects, as in the Arrow approach, we encounter fundamental difficulties. It appears that a satisfactory basis for social decisions must involve the making of interpersonal comparisons, either explicitly or implicitly. Various methods of making such interpersonal comparisons can be studied to best advantage, however, only after some further investigations have been made into the relation of the individual utility function to the making of choices in circumstances involving risk, and, accordingly, further discussion of the social-welfare function is deferred until after this topic has been more thoroughly covered.

EXERCISES

A LEGISLATURE is considering three alternatives, x, y, and z; its members are divided into three equal groups, group A having the preference xyz, B, yxz, and C, zyx.

a. Show that these preferences admit of a single-peaked representation.

b. Show that the outcome based on majority vote between successive pairs of alternatives is independent of the order of the choices.

c. Suppose group A to be highly disciplined, the other two groups being composed of unorganized individualists. Under what circumstances could group A gain by misrepresenting its preferences?

PART III

Monopoly and Imperfect Competition

CHAPTER SEVEN

Monopoly

Simple Monopoly

HAVING developed the elements of a theory of how to deal in the public interest with cases in which competition does not work effectively, we now come to the much more difficult task of developing a theory of how firms will react if they are subject neither to the pressures of perfect competition nor to the restraints of effective public control. The simplest case, and one which furnishes the tools needed for the analysis of other more complicated cases, is that of monopoly.

To consider first the simplest form of monopoly, we will assume that the monopolistic firm produces a single output with factors purchased in competitive markets, and sells the product in a market in which it is the sole supplier. The monopolist is supposed to know what the demand curve in this market is, and is supposed either to set a price, supplying whatever is demanded at that price, or to determine his output, selling this output for whatever it will bring. The first and more common policy is called a "price policy," the second an "output policy." In the case of simple monopoly, it usually makes no difference which of the two types of policy is pursued, the outcome is the same, though we shall see that for other forms of imperfect competition which type of policy is pursued may make a drastic difference in the outcome.

In simple monopoly, then, the monopolist is assumed to set the price or the quantity produced at the level which will maximize the net profit. This may be illustrated in FIGURE 70. Here the demand curve is shown as *GBAF* in the lower part of the diagram. By taking each point on the demand curve and multiplying the price by the quantity we get the total revenue, which can be plotted against the quantity sold to get the total-revenue curve shown in the upper part of the figure as *obhf*. When no units are sold, total revenue is of course zero; total revenue in general rises to a maximum at *h*, then falls off again, becoming zero again at *f* when the amount supplied becomes great enough to drive the price down to zero. The total-cost curve *oe* can be plotted on the same diagram, and the profit for any given output will then be the vertical distance between the two curves. This will obviously be at a maximum when the tangents to the two curves at points representing the same output are parallel, as occurs in this case at an output of *om*, where the profit will be *eb*.

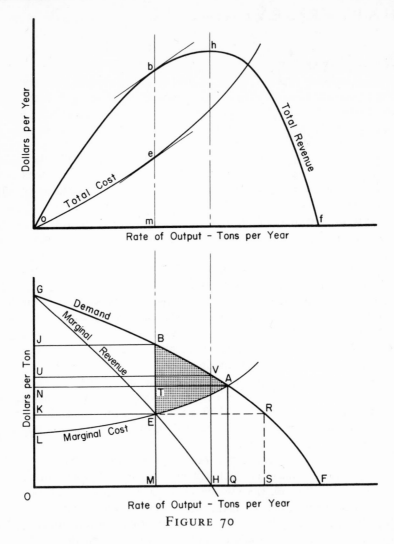

FIGURE 70

For purposes of analysis, however, it is desirable to show this equilibrium determined in terms of the demand curve as given in the lower part of the diagram. To do this, we derive from the total-revenue curve a marginal-revenue curve *GEH*, which represents at each point the additional revenue resulting from the sale of an additional unit of output, after allowing for the necessary reduction in the price at which the previous units would be sold. The height of the marginal-revenue curve thus varies with the slope or steepness of the total-revenue curve, and the marginal-revenue curve becomes zero at the point where the total-revenue curve is at a maximum. We can also draw

286]

in the marginal-cost curve *LEA*, which likewise corresponds to the slope of the total-cost curve *oe*. The point of maximum profit is determined by the intersection of the marginal-cost curve and the marginal-revenue curve at *E*, beyond which point it is clear that the marginal revenue brought in by selling additional units of product would be less than the cost of producing it; conversely, curtailment of output below the level indicated by *E* would lose more in revenue than would be saved in costs. The price that can be obtained for this output is *MB* as indicated by the demand curve; total revenue is indicated by the rectangle *oJBM*; the (variable) costs are indicated by the area *oLEM* under the marginal-cost curve, and the (gross) profit is the remaining area *LEBJ*.

We can compare this result with the results of competition if we assume that the specialized factors, the limited supply of which causes the marginal-cost curve to slope upward, are owned by the monopolist, as would be the case, for example, if a tin monopoly owned all the tin deposits. In this case, the marginal-cost curve to the monopolist would also be an industry marginal-cost curve for the competitive case where each tin deposit is owned separately and operated separately. For a given level of output in the industry, the price or "rent" the specialized factors would obtain under competition will be just such as to bring the minimum average total cost for each firm up to the level of the prevailing market price, and a competitive equilibrium for the industry will be reached at *A* with a total output *oQ*, a price *QA*, total revenues of *oQAN*, and total costs equal to total revenues, of which *AELN* would represent the rent paid or imputable to the specialized factors, the remainder being payments to general factors (including that part of the payment to specialized factors that merely equals what they could obtain in their next best use outside the industry). The consumer's surplus would be *ANG*, and the total surplus resulting from the operation of the industry would be *ALG*. Under monopoly the total surplus would be merely the sum of the monopolist's gross profit *JBEL* and the consumer's surplus *BJG*, which together amounts to less than the competitive surplus by the amount *AEB*.

The effect of shifting from competition to a monopoly may then be summarized as a transfer of income of the amount *NTBJ* from consumers to the monopolist, plus the reduction of aggregate incomes by *AEB*, of which *ATB* represents loss taken from consumers and *ATE* represents loss taken from suppliers of the factors. The effect is very much as though a tax of *BE* had been levied on the output of the industry and turned over to the producers or monopolists.

Exactly the same analysis can be carried through without assuming any specialized factors; in this case it is necessary to assume constant returns to scale for the industry, and hence a horizontal marginal-cost curve such as *KER*. In such a case competitive output would be *KR* as compared with *KE* for the monopoly; the social loss would appear entirely in the form of loss of consumers' surplus *REB*. If on the other hand the industry constitutes such a large part of the market for the factors that it uses that expanding the industry would drive factor prices up, then a monopoly taking over the industry would find that in addition to its monopoly powers in the product market it has monopsonistic powers in the factor markets and a more complex analysis is necessary, which will be presented later. Or if specialized factors are owned by individuals independent of the monopoly, as, for example, if particular tin deposits were in the hands of individual owners, the exact outcome might be somewhat uncertain, since each such owner is in a position of bilateral monopoly vis-à-vis the tin-smelting monopoly, and considerable uncertainty would exist as to what rental would be paid for each property and even as to which properties would actually be operated.

The analysis for a case of decreasing cost is also quite similar, except that of course it is not possible to compare monopoly operation directly with perfect competition, but only with regulated monopoly or subsidized operation at the prices equal to marginal cost.

The Geometry of Marginal and Average Curves

To SIMPLIFY further analysis, it is desirable to be able to derive marginal-revenue curves directly from average-revenue or demand curves without having first to construct a total-revenue curve. This can readily be done as shown in FIGURE 71. If we have a point *A* on a demand curve *EAD* and wish to find the value of the marginal revenue at this level of output, we can simply draw the tangent *AC* to the demand curve at *A*, and also a horizontal line *AL*; if the

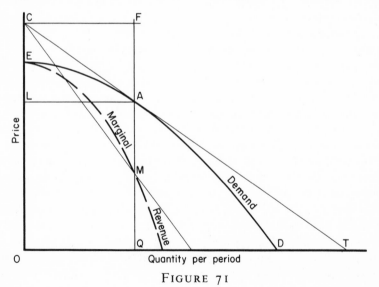

FIGURE 71

288]

distance LC which these two lines cut off on the price axis is laid off downward from A, giving the point M such that $AM = FA = CL$, then the resulting point M will be the required point on the marginal-revenue curve. In particular, if the demand curve were taken as the straight line AC, the corresponding marginal-revenue curve will be the straight line MC, i.e., just twice as steep as the demand curve.

Indeed, if the marginal-revenue curve is CM, it is easy to see that the average revenue for the output oQ must be QA, for the total revenue is the sum of the

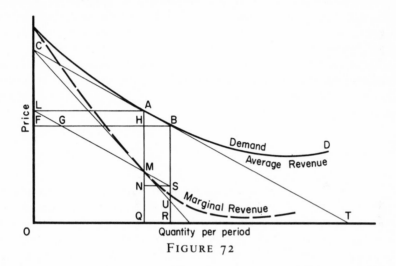

FIGURE 72

successive marginal revenues, or the area $oQMC$, which must be equal to the total revenue $oQAL$ obtained by multiplying output oQ by the price QA. In effect, QA is the average of the successive marginal revenues of the successive units of output up to the point Q, and if CM is a straight line, QA will be half way between the highest marginal revenue $OC = QF$ and the lowest, QM. Similarly, for nonlinear curves, if the marginal-revenue curve is EM, QA will be the average of the marginal revenues along EM.

To show this relation in the reverse direction, we take, in FIGURE 72, two points A and B close together on the demand curve ABD. Total revenue at A is the rectangle $oLAQ$, and at B it is $oFBR$. Going from A to B loses revenue equal to $ALFH$ from the reduction in the price charged the old customers, while gaining $QHBR$ from the new customers at the new price. Now if we lay off $AM = CL$, then LM and CA will be parallel, and $ALFH = LGBA = MSBA = HBSN$ (since parallelograms with the same bases and altitudes have equal areas); thus the net gain in revenue is $QHBR - ALFH = QHBR - HBSN = QRSN$. Dividing $QRSN$ by the increment of output QR gives an "average marginal revenue" over the arc AB of oN. Now as we make

[289

the increment in output smaller and smaller by moving *B* closer and closer to *A*, the point *N* approaches *M* and the line *CA* becomes a tangent, so that the desired marginal revenue at *A* is *QM*.

Elasticity

IN THE ANALYSIS of various forms of imperfect competition, it becomes more important to consider the elasticity of demand and other curves as numerical quantities rather than as mere qualitative descriptions. Actually, there is a very useful relationship between elasticity and the ratio of the marginal to the average revenue. Elasticity is a measure of the relative response of one magnitude to small relative changes in another. The elasticity of demand, for example, is the relative change in quantity divided by the (small) relative change in price that produces it. Thus in terms of FIGURE 72, if we consider *B* to approach *A*, we have:

$$\epsilon = \frac{\dfrac{dq}{q}}{\dfrac{dp}{p}} = \frac{p}{q} \cdot \frac{dq}{dp} = \frac{oL}{LA} \cdot \frac{HB}{AH} = \frac{oL}{LA} \cdot \frac{LA}{CL} = \frac{oL}{CL} = \frac{QA}{AM} = \frac{TA}{CA} = \frac{TQ}{oQ}$$

In this series of expressions, the first equation is the definition of elasticity; the second results from the rearrangement of terms in the definition, and the third is an interpretation of the definition in terms of FIGURE 72. The fourth equation is a consequence of the similarity of triangles *ABH* and *CAL*, the fifth obtains by cancelling *LA*, the sixth from the fact that *LAM* and *ALC* are congruent since *LM* and *CA* are parallel, the seventh from the fifth by observing that *LA* is parallel to the base of triangle *oCT*, and the last, similarly, from *AQ* being parallel to the side *Co* of triangle *oCT*.

Elasticity of a demand curve is, strictly speaking, a negative number, inasmuch as the changes in demand and price are in opposite directions. This is reflected in the fact that if we take account of the direction implied, for example, in writing *AH* rather than *HA*, the quantities *AH*, *CL*, *AM*, and *TQ* are negative. However, economists, for better or worse, are not very meticulous about such things, and often speak and write about elasticity of demand as though it were positive, so that a little attention to the context is often required to be sure of interpreting statements in the sense intended.

Keeping to the negative convention, here, we may note that *QA* is the average revenue, while *AM* is the negative of *MA*, which in turn is the excess of average over marginal revenue. If we put *p* for average revenue and *m* for marginal revenue, then we have

$$-\epsilon = \frac{p}{p - m}, \quad \text{or} \quad m = p\left(1 + \frac{1}{\epsilon}\right), \quad \text{or} \quad \frac{m}{p} = \frac{1 + \epsilon}{\epsilon}$$

Thus we find that if demand has unit elasticity, so that $\epsilon = -1$, marginal revenue is zero regardless of price. If ϵ lies between 0 and -1, marginal revenue is negative. As the demand becomes more and more elastic and ϵ approaches $-\infty$, marginal revenue approaches price.

The relation $\epsilon = OL/CL$ furnishes a useful means of determining the elasticity of a given curve at a given point graphically, by drawing a tangent to the curve and noting the relation of its intercept on the y axis with the ordinate of the point being observed. The relation $\epsilon = TA/CA$ has been used for this purpose by Joan Robinson, but seems on the whole more awkward to evaluate; we can also use $\epsilon = TQ/oQ$, which in some ways is more instructive than the others: if oQ is taken as a unit, the relative magnitude of TQ gives the elasticity and shows directly how elasticity varies as the curve at A shifts in various ways.

These relationships between an average curve, its elasticity, and the corresponding marginal curve are quite general and hold also for productivity curves, cost curves, and others. For the normally sloping supply curve, for example, the application of the above methods will give an appropriately positive value for the elasticity, as then C will be below L and T will be to the left of Q, so that CL and TQ will be considered positive. An elasticity of $+1$ will indicate that the tangent to the curve passes through the origin, a smaller elasticity that it passes below the origin, and a larger elasticity that the tangent passes above the origin.

Monopsony ("One Buyer")

THE ANALYSIS of simple monopsony is quite symmetrical with that of simple monopoly. We assume that the monopsonist is buying in a market in which he is the sole purchaser, that he knows what the supply curve in this market is, and that otherwise he is confronted with competitive conditions. This might mean, for example, that the monopsonist (or a group of consumers organized to purchase as a unit) uses the commodity purchased directly, or uses it in conjunction with other factors purchased competitively to produce a product that is sold in a competitive market. Or if we can assume a smooth production function without "creases," it would be possible to carry through the analysis on the assumption that the other inputs are held constant and get the correct result; in this case the conditions under which the other factors are supplied would not affect the form of the partial analysis.

In simple monopsony we have the situation depicted in FIGURE 73. The supply curve LEA represents the average cost that the *purchaser* must pay for the various outputs. This curve should not be confused with the average cost to the *supplying industry*, which will in general be lower than the supply curve by an amount reflecting the rents imputable to the specialized factors owned and used within the supplying industry. If all specialized factors were

[291

so owned, an average-cost curve for the industry which excluded such rents would be as shown in the curve *LP*, which is the average-cost curve for which the supply curve *LEA* is the marginal-cost curve. Only if rents are charged for all specialized factors, either by imputation or through their being owned outside the supplying industry, would the average cost to the supplying industry coincide with the supply curve. In either case the supply curve will tend to reflect the marginal social cost of the commodity being supplied.

On the other side of the market, the curve *WYZBA* is what the demand curve would be if the monopsonist were behaving competitively on the

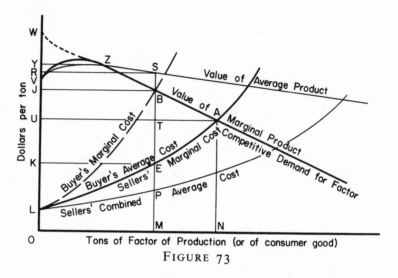

FIGURE 73

assumption of a price not subject to his influence. For an ultimate user the *ZBA* portion of this curve represents marginal utility. For a purchaser using the commodity as a factor of production, it is the "marginal revenue-product" of the input, i.e., the addition to money gross revenues obtainable as a result of adding an increment of this factor, which in turn is the result of multiplying the marginal physical product of an increment of the input by the marginal revenue derivable from the sale of the final product. Where the final product is sold competitively, as we have for the time being assumed, marginal revenue is equal to price, and in this case the marginal revenue-product is also the "value of the marginal product."

To determine the output that will maximize the monopsonist's profit in such a case we first construct the buyer's marginal-cost curve *LB* from the buyer's average-cost curve *LEA*, which is also the supply curve. The volume of purchases that will maximize profit is then indicated by the intersection of this marginal-cost curve with the demand or marginal-value curve at *B*. The amount purchased will then be o*M*, and the price that must be paid for it will be *ME* as indicated by the supply curve. The total revenue from sales of the final product will be *RSMo*, of which *RSBJ* would be required to pay for other (fixed) factors, or will represent rents imputable to specialized factors owned and used by the monopsonist; *ELK* will be the rents arising in the supplying industry by reason of the demand of the monopsonist, *oLEM* is the amount the factors in the supplying industry could earn in their next best use, and *EBJK* is the monopsony profit. Similar to the monopoly case, the monopsony has produced a loss of aggregate net surplus by an

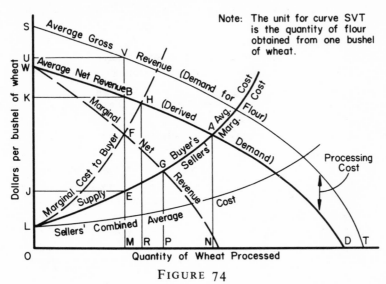

FIGURE 74

amount approximately represented by the area *AEB*, as compared to a competitive equilibrium at the price *NA* and an output o*N*.

A case of combined monopoly-monopsony may also be analyzed where the producer buys factors in a monopsonistic manner and sells his product in a monopolistic manner. If the exposition is to be kept within a single diagram in such a case, it is necessary to assume a rigid relationship between the monopsonized input and the monopolized output, so that we can measure the output and the input on the same axis. The case of a flour mill that is the sole buyer of wheat and the sole seller of flour in an area can be represented in this way in FIGURE 74. Here the axes are set up in terms of bushels of wheat, but a demand curve for flour can be transferred to these axes by taking any given output of flour, determining the price at which it can be sold and the amount of wheat required to produce it, obtaining the total revenue from the sale of the flour at that price and dividing by the required amount of wheat to get an equivalent price in terms of wheat, and plotting this price against the required input of wheat as curve *SVT* in FIGURE 74.

[293

From this we can subtract the average cost of processing the various quantities of wheat, to obtain the "derived demand" for wheat, shown as the curve *WBHAD*, which is in effect the average net revenue product of the inputs of wheat, at various levels of operation. Then if from the supply curve *LEGA* we construct the marginal-cost curve *LFH*, and from the average-net-revenue-product curve a marginal-net-revenue-product curve *WFG*, their intersection at *F* will determine the output o*M* that maximizes profits.

At this level of output, the price of wheat will be *ME*, while the price of flour will be the equivalent, in terms of the wheat needed to produce it, of *MV*. Consumers' surplus can be indicated by the area *SUV* (=*KWB*); *KUVB* is the processing cost, *KBEJ* the monopoly profit, *JEL* the rents of the suppliers, and o*LEM* the alternative product of the factors used. This compares with the output o*R* under simple monopsony determined by the intersection of the marginal-cost and average-net-revenue curves at *H*, or the monopoly output o*P* determined by the intersection of the marginal-revenue and the supply curves at *G*.

In a more severely simplified case where the monopolist-monopsonist is merely a middleman purchasing in one market in which he is the only buyer and selling in another in which he is the only seller, the output and input can be measured in identical units, and the average-net-revenue curve *WBA* can then be considered as a "net-demand" curve derived from a "gross-demand" curve simply by subtracting the costs of transferring the commodity from one market to the other, which costs may be considered to be fairly closely proportional to the volume of sales. Thus in this case the net demand is merely the gross demand lowered by a constant cost of conversion *SW*.

Another way of handling this and more complicated problems involving an entrepreneur who has monopoloid positions in several markets is by separating off the buying and selling operation in each such market and treating it as a separate enterprise, exchanging the factor or product with the production unit at the marginal cost of the factor or marginal revenue of the product as determined in the respective markets. Maximum profit will then be obtained when the manufacturing unit operates as it would if these artificially determined prices were beyond its control, as in competition, while each buying or selling unit is operating as a simple monopoly or monopsony.

Discriminating Monopoly

ONE IMPORTANT case where a monopolist has dealings in several markets is that where he sells substantially the same product to different classes of customers. Where it is not possible for customers of one class to resell the commodity or service to those of another, or to act as agents for them, there may be opportunity for the monopolist to increase his profit by charging different prices to the different classes of customers. A case involving two classes of customers is shown in FIGURE 75. In the two markets, the two demand curves are BA and SR, respectively, and the corresponding marginal-revenue curves are BFG and SL. If the commodity is completely identical in the two markets, the marginal cost will depend on the combined output in the two markets, and may be shown in the curve TGA. To determine the sales pattern that will maximize total profits, we can consider what the sales

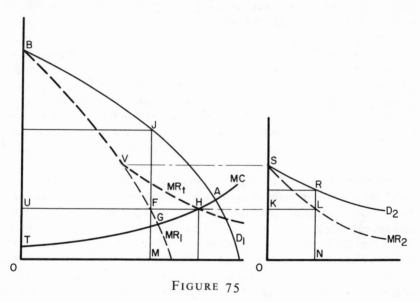

FIGURE 75

would have to be in the two markets if the level of marginal cost were given, which will be indicated by the two marginal-revenue curves. Thus if we add horizontally the two marginal-revenue curves, we obtain a curve BVH which indicates the aggregate sales that would maximize total profits for each level of marginal cost. The intersection of this curve with the marginal-cost curve at H will then indicate the most profitable output and the corresponding level of marginal cost. Setting marginal revenue equal to this marginal cost in the two markets at the points F and L, respectively, determines the sales oM and oN in the two markets, and the demand curves give the corresponding prices MJ and NR.

A similar result is obtained if we follow the suggestion in the preceding section and set up two agencies in each market, each acting as would a simple monopolist getting its supplies under competitive conditions at a price equal to marginal cost from the producing unit: if each agency treats this price as a fixed datum, their "demand" will follow the marginal-revenue curves of the respective markets, and the curve *BVH* becomes an aggregate-demand curve. The operating unit, if it behaves "competitively," treats the price it obtains as fixed and adjusts output to the amount *UH*.

It is important to note that such discrimination in prices between different markets will increase profits only if there is a difference in the elasticities of demand in the two markets. If the elasticity is the same, then, as we saw on page 290, $m = p(1 + 1/\epsilon)$, equal marginal revenues imply equal prices in the two markets, so that there will in effect be no discrimination. Or at least if there is discrimination in such cases it will in general produce less than the maximum possible profit and must be explained on other than profit-maximizing principles.

An interesting variant of this case occurs where there is some limit to the discrimination in price that can be made to stick—for example, when a differential in the delivered price between two localities cannot be made greater than the cost of shipping the commodity from one place to another, lest the customers in the higher-price locality purchase the commodity at the lower price and ship it to where it is to be used. Discrimination is thus aided where transportation costs are high. Sometimes artificial barriers such as tariffs are imposed in addition; discrimination made possible by tariff walls is often referred to as "dumping." Of course, if the prices that would be set according to the preceding analysis differ by less than this critical amount, there is no problem: the result can stand. If the difference would be greater, then the monopolist is constrained to keep the difference in price just below this critical level, otherwise in effect he will sell only at the lower price. One can then proceed by trying various levels for the lower price, with the higher price at corresponding levels, higher by just less than the critical differential; total sales and total revenues can be determined in each case, and marginal revenue can be derived and equated to marginal cost to determine the total output. The general case of this sort does not appear to lend itself readily to simple diagrammatic treatment, although Stigler has produced a diagrammatic solution for the special case where the demand curves can be treated as straight lines. And the still more general case where the "leakage" is not an all-or-nothing matter but varies according to the price differential is too complicated a problem to deal with in detail here.

Often, of course, the products sold in the two markets will not be identical with respect to cost, but in many cases this can be dealt with analytically by deducting any cost differentials from the demand curves for the higher-cost items, as where the cost of an item delivered in a remote market implies heavier transportation costs. More perplexing is the fact that where there are substantial cost differentials, it is often difficult to distinguish discrimination from mere differential pricing based on differences in costs. At one extreme one might take the position that all deviations of price from marginal cost involve discrimination, though this would rob the term of much of its impact. At the other it would be possible to insist that discrimination exists in the strict sense only in the obvious case where the two products are identical in terms of their costs, or where the cost and price differentials are in reverse directions. But most of the interesting cases come under neither of these extremes.

Indeed, the stigmatization of a given price practice or relationship as discriminatory is more often a legal or ethical operation to which economic theory can offer but little assistance. Particularly where a decreasing-cost industry is trying to break even, the distribution of the intra-marginal residue of costs over the various products can be made in a number of ways. Distributing this excess in inverse proportion to the elasticity of demand will in general come fairly close to minimizing the net social loss arising from failure to set prices at marginal cost, but to use this as a standard of discrimination seems much too difficult, since it would be required to know the elasticity of the various demand curves. Indeed, such a method of pricing is substantially what is meant by "charging in proportion to what the traffic will bear," ordinarily considered to be a highly discriminatory practice.

It might be considered appropriate in some cases to consider a non-discriminatory price structure to be one in which all prices are raised above marginal costs by a given uniform percentage. But cases will arise where such a pricing pattern would be entirely unsatisfactory. For example, if product A is convertible into product B by an operation that can be performed outside the production unit under consideration at a cost only slightly higher than inside, then to load this cost differential for inside conversion with a uniform portion of the intra-marginal residue for all operations combined would result in no product B being sold directly, but only product A, part of which will be turned into B by outside operations at an unnecessarily high cost. On the other hand, to increase prices over marginal cost by a constant amount per some unit in which the various products are commonly measured may also lead to difficulties. Indeed, the choice of the unit for this purpose may be somewhat arbitrary. One would get different results, for example, if the price of trucks were fixed by adding a fixed amount per vehicle to the various marginal costs of trucks of different models and sizes, rather than by adding a fixed amount per ton of truck capacity or per pound of net weight. It is not even clear on the surface which of these methods of pricing, or whether pricing at marginal cost plus a percentage thereof, would be most likely to lead purchasers of trucks to a correct decision (in terms of the community's total use of resources) in their attempt to select a truck that will be most economical for their purposes, everything considered. Probably the theorist would do well at this point to leave the use of the term "discrimination," at least in its more invidious applications, to lawyers and institutionalists.

[297

Caveats to the Use of Monopoly Theory

THE SIMPLE theory of monopoly and monopsony, given above, assumes fixed demand and supply curves, presumed to be known to the monopolist. We have already dealt with the possibility that the monopolist may be uncertain or mistaken as to the shape of his demand curve in connection with the discussion of the pure exchange economy on page 113. Another possibility that is ignored in this simple analysis is that the curves might respond, in some way other than the passive reaction assumed, to the actions of the monopolist. If, for example, there is a possibility that by setting too high a price the lure of profit might entice competitors into the field and thus lower the demand curve to the original monopolist, this potentiality is here to be treated, if at all, by modifying the demand curve to reflect this long-run possibility. Other possible threats to the enjoyment of unrestricted monopoly are less amenable to inclusion in a rigorous analysis, and their implications can only be considered qualitatively. Among these are the possibility of bringing on public regulation, or antitrust action, or stimulating the development of defensive monopolies of customers that would result in a state of bilateral monopoly. In some cases the "tastes" of consumers may be adversely affected by too full an exploitation of a monopoly, in that too high a price might lead consumers to experiment with alternative products and possibly to a complete shift. Maintenance of the good will of customers may affect their tastes, also. On the other side, potential competitors may possibly be kept out of the field by threats of price wars, or by temporary price-cutting; this, however, properly belongs in the strategy of oligopoly rather than the theory of monopoly.

Selling Costs

ONE RATHER important phase of monopoly that is fairly easy to incorporate in a formal analysis is that of selling costs. Very often the market in which a monopolist sells is imperfect in that the demand curve is not a fixed datum, but can be influenced to varying degrees by advertising and other types of promotional effort. While in practice the determination of the optimum amount to spend on sales and promotion is an extremely difficult problem, the formal analysis presents no difficulty, provided that we regard sales effort as a means of obtaining a higher price for a given level of output, rather than, as is more common, as a means of increasing sales at a given price. As sales effort can be regarded as having the effect of shifting the demand curve away from the origin, we are still free to measure this shift in terms of the vertical distance between the before and after demand curves, rather than in terms of the horizontal distance. If this is done, it is a simple matter to inquire, for each level of output, what level of sales effort will result in the maximum net revenues after deducting from the gross price obtained the cost of the sales effort. This net revenue per unit of output, plotted against output, then can be treated as a "net-demand" curve and the analysis can proceed substantially as before. In effect, for analytical purposes one can again separate the productive function from the marketing function, the marketing function being one of securing the maximum possible net revenue from any given level of production, and of ascertaining the marginal net revenue obtainable from an additional unit of product, and the productive function simply being the matching of marginal cost and marginal net revenue.

Of course, none of this actually helps the sales agency perform the task of maximizing net revenue; the theory merely assumes that it can be done, in exactly the same fashion as theory assumes that the production function is known to the entrepreneur. The problem that is of more direct concern to the economic theorist is how to evaluate the welfare consequences of selling activity and the costs involved. Not all selling activity is wasteful: while much advertising is actually misleading rather then helpful to the consumer, some does actually help him secure a better satisfaction of his ultimate wants than he would be able to secure without its aid. And some sales activity is in the form of subsidiary service to customers that in effect enhances the value of the product they buy. Methods of appraisal of these values, however, are still practically nonexistent, so that this phase of economic analysis must for the time being be skipped over with merely this passing reference.

Mathematical Appendix

IF A MONOPOLIST'S demand curve is given by $q(p)$, total revenue is $R = pq$, and marginal revenue is

$$m = \left(\frac{dR}{dq}\right) = p + q\left(\frac{dp}{dq}\right) = p + q\frac{1}{\left(\frac{dq}{dp}\right)} \qquad 7.1$$

The elasticity of the demand curve is a negative number defined as

$$\epsilon_d = \frac{p\,dq}{q\,dp} = \frac{d(\log q)}{d(\log p)} \qquad 7.2$$

We immediately have the important relation given in the text:

$$m = p\left[1 + \frac{1}{p}q\frac{1}{\left(\frac{dq}{dp}\right)}\right] = p\left(1 + \frac{q\,dp}{p\,dq}\right) = p\left(1 + \frac{1}{\epsilon_d}\right) \qquad 7.3$$

[299

EXERCISES

THERE are 1,000 consumers of elbow grease, each of whom consumes monthly the amount given in the following table, according to the price. There are also 100 plants engaged in the manufacture of elbow grease, the variable costs at the various outputs being, for each plant, as given in the table below.

1,000 Consumers		100 Plants	
Price, dollars per quart	Consumption, quarts per consumer per month	Output, quarts per plant per month	Variable costs, total, dollars per plant per month
26	0	0	0
14	1	10	30
10	2	20	62
8	3	30	96
6	5	40	132
5	7	50	170
4	11	60	212
3	23	70	259
(2.5	47)	80	312
(2.2	119)	90	371
		100	442

a. If there is competition on both sides of the market, how much will be produced and consumed, in the short run, before plants can be built or dismantled? What will be the price? What will be the gross profit?

b. If the producers organize a monopoly while the consumers act competitively, what will be the price, output, and gross profit (still in the short run)?

c. What will be the approximate consumer's surplus in case *a*? In case *b*? What will be the net social loss resulting from the monopoly (short run)?

d. If the consumers organize a monopoly while the producers compete with each other, what will be the output, price, gross profit, consumer's rent? (Hint: Consider the consumers to be manufacturers who use elbow grease to run the robots in their factory. What does their demand curve, in the competitive case, represent? What, as monopolists, do they maximize [short run]?)

e. What plausible reason might there be for the large increase in demand as the price decreases below $3 per quart?

f. New plants can be built and placed in operation for fixed charges and overhead amounting to $30 per month, including normal return on the investment. With free entry and full competition, what are the results?

g. Total fixed charges and overhead amount to $214 per month per plant, of which $136 consists of current items incurred only if the plant is kept in operation, the remaining $78 being unavoidable "sunk" costs. Plants wear out with catastrophic suddenness, like the deacon's one-horse shay, after 100 months of use, one of the existing plants wearing out each month. What are the immediate results? What tends to take place over a period of time? What is the ultimate equilibrium position? How long does it take to reach it? How is it maintained thereafter?

h. Returning to a competitive short-run situation, as in *a*, suppose that a tax of $1 per quart is imposed on the manufacture of elbow grease. What are the results?

i. What happens if the tax is increased to $2? Compare the net social loss in this case with that in case *h*.

j. Suppose that in case *f* a tax of $.50 per quart were imposed; what would be the results? Compare the incidence of the tax in this case with that in cases *h* and *i*.

k. Suppose that in case *g* there were a tax of $1.50 per quart in addition to other costs; what would the immediate and final results be? Compare the immediate and final incidence of the tax.

l. Returning to case *f*, suppose that in competition with the new plants with annual charges of $30 and variable costs as shown in the table there are in existence a few old and partially obsolete plants with variable costs $.50 per quart higher than those of the new plants, at corresponding rates of output. What would such plants rent for if other annual fixed costs to be borne by the user amount to $5 per month? If these costs are $10 per month?

CHAPTER EIGHT

Imperfect Competition

Approaches to Imperfect Competition

ONCE WE LEAVE monopoly, which is a situation that can be analyzed in fairly definite terms with on the whole a fairly close correspondence between cases encountered in the real world and the simplified models of the analysis, we come to an area in which the analysis is in a much less satisfactory state. Situations intermediate between monopoly and perfect competition are many and diverse; the various aspects of most situations are in practice closely interrelated in a way that rapidly becomes too complex for complete analysis, and the results often depend in a crucial way on the operation of volatile psychological factors that are difficult to reduce to any precise formulation. Analysis in this area consists very largely of independent investigations of a number of fairly distinct special cases, each featuring in a much oversimplified form one of the many elements that may be factors in real situations. And while some of the interrelations between the various types of analysis have been discussed fairly precisely, and others can be perceived in a rather vague way, very little has as yet been done to build an integrated structure from the whole set of analyses. In a sense, we have succeeded in beating some paths part of the way into the jungle from different starting points, sufficiently to begin to get an idea of the general topography, and to get within shouting distance of each other; this is still, however, a long way from being able to say that the jungle has been fully explored.

There are three main categories of starting points: one is pure duopoly and oligopoly, another is product differentiation, and the theory of games is a third. Duopoly is the study of the behavior of two sellers selling in the same market; oligopoly is the case where the sellers are few, but insufficiently numerous to produce the competitive result. In pure duopoly or oligopoly, the consumer has absolutely no preference for the product of one seller over the product of any other: the products of the various sellers are identical in every relevant respect. This is also expressed by saying that the products are perfect substitutes for each other, or that there is perfect cross-elasticity of demand for each product in terms of the prices of the others.

Product differentiation refers to cases where there are differences between the products of the various sellers, but the differences are not so great that changes in the price for one seller's product will not influence appreciably the demand for the products of his competitors. Where the differences consist of differences in location, we have spatial competition, a class of cases that are of special interest because of the relative simplicity of the interrelationships between the demands for the products of various suppliers. Monopolistic competition and nonprice competition also belong in this category. The difference in products may be objectively significant and measurable, or it may exist only in the imagination of the consumer: the differentiation of trademarked articles can sometimes be of this character.

The theory-of-games approach focuses attention on cases where sellers are acutely conscious of the effects of their actions on the actions of their competitors, and of the actions of their competitors on their own profits. It attempts to solve (but with only limited success) the problem of enumerating possible outcomes where strategy and possible coalitions between firms are important elements of the situation. The theory-of-games approach can be applied both where products are differentiated and where they are not, but for successful application it requires that the nature of the situation be specified with great accuracy, something that is often not possible for product differentiation cases.

Duopoly and Oligopoly

IN DUOPOLY we have for the first time to distinguish fairly carefully between price policy, in which the seller fixes his price and expects to supply all the demand that presents itself at that price, and output policy, in which the seller determines his output and throws it on the market for what it will bring. Under perfect competition only an output policy was possible, since by hypothesis a seller could have no influence on the price: if he were to set a price higher than the market price he would make no sales, while if he were to set a lower price he would have more orders than he could fill. Under simple monopoly both kinds of policy were possible, but as the same result would be obtained with either policy, it made no difference which was assumed. Here, however, it will make all the difference to the results whether competitors are assumed to select an output, and stick to it at least for a brief period, or to select a price and hold to that for some brief period.

Analytically, the easier case to deal with is that where an output policy is followed. In general, this assumption leads to fairly determinate results. The several sellers determine their outputs, whereupon the market price is determined by the demand price for this aggregate output.

Where a price policy is followed by sellers of undifferentiated products, however, usually some additional assumptions will be needed in order to determine how the total demand is distributed among the various sellers. If one seller has the lowest price, it is of course natural to assume that he will get all the sales and the others none, unless indeed his capacity is limited and he turns some customers away, in which case the demand will go to the successively higher-priced sellers until the demand is satisfied. Here, as we saw in the case of hotel rooms on pages 225–35, it is in principle necessary to make some assumption as to how the fortunate customers able to secure the commodity at the lowest price are to be determined, in order that it be possible to specify the number out of those remaining who will be willing to pay the next higher price. However, in most models of this sort the difference at any given time between the various prices being charged is ordinarily so small as to make the possible differences on this score of little importance. More awkward is the case where there are two or more sellers with the lowest price, and where these sellers have sufficient capacity to supply more than the demand at this price; in this case an additional assumption becomes necessary in order to determine how the total demand is to be allocated among these suppliers. Often for the sake of simplicity it is merely assumed that each supplier will get an equal share, although there is ordinarily nothing to compel this result or even to make it particularly probable.

There are of course other "policies" possible: for example, one competitor may follow an output policy while others follow a price policy; or a price may be specified together with an upper limit on sales, or a firm may attempt to insist on getting a certain share of the entire market. To start with, however, we will turn our attention to the simplest case, that of output policies.

The Cournot Case

THE FIRST case of pure duopoly to be analyzed with any precision is that where two or more producers follow an output policy, and where each adjusts his output on the assumption that the others will continue to supply their current output. This is referred to as the Cournot case, it being the case treated by Augustin Cournot in *Recherches sur les principes mathématiques de la théorie des richesses*, published in 1838.

FIGURE 76 shows the simplest case where there are two firms, each producing an identical commodity at no cost (Cournot's original case was that of owners of identical mineral springs). If the demand curve is a straight line *FLHJ*, we can start with one of the firms, say *A*, supplying the market as a monopolist, and supplying an amount equal to half of what could be sold at the marginal cost price of zero, or an output of o*G* at the price *GF*. If *B* now enters the market, and considers *A*'s current output o*G* to be fixed, he will find himself faced with a leftover demand given by the portion of the demand curve *FJ*, considering now the point *G* as the origin for *B*'s output. The greatest net revenue that *B* can secure for himself will be obtained by supplying half of this remaining demand, so that the price now drops to *KH*, with three-fourths of the total demand being supplied, half by *A* and one-fourth by *B*.

304]

But now *A* in his turn looks at the situation, and finding *B* supplying one-fourth of the total demand, has three-fourths left to deal with himself. On the assumption that *B* will continue to produce at the one-fourth level, *A* finds that he will maximize his own profits by supplying an amount equal to half of this new "leftover" market, or three-eighths of the total. When *A* has so adjusted his output, it will again be *B*'s turn to adjust, and a series of adjustments will continue, approaching as a limit a final equilibrium position indicated at *L*, in which *A* and *B* are each supplying one-third of the total demand, one-third being left unsupplied. As long as *A* maintains the same

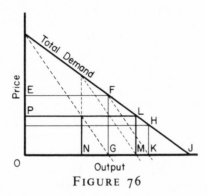

FIGURE 76

output, *B* cannot increase or decrease his output without reducing his profits, and the same is true for *A* if *B*'s output remains unchanged. Each will make a profit of four-ninths of the profit made by the single monopolist; i.e., together they will make one-ninth less profit than the monopolist. Consumer's surplus will of course be substantially increased.

This result is the one reached by Cournot. However, it tends to last only so long as both *A* and *B* persist in believing, contrary to experience, that changes in their own outputs will not induce any change in the output of the other. Thus this case could be termed the "naive-naive" case. If *A*, for example, finally realizes that *B* is not keeping his output constant after each change in *A*'s output, but is always adjusting so as to supply half of the market not supplied by *A*, so that in effect *A* always gets a price just half of what he would get if *A* were the only producer, then assuming this reaction will persist, *A* would maximize his profits by going back to an output equal to half of the total demand, leaving *B* to adjust as best he can by supplying one-fourth of the total demand, with one-fourth left unsupplied. The total profit is smaller than in either of the preceding situations, but *A* gets a profit equal to half that of the monopolist, *B* only one-fourth, instead of four-ninths each.

This result is asymmetrical; indeed, it can be identified as the "sophisticated-naive" case, in that *A* anticipates his competitor's reaction while *B* does not.

But at this point, even if B should become aware of what has been happening, it is difficult for him to know what to do next. A has just demonstrated that his action can no longer be determined on the basis of maximizing profit on the assumption that B's output will remain unchanged. As long as A persists in producing an output equal to half of the market, the best that B can do is to supply one-fourth. If B reduces his output, this increases A's profits and reduces B's. If B increases his output beyond one-fourth, his profits and A's will both be reduced, at least at first. B may increase his output to one-third and keep it there, hoping that if he keeps it there long enough, A will accept this as a fixed datum and himself cut his output to one-third. Or B may attempt to drive A out of the preferred position by increasing his output to one-half, thus driving the price to zero until one or the other decides to cut his output, and if A eventually does so he will then find himself in B's former disadvantageous position. But which of these events takes place is essentially a matter of tactics in a struggle for economic advantage; it is not the resultant of a balancing of forces and does not result in anything that could be described as an equilibrium.

Thus even in this simple case, duopoly yields a determinate solution only so long as a fairly unrealistic assumption is made by one of the duopolists concerning the behavior of the other. The moment one of them begins to think much about the possible reactions of the other, the solution shifts, and if both become sophisticated the solution breaks down into a series of tactical maneuvers, the outcome of which it is hard to predict. Of course, one ultimate possibility is always collusion between the two duopolists against the consumer, in which case the monopoly output will be produced and the price will be the monopoly price; there may still be a problem, however, of determining how this output, or the profits, will be distributed between the two parties. In the present case, symmetry may be held to dictate an equal division, but there will be other cases where this argument cannot be appealed to and the outcome will be still uncertain. Attempts to resolve problems such as this one generally belong in the domain of the theory of games, to be considered later.

Some slight additional justification for regarding the original Cournot solution (the naive-naive case) as an applicable one may be derived from considering that approximately this same result would be likely to arise if each duopolist were to regard himself as a monopolist unaffected by the actions of the other, as would be the case, for example, if each ignored the existence of the other and attributed fluctuations in his demand schedule as being the result of ineluctable forces outside his own influence, or if each was convinced (contrary to fact) that his own product was so completely differentiated from that of the other, as by brand name, that no customers attached to the one brand would ever desert it in favor of the other. Each seller might be assumed to make occasional experimental variations in his output in order to explore the current degree of elasticity of demand. The results of such experimentation by one of them will of course be obscured by variations in his demand induced by simultaneous experimentation of the other, but if each acts fairly randomly and in ignorance of the other, these variations may be assumed to be random, and the two sellers will each arrive at an average estimate of their demand and of its elasticity corresponding to the actual demand that exists when the output of the other is fixed at its average level. The two sellers would thus

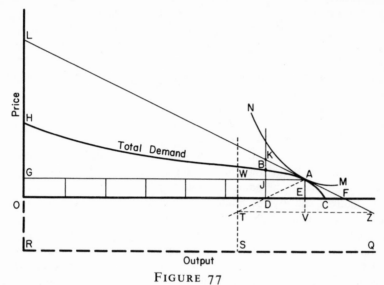

FIGURE 77

ultimately be led to the conclusion that the output that maximizes their profit is the output determined by the Cournot solution.

The treatment can be generalized (as it was by Cournot) to cover n sellers and a demand curve that is not necessarily linear, as in FIGURE 77. Considering first the linear case, if the total demand is $LKAF$, and each supplier considers the supply of the others, aggregating oD, as fixed, he will supply an amount determined so as to maximize his profit $DJAE$. As each seller in turn puts himself on the end of the supply, equilibrium requires that he supply the amount DE, or half of the demand not supplied by others. The total amount supplied will thus be $n \cdot DE$, and the total demand oF will be $(n + 1)DE$; the total amount supplied is thus $[n/(n + 1)]$oF. The elasticity of demand at A will be FE/o$E = -1/n$.

Now if we consider the case of the nonlinear demand, we note immediately that the point A is still an equilibrium point for any demand curve which is tangent to the line $LKAF$ at A (although it may be an unstable equilibrium if the demand curve is convex to the origin as is NAM). Thus we can say that for zero marginal cost and n sellers, the Cournot equilibrium point will be a point where elasticity of the demand curve is $-1/n$. Moreover, as long as the demand curve is such that it becomes less elastic as the price declines, we observe that as we make n larger and larger, the equilibrium output approaches nearer and nearer to the competitive output. This result led to a feeling that the Cournot solution supplied a neat continuous series of cases ranging from monopoly at one end to perfect competition at the other.

If production is not costless, but involves a constant marginal cost that is the same for each producer, the analysis and the results are much the same, the only difference being that the line oDEF now represents not a price of zero, but a price equal to the marginal cost, the zero price line now being the dotted line RQ in FIGURE 77. The elasticity of point A will no longer be equal to $-1/n$, but we will still be able to compute a "pseudo-elasticity" in which instead of putting

$$\epsilon = \frac{p}{q}\frac{dq}{dp} \quad \text{we put} \quad \epsilon' = \frac{p-m}{q}\frac{dq}{d(p-m)}$$

That is, we still treat o as the origin to which to refer this "pseudo-elasticity," even though it no longer represents zero price. This pseudo-elasticity will then be equal to $-1/n$ at the point of equilibrium.

The analysis can also be modified to consider variations in marginal cost among the competitors. Thus if GA represents aggregate output at equilibrium, and a given seller has a marginal cost represented by ST, he will be individually in equilibrium if he is producing an amount TV, which maximizes his profit $TVAW$. If we extend the tangent to the demand curve at A to meet the horizontal line TV at Z, TV will be half of TZ. The relative amounts supplied by the various suppliers will in each case be proportional to the difference between the uniform market price RG and their respective various marginal costs; thus the suppliers with the low marginal costs will supply more than those with higher marginal costs.

The above analysis tacitly assumes that each supplier knows the aggregate-demand curve $HBAC$, or at least knows its elasticity in the neighborhood of the equilibrium point A. Actually, the equilibrium depends not on the actual demand curve, but on the demand curve as it is imagined by the various suppliers. If all have the same estimate of the elasticity of the demand curve, then the above analysis applies without modification, provided we treat $HBAC$ as the demand curve imagined by all the suppliers and that the "real" demand curve also passes through A so as not to provide an experience that would compel a revision of estimates. Subject to this condition, it actually makes no difference to the outcome what the real demand curve happens to be.

It is likely, however, that different suppliers will have different ideas as to the elasticity of the aggregate-demand curve. In this case, their outputs will also vary even when marginal costs are all the same: the more elastic the

308]

individual seller's idea of the demand curve, the greater will be his relative output. If the putative elasticity is expressed as a pseudo-elasticity referred to the marginal-cost level as a base line, the several outputs will be proportional to the respective putative pseudo-elasticities. It is even possible for the total amount supplied by an oligopoly in which each supplier believes the demand to be very inelastic to be smaller than the output of a monopolist with a higher (and possibly more correct) estimate of the elasticity of demand. Also, in such a situation it is to the interest of each supplier to persuade the others that the demand is very inelastic so as to induce them to reduce their output and raise their price. A faint echo of this in the real world may perhaps be read into some materials found in trade literature that proclaim the inelasticity of demand, at least for the industry as a whole.

Oligopoly with Price Policies

THE ABOVE approach to oligopoly can be criticized as highly unrealistic in that in the contemporary economic world few if any firms in a monopoloid position follow an output policy; rather, most firms actually set a price and let output be determined by this price and by the reactions of other firms, possibly with considerable effort on the side to influence demand through sales effort. If firms thus have price policies rather than output policies, i.e., have "administered prices," the results are found to be quite different from those obtained in the output policy case, and generally less stable.

First, if each seller assumes the other will keep his current price unchanged, and if each has sufficient capacity to supply the entire demand, then we have substantially "cutthroat competition." On these assumptions, each seller can gain all the customers of the others by lowering his price to just below that of the other. Undercutting will continue back and forth in this manner until there is no longer anything to be gained by further undercutting by any of the sellers. If all have the same costs, the end result is likely to be substantially the competitive position, even with only two sellers: price will be reduced to marginal cost, and each seller, having first set a price uniform with all the others, adjusting his sales to the level at which marginal cost is equal to this price.

A slight modification of this case occurs where one seller has a marginal cost lower than any of the others: in this case, the price will be driven down by undercutting only to the level of the next higher marginal cost; below this level, the low-cost producer is in a position of limited monopoly and can obtain a profit equal to the difference between his cost and that of the next seller. However, since he can presumably expand his sales greatly by just slightly undercutting his competitors, he will presumably do this and expand his output until his marginal cost rises to the level set by the costs of his next competitor, or until he has in fact absorbed the entire market and is in the

[309

position of a monopolist restrained by the threat of the re-entry of competitors. But these cases are hardly significant departures from the competitive result: in the last case the profits of the low-cost producer are presumably a form of rent imputable to whatever scarce resource is responsible for his costs being lower than those of others.

But here, even more than when output policy is the rule, it is absurd for a seller to assume that a competitor would keep his price constant in the face of loss of most or all of his business. But is there any definite rule of behavior that it would be reasonable to expect one's competitor, selling an identical commodity in a perfect market, to adhere to? This is, indeed, the rock on which most attempts to construct a theory of pure duopoly in terms of price policies have foundered. We can, however, take a passing look at some of the results of the simpler assumptions.

One assumption might be that any price set by A would be matched by B, provided that this price is not higher than that which B considers would give the maximum monopoly profit for the two sellers together, and that sales at the uniform price will be divided between the two in some fixed ratio. Then no matter what price A sets, he gets this fixed proportion of the total demand at that price, and he is in substantially the same position that he would be in were he a monopolist in a market proportionally smaller than the one he shares with B. The tendency in this situation is then for the price to be the monopoly price, the maximum monopoly profit being shared between A and B according to the fixed proportions in which sales are divided.

There is, however, one difference between this situation and that of simple monopoly: with a single seller, the price actually set depends on the monopolist's idea of the demand curve, whereas with two sellers in the field, there may be disagreement as to what price actually is the profit-maximizing price. If A sets a price higher than B thinks will produce the maximum net revenue, B may stick to the lower price, which he thinks is most profitable, and A will be helpless to do anything but come down to B's price; otherwise A would be out in the cold and B would be left with the entire monopoly profit. B on the other hand has no incentive to follow A's lead as to price since he believes that A's price would give a lower total profit. Accordingly, the price set in this situation tends to be the lowest of the various monopoly prices as estimated by the various sellers. A similar situation can arise through differences in marginal costs among the sellers: the seller with the lower marginal cost would be the one to determine the price: he will set it at a level such that marginal revenue becomes equal to his own marginal cost.

Another possibility, suggested by Edgeworth, exists where the capacity of the sellers is limited, so that at some stage it will be possible for a seller to raise his price above that charged by others and still be able to sell to those customers who have not been able to satisfy their demand from the limited capacity of those with lower prices. In such a model there comes a time in the price-cutting process where price-cutting becomes less attractive than exploiting at a higher price the demand which the low-price seller cannot satisfy. For example, *A* may realize that *B* cannot supply the entire demand at the price that *B* is currently quoting, and that hence *A* is in a position to exploit whatever part of the demand *B* turns away as a monopolist, and if *B*'s price is down close to *A*'s cost, such exploitation may yield more profit to *A* than an attempt to undercut *B*. *A*, therefore, instead of undercutting *B*, jumps his price back up to the monopoly level. If we assume here, as in the hotel problem, that the successful purchasers of the limited amount of the lower-priced product offered by *B* will be a random sample of all those willing to pay the low price, the monopoly price for the unsatisfied demand will be the same as the monopoly price for the entire market. *B*, however, may now either match *A*'s price, or just undercut it, since at the higher price he may have the capacity to supply a much larger proportion of the effective demand, or even the whole of it. The process of price-cutting then begins all over again in a cyclical pattern that has, however, no time period.

Such a model rather suggests the repeated price wars that break out spasmodically in some commodities. But it can hardly be expected that this process would repeat itself more than a few times before some rather significant change occurred in the expectations of sellers as to the reactions of others to their own changes in price. And in any case a strictly limited capacity is likely to be only a short-run phenomenon.

A more modern version of this model expresses the limited capacity not as a fixed limit, but as a rising marginal-cost curve. After price-cutting has driven the price down to the competitive level, given by the intersection of the demand curve and the horizontal sum of the marginal-cost curves, the more perspicacious of the two competitors may realize that an increase in his price will shift only a part of his demand to his competitor: even if his competitor were to allow his price to rise to just below his own increased price, the competitor's output would not be increased by more than is indicated by his marginal-cost curve. The situation may be illustrated in FIGURE 78. The marginal-cost curve of each supplier is *ANGF*, so that by adding two of these curves together we get the competitive supply curve *AJ*, and *J*, the intersection of this curve with the demand curve *EFJHK* is the point of competitive equilibrium reached after price-cutting. At this point, supplier *A* may realize that if he raises his price, say to *oQ*, then even if *B* keeps his price just below *A*'s so as to get the first chance at all the customers, *B* will limit his sales to the amount *QR* indicated by his marginal-cost curve, and will turn away any additional customers. *A* will thus be left with sales of *RT*. Thus on this most pessimistic assumption (from *A*'s point of view), we can subtract *B*'s marginal-cost curve *ANGRF* horizontally from the demand curve *EFJHK*, to get the curve *BSGHK*, which is the amount that *A* can sell at various prices, assuming that *B* will just undercut him and sell the amount indicated by his marginal-cost curve. From this partial demand curve we can derive the corresponding marginal-revenue curve $BNLM$. If then A's marginal-cost curve is the same as B's, namely, $ANGRF$, A's output will be determined by the intersection at N, so that the final price is oQ, A's output is $QS = RT$. A's gross profit is $ANSQ$, but B's profit is $QRGNA$, or perhaps slightly less than this because of the price differential that B is supposed to maintain.

This case is perhaps a bit peculiar in that A who takes the initiative in raising the price above the competitive level and perhaps may be termed the

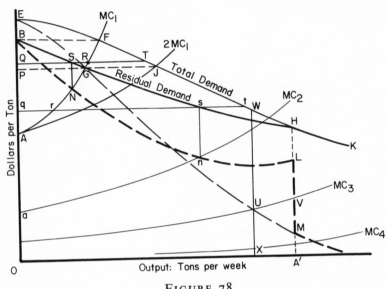

FIGURE 78

"price leader" winds up with a smaller profit than does B, whose role, ostensibly at least, is passive. This fact may tend to produce a slight instability in the result, in that at the competitive position there may be some jockeying to induce the other seller to make the first move, while at the price oQ there would still be a temptation to cut prices, not only for the immediate advantage, but for the sake of inducing a possible reversal of the roles of A and B.

Some escape from this indeterminacy is obtained when there is a substantial difference between the marginal-cost curves of the two sellers, particularly if the lower one also has a greater elasticity. Under these circumstances there may be a fairly definite tendency for the low-cost seller, say A, to assume and retain the role of price leader, since if B were to assume this role, A would be selling much the larger part of the demand and obtaining much the larger share of the profits, and this would hardly sit well with B.

Or a similar analysis may be carried out in which A is the dominant seller, while instead of *B* there are a group of small sellers none of which is large enough to have an important influence on the price, and who are thought of as having an output policy rather than a price policy. In this case *A* is sometimes said to be "holding up the umbrella" for the smaller, possibly higher-cost, producers. Still another case occurs where *A*'s marginal cost is so much lower than that of his competitors, actual or potential, that it intersects the marginal-revenue curve below *L*. In such cases, other sellers will be cut out of the market entirely. Indeed, if *A*'s marginal-cost curve passes below *M*, as

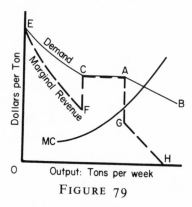

FIGURE 79

does the curve MC_4, then this means that *A*'s position in the market is so secure by reason of having marginal costs so much below that of the nearest competitor that the presence of such potential competitors has no effect on his actions, and he behaves in every respect as a pure monopolist. Where the marginal-cost curve passes between *M* and *L*, however, the presence of competitors with marginal costs starting at *A* means that *A*'s output will be determined by the intersection at *V* rather than the intersection at *U* with the curve *EUM* that is what the marginal-revenue curve would have been had *A* been the only seller in the market. The price and output corresponding to *V* are o*A'* and *A'H*, respectively; i.e., the price is just low enough to preclude any profitable sales on the part of a competitor, whereas with an unthreatened monopoly the output would have been o*X* and the price *XW*. The same output and price, as indicated at *H*, will result for any marginal cost falling within the range *LM*. It is only when *A*'s marginal cost rises above *L* that the price will be set high enough for competitors to enter with profit.

Still another interesting case occurs if each seller assumes that any attempt to expand sales at the expense of other sellers by cutting his price below the prevailing level will induce competitors to meet the cut fairly promptly, whereas an increase in price will be matched perhaps only slowly if at all. The individual seller would then regard his demand curve as having some such shape as shown in FIGURE 79, where starting from the point *A*, any reduction

[313

in price will increase sales only to the extent of a proportionate share in the increase in total demand, as along the segment AB. On the other hand, any increase in price above the prevailing level will immediately lose a substantial portion of sales, the seller retaining only those customers who either have a special preference for his product (which would imply at least some differentiation) or who cannot satisfy their demand from others because of their limited capacity; thus the demand curve in the other direction would look something like ACE. Corresponding to the demand curve $ECAB$ is the marginal-revenue curve $EFCAGH$. It will be seen that for any marginal-cost curve in the entire range AG, the maximum profit point will be at A. Thus over a wide range of conditions, sellers will tend to keep their prices at the prevailing level rather than attempt to change them. This analysis, then, presents one possible explanation for the "stickiness" of prices that goes beyond mere inertia and costs of administering a change; it applies primarily to "administered" prices and not to "market" prices. The trouble with this analysis is chiefly that while it indicates why prices tend to stay where they are, it furnishes little or no information as to how any particular level of prices happens to get established in the first place. For this we would probably have to go over the history of the industry, which would take us out into dynamics. Indeed, perhaps the most useful way to apply such an analysis is to use it as a background for explaining lags in dynamic price changes.

Product Differentiation

THUS AS LONG as the products of the various sellers are perfect substitutes for each other and consumers shift completely from one seller to another in response to any price differential, no matter how small, any price higher than the competitive price has only a relatively precarious stability, particularly where the tendency is toward price policy rather than output policy. And of course where there are increasing returns to scale, even the competitive price is an untenable one in the long run. And in view of these rather unsatisfactory and even rather unrealistic results of analysis based on strict identity of the products, many attempts have been made to proceed in the direction of a less perfect "workable competition" by relaxing the conditions somewhat. And indeed in practice substitutability between the products of different sellers is usually less than perfect, and recognition of this fact will lead to a substantial modification of the analysis and its results. Even where differentiation of product does not arise naturally, producers will often attempt to introduce an artificial differentiation, either through some genuine variation in the characteristics of the product, or through branding and advertising, in the hope of protecting themselves in some degree against the rigors of competition and the effects of price-cutting by others. Or by tacit mutual consent, after having found price competition to result in relatively low profits, price competition may be set aside in favor of various forms of nonprice competition such as sales promotion, auxiliary services, and the like, such as may be difficult for competitors to copy promptly, and so may have some chance of increasing profits more than momentarily.

The introduction of product differentiation, however, will enormously complicate the analysis unless some rather drastic simplifications are introduced. Now each competitor has not only a price to determine, but is also at liberty to vary a large number of parameters pertaining to the characteristics of the product that he is to offer, if indeed he does not go further and offer several varieties. And on the demand side, we no longer can simply assume that each customer seeks to buy first from the lowest-priced seller; quality differences may lead individual consumers to select a higher-priced article in preference to one with a lower price, and the demand for the product of any one seller is likely to depend in a fairly complex way on the whole array of prices prevailing in the group of more or less closely substitutable commodities.

To reduce the problem to manageable proportions, some fairly drastic simplifying assumptions are required. One way of doing this is to concentrate first on the price aspects of the problem, and to assume that in some way, either by historical accident or otherwise, the characteristics of the product to be offered by the various sellers has been determined, in which case the remaining problem is simply one of determining how each seller will then set his price. Another simplifying assumption often made is that of symmetry; i.e., while the products of the various sellers are different, each one of them bears the same relation to the others; none is superior or inferior, but each one is merely more closely adapted to the needs and requirements of its own particular group of consumers. On this assumption it is possible to set up an analysis for a single seller, and by virtue of the symmetry assumption this analysis will also apply to all the others and we can assume that they all behave in the same way. After the analysis has been carried through on this basis, the results can then be carried over in a rough qualitative way to the cases where the symmetry assumption does not apply. This is the general approach of the "monopolistic-competition" analysis introduced by E. H. Chamberlin.

Another way of reducing the problem to manageable proportions is to assume a comparatively simple, or at least systematic, relationship between the various prices and the demand for the various products. One ready way to visualize such a systematic relationship is to represent the differences between the various products by differences in location of the producers, and, similarly, to represent the different preferences of the consumers by locating them at different points geographically, in relation to the location of the producers. Costs of transportation then induce customers to buy from one seller in preference to another unless price differentials are sufficient to

[315

overcome this preference. This type of analysis, developed by Hotelling, Lerner, Singer, Smithies, and others, is sometimes termed "spatial competition."

As an example of "monopolistic competition" we can again make use of the hotel industry, but in this case instead of all hotels being alike with no individual having any preference for one hotel over any other, we now assume that they differ from one another in style, location, or other characteristics, so that we can have a substantial difference in price without necessarily inducing all prospective guests to apply first at the hotel having the lowest price. But while the hotels differ, they are sufficiently similar so that demand at any one hotel will be substantially affected by the prices charged at others. The symmetry assumption, however, precludes any hierarchy in these differences: at a uniform price, each hotel has a clientele which considers it the hotel best suited to its needs and tastes, and in no case is one hotel considered generally superior or inferior to another one. Perhaps the easiest way to specify such symmetry is to consider all hotels as being similar in every respect except as to location, and to suppose that they are all located equally spaced in a circle about the center of town, in such a way that if all hotels charged the same price, the total demand would distribute itself evenly among them.

The aggregate demand for rooms will of course depend in general on the entire price structure for the different hotels; however, the symmetry assumption makes it natural to give special attention to the case where all prices are equal, and on this assumption we can draw an aggregate-demand curve giving the relation between the common price and the aggregate demand. This aggregate demand can be divided equally, according to the symmetry assumption, among the various hotels to give a demand curve for each hotel shown as D_1 in FIGURE 80, with its corresponding marginal-revenue curve MR_1. Average-cost and marginal-cost curves for each individual hotel are also shown as AN and $ABMG$, respectively.

Now if an individual hotel operator thinks that D_1 represents the alternatives actually open to him, as it actually does represent the alternatives available to all the hotels simultaneously, and if he attempts to maximize his profits on this assumption, his policy will be indicated by the intersection of the marginal-cost curve with the curve MR_1 at B, giving a volume oE at a price EF. If all hotel operators do likewise, there will actually result an equilibrium at F, which is in effect a result substantially the same as the monopoly result, except for the fact that if all hotels were operated by a single monopolist, costs might be reduced by shutting down some of the hotels and operating the others at the minimum point of their average-cost curves, U, so that marginal cost would be oY and the profit-maximizing policy would be indicated by the intersection with the curve MR_1 at V, giving a price WX and an output YV. Depending on the shape of the marginal-cost curve, this price may be either higher or lower than EF.

Such an equilibrium may be maintained at close to the monopoly output as long as each operator feels that any price cut on his part would be met by all of the others, or if this price is kept by a more or less tacit agreement. But one or more of the operators is likely to feel that if he lowers his price he will increase his volume by more than his share in the total increase in demand that would result if everyone cut his price equally; i.e., he expects to attract some additional customers from other hotels, or perhaps merely gain more than his share of the new customers generated by the price reduction. He may feel that not all of the other hotels will copy his price cut immediately, especially

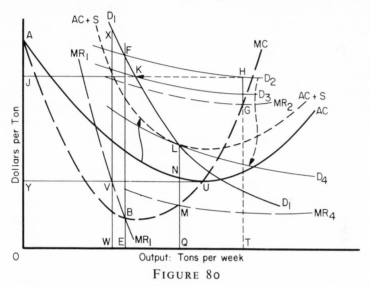

FIGURE 80

if some of them are on the other side of town, and if, contrary to our assumption, there are differences of rank as well as of variety so that not all prices are identical and there is some uncertainty as to exactly what price response by his competitors would be required to restore the relative status quo ante. Or one operator may merely feel that someone is going to upset the apple cart anyhow, and he might as well get the temporary advantage of being the first as well as perhaps gaining some customer good will. However this may be, we can express the operator's feeling as to the consequences of lowering his price by drawing a demand curve D_2 passing through the current operating point F, but having a greater elasticity than D_1 by reason of the expectation that he will improve his relative share of the market. To determine the profit-maximizing policy on this basis, we draw the marginal-revenue curve MR_2 that corresponds to the demand curve D_2, and the intersection of this MR_2 with the marginal-cost curve at G indicates that the appropriate output is JH attained by setting a price of oJ. For a time this operator may actually enjoy the volume JH, as expected. But sooner or later, other operators, similarly situated, may be assumed to have been going through approximately the same reasoning, and may be further stimulated to action by the action of the first to change; as all of them lower their prices to oJ, the volume of each becomes JK rather than JH, since an individual hotel could attain the volume JH only if some other hotel got less. Arrived at K, operators may again imagine their individual demand curves to be more elastic than the aggregate-demand curve, as indicated by D_3, and cut prices again.

This process can continue until a point such as L is reached, where the marginal revenue derived from the demand curve D_4 which each operator considers to be his individual demand curve is just equal to the marginal cost at the current output, as shown at M. At this point, as long as the demand curve D_4 continues to be regarded as the expression of the consequences to each individual of lowering or raising his own price, there will be no incentive to change. Even if demand behaves as expected, marginal revenue is equal to marginal cost and no gain in profits could be obtained. In the case illustrated in FIGURE 80, this results in a price QL greater than the average cost QN, leaving a unit profit of NL. On the other hand, in an overexpanded industry with a larger number of firms, a relatively smaller total demand, and perhaps more elastic conceptions of their individual demand curves by individual operators, a situation could easily arise where the equilibrium at this stage would result in a loss. As long as no firms enter or leave the industry, such a situation would continue, producing either a loss or a profit.

However, if firms are free to enter or leave the industry, this is not the end of the process. In the case illustrated, the presence of the profit per unit of NL will be an inducement by the construction of new hotels, for new firms to enter. We may overlook at this point the practical problem of how the symmetry assumption can be preserved: if the differentiation is a purely spatial one and the original hotels are symmetrically spaced, it will usually be difficult to fit additional hotels into the pattern without disturbing the symmetry, unless perhaps the number of hotels is to be exactly doubled, or the hotels can somehow be relocated without cost. Where differentiation is in terms of a number of quality parameters, preservation of symmetry may not be so difficult to conceive, although perhaps more difficult to define. Assuming that the symmetry is somehow preserved, the result will be that the total business will be divided among a large number of units. Some additional business will be attracted, at any given price, by the fact that a greater variety of service is being offered, and some customers who were not formerly able to find a variety that they considered to be worth the price may now find themselves part of the effective demand. But in general this increase will be far less than in proportion to the number of new firms, and the result will be that the share in each hotel in the total demand, for any given uniform price, will be reduced, and this can be indicated by a shift of the demand curve D_1 to the left.

318]

As the number of competitors increases and the demand curve indicating the share of each in the total demand shifts to the left, the equilibrium price at each stage in the addition of competitors will be such that it will exceed marginal cost by a proportion dependent upon the elasticity of the individually imagined demand curve, according to the relation $p = m\epsilon/(1 + \epsilon)$ where ϵ is considered negative. In the long run, the adjustment of the number of competitors (up or down) will continue until price is just equal to average cost, as is indicated at T in FIGURE 81. Dividing the total demand by the

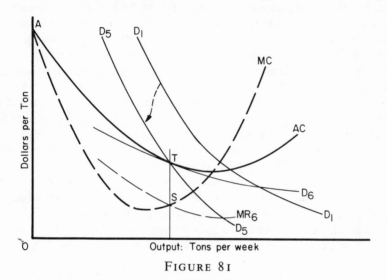

FIGURE 81

larger number of sellers yields the curve D_5 instead of D_1; along this demand curve equilibrium is found at the point T where the elasticity of the imagined individual demand curve D_6 is such as to produce a marginal-revenue curve MR_6 that intersects the marginal-cost curve at the same volume of output at S; this in turn implies that the curve D_6 is tangent to the average-cost curve at T. At this final equilibrium, there is no incentive for anyone to enter or leave the industry, as there is neither profit nor loss; and there is no incentive for any individual firm to raise or lower its price, since marginal cost and marginal revenue are equal; indeed, if we consider D_6 to be a locus of points that are considered to be possible points of operation by some individual firm, T is the only point where price will equal average cost, and at all other points along D_6 the price will be below average cost indicating operation at a loss.

In this final equilibrium, each firm operates at a smaller output than would result in minimum average cost, and there are, accordingly, more producing units than would be required if each were of the optimum size. The price is

[319

also higher than would be required if it were necessary to cover only the minimum average cost; this higher price, however, does not appear as profit, but is absorbed by the higher costs of operating a larger number of firms of a smaller size. In making such statements, however, one must take care not to jump too precipitously to the conclusion that this higher price represents waste. If indeed the imperfect elasticity of the demand curves of the individual sellers is ascribed to frictions in the market, ignorance on the part of consumers, or purely fictitious differences in the products being sold, then it would be possible to compare the consumers' surplus obtained in the monopolistic-competition case directly with that in a prefectly competitive situation in which the minimum average cost is achieved with a corresponding price, and the difference would indeed represent a net social loss resulting from the regime of monopolistic competition rather than a regime of perfect competition. Where, however, the inelasticity of demand represents genuine and informed preferences of consumers for one product over another, it will in general be desirable to sacrifice the minimization of cost to some extent for the sake of greater variety, so that limiting the number of varieties to the number that can be produced and marketed on a scale sufficient to minimize unit costs represents something less than a Pareto optimum adjustment. It is not obvious, at this stage of the analysis, just how far this increase of costs for the sake of variety should go; it will appear in due course that the degree to which this is carried under a regime of monopolistic competition is normally too far, but it nevertheless may be improper to measure the wastes resulting from monopolistic competition by reference to the point of minimum average costs.

The final equilibrium point T indeed may lie at any point over quite a range of the average-cost curve, depending entirely on the elasticity of the estimated individual demand curve D_6. While to some extent this elasticity will depend on the objective degree of differentiation of the various products and the intensity of consumers' preference for the product of one seller over that of his competitors, it must also be considered to a very large extent a subjective matter, relating to the state of mind of the seller and his expectations and degree of forethought concerning the reactions of his competitors to changes in his own price. At one extreme perhaps, D_6 may be considered to be what the variation in volume would be if the price of the particular seller were varied while the prices of the others remained fixed. Indeed, we could here again invoke the model where each seller makes no direct allowance for the reactions of his competitors, but determines the elasticity of his own demand by making experimental excursions away from his equilibrium price. If all sellers do this in a more or less random fashion, and if the only way a change in one seller's price reacts on the behavior of other sellers is through the effect on the estimate of demand elasticity made in this way, then if the reaction of consumers is fairly prompt, estimates of elasticity are likely to approach the value that obtains if all other prices are kept constant. On the other hand, if consumers' reactions are slow and price changes are not left in effect long enough for the reaction to become complete, elasticity may be underestimated, while if experimental price changes are left in effect long enough for others to be induced to change their prices similarly, the estimated elasticity of demand is again reduced. Ordinarily, moreover, each seller has direct information concerning the prices quoted by his competitors, and in addition will often have some more or less vague idea of probable reactions of his competitors to changes in his own price that will tend to make D_6 steeper than it would be if it could be assumed that all other prices would stay constant. Thus for a variety of reasons D_6 will tend to be steeper than the "other-prices-constant" curve would be, and of course the steeper D_6 is, the higher will be the equilibrium price and the greater will be the loss from having too many units of too small a size.

Where the subjective-demand curve through L, i.e., D_4, contains a strong element of allowance for the reactions of others to one's own changes in price, there is also the possibility that L may still not be an equilibrium position for the firms already in the industry, but that having exhausted the possibilities of price competition they turn to other measures in an attempt to increase their profits. Instead of trying to secure more business by price reductions that he feels are likely to be met promptly by reductions on the part of others, a seller may turn to embellishing his product, to advertising, or to other methods of sales promotion. If all sellers do the same, this may have some effect in increasing the aggregate demand for the entire industry, but this effect is likely to be slight, and for most sellers the main objective of selling expense will often be to attract customers away from competing firms. The net result of these attempts is a relatively minor increase or perhaps none at all in the demand curve for each individual firm, but a substantial increase in their costs. The process may well continue until the average-cost curve, inclusive of selling costs, rises until it is tangent to some curve such as D_4 at some point such as L, at which point profits will again have vanished, this time in selling expense rather than in the higher costs of smaller-scale operation.

Monopolistic competition is thus a situation which in general leads to a somewhat higher price than would cover the minimum average cost of production; some of this price excess may be considered a price paid for increased variety, but in some cases at least the premium so paid will be unwarrantably high. Some of the increase in price that the consumer pays represents a loss of consumers' surplus without any corresponding advantage in the long run to the sellers. In general, for the sellers to obtain some advantage in the long run, it is necessary that there be some form of restraint to prevent competitors from entering the field.

There is, however, a case where the inhibition to the entry of competitors is inherent in the circumstances. In the analysis of FIGURE 81 it was assumed that it would be possible to bring in just the right number of sellers to bring the share of the individual firm in the total demand down to a level where the conditions of point T could be realized. Of course, where there are only two or three firms in a given field to begin with, the addition of one more might push the demand curve D_5 to the left of T and bring about a situation in which the equilibrium level of operation would result in a loss, given the opinions of the competitors as to the elasticity of the individual demand curves D_6. Given the possibility of such cases, competitors may indeed refrain from coming into a field where there is a possibility that their entry would drive prices below a profitable level; if this is the case, such a field may remain mildly profitable for a considerable time or even indefinitely. But as the precise location of the point T depends on so many uncertain factors, including subjective estimates of the elasticity of demand, the exact shape of the average-cost curve, appraisals of the response of competitors, and the like, that it is hard to say how much monopoly profit is to be accounted for by these cases of "indivisibility."

In any event, the situation is always changing with some rapidity, and the really determining factors in any situation involving monopolistic competition are likely to be processes of growth, innovation, and change. A field in which the over-all demand is growing relatively to the volume of output of a firm capable of exploiting all of the economies of scale will gradually open up areas where an additional firm can come in and for a while make a more than normal profit. But if this fact is foreseen, firms may attempt to establish themselves in the field at a time somewhat in advance of that at which demand is sufficient to bring them a profit, and losses during such a period of anticipation may in extreme cases eat up much of the later profits. Indeed, the economic landscape in newly developed areas is strewn with the skeletons of firms that sought to "get in on the ground floor," only to be starved out before they reached the more profitable stages. In this area of analysis, a static approach is more than usually a bare framework or outline that requires a great deal of modification and qualification if it is to bear any resemblance at all to the real world. The determining factors in a situation may indeed be such matters as how long it takes customers to react to a changed price or to a reduction in price below one's competitors; or how long customers attracted by the initiation of a change by one competitor will stay after the price cut has been met; or how rapidly a firm can expand through its own internal resources; or how far one firm can keep ahead of others in the addition of new features to its product, or perhaps of new claims to its advertising. Indeed, the main service of static analysis of imperfect competition at this point may well be to point up, by its own indeterminacy, the strategic importance of these factors that might otherwise be thought of as having only a minor or subsidiary influence on the outcome.

Spatial Competition

SPATIAL-COMPETITION models are usually more precisely defined than the monopolistic-competition model, but for that very reason are usually more artificial and remote from actual economic phenomena. They come in many varieties, of differing degrees of oversimplification, but some of the very simple models nevertheless provide valuable insights. The great danger lies in being too quick to generalize from simplified specific models to classes of cases involving many more complexities.

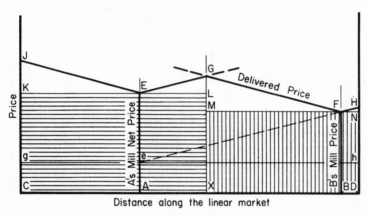

Distance along the linear market

FIGURE 82

Indeed, Hotelling's original trail-blazing article, published in 1929, was itself a rather striking example of rather wild generalization from an extremely artificial special case. He studied the case where customers are uniformly distributed along a straight line of length m, each customer having a completely inelastic demand for a specific quantity of a commodity furnished by two sellers A and B located at different points along this market line, each seller setting his own uniform mill net price, with consumers buying from the seller whose product has the lower delivered price, inclusive of a transportation cost proportional to the distance from the seller to the customer. This is illustrated in FIGURE 82, in which the producers are located at A and B along the road CD that constitutes the market along which consumers are evenly spread. If A charges a mill net price equal to AE, and B a price BF, then the line $JEGFH$ can represent the effective delivered price at each point along the road CD, the slopes of the lines EJ, EG, FG, and FH being equal and representing the cost of transportation per mile. The intersection of the two lines from E and F at G determines the division of the market between A and B, A selling to the customers on the segment CX, and B selling to the customers XD. Assuming, for simplicity, a zero cost of production, A's

[323

profits can be represented by the rectangle *CKLX*, and *B*'s by the rectangle *XMND*, the location of *X* of course depending on the relation between the two prices. (As with the Cournot case, the analysis of this case can be applied to the case of constant marginal cost merely by lowering the origin of the price axis, so that o*C* represents this constant marginal cost.)

Hotelling's approach to the problem was straightforward in terms of algebra and calculus, and while most spatial-competition cases seem to call for the use of fairly involved mathematics for their analysis, it is possible, in this

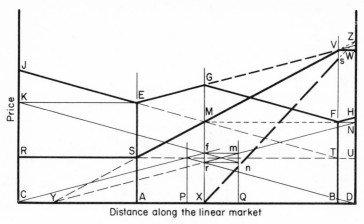

Distance along the linear market

FIGURE 83

case, to provide a reasonably simple graphical analysis that helps one see into the nature of the problem.

If in FIGURE 83 we take *A*'s price and position as given at *E*, then *A*'s delivered price will be given by the V-shaped line *JEGV*; if *B* sets a price greater than *BV*, he will sell nothing, but as soon as the price is lowered to *BV* or just below, he will sell to the buyers in his "hinterland" *BD*. Lowering the price further will gradually increase his sales; at a price *BF*, the sales *MN* are determined by the intersection at *G* of *B*'s delivered price with that of *A*. However, if *B* lowers his price to just below *BT*, he will then undersell *A* at all points on the market, and will thus sell to the entire market as long as *A* makes no change in his price. If we plot *B*'s share of the market, measuring from *D*, against the price *B* sets, considering *A*'s price to be fixed, we can obtain as a kind of short-run demand curve for *B* the broken line *RSMVW*. The segment *SMV* of this demand curve will be a straight line having twice the slope of the delivered price line *EGV*, since obviously *VF* = 2*GM*.

Now if conditions are such that neither *A* nor *B* is completely eliminated from the market, the equilibrium point must be somewhere along the line segment *SMV*, and in fact in the neighborhood of the equilibrium point conditions will be exactly the same as though the whole demand curve were a straight line $YSMVZ$ including SMV as a part of it. For such a straight-line demand curve we know that with zero marginal cost, profit maximization occurs at its midpoint M, indicating a price DN equal to half of DZ. Since YZ has a slope equal to twice that of the delivered price line EGV, the distance WZ represents twice the cost of transporting a unit of the commodity from B to D, and DZ is thus equal to A's price AE, plus transportation cost from A to B, plus twice the transportation cost from B to D. $BF = DN$ is then half of this, or

$$P_B = \tfrac{1}{2}(P_A + t\overline{AB} + 2t\overline{BD}) = \tfrac{1}{2}P_A + t\overline{QD}$$

where Q is the midpoint between A and B. Similarly, A's equilibrium price, given B's price, will be half of B's price plus freight from Q to C.

These two relationships can of course be solved algebraically, giving

$$P_B = \frac{2t}{3}(\overline{CD} + \overline{QD}) \quad \text{and} \quad P_A = \frac{2t}{3}(\overline{CD} + \overline{QC})$$

The process by which equilibrium is reached is more clearly illustrated by the construction of "reaction curves" as illustrated in FIGURE 84, in which the axes represent the two prices, and the curve R_A, which in this case is a straight

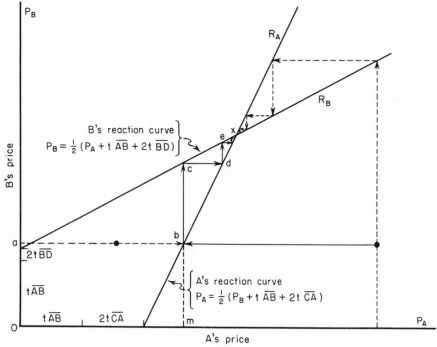

FIGURE 84

line, represents A's reaction in adjusting his price to a given price established by B, and, conversely, R_B shows the price that B will adopt in response to any given price he observes A to be selling at. If B initially has a price indicated by the abscissa oa, A's reaction will be to set his price at the corresponding point on his reaction curve, i.e., a price of ab; B, in turn, observing this price set by A will adjust his price to the level given by R_B or a price of mc; and further reactions trace out a zigzag path $abcde$ . . . approaching a final equilibrium at x. The fact that x is approached in this way from any starting point indicates that x represents a stable equilibrium, given the fixed locations of A and B.

Hotelling showed that if A set his price so as to maximize his profit on the assumption that B would keep his price constant, and if B did the same, an equilibrium would be established that would have a certain stability, as contrasted with the instability found in the case where two competitors located in the same spot try to follow the corresponding naive price policy. So far so good, and we have in effect a particular model that could be used as a background for the theory of monopolistic competition. But Hotelling went further and noted that if A was free to adjust his location as well as his price, and assumed that B would keep his location unchanged, he would find it advantageous to move toward B. A's gain in so doing is obvious if he simultaneously shifts his location and raises his price so that E moves along the line EG: A's share of the market will remain unchanged while the net price he receives increases. At the same time, as long as A does not get so close to B that B is tempted to lower his price enough to cut A out of the market entirely, B would have no occasion to change his price policy by reason of such a shift, since for any change in B's price short of that which would undercut A entirely, B will get exactly the same results as before A shifted. (Hotelling's argument was slightly different, implying that A would consider B's price reactions when choosing a location, but not when setting his price; he tended to disregard altogether the increased danger of B undercutting A entirely). Hotelling argued that although to minimize the transportation costs in the interests of over-all economy, A and B should obviously be located at the quartile points, in this model they would tend to congregate in the middle of the market. At least, it can be argued, they would tend to locate closer to the center than the quartiles. Taking geographical distance as a representative of all types of quality variation, Hotelling generalized this result to a statement that all products tend to be too much alike, and that even political platforms and religious denominations have too much in common.

Taken with a grain of salt, there is a good deal of validity in such a generalization. However, it is possible to exhibit models in which the tendency to concentration does not exist, and also to show that where there are three or more competitors, rather than two, the concentration tends to be very much less extreme. For example, if instead of assuming that demand is completely inelastic, we assume that it falls off as the delivered price is increased, then in many cases A will be deterred from moving toward B by the fact that in doing so he must either lower his base price or increase the delivered price to consumers on the segment CA and thereby reduce his sales in this segment. While A and B may still locate closer together than would minimize transportation costs, an equilibrium may now be reached with A and B a considerable distance apart. A number of such cases have been analyzed by Arthur Smithies. And even in Hotelling's original case, it must be noted that if A and B locate at the same point they will then be in the position of ordinary duopolists, and the differentiation between their products will have vanished. In the resulting instability, A and B may well be worse off than they would have been had they stayed a certain distance apart. Indeed, even with some distance between them, instability may be introduced if A is in a position to increase his profits, at least temporarily until B reacts, by lowering his price sufficiently to make his delivered price at B less than B's base price and so cut B out of the market entirely. B and A may therefore both be under some inducement to locate far enough apart so that this cannot happen, or at least so that it is unlikely.

For example, if A and B are located as they are in FIGURES 82 and 83, B might even consider lowering his price to BT in order to secure the entire market for himself, for if A maintains his price, the resulting profit $RUDC$ is slightly larger than $XMND$, which is the profit obtainable with the price BF. However, even though B might plausibly ignore possible reactions of A to a small change in B's price that would still leave a considerable market to A, it is almost absurd for B to assume that he can cut A completely out of a profitable market without provoking some reaction on the part of A. B, therefore, may well decide not to make such a cut even though it might offer a temporary increase in profits.

In the case illustrated in the diagrams, A would not even consider an attempt to undercut B entirely, for lowering the price to Ae (FIGURE 82) would yield a profit of only $CghD$, which would be less than $CKLX$, which is what he enjoys at the equilibrium price AE. And indeed if the two sellers are far enough apart, neither will have any temptation to undercut the other. It is perhaps a curious coincidence that if A and B locate at the quartiles, where freight costs are minimized, this is exactly the closest that they can approach each other without giving rise to a temptation to undercut. But in view of the probable recognition by both A and B that undercutting would provoke reactions, a mild temptation to undercut would probably be withstood, so that a sort of stability may persist even if A and B are considerably inside the quartile points. But how far this stability would persist it is impossible to say on a priori grounds.

A still simpler model has been employed by Lerner and Singer to illustrate the possibilities inherent in shifting location alone, independent of price variation. If we assume that there is one rigid price at which a product must be sold (as with fair-traded articles or articles with a well-established customary price, such as periodicals, candy bars, and the like), then the only thing that is important is location (at least if we neglect variations in associated services). We may assume that each customer will patronize the nearest dealer.

Under these circumstances, it makes no difference to a single supplier A where he locates, for he has the market to himself, while price and demand are fixed. But a second supplier B, finding A already located, will tend to locate so as to secure as large a part of the market for himself as he can. In the case of demand uniformly distributed along a line, this will be when he locates just far enough away from A to create a preference in favor of B on the part of those coming from B's end of the market, and on the side of A, which has the larger part of the market. If A originally located away from the center of the market, A will then have the smaller share. If, however, A is free to move his location, and assumes B to be fixed, he will, once B has fixed his location, move to the other side of B (between B and the center) so as to obtain a larger share. B in turn may do likewise, so that a series of moves of this sort will end with both A and B near the center of the market. Or the whole process may be anticipated and short-circuited by either A or B moving directly to the center. Indeed, if one seller is inhibited in some way from locating closer to an established competitor than some small distance, say d, then the one establishing himself first would be prudent to locate exactly at the center, forcing the other to locate a distance d away from the center, securing a market of $(1 + d)/2$ for himself, and leaving for the other only $(1 - d)/2$. Thus if A anticipates the advent of a second seller B, he may locate in the center in the first place.

The introduction of a third seller C, however, tends to break up the concentration at the center of the market. He may initially locate close to A, on the side opposite to B, thus leaving A a market of only d. But if A is free to move, he will escape from between B and C, moving, say, outside of B. B in turn will then want to escape from between the other two, and the leap-frog process will continue as long as the market secured by the center seller, which is half the distance between the other two, is less than he might secure by going just outside of the others. The process ceases when the two outside sellers are located at the quartiles of the market, in which case the inside seller will get one-fourth of the market regardless of where he locates, and the outside sellers will get between one-fourth and one-half, the division between them within these limits depending upon the location of the middle seller. A seller can enhance his chances of being the one with the largest share by being the first to move to one of the quartiles, moving to the one farthest from the other two sellers.

To be sure, at this point one or both of the outside sellers would be in a position to gain, temporarily, by moving in toward the center seller, thus increasing their immediate share of the market. As soon as one of them does this, however, the center seller will gain by moving to the quartile just vacated, and the outside seller who moved would then find himself on the inside with only one-fourth of the market instead of the larger amount he had previously. If the outside sellers are thus not sufficiently perspicacious to avoid jeopardizing their current superior position for the sake of such an evanescent advantage, they will soon learn, the hard way.

With four sellers, *A*, *B*, *C*, and *D*, an equilibrium of sorts is reached when *A* and *B* locate close together (or are separated by the minimum distance *d*) at one of the quartiles, with *C* and *D* similarly close together at the other quartile. In this case, no seller has an advantage over any other; each gets one-fourth of the whole market. But the sellers are located in such a way that the transportation costs are greater than they need be: if the four outlets were spaced at equal distances, with the end outlets being one-eighth of the length of the market from the ends of the market, the average distance from customers to the nearest outlet would be cut in half.

This equilibrium is somewhat peculiar, however. While no seller can gain any immediate advantage by moving, and *A* and *D* cannot move without losing (considering *A* and *D* to be located just outside the quartiles, *B* and *C* just inside), *B* can move toward the center of the market without himself losing, although by so doing he will be increasing *A*'s market at the expense of *C*'s. Thus we have the possibility that *A* may be able to persuade, induce, or bribe *B* to move in this direction, as long as *B* loses nothing directly by this move. (The same relationship of course exists between *C* and *D*.) Or if we reintroduce an element of elasticity of demand into the picture, so that those farther from the source will no longer purchase as much, or perhaps as frequently, *B* and *C* will have an incentive to move toward the center to decrease the average distance to their customers and thus increase the volume of sales obtained from a constant length of market. More important, as soon as *B* does move toward the center, the others are no longer in equilibrium and *C* now has an incentive to move outside either *A* or *D*. *A* also has a short-run incentive to move in, following *B*, but may hesitate to do so lest this definitely decide *C* to move outside *A* rather than outside *D* and thus squeeze *A* between *B* and *C*. If *B*, once having moved, is now assumed to stay at the new position, *A*, *C*, and *D* may then proceed to a whole series of moves, the end result of which is difficult to determine with any precision. In the process, however, it is at least possible that *B* would enjoy for a greater or shorter period more than his original quarter of the market, thus justifying his original move. Thus while Lerner and Singer give a definite equilibrium for this case, as well as for cases with larger numbers of sellers, it rather seems that the full solution for this type of case has not yet been determined. Indeed, in this case we already see a certain resemblance to a parlor game.

Of course, markets are not usually capable of being represented at all closely by a uniform distribution of customers along a straight line. Actual situations are ordinarily too complex to conform to any simple model, but many attempts have been made to approach closer to reality. For example, it is natural to extend the idea of spatial competition to a market spread evenly or otherwise over a plane, transportation being in a straight line from the supply point to the consumption point. Simple as it may seem, however, this model is quite difficult to deal with, as the boundaries between the markets of the several suppliers will ordinarily consist of hyperbolas, and the problem of analytic integration becomes quite difficult. Actual situations in fact more nearly approach the idea of a market being distributed along the lines of a transportation network, consisting of a pattern of streets, highways, or railroads.

One of the simplest possible patterns is a simple loop (which may or may not be circular), with consumers distributed evenly along it. If transportation can take place only around the loop, then the resulting analysis becomes even simpler than for the straight line, since here all points are geographically similar. And in this case, at least, the famous generalization about firms locating too close to each other breaks down, for assuming that firms are free to move at negligible cost, and that there is enough elasticity of demand to induce a firm to move to the midpoint between his two neighbors, the equilibrium is reached for any fixed number of firms when they are equally spaced around the loop, thus minimizing transportation costs.

In actual cases of spatial competition, the assumption that cost of movement can be neglected is very unrealistic. Where "location" is merely a symbol for quality variation, however, the costs of "movement" in terms of changing the quality characteristics of the product may indeed be small or negligible, especially where there is rapid obsolescence in any case. But in most cases such costs will exist, and where they do they will in general affect the result, even in the long run, since there will nearly always be points at which the advantages of moving will be so small that even if the gain from the move were to continue in perpetuity, this gain might constitute an inadequate return on the investment in the moving. And in the spatial case, at least, the costs of moving cannot be eliminated by waiting until existing plant wears out, for it is not ordinarily possible to plan, without loss, for a plant to wear out all at once like that so conveniently wonderful one-horse shay (probably if Holmes hadn't invented it, economists would have had to!). To allow for cost of movement, we might want to assume that no seller would move unless the expected advantage is greater than the cost, thus introducing a kind of friction into the model. If the level of "friction" is such that repeated moves are possible, the analysis becomes very complicated and possibly not correspondingly instructive.

Reasonably simple cases occur, however, if we assume that a given number of sellers are to enter the market in sequence, knowing that once having taken up their positions they will find moving prohibitively expensive. In the simplest case, that of the loop market, if there are only two sellers, it makes no substantial difference where the two locate: they will share the market equally in any case. Presumably, if there is any elasticity of demand they will locate opposite each other.

If there are to be three sellers, however, the symmetry disappears. We may assume that the third seller to locate, C, will locate in the middle of the larger of the two spaces between A and B, and that thus A and B will share equally what is not obtained by C. B, anticipating this, will act so as to make C's share as small as possible, by locating so as to make the larger of the two spaces between himself and A as small as possible, i.e., by locating opposite A. Thus A and B get three-eighths of the market, and C only one-fourth.

In general, problems of this sort can be attacked by considering the decisions made by the sellers in the reverse order of their entry, in terms of all possible configurations of the preceding entrants and of the policy already determined for the subsequent ones. For example, for four sellers, D will locate in the middle of one of the largest of the segments left by A, B, and C. C, anticipating this, locates in the middle of the larger of the two segments left by A and B, and B, anticipating in turn the actions of C and D, will locate just short of one-third of the circuit away from A (so that at least one of the segments adjacent to himself will be safe from the intrusion of D). D then gets just over one-sixth, C just over one-fourth, and B and A get just under one-fourth and just under one-third, respectively, or vice versa, depending on which segment D chooses to locate in, of the two equally attractive segments that C leaves.

For n expected sellers, one solution results when each successive seller locates himself just a little less than $1/(n - 1)$ of the circuit away from the preceding sellers, leaving the penultimate seller to split evenly a remaining space of just over $2/(n - 1)$, with the last seller locating in the middle of one of the spaces adjacent to the penultimate. In this model it is in general an advantage to be one of the earlier locaters, in that an earlier seller is less likely to get crowded by the last seller, while the last and next-to-last sellers are at a definite disadvantage, the last getting just over $1/2(n - 1)$, the next to last just over $3/4(n - 1)$. In general, a slight irregularity remains in the spacing of the sellers, and there is thus more transportation required, even for a loop configuration, than there would be with an optimum spacing of the same number of sellers. The amount of excess transportation, however, seems relatively small when it is compared with the Hotelling models.

A similar and somewhat more realistic case can be set up by assuming that the number of sellers is not fixed in advance, but is limited only by the fact that it will not pay to open an outlet unless a market of at least some minimum amount k can be secured. In this case, successive entrants would tend to locate themselves at distances of just under $2k$ from the preceding established sellers, until the remaining gap becomes less than $4k$, at which point the remaining seller would have to content himself with half of this interval, presumably locating in the middle of it. It may be noted that in this case profits persist in spite of free entry. And although freight costs are higher than they are for an equal number of sellers evenly spaced, the model is such that without further information it is not possible to tell whether the number of sellers that would minimize total cost would be greater or smaller than the number that enter the market.

There is a fairly close similarity between the results for a loop and those for a straight-line market configuration where the location chosen must be the final one. The straight-line results, indeed, can be obtained from the loop results for three or more sellers merely by cutting the loop halfway between the first two sellers and straightening the loop. In effect, in the straight-line case, the first two sellers, locating so close to the ends that no subsequent seller finds it profitable to locate nearer to the ends, insulate the remainder of the maneuvering from the effects of the ends. For two and three sellers, the final results are similar to those where free movement is assumed. For four sellers, A and B locate one-fifth of the market in from the ends, C will locate in the center, and D will choose the middle of the space on either side of C. This case thus differs from the free-movement case. For the indefinite-number case, the first two sellers locate a distance k from the ends, after which the procedure is the same as for the circle.

Especially in the cases with the larger numbers of sellers, such models must assume a rather high degree of perspicacity on the part of the successive sellers, and indeed confidence in the perspicacity of the succeeding sellers by the ones who commit themselves earlier, and we are already approaching the degree of overrefinement often found in the theory of games. In practice it seems unlikely that any seller would know the prospects sufficiently accurately, or have the confidence that succeeding sellers would locate according to the ideal principle, to make results of this type a reliable guide.

It is of course possible to examine more complicated models in which the market may be unevenly distributed, or where there are junctions and other complications in the network, and so on, but the difficulties increase rapidly and the number of possible variations is so enormous that few economists have considered it worthwhile to attempt very much in the way of further analysis in this direction. The above examples are merely sufficient to show that the effect of spatial considerations in producing a concentration of sellers can be quite moderate, and appears to be related primarily to the proximity of an "edge" to the market. Another interesting type of case not examined here is that in which because of the growth of demand over time, or because of technological improvement, the size of the market needed to support an outlet decreases (or increases) gradually through time. Consideration of such a model might require assigning a less important place to the possibility illustrated in the above models for net profits to persist under conditions of free entry.

Of course, we do in the real world observe some quite remarkable cases of geographical concentration: the automobile industry in Detroit, "book row" on lower Fourth Avenue in New York; or in terms of quality, standardization of a great many things from electric-light bulbs to men's shirts. In most cases, however, the principal reasons for this concentration appear to be considerations other than the "spatial-competition" considerations. Concentration of an industry is very likely to occur by reason of the "external economies" of the industry, particularly the "internal economies of scale" in the various associated specialty-supply industries. A concentration of shops may be effective in attracting customers by means of a larger selection concentrated in a small area; "price-lining" may have a rationale in avoiding too confusing an array of qualities and prices. Some types of firms may tend to concentrate at nodal points in the transportation network, which is a spatial effect, to be sure, but one that need not involve excessive concentration from the point of view of maximum economic efficiency.

Perhaps the main usefulness of a certain exploration of spatial models is to furnish a concrete model that will illustrate some of the workings of monopolistic competition. Thus if firms are free to move or to change the nature of their product without cost, we can see that in the long run the equilibrium position is likely to be very close to the no-profit position, the addition of new firms ceasing only when there is no longer room for another firm to squeeze in, with the other firms adjusting themselves to the newcomer in such a way as to make a profit. If firms are unable to change their position or the characteristics of their product without appreciable costs, then a long-run equilibrium may be reached with a somewhat smaller number of firms and a somewhat greater margin of profit, representing a situation in which there is insufficient "room" between the established positions of the sellers for a new seller to establish himself profitably, even though it would have been possible for more sellers to have established themselves in profitable positions had they adopted different positions originally.

Thus there is room for profits to arise out of product differentiation combined with declining average cost prevailing at least up to a modest volume. The amount of profit in any particular case is likely to depend in large measure on the entrepreneur's ability to appraise the market situation and find a "gap" into which he can fit a product, but into which, after he is in, others will not be tempted to follow, at least for some time. In such a situation, a great deal depends on being the first to see the situation, and, in a rapidly changing environment, even to foresee developing trends. To some extent, of course, in an uncertain situation perhaps a sufficient number of entrepreneurs would attempt to try to extract a profit in this way so that enough would overshoot the mark to bring the profit on the average back down to the zero of classical competition. But on balance it would seem that there would be enough accuracy in the entrepreneurs' estimates of the various situations so that on the whole fewer would venture where the situation tends to result in a loss than where a profit results, and that thus on the average profits would emerge, even on a purely static basis. But it seems likely that in practice these interstitial profits will be overshadowed by instances of genuine monopoly enforced by some specific barrier to entry, and by the effects of dynamic changes and innovations.

Moreover, in a dynamic world in which the profitable gaps are continually opening and closing, there may be an advantage to establishing a firm in an opening gap somewhat ahead of the time at which the situation is currently profitable, in order to pre-empt the position and enjoy the later profits. The earlier losses due to the attempts at pre-emption would then have to be offset against later gains. Indeed, in a situation of perfect foresight and vigorous competition, some entrepreneur would presumably jump in as soon as the expected pre-emptional loss has diminished to the point where it will just be outweighed by the prospective profits to be enjoyed later. On the other hand, in a situation where profits are diminishing—for example, due to falling demand—it may not be obvious which of the various firms in the "neighborhood" should drop out, and each may stick, even after profits have vanished, in the hope that one of the others will drop out soon, after which some remaining firms might be able to reap a profit again, at least for a time. However, if it is clear which firm is the one that will eventually drop out first, this certainty will result in its dropping out as soon as the losses begin, and there will thus be no operation at a loss in the declining phase to correspond to the pre-emption losses in the growing phase. Where there is uncertainty as to which firm will drop out first, it is only a short step to price wars and similar attempts to induce the dropping out of competing firms.

In any event, any close calculation of the time when it becomes appropriate to attempt to pre-empt an improving position requires estimates of the behavior of both existing and potential competitors, who will themselves be attempting to estimate the behavior of others ad infinitum. In analyzing such situations, one either abandons all pretense at precision and sharp definition, the analysis becoming loaded with intangible psychological factors, or turns to explicit consideration of the strategic aspects of the situation in terms of the theory of games, which we will discuss in the next chapter.

Monopolistic Competition and Optimum Variety

SPATIAL-COMPETITION models can also be used to throw light on the question of the extent to which the added costs of smaller-than-minimum-cost scale of output resulting from monopolistic competition can be justified in terms of the increased value to consumers of the greater variety of products offered. Whereas with generalized variation in quality the value of the wider range of choice is difficult to relate in any direct way to the costs of providing variety, where the difference is merely geographical the advantages of having a larger number of points of supply to choose from can be directly evaluated in terms of transportation cost.

Consider, for example, a market in the form of a loop of length L, with a perfectly inelastic demand distributed uniformly along it, served by N evenly spaced outlets, each of which involves a fixed cost C, in addition to the variable costs of supplying the commodity, which for simplicity we can set at zero. The distance between outlets is then L/N, the maximum distance from a customer to an outlet is then $L/2N$ and the average distance $L/4N$ so that if total demand is Q and the freight rate is t, the total transportation cost is $T = QtL/(4N)$. If the cost C of the Nth outlet was justified in terms of transportation-cost saving, we must have

$$C < \frac{QtL}{4(N-1)} - \frac{QtL}{4N} = \frac{QtL}{4N(N-1)}$$

Similarly, if the installation of another outlet (shifting the outlets to keep the spacing even) is unprofitable, we should have

$$\frac{QtL}{4N} - \frac{QtL}{4(N+1)} = \frac{QtL^-}{4N(N+1)} < C$$

Thus to insure that the value of N is optimal, we must have

$$4CN(N-1) \le QtL \le 4CN(N+1)$$

If on the other hand the number of sellers is arrived at as a result of monopolistic competition, we may assume that new firms enter the market with additional outlets as long as the addition of another will not depress gross profits below the cost C. If the firms are spaced at intervals L/N, and the neighbors of a particular firm set a price P, their delivered price at his location will be $P + tL/N$ so that his demand curve will be linear with a maximum price equal to $P + tL/N$; he will, accordingly, maximize his profits at $p = P/2 + tL/2N$, using the midpoint of this linear demand curve. Equilibrium among all the sellers will be reached when $p = P$, or $p = P = tL/N$, so that gross profits are $QP/N = QtL/N^2$. If new firms enter until the entry of one more firm would drive profits below C, we have, as the condition determining the number of firms,

$$N^2C \le QtL \le (N+1)^2C$$

Comparing this condition with the one for the optimum number of outlets we find a tendency for monopolistic competition to result in about twice as many outlets as would be optimum.

However, new firms in considering entry into the field may look not at the situation that would be reached after locations have been adjusted to the new number of firms (which, however unrealistic it might be in static terms, given the heavy expense involved in moving from an established position, whether in terms of geography or an established-product reputation, may well serve as a rough approximation to the case of pre-emptive entry into an expanding or changing market), but rather at the immediate prospects for profits under the existing pattern of delivered prices. If N firms are established with a price $P = tL/N$, the delivered price to the point midway between them where a new firm might establish itself would be $tL/N + tL/(2N) = 3tL/(2N)$, so that the new firm would maximize profits by setting his price at half of this, or $3tL/(4N)$ (assuming no reactions on the part of the existing firms), obtaining a sales volume of $3Q/(4N)$, or a profit before fixed charges of $9QtL/(16N)^2$. The value of N such that no further entry takes place is then given by

$$16N^2C \leq 9QtL < 16(N + 1)^2C$$

The number of outlets will be approximately 50 per cent greater than optimum.

One might even consider the case where new entrants are so cautious as to consider not only that there will be no favorable readjustment of locations in response to their entry, but that the competitors in their immediate vicinity will respond by lowering their prices, with diminishing repercussions throughout the market. Determining the equilibrium to be expected under these circumstances is a fairly involved process, possibly even too abstruse for the potential new firm to be expected to follow, but if we assume that the entrepreneur has some sort of intuition that enables him to feel approximately what the answer is, we may expect him to enter if the existing number of firms is such as to enable him to make a profit at a price of $.634tL/N$, selling $.634Q/N$ and obtaining a gross profit of $.402QtL/N^2$. The number of firms in this case would be 26.8 per cent in excess of the optimum. But this is getting perilously close to the case of the man who wanted to know whether the dog knew that he wouldn't bite.

One would be tempted, even so, to claim as a general proposition that even where aggregate demand is so inelastic that monopolistic competition causes no misallocation of resource in terms of the aggregate output for the industry as a whole, there remains misallocation in terms of wastefully small-scale operation and proliferation of firms beyond the point where this can be justified on the basis of the value of variety. While on the whole this would appear to be the general rule, examination of cases having more dimensions, either because the market is in fact distributed over a plane rather than along a line, or because other quality attributes than mere location are involved, indicates that particularly where the short-run rather than the long-run criterion for entry is used, it is possible to find equilibrium with too few rather than too many outlets.

Selling Costs: Non-price Competition

IN ADDITION to the selection of a specific quality to be offered, among the many qualities of goods that are potentially producible, which can be moderately well represented by the selection of a "location" in the space of commodity characteristics, competition also takes the form of attempts to modify the attitudes of consumers toward the product, partly through advertising and selling effort, but also through the embellishment of the product with "selling points." Qualitatively, this is one of the most interesting and varied aspects of imperfect competition, but analytically there is very little that can be said about it in any precise way. Where a firm operates naively in that it does not explicitly attempt to take into consideration possible reactions of other firms to its policies, selling expense can be handled simply by separating out the selling from the manufacturing activities of the firm. Selling expense operates to raise the demand curve. For each level of output, there will be a volume and type of selling expense that will permit this output to be sold at a price that will yield the highest net revenue over the selling expense. In other words, for each output the optimum selling expense is reached when a marginal increment of selling expense will raise the price obtainable for the given output by the increment of selling cost. For each output there is thus a maximum obtainable net revenue, and from this a marginal net revenue can be derived and compared with marginal cost. This much is fairly trivial, when expressed in this form.

The really interesting questions regarding selling expense are such conundrums as how to determine the extent to which such expenses are beneficial to a consumer through permitting him to make a better or more intelligent choice, and how far they are merely wasteful or even injurious, or how the analysis should be carried out where increased selling expense may provoke reactions from competitors. Indeed, it is precisely the factors responsible for the difficulty of the analysis that make the use of selling expense as a means of competition more attractive than that of price-cutting: a price cut is something that can be fairly easily met in kind by a competitor, but an advertising campaign is *sui generis*: even though the competitor may be able to match in some sense the advertising appropriation, he may not be able to find the appropriate countervailing slogan, appeal, or what have you. The response is thus much less certain, and being less certain, is harder, if not impossible to analyze on an a priori basis with a strictly specified model. Here, too, competition begins to take on some of the aspects of a game of strategy.

Mathematical Appendix

AN INTERESTING and fairly simple generalization of Cournot's analysis, which contains Cournot's results as a special case, is as follows. Let there be n producers of an identical product, the output of the ith producer being q_i, and the cost of this output $C_i(q_i)$. Total output is $Q = \sum_i q_i$ and the market demand curve is given by $p = p(Q)$. Total profit for each producer is then

$$G_i = q_i \cdot p(Q) - C_i(q_i) \qquad (i = 1, 2, \ldots n) \qquad \text{8.1}$$

Each producer then adjusts output q_i to maximize G_i, taking all of the q_j, $j \neq i$ to be fixed. Accordingly,

$$\frac{\partial G_i}{\partial q_i} = p(Q) + q_i \frac{dp}{dQ} \frac{\partial Q}{\partial q_i} - \frac{dC_i}{dq_i} = 0 \qquad (i = 1, 2, \dots n) \qquad 8.2$$

We will write m_i for the various marginal costs: $m_i = (dC_i/dq_i)$, and since $(\partial Q/\partial q_i) = 1$, we have:

$$p + q_i\left(\frac{dp}{dQ}\right) - m_i = 0 \qquad (i = 1, 2, 3, \dots n) \qquad 8.3$$

If we add all of these equations, we get

$$np + \left(\frac{dp}{dQ}\right)\sum_i q_i - \sum_i m_i = np + \left(\frac{dp}{dQ}\right)Q - \sum_i m_i = 0 \qquad 8.4$$

If we divide by n, this can be written

$$p\left(1 + \frac{1}{n}\frac{Q}{p}\frac{dp}{dQ}\right) - \bar{m} = 0 \qquad 8.5$$

where $\bar{m} = \dfrac{1}{n}\sum_i m_i$ is the "mean marginal cost" of the various competitors;

if we put $\epsilon_d = \dfrac{p}{Q}\dfrac{dQ}{dp}$ for the elasticity of the market demand, we have, by solving for p,

$$p = \bar{m}\left(\frac{1}{1 + \left(\dfrac{1}{n\epsilon_d}\right)}\right) \qquad 8.6$$

This result of course holds only if all of the m_i will be less than p, when this formula is applied; if some m_i is greater than p, then this producer will drop out and we must repeat the analysis for the remaining producers. As n becomes large, p approaches $\bar{m}$, giving the competitive result.

More sophistication can be introduced into the mathematical model, but if it is done symmetrically or multi-laterally, an impasse is reached almost immediately. Let x and y be parameters under the control of competitors A and B, respectively, and in general the profits of each will depend jointly on these two parameters, which may represent outputs, prices, or perhaps even outlays for advertising. If the situation is well defined, it will be possible to determine the form of this dependence so that we can consider $G = g(x, y)$ as giving the net profits of A, and $H = h(x, y)$ as giving the net profits of B. The naive model results from putting $(\partial g/\partial x) = 0$ and $(\partial h/\partial y) = 0$, y being held constant in the first case and x being held constant in the second. To allow for sophistication we may put

$$\frac{dg}{dx} = \frac{\partial g}{\partial x} + \frac{\partial g}{\partial y}\left(\frac{dy}{dx}\right)_e = 0 \quad \text{and} \quad \frac{dh}{dy} = \frac{\partial h}{\partial x} + \frac{\partial h}{\partial y}\left(\frac{dx}{dy}\right)_e \qquad 8.7$$

where the term $\left(\dfrac{dy}{dx}\right)_e$ represents the "conjectural variation" that A expects to occur in y as a consequence of his varying x, and, conversely, for $\left(\dfrac{dx}{dy}\right)_e$. But there exists no very satisfactory way of determining what these conjectural variations should be on any rigorous basis; their values will depend very strongly on the institutional and psychological environment.

For Hotelling's case, we can take CD as the unit of distance, write $CA = a$ for the length of A's "hinterland," and, similarly, $b = BD$, and c for the cost of transportation. If x is the distance from A to the market division point at X, then we have $P_a + cx = P_b + c(1 - a - b - x)$, so that

$$x = \frac{1}{2}\left[1 - a - b + \frac{P_b - P_a}{c}\right] \qquad 8.8$$

A's gross profits are

$$G_a = P_a(a + x) = \frac{1}{2}P_a\left[1 + a - b + \frac{P_b - P_a}{c}\right] \qquad 8.9$$

If he maximizes profits on the assumption that P_b, a, and b are all fixed, we have

$$\left(\frac{\partial G_a}{\partial P_a}\right) = \frac{1}{2}\left[1 + a - b + \frac{P_b - 2P_a}{c}\right] = 0 \qquad 8.10$$

And, similarly, for B we have

$$\left(\frac{\partial G_b}{\partial P_b}\right) = \frac{1}{2}\left[1 - a + b + \frac{-2P_b + P_a}{c}\right] = 0$$

Solving these for P_a and P_b gives

$$P_a = c\left[1 + \frac{a - b}{3}\right]; \qquad P_b = c\left[1 + \frac{b - a}{3}\right] \qquad 8.11$$

and putting these results back in 8.9 gives

$$G_a = \frac{1}{2c}\left[1 + \frac{a - b}{3}\right]^2 \quad \text{and} \quad G_b = \frac{1}{2c}\left[1 + \frac{b - a}{3}\right]^2 \qquad 8.12$$

Profits are thus proportional to the transportation cost; if the sellers are symmetrically located, so that $a = b$, we have $P_a = P_b = 1/2c$ and $G_a = G_b = 1/2c$, independently of how close together they are.

EXERCISES

1. A demand curve for commodity x, and a horizontal line indicating the constant marginal cost of production, is drawn in the accompanying figure.

  a. Construct the marginal-revenue curve.

  b. Indicate the monopoly output and price.

  c. Estimate the elasticity of demand at A; at B.

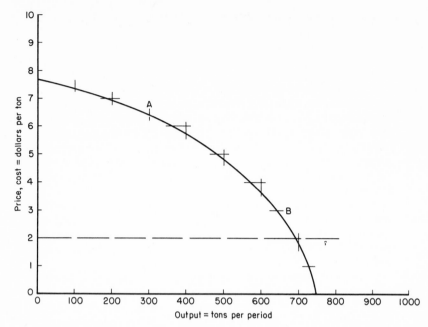

(NOTE: Use appropriately different methods to avoid having to extend the diagram.)

2. Four Cournot oligopolists are supplying an identical commodity *x*, each assuming that the output of the others will not change. What are the results? (Hint: Find appropriate pseudo-elasticities for various points on the demand curve.)

3. Four competitors supply differentiated varieties of *x*, each competitor estimating the elasticity of his own demand to be −3. What will be the results?

4. In question 3, if fixed costs are $10 per period for each seller, and there is free entry, subject to trademark restrictions that keep a certain minimum differentiation between products, what are the results?

5. Four sellers, *A*, *B*, *C*, and *D*, each determine their own output of an identical product *x* in the light of a known (linear) aggregate-demand curve and the following assumptions regarding the output behavior of the others: *D* takes the outputs of *A*, *B*, and *C*, as given; *C* allows for this reaction on *D*'s part, but takes the outputs of *A* and *B* as fixed; *B* allows for the reactions of *C* and *D* and takes *A*'s output as fixed; *A* anticipates the reactions of all the others. Discuss the results.

6. Travel from *A* to *C* involves a rail trip from *A* to *B* plus a ferry ride from *B* to *C*. Demand for such travel is linear in terms of the total fare for the two segments of the trip combined, and there is no significant traffic to or from the ferry landing *B* itself. Determine the equilibrium price under the following varying assumptions:

a. The fare for the rail portion of the journey is fixed at r, perhaps because this line is a branch of a larger system over which a uniform rate of fare is maintained. The ferry company is independent, and sets its fare to maximize its profits. Marginal costs may be assumed to be negligible.

b. The constraint on the rail fare is lifted; the ferry company and the railroad each adjust the fare for their segment of the trip on the assumption that the other company will maintain the previously quoted fare. What influence will the relative lengths of the rail and boat trips have on the fare structure? What will be the equilibrium fare structure if the fixed costs are small in relation to revenues? What are the possible consequences if the fixed costs are of the same order of magnitude as the revenues?

c. The ferry company continues to adjust its fare on the assumption that the rail fare will not be affected by what it does; the railroad on the other hand takes account of the reactions of the ferry company to changes in the rail fare. What are the results for various levels of fixed costs?

d. The ferry company is absorbed by the railroad company and the joint operation carried out as a simple monopoly. What are the results?

e. Generalize the case to that of n mutually complimentary products, and compare this case with the Cournot case. What are the welfare implications for appraising vertical integration?

7. Demand is distributed along the three legs of a Y pattern, two legs having 12 units of demand, the third six units, the density of demand being uniform in each case and the price a fixed datum. Discuss the possible equilibrium configurations for 2, 3, 4, 5, 6, and 7 sellers, and compare this with the efficient configurations.

8. Two coal-mining areas are located 100 miles apart; A, a deep-mine area, produces coal of 14,000 BTU per ton, at a marginal cost of $7 per ton; B, an open-pit mine area, produces coal of 7,000 BTU per ton at a marginal cost of $2 per ton. The market area for these mines is distributed along a railroad route passing through both A and B, the market area extending 500 miles beyond A and B in each direction. Show that the most efficient supplying of the demand may involve (a) "hauling coals to Newcastle," and (b) "cross-hauling." Assume for simplicity that transportation costs per ton-mile are constant, but otherwise consumers are interested only in the BTU content, and are not inconvenienced by the extra tonnage of the inferior coal.

CHAPTER NINE

The Theory of Games

THE THIRD major method of approach to the problem of imperfect competition is that of the theory of games. The theory is still so new, and, because of the mathematical terms in which it has been presented, so little understood by economists generally, that its place in the structure of theoretical economies is still uncertain. The following discussion is aimed merely at outlining the nature of the theory-of-games approach and indicating the very limited contribution that it makes to the analysis of problems of imperfect competition.

Fundamentally, the theory of games attempts to answer the question of what can be considered to be rational behavior on the part of an individual confronted with a situation the outcome of which depends not only on his actions but also upon those of others who are in turn faced with a similar problem of selecting a rational course of action. In dealing with this problem, the theory of games examines not only the possible strategies of the individual players, but also the possible ways in which players may cooperate in coordinating their strategies, possibly with the use of side payments as inducements. By examining a wider range of possible types of conduct than is usually considered in other types of economic analysis, the theory of games has succeeded in turning up some possible outcomes of imperfect-competition situations that had been overlooked, thus widening the field of inquiry. In most cases, indeed, the theory of games gives us no greater certainty regarding any particular result, but rather diminishes our confidence in the outcomes indicated by the older theory by pointing out that still other outcomes are possible.

The Concept of a Strategy

IN THE "NORMALIZED" FORM of the theory of games, each of the participants, or "players," in a given situation is supposed to choose one of a number of programs, or plans of action, called a "strategy," which strategy will contain a complete specification of all of the actions or "moves" to be taken at each opportunity as a function of the state of information possessed by the player at the time the action is to be decided upon. A strategy is thus a complete set of plans of action specifying what the player is to do under any possible future contingency occurring in the playing of the game. When each of the players has chosen such a strategy, the interaction of these strategies with each other and with the rules of the game will determine the resulting outcome, or set of consequences, to the several players. In general, these outcomes may be any consequences whatever, such as A losing a leg, or B winning a trip to Paris; in much of the discussion the consequences are, however, limited to the winning or losing of sums of money or the equivalent. In many games or situations, the outcome may not be determined with certainty, but may depend on the values taken by certain chance variables, such as the fall of a die, or the state of the weather. In such cases, the rules of the game or the given data of the situation are assumed to determine the probability that these random variables will assume specific values on a given occasion, and hence the probability of each of the various possible outcomes resulting from a given choice of strategies by the various players.

Interaction of Strategies and the Payoff Function

EACH PLAYER, in selecting his own strategy, is supposed to know the complete set of strategies open to himself and also those open to the other players, and for every possible combination of choices of strategies by the players, he is supposed to know the probability of each of the possible outcomes. Each player is also supposed to know how each of the other players values or ranks the consequences to himself under each of the possible outcomes. One player may or may not know, when selecting his own strategy, what the strategy of any of the others is to be, except as this choice may be predicted by the theory of games itself. It is indeed an essential element of many games, and of many economic situations, that it is desirable to avoid giving any unnecessary information to the opponents concerning the strategy one is to choose for any particular play of the game.

It should of course be clearly understood that to assume this degree of knowledge on the part of the participants is rather extreme, particularly when the situations are fairly complex. If chess players possessed such knowledge about their game, for example, there would cease to be any point to it, as the outcome of the game would always be the same. Either there would be a strategy for white that would insure his winning, or a winning strategy for black, or strategies for both white and black that would insure against losing. Yet on an analytical level it is hard to get away from such an assumption, except in the very simplest and most naive models: as soon as one tries to specify a particular plausible degree of partial knowledge, including uncertainty, misinformation, and differences of opinion about the probabilities of various possible results of a given combination of strategies, the analysis becomes intractable.

The theory naturally builds up from the simplest cases. The case of a single

[343

player is merely the problem of an individual maximizing his utility already adequately treated in economic theory, and the theory of games proper has nothing new to add, although as a stage in the development of the theory John von Neumann and Oskar Morgenstern made a valuable contribution to the logic of choice that they required as a basis for bringing the theory of games to bear upon economic situations.

The Two-Person Strictly Adversary Game

THE SIMPLEST significant category is the "strictly adversary" game between two players. In such games the two players rank the various possible outcomes in exactly opposite order, so that any shift from one outcome to another that would be desired by one would be opposed by the other. This opposition of interest must extend to probability combinations of the outcomes, as well as to the "pure" outcomes, which in effect requires that the utility of the various outcomes to one player must be a linear function of the utility of the outcomes to the other. This condition is met, for example, if the outcomes consist of the payment of a specified sum from one player to the other, the marginal utility of money being deemed constant over the range involved in the playing of the game, for each player. Such a game is called "constant sum" in that the amounts gained or lost by the various players in any outcome of the game add up to a constant. In this particular instance, the constant is zero and the game is a "zero-sum" game; there is no significant difference between the theory of zero-sum games and the theory of constant-sum games. In such games, the two players necessarily operate independently of each other: there is nothing to be gained by attempting to cooperate with the other player, since the only way one player can gain is at the expense of his opponent.

If we assume that the number of strategies available to each player is finite (though possibly astronomically large), any two-person constant-sum game may be fully described by a rectangular array of numbers representing the amounts that will be obtained by *A* if *A* chooses a strategy corresponding to a given row of figures and *B* chooses the strategy corresponding to a given column. The results of the game for any combination of such choices is that *A* will receive the number in the array at the intersection of the row corresponding to *A*'s choice and the column corresponding to *B*'s choice; *B* will get the amount obtained by subtracting *A*'s winnings from the specified constant sum. This is illustrated in TABLE I, where *A* has three choices and *B* four.

Now if *A* chooses his strategy first, and if *B* then makes his choice with full knowledge of *A*'s choice, *A* will in effect first determine a row, and *B* will pick the smallest number in that row by a suitable choice of column (i.e., by the selection of the corresponding strategy). These smallest numbers for each row can be listed at the right, and are what *A* can expect as a result of initially choosing each row. A, under these circumstances, will pick the row having the largest minimum value, in the present example b, after which B will choose strategy z, resulting in a payment of 6 to A, and of $k - 6$ to B, k being the "constant sum" of the game.

If the procedure is reversed and B must choose and disclose his strategy to A before A makes his choice, then A will choose the strategy in each case that gives the highest value for the column previously selected by B, and B, anticipating this choice on the part of A, will choose the column having the smallest

TABLE 1

Strategy chosen by B:		x	y	z	w	
		Amount A wins from B:				ROW MINIMA
	a	1	2	3	12	1
Strategy chosen by A:	b	7	8	6	10	6
	c	5	11	4	3	3
COLUMN MAXIMA		7	11	6	12	6

maximum. In TABLE 1 this is again z, and A will again pick b. In this particular case, we see that the greatest minimum of the rows is equal to the smallest maximum of the columns, 6 in each case, and there is no advantage to be gained by finding out what strategy the opponent is going to use in advance of selecting your own: the result is the same whether A's strategy is known in advance to B or B's strategy is known in advance to A. Moreover, once the "minimax" strategies b and z, respectively, have been chosen, neither A nor B can gain by changing his own strategy while the other keeps to the minimax strategy. Games having this property are called "strictly determined" and sophisticated players having a complete knowledge of the game can be expected to play only the minimax strategies, yielding a unique result.

The results are substantially the same if more than one row has the same largest minimum value, or if more than one column has the same smallest maximum value. The outcome of the game will still be uniquely determined, but there will be several combinations of strategies that will produce the same result: the choice between these alternative minimax strategies will be a matter of indifference to the players as long as neither is expected to make a mistake. In any case, the important result for use in further analysis is the determination of a unique value for the game; the fact that this value may be achieved by alternative strategies is of no importance in the further theory. For example, if in TABLE 1 we replace the number 7 by another 6, then B would have no reason to prefer strategy z to x or vice versa (except possibly in consideration of the remote possibility that A might by mistake choose a or c), and the same ultimate payment can be obtained either by the combination of strategies (b, x) or (b, z).

The same general line of reasoning can be applied, in principle, no matter how numerous are the strategies that are available to the two players, or, within limits, even if the strategies are not discrete alternatives but contain parameters that can be given any values within a continuous range, such as the determination of a location or a price. For example, in the case discussed on page 328 of two sellers in a linear market with a predetermined price and a completely inelastic demand, we have essentially a constant-sum game with strategies consisting of the choice of a location. The constant sum is the total market that will be divided between the two sellers as a result of their choice

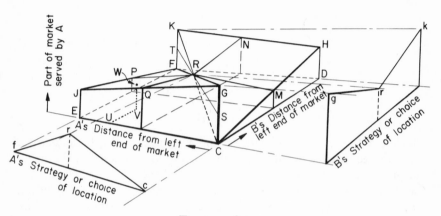

FIGURE 85

of location. The results of various combinations of strategies, or choices of locations, can be represented by a three-dimensional figure such as FIGURE 85, where A's location, measured from the left end of the market, is represented along the axis CE, B's distance from the same end along the axis CD, and the resulting share of the market secured by A is measured vertically up from the horizontal plane CEFD. Thus if A locates a distance CU from the left end, while B locates at a distance UV from the left end, A's share of the market will be given by the vertical distance VW (where V is in the base plane CEFD and W lies in the surface JPRQ). Plotting all of these points W for various possible locations of A and B gives the upper surface of the figure, which consists of the two slanted planes GRFPJQ and CMHNKR, there being a sharp break along the diagonal CF corresponding to the shift of customers from one seller to the other as either seller shifts his position from one side to the other of his competitor. To make the picture complete, it is necessary to specify what happens when both sellers pick the same spot: it is convenient in this case to assume that they will then share the market equally, so that the result in such cases is given not by points on the line FRG or the line CRK, but rather by the horizontal line SRT at a height of one-half.

346]

If A chooses a location first, and then B chooses his location so as to minimize the market secured by A, the results are shown by the curve *frc*, which is the projection of a line close to but not quite identical with *FRC* in the main diagram. Similarly, the maximum selected by A after B first chooses and discloses his choice is given by the curve *grk*, reflecting combinations close to those along *GRK* in the main diagram. The largest minimum is equal to the smallest maximum, so that it makes no difference "who goes first"; each seller obtains one-half of the market, and indeed there is only one

TABLE 2

B's strategy:	Heads	Tails	
	Amount B pays A:		ROW MINIMA
A's strategy: { Heads	$+1$	-1	-1
Tails	-1	$+1$	-1
COLUMN MAXIMA	$+1$	$+1$	$+1/-1$

TABLE 3

B:	Scissors	Stone	Paper	
	Amount B pays A:			ROW MINIMA
{ Scissors	0	-1	$+1$	-1
A: { Stone	$+1$	0	-1	-1
{ Paper	-1	$+1$	0	-1
COLUMN MAXIMA	$+1$	$+1$	$+1$	$+1/-1$

equilibrium position, at R, where both sellers locate at the center of the market.

Not all games, however, lead to a determinate equilibrium in this simple way. In the more interesting cases, the largest of the row minima will be less than the least of the column maxima (a little thought will show that the reverse cannot occur). In such cases it does make a difference which player finds out what his opponent's strategy is to be, and in fact this is the essence of many common games. For example, "matching pennies" and "scissors, stone, paper" can be described by the following tables: in TABLE 2, A is supposed to win on "even"; TABLE 3 expresses the formula, "stone dulls scissors, scissors cut paper, paper wraps stone." In these cases the difference between the largest of the row minima and the smallest of the column maxima as shown in the lower-right-hand corner expresses the degree to which the results of the game may be influenced by the degree to which one player discovers or predicts what the strategy of the other is to be.

A similar situation can be constructed in terms of a spatial-competition model. Let us suppose that we have a market in the form of a loop twelve units long, as in FIGURE 86, points on which can be labeled with the hours of the day, with three branches, 5, 9, and 12 units long, respectively, leaving the loop at the 5 o'clock point, the 9 o'clock point, and the 12 o'clock point. As a further simplification, let us consider that sellers can locate only at three

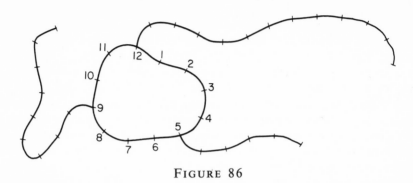

FIGURE 86

points on the loop, namely at 3, 8, and 11 o'clock. Consumers are uniformly distributed over the loop and the branches, and buy uniform amounts at fixed prices from the nearest seller; if two sellers happen to choose the same location they split the customers equally between them. If there are just two sellers, they will split the customers on the loop evenly between them regardless of where they locate, so that the issue is over the division of the markets

TABLE 4

B's choice of location:		3	8	11	
		A's share of the market			ROW MINIMA
	3	19	23	11	11
A's choice of location:	8	15	19	20	15
	11	27	18	19	18
COLUMN MAXIMA		27	23	20	20/18

on the branches. TABLE 4 gives the market obtained by A for various possible combinations of choice of location, with B of course getting the balance of the 12 + 9 + 5 + 12 = 38 units of market.

Thus if both A and B locate at 3 o'clock, they will share the total market between them, getting 19 each. If, however, B finds out that A is committed to locating at 3 o'clock, or can in any way predict with assurance that A will locate there, B will locate at 11 o'clock, securing for himself both the 9 o'clock and the 12 o'clock branches, leaving A only half of the loop plus the 5 o'clock branch, or a total of 11, as shown in the table. But *A*, in turn, if he discovers that *B* is at 11 o'clock, will want to move to 8 o'clock (at least, as we assume here, if moving is costless), thereby obtaining a market of 20. *B* now has an incentive to move from 11 to 3, and no equilibrium emerges, but a continuous chase around the circle. Substantially the same thing happens if we remove the restrictions on location and permit *A* and *B* to locate at any point along the loop or the branches.

Thus in such a situation there is no equilibrium possible, in the usual sense of the term "equilibrium," and if a cost of moving is injected as a means of putting a stop to the continuous chase, the "game" is no longer "constant sum" but must be analyzed by more elaborate methods. To save the situation, the theory of games at this point borrows an idea from such games as "matching pennies" and introduces the idea of "mixed strategies." It is fairly obvious that if one is engaged in a long series of plays of "matching pennies" or "scissors, stone, paper," a good, or at least a safe, way to play the game is to choose the strategy used on each occasion by reference to some chance device, so that since the player himself does not know in advance what his strategy for a particular play is going to be, neither can his opponent, so that there is then no danger of being "found out." More generally, a "mixed strategy" is any assignment of probabilities to the various "pure" strategies such that the sum of all such probabilities is unity. If such mixed strategies are admitted, then each player is permitted the much wider choice of determining the probability assigned to each strategy (which will include the case in which a pure strategy is chosen by assigning a probability of one to it and zero to all others). The pure strategy to be used on any particular occasion will then be determined not by any further action of the player, but by resort to some chance device that has the required probability characteristics, as, for example, by drawing from a shuffled deck of cards, or consulting a table of random numbers, having previously determined what pure strategy will be indicated by any particular drawing.

If one or both players resort to such mixed strategies, the outcome, even if certain in the pure-strategy case, will now no longer be so, and it becomes necessary to determine an average or expected outcome for each choice of mixed strategies. This can be done by taking each element in the outcome matrix, multiplying it by the probability assigned by *A* to the corresponding one of his pure strategies, and then by the probability assigned by *B* to the corresponding one of *B*'s pure strategies, and summing these products for each element of the outcome matrix. In this process, it is assumed that *A* and *B* pick their strategy for any given occasion independently of each other so that there will be no correlation between the choices of *A* and *B*. For example, if in matching pennies each player chooses heads with probability 0.5, the frequency of each of the four cells is 0.25, and the expected value of the game to *A* is zero. On the other hand, if *A* picks heads with probability

[349

0.6, and *B* picks heads with probability 0.7, the cells have probabilities of 0.42, 0.18, 0.28, and 0.12, and *A*'s expected gain is $.42 - .18 - .28 + .12 = .08$.

It is a fundamental theorem of the theory of games that if mixed strategies are admitted, then any two-person constant-sum game has a minimax value. That is, there exists for each player one or more minimax strategies such that if one player follows a minimax strategy, the other player can never do any better against it than employ his own minimax strategy, and all combinations of minimax strategies produce the same minimax value for the game. It is not easy to give a simple demonstration of this theorem (the usual proofs have recourse to the theory of convex sets), so that for most economists its validity will have to be taken on faith. It does not seem to be intuitively unlikely, however, although prior to the discovery of the proof at least one well-known mathematician expressed doubt as to its universal validity. In the matching-pennies case, the minimax strategy is obviously to choose heads and tails with probability of one-half each. Any other probability consistently adhered to over a long series of plays could be assumed in the long run to be observed by the opponent and acted upon to the loss of the player who persists in using the wrong probabilities. Or if any valid theory based on other lines of reasoning indicated a different strategy, this theory would itself be known to a rational opponent, so that, for example, *B* might use the theory to predict *A*'s behavior, and take advantage of this knowledge, so that *A* would be worse off than if he used the minimax strategy, indicating that this would be a bad theory for *A* to follow.

Where the game is symmetrical as between different strategies, the optimum mixed strategies are fairly obvious. Where this symmetry is lacking, and especially where the number of pure strategies is large. the procedure for determining the various probabilities to be used in forming the minimax mixed strategy is not so obvious. In the spatial-competition case, which, though symmetrical as between *A* and *B*, is not symmetrical as between different strategies, it so happens that we can determine the probabilities *x*, *y*, and *z* with which *A* should choose locations 3, 8, and 11, by imposing the condition that the expected result should always be some constant value *k*, for all three of the pure strategies available to *B*. If this condition can be met, then no matter in what proportions *B* combines his strategies, the outcome will always be the same. Solving the resulting equations gives for the probabilities *x*, *y*, and *z* the values 1/13, 8/13, and 4/13, respectively, and for the constant outcome *k* the value 19. This value of *k* is what would be expected from the symmetry between the positions of *A* and *B*: since there is no reason to expect that one would get more than the other, they must each get half of the total. *B*, symmetrically, must choose the various locations with the same probabilities as *A*; of course, on any particular occasion, they are likely to choose different locations.

The determination of the probabilities in the minimax mixed strategy is of course not always so simple as it is in the above examples, but there is a general procedure available, too complicated to give here in detail, by which one can always obtain the answer in a finite number of computational steps. This procedure is of considerable interest in other connections, in particular in the solution of the type of problem known as linear programing, examples of which are the distribution of coal from a number of mines to a number of steel mills so as to minimize the total cost of transportation, assumed for each route to be a linear function of the amount shipped; or to obtain certain specified quantities of nutrients present in various foods in specified proportions by purchasing foods at fixed prices so as to minimize the total cost.

But while the computations can be carried through in principle, the amount of work required mounts up rapidly as the number of pure strategies to be considered increases. If the number of strategies for each player is of the order of 100, electronic computing machines would be indicated for the work of solution, unless the payoff matrix has systematic properties that permit short cuts. Thus to say on the one hand that the problem is in principle solved, and on the other that real players or participants in economic life can be expected, even in the most idealized circumstances, to come anywhere close to the theoretical result, may be quite different things.

Even abstracting from the difficulties of carrying through the calculations, it is admittedly somewhat difficult to fit such a notion of mixed strategies into economic problems, as costs of moving, historical preconditioning, costs of securing information, and uncertainty and difference of opinion as to the probability distribution of consequences are likely to bulk large in an actual situation. In the above model one may perhaps think of a pair of super-rational produce vendors who truck their produce in from the source each night and set up shop for the day at dawn, each in complete ignorance of the whereabouts of the other, except as inferences may be drawn from the general situation, assumed to be fully known. The most rational act for the vendors in such circumstances would be for both A and B to provide themselves with a little bag with one white, eight red, and four blue balls, draw one of these balls from the bag each night, and locate at 3 if a white ball is drawn, at 8 if red, and at 11 if blue. Then even if A were to find out about B's bag of balls, or even if A were to deduce from the theory that this is what B would do, it will do him no good unless he is able to hold off his own decision until he has some further information as to what B is going to do on a specific occasion—for example, until after B has actually drawn the ball and A has in some way found out about it. But if B uses a bag with balls in any other proportion, and A finds out about this, either directly or by observing B's behavior over a long enough period of time to be able to estimate the relative frequencies, A can then derive an advantage by changing

[351

his own behavior accordingly. But of course he can do this only at the risk of being found out in turn by *B*.

Or we can imagine *A* and *B* both planning to construct a plant, each expecting to be fully committed as to location before he is able to learn of the plans of the other. In such a case, again, in strict theory there is no better plan for each than to draw lots from an urn containing the appropriate proportions of balls of various kinds. For if there were any rational basis for making a decision in any other way, then on the basis of perfect rationality, *B* would know just as much about this rational basis for *A*'s decision as would *A*, and would therefore be able to take advantage of this knowledge, with the result that *A*'s expectations would be diminished below the level of the minimax value, and the alternative theory proves to be less advantageous to *A* than the minimax.

But whatever reservations one may have about the analysis of two-person strictly adversary games in terms of mixed strategies, the theory of games proceeds on the basis that by their use every two-person constant-sum game will have a determinate value to the two players, representing the amount that on the average they can expect to get from each occasion on which the game is played when each uses a minimax strategy. Indeed, much of the theory involving more than two players is built on this as a foundation, by the device of regarding any constant-sum game between any number of players as being capable of being played as a two-person game between two opposing factions or "coalitions." Each opposing group is supposed to coordinate the strategies of its members into a group strategy: the strategies thus open to the group as a coalition will then consist of all of the possible combinations of the strategies of its members. The game as played by some particular group against the rest of the players likewise coordinating their strategy will then have a distinct value for the group, resulting from both groups adopting their respective minimax strategies, either pure or mixed. This value or aggregate gain for the group can be determined with respect to each of the various possible coalitions of players, being in each case the amount that such a group can secure for itself in the aggregate by coordinating the strategies of its members against the most unfavorable strategies that the remaining players can possibly use. The whole set of values so determined for each of the $2^n - 1$ subsets that can be formed from the set of *n* players is called the "characteristic function" of the game. Much of the theory of games of three or more persons is based entirely on this characteristic function.

Constant-sum Games with Three or More Persons

CONSIDER, FOR EXAMPLE, the case of three sellers choosing locations in turn along a market 24 miles long, demand being inelastic and the price fixed. The characteristic function in this case can be derived as follows. The coalition of all three sellers obviously secures the entire market, so $v(ABC) = 24$. For some purposes, it is also convenient to assign a value to the "empty" or "null" coalition, $v(\emptyset) = 0$. But the important values are obtained when the players are divided into two nonempty groups, which in this case can be done in three ways, yielding six coalitions. If A, the first to locate, plays a lone hand against B and C, then no matter where A locates, B and C can locate on either side of him, securing substantially the entire market for the coalition BC, leaving A with nothing; thus we put $v(A) = 0$; $v(BC) = 24$. If A and B form a coalition, A and B can agree to locate at the quartiles, after which C can get at most one-fourth of the market, leaving the remaining three-fourths to be shared in some way between A and B. Thus we put $v(C) = 6$, $v(AB) = 18$. Finally, if A and C form a coalition, then C will locate next to B in such a way as to cut down B's share of the market as much as possible. B, anticipating this, will maximize his ultimate market by making the smaller of the two sides of his market as large as possible, i.e., by locating one-third of the distance toward A from the end of the market farthest from A. A, in order to do his part in minimizing B's ultimate market, will locate in the center, so that B then locates 4 miles from one end, and C locates next to B. B and C then each get 4, and A gets 16, so that $v(B) = 4$, $v(AC) = 20$.

The characteristic function tells us how much a given coalition can secure in the aggregate, but it does not directly specify how this aggregate gain is to be divided up among the members of the coalition. To be sure, the specifications of the game or situation may give an initial distribution of the proceeds among the members of the coalition, but this distribution need not be, and in some cases cannot be, final, for it may be necessary for some members of a coalition to pay a bonus of some sort to other members in order to persuade them to stay in the coalition and coordinate their strategy with those of the other members. For example, in the above case where the coalition AC was formed, A would end up with 16, and C with only 4. But if this is all C is to get out of this arrangement, he will never consent to entering such a coalition, for he can secure at least 6 by operating independently, even if A should join with B against him. He may indeed get even more than 6 if he succeeds in forming a coalition with B. Hence if A is to have any hope at all of holding this coalition AC together, he must pay C a bonus out of his share of the gain, so as to bring C's share up to more than 6 miles.

But if the rules of the game, or the specifications of the model, do not give us the distribution of the gain within a coalition, how is this to be determined? At this point there is a considerable divergence of approaches. Indeed, even before coming to the characteristic function, there is an approach in terms of the "noncooperative game" in which each player is required to act entirely independently of all of the others. Many parlor games are in effect of this type, where collusion between players is regarded as unethical. For such games, one of the interesting results is an extension of the minimax principle, due to Nash, which says that there always exists a set of (possibly mixed) strategies for the players, such that for each player separately his strategy is the best for him if the others all persist in their existing strategies. In other words, there exists a "Nash equilibrium point" such that no player can gain by changing his strategy if all the other players keep their strategies unchanged. In effect, this is an analogue of the proposition that a competitive equilibrium point always exists. It is often possible, however, for two or more players to move away from a "Nash point" in such a manner as to improve their combined gains, so that a Nash point is stable only if coalitions are effectively proscribed—as in some instances the coordinating deviants can even improve the gains to each separately, not only explicit coalitions with the payment of side inducements, but tacit coalitions where no such overt behavior is involved must be prevented. In addition, Nash points may, in the case of non-constant-sum games, occur when the aggregate gain is less than the maximum possible, i.e., when the equilibrium point is not "efficient," which is another reason for regarding such points as unsatisfactory as solutions. Still another possibility is that there may be more than one such Nash point, yielding different distributions of gains to the players, and since in general an individual strategy that is "good" at one Nash point, i.e., cannot be unilaterally changed with profit, may not be good at another, there is no basis for predicting which strategy the individual will choose, or even that there is any tendency for the situation to approach the Nash point, even under assumptions of continued "noncooperation" and naïveté concerning the reactions of other players. This result reflects, for example, the situation in the Edgeworth duopoly problem.

Another approach is that of Shapley, who constructs a value of the game for each individual from the increments that the accession of a given individual to a coalition will bring to the characteristic function for that coalition. We can imagine a coalition starting with one member and adding one member at a time, with each new member being given the entire increment in the value of the coalition due to his joining it, until a coalition of all players is formed. This can be done in $n!$ ways,[1] each of which will give a distribution of gains among the players. By averaging all of these gains, a figure can be obtained for each player that may be considered what he can expect from the game, supposing that we consider the formation of all of these sequences of coalitions as equally likely. The value so determined has many unique properties, and if a single value is to be found for each player representing his expectations from the game, the Shapley value may well be considered the only acceptable one. There is, however, no special reason to suppose that the Shapley value actually represents anything likely to occur on any

1. $n!$ represents n factorial, also written $\lfloor n$, and is equal to $1 \cdot 2 \cdot \ldots \cdot (n-1) \cdot n$.

354]

one occasion, or even as an average of actual occasions, at least unless more is said concerning the relative likelihood of different sequences of coalition-formation, and particularly of the new member of the coalition being able to secure for himself the entire amount that his accretion adds to the strength of the coalition.

The more voluminous, if indeed not the more significant, development of the *n*-person game theory follows a rather subtle line of reasoning. In general, this part of the theory fails to specify any one result from a given situation, but rather presents a class of possible results from which the one that can be expected to occur on any occasion must be considered to be determined in large measure by chance, history, custom, or any of a number of other factors too subtle or complex to permit their being included in the analysis. And the process of specifying this class of results is itself somewhat indirect and involved.

We begin by defining an "imputation" as a set of numbers giving the net amount of gain (or loss) to be received by each player, net after all compensations or bonuses have been paid between the members of the various coalitions, provided that each player gets at least as much as he could secure playing a lone hand against a coalition of all the rest. Thus the imputation (12, 6, 6) is one that might result if *A*, *B*, and *C* locate without any coalitions being formed, *C* happening to choose to locate near *B*, *A* and *B* being at the two quartiles. The distribution (16, 4, 4) would be the shares of the markets secured by *A*, *B*, and *C*, respectively, if *A* and *C* cooperate to minimize *B*'s share, but this is not an imputation, since *C* can get more than 4—namely, 6—by his own unaided effort. If *A* pays *C* 8 for his cooperation, giving the distribution (8, 4, 12), this would be an imputation.

The next important concept is that of the "domination" of one imputation by another. One imputation *a* is said to be dominated by another imputation *b* if there exists a coalition *T* such that each member of *T* prefers *b* to *a*, and *T* is powerful enough to secure for its members the amounts they are assigned in *b*. *T* is called the "effective set" for the domination of *a* by *b*. Loosely speaking, *b* dominates *a* if there exists a set that unanimously desires and can enforce a shift from *a* to *b* (in games of five or more persons, a distinction can sometimes be made between "strict domination," in which the effective set *T* can actually enforce a shift from an existing *a* to a completely specified *b*, and "loose domination," in which the effective set *T* can insure for its members the amounts they get in *b*, but cannot control the distribution of the balance of the gains among the players not in *T*). Thus in the above example we can say that the imputation *b* = (12, 6, 6) dominates *a* = (8, 4, 12), since *A* and *B* are both better off in *b*, and the coalition *AB* can actually secure for itself a total of 18, which is the amount *A* and *B* together get in *b*.

Unfortunately, the relation "dominates" (unlike the relation "is preferred

[355

to" encountered in utility analysis) is not transitive; i.e., if b dominates a, and if c dominates b (but perhaps with a different effective set), then it is not necessarily true that c dominates a; indeed, it is quite possible for a to dominate c, completing the circle (with loose domination and five or more players, it is even possible for a to dominate b and b to dominate a). Thus if in the above example we consider a third imputation $c = (4, 12, 8)$, this imputation dominates b, since both B and C are better off in c and since together they are able to obtain almost the entire 24 miles of market, which is greater than the total of 20 miles allotted to them in c. On the other hand, A and C are both better off in a than in c, and can as a coalition secure the 20 miles imputed to them in a, so that a dominates c, and we saw above that b dominates a.

Thus in general we can set up an infinitude of circular movements in which we go successively from one imputation to another through the formation of successive different coalitions, with no resting place in sight. Two somewhat different approaches to the problem of putting a limitation on this process and perhaps bringing the endless shifting process to a halt have been followed. One, due to Duncan Luce, is fairly straightforward, but somewhat arbitrary; the other, more general and of long standing, is that developed by von Neumann and Morgenstern.

The Luce procedure is to consider a situation as consisting of a conjunction of an imputation and a partition of the players into coalitions, and then to consider only those dominations for which the effective sets are not too radically different from one of the coalitions in the situation, which we may call proximate coalitions. The way in which the set of proximate coalitions is defined is at best arbitrary: for example, we may consider only those coalitions that can be formed by dropping one member from or adding one member to one of the situation coalitions. Or coalitions may be considered that require two changes of membership, or that are the union of the situation coalitions. However we decide to define this proximate set (with the idea being to include in this set all coalitions that could be formed from the existing ones with a given degree of ease), a situation can be considered stable if the existing coalitions have something to hold them together (i.e., if each member of the coalition in the situation gets more than he would get acting alone), and if there is no domination of the existing imputation with an effective set for the domination among the proximate coalitions, then the situation is considered stable, with respect to the proximate set as defined. A given game may have no stable situations, or one, or several, depending upon the strictness with which the proximate coalitions are defined.

This method of singling out stable situations has a certain appeal, in that it is mathematically simpler than other methods, and both on a priori grounds and on the basis of observed experimental behavior, changes in coalitions are somewhat more likely to take place one person at a time, so that there is some sense in trying to draw a line between the coalition shifts that can and those that cannot take place on the basis of the degree of complexity of the shift. On the other hand, there is little information available, either observational or a priori, as to just how this line should be drawn. Situations that are stable with respect to a significantly large proximate set of coalitions appear to occur chiefly for the games with larger numbers of players: there are no such stable situations for three-person constant-sum games, which of course include the above example (except for the trivial case where the proximate set includes only the sets of the partition in the situation).

The von Neumann–Morgenstern Theory

THE VON NEUMANN THEORY, on the other hand, proceeds by grouping imputations into sets that he terms "solutions." The word "solution" is perhaps misleading in that each "solution" (and there may be many to a given game) consists of several imputations or possible outcomes; possibly the term "coherent pattern," or "coherent set," or, for short, "coherence," will come closer to conveying the underlying meaning, and these terms will be used in what follows. A "coherent set," or "coherence," is a set of imputations such that no imputation in the set dominates (or is dominated by) another imputation in the set, while each imputation outside the set is dominated by some imputation in the set. The idea behind this definition is that if we can consider some such set of imputations to be established as conforming to accepted standards of conduct, or normal trade practices, or otherwise singled out as preferred, and if imputations outside such a set are considered in some way inferior or improper, then an imputation within such a set may have a good chance of persisting, once it has been reached, for a longer period or in the face of more powerful disturbing influences than an imputation not in the socially approved coherent set. There can be no movement within the set, since no imputation in it dominates another; moreover, a movement against the mores to an imputation outside the set will be rather rapidly discredited by the domination of that imputation by an acceptable one in the coherence.

A set of imputations that fails to contain an element dominating an outside imputation will be too vulnerable to movement to such an imputation to be considered stable, and more than mere normal suasion might be necessary to keep the participants to the accepted pattern: this might take the form of regulation or law, tantamount to a change in the rules of the game. Or a set that contains imputations dominated by others in the set may contain one or more rings of successive dominations, with the likelihood that movements within the set would occur. If any of the dominated elements belong to no such ring, they would sooner or later be moved away from, and thereafter will be unused, so that they should preferably have been left out of the

[357

proposed pattern in setting it up. Thus any set of imputations proposed for use as a standard of conduct that does not conform to the above criteria for a coherence will either lack stability, contain redundant elements, or fail to provide a direct path to the set from outside imputations.

The Three-Person Constant-sum Game in the von Neumann–Morgenstern Theory

THE NOTIONS of domination between imputations and of a coherent set of imputations can be illustrated for our three-person game in FIGURE 87.

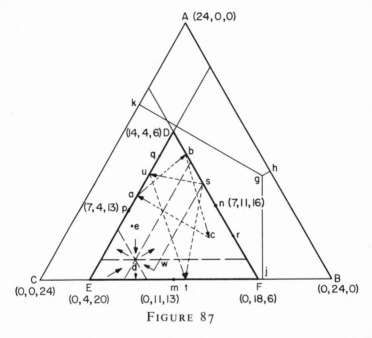

FIGURE 87

ABC is an equilateral triangle with an altitude of 24. If we take any point inside this triangle, the sum of the distances from the point to the three sides will always equal 24, so that we may take any such point as representing an imputation in which the gains of *A*, *B*, and *C*, respectively, are represented by the distances from the point to the sides *BC*, *AC*, and *AB*, respectively, opposite the angles *A*, *B*, and *C*. Thus the point *g* represents a distribution in which *A* gets the amount *gj*, *B* gets the amount *gk*, and *C* gets the amount *gh*.

C acting independently can secure for himself at least 6, and *B* at least 4, so that in effect only the points within the triangle *DEF* are, strictly speaking, imputations, and only these points need be considered. If we consider an imputation *d* within *DEF*, then we can draw through *d* three lines parallel to the sides of the triangle, dividing the space around *d* into six sectors. Any point *e* within the sector containing the apex *D* will be dominated by *d*, since both *B* and *C* will be better off at *d* than at *e*, and since *B* and *C* in a coalition can, if they exert their powers, achieve any total gain up to 24, represented for them by points along the line *EF*, and a fortiori can enforce *d*. Similarly, *d* dominates any imputation *within* the sectors containing the points *E* and *F*, the effective coalitions for these dominations being *AB* and *AC*, respectively. On the other hand, *d* is dominated by any point within the three other sectors.

The sectors dominating *d* and dominated by *d* are indicated in the diagram by the arrows, which go in the direction of possible movement. It is easily seen in applying these rules to *a*, *b*, and *c*, that *b* dominates *a*, *c* dominates *b*, and *a* dominates *c*, as indicated by the arrows. No points outside *DEF* dominate any point inside *DEF*.

It is important to note that points *on* the lines dividing the sectors from each other neither dominate *d* nor are dominated by *d*. Changes along these lines benefit only one person at the expense of another, the third player being unaffected; within the triangle *DEF* no person acting alone is powerful enough to bring about any change. Accordingly, if two imputations are to belong to the same coherence, they must both lie along a line parallel to a side of the triangle *DEF*, since neither must dominate the other. If there is a third imputation in the coherence, and if it is not to lie on the same straight line, it must be at the third apex of an equilateral triangle with the other two, and a fourth imputation in the coherence becomes impossible. Thus if coherences exist, they must consist either entirely of points on a line parallel to a side of *DEF*, or of three points at the vertex of an equilateral triangle with sides parallel to those of *DEF*.

Taking the equilateral triangle case, we can fairly easily see that the only way in which the vertexes of such a triangle can be placed so as to dominate all other points in or on triangle *DEF* is to place them at the mid-points of the sides of *DEF*. These three imputations, then, taken together, form a coherence, and it would therefore be plausible for a standard of behavior or norm to be set up that would give some degree of approval to arrangements that result in one of these three distributions of gains, while giving some degree of disapproval to all other results.

We have yet, however, to determine why, except for the strength of the social sanctions themselves, players would feel impelled to adhere to such a coherence. It turns out, happily, that this particular coherence has special properties, not possessed by all coherences, that make it to a considerable extent "self-policing," in that if the pattern or coherence gains an even slight degree of customary acceptance, there will be a strong tendency for an imputation in this coherence, once reached, to maintain itself without the need for any further outside sanctions. The members of the coalition in existence at any time will strongly resist any blandishments proffered by the shut-out player to break up their coalition. This condition comes about as soon as it becomes apparent that a shift from an imputation outside the coherence, which we may term a "heresy," to one within the coherence, which we may call a "conforming imputation," or simply a "conformity," is to any extent likely to take place or develop more quickly or more easily than a shift from a conformity to a heresy.

This self-policing tendency results from the following considerations. Suppose that A and B have formed a coalition and have pushed to the conformity $n = (7, 11, 6)$, this being the midpoint of DF and thus part of the coherence consisting of the points n, p, and m, which we assume to be socially approved in some way. C, being the loser under this arrangement, may attempt to break it up by offering to form a coalition with A in which the split will be such as to produce the heresy q, which will be better for both A and C. A may at first be tempted to accept this offer. But if he does accept, the heresy q will be vulnerable, and indeed B, being the loser at this point, would immediately set about trying to persuade C to join B in a coalition with the conforming result m. Because this is a "policing" move from a heresy to a conformity, B should have a much easier time persuading C to join him in a coalition for this move than C did in persuading A to join him in the heretical move to q. This is not only because it may be easier to conform than to dissent, but also because the uniqueness of m provides a focus for bargaining, making it easier for C and B to agree on the way the gain is to be shared than it was for A and B to come to an agreement. Accordingly, A, after enjoying the benefits of q for a relatively short time, may be chagrined to find the situation winding up at m. Moreover, if A now in his turn tries to break up the coalition BC to form a new heresy, not only will he have to offer some point such as r as an objective that is less advantageous to him than the original point n, but he will see his chances of getting his offer accepted become very dim indeed as B learns from A's experience that it may not pay to be too greedy. Indeed, if A is sufficiently perspicacious to anticipate all this from the start, he will probably refuse to budge from n despite all the persuasive wiles that C can bring to bear, unless perhaps C can invent a more permanent and binding form of agreement or contract than that which binds A and B together, so that A can be guaranteed a long enough sojourn at q to allay his fears that B and C will eventually get together at m. But of course in static long-run analysis, all contracts run out sometime.

For the three-person constant-sum game, this triangular coherence turns out to be the only one that has this self-policing feature. If we consider the other alternative, where all points of the coherence must lie along a line, then if the entire triangle DEF is to be dominated by conforming imputations, these must include all the points on the line, as any point left out would be

360]

undominated. Moreover, the line must lie closer to the side of *DEF* to which it is parallel than to the midpoints of the other two sides, otherwise the midpoint of the parallel side would be left undominated. The set of points on any line segment conforming to these requirements will then constitute a coherence according to the definition above. In effect, such a coherence consists of a rule that one of the participants must always get a constant amount, which is of course at least as much as what he could get for himself unaided, but exceeds it by less than half of the altitude of triangle *DEF*.

But the self-policing feature is lacking in such coherences. For example, if the accepted coherence consists of the points on the segment *DF*, and again we are originally at *n* with the coalition *AB* exerting itself, then *A* would have relatively little to fear from accepting an offer from *C* to join him in a change to the heresy *q*, for now there is no conformity that can be reached directly from *q* that is worse for *A* than *n* was. While *B* and *C* may subsequently get together at some such point as *m*, *m* is now also a heresy, and the switch from *q* to *m* is not likely to occur quite so promptly. Moreover, even arrived at *m*, *A* has now a fairly good chance of bringing about a shift to *r*, since *r* is now a more respectable imputation than *m*. And from *r* he may get back to *q* and start over again. Indeed, in this case it is difficult to see any real tendency to adhere to the accepted standard that arises from the nature of the game itself, and it seems rather likely that a coherence of this type would not long retain its status as a generally observed social code unless adherence is enforced by some fairly strong institutional pressures of an unspecified character. This is especially true where, as in this instance, *C* has little or nothing to lose by breaking away from the standard.

One may of course run across fairly strongly held ideas of proper behavior that do not conform to one of the coherent patterns here defined. We have already seen how a prejudice against paying bonuses (or "bribes") may have to face strong pressures from the exigencies of the situation, especially when this proves to be the only way to secure the participation of one of the needed members of the coalition. One might, for example, propose as a standard of proper behavior that every coalition should split its gains evenly among its members. This would give coalitions $s = (9, 9, 6)$ if the coalition *AB* is formed, $t = (0, 12, 12)$ for *BC*, and $u = (10, 4, 10)$ for *AC*. In this case, the coalition *t* dominates the other two, and there would, accordingly, be a tendency for the coalition *BC* to form to the exclusion of the other two. But this is not all; the imputation $w = (2, 9, 13)$ dominates *t* and is not dominated by *s* or *u* so that it would be quite possible to have a shift from *t* to *w* with *w* persisting for quite some time. This might come about, for example, by the formation of the coalition *AC*, which, however, would not exploit *B* completely, leaving enough over for *B* so that *B* would not be tempted to push for a change to the approved imputation *s*. Thus it would seem that a group of sophisticated and hard-pushing participants would rather soon put an end to adherence to any standard that did not constitute a coherent set of imputations, unless indeed such a standard were enforced with such substantial externally applied sanctions as to make adherence to such standards a part of the rules of the game or of the underlying circumstances rather than a tenuous ethic, habit, or custom.

The three-person constant-sum game can thus be fairly completely analyzed, at least within the limits of the restrictive assumptions made. Indeed, there are only two significantly different varieties of this game, in terms of the strategic behavior produced: the "essential" game, just analyzed, and the "nonessential" game, in which the gain obtainable by each coalition is merely the sum of the gains obtainable by each member of the coalition acting separately against a coalition of all the other players. In such a nonessential game, there is nothing to be gained by the formation of coalitions, and only one imputation will result from the rational playing of such a game: the imputation that gives to each participant precisely the amount that he can obtain for himself, i.e., the value of the characteristic function for the one-person set of which he is the sole member.

It is fairly easy to see that these two types exhaust all the possibilities for the three-person constant-sum game if we consider that the rational behavior of the participants of a game should not be influenced if we modify the characteristic function in such a way as to add (or subtract) a constant amount to the respective gains which a participant, and any coalition of which he is a member, can secure. Rational behavior depends upon a comparison of alternatives, and if all of the alternatives are improved or worsened by a constant amount, the choice should be the same. Concretely, if in the spatial-competition case each seller must meet a certain fixed cost regardless of choice of location (and even if he stays out of the market altogether), then his behavior should be unchanged whatever his cost happens to be. To be sure, in a real situation, irrational or habitual behavior may prevail in terms of covering costs, bolstered perhaps by a notion of "just price." But such considerations must be excluded here, if tractability is to be preserved.

One game then can be said to be "strategically equivalent" to another if its characteristic function can be obtained from that of the other by adding or subtracting a constant amount to each of the values of the characteristic function obtaining for sets of which a given player is a member, or by any series of such changes. In particular, we can subtract, with respect to each player, the value of the single-player coalition, to obtain a characteristic function in which each player acting alone gets zero. If the original game was nonessential, this transformation will produce a characteristic function that is zero for all coalitions, and no player will be able to win or lose anything from the playing of this "normalized," nonessential game.

For essential games, the equivalent game produced by the above process can be further normalized by dividing all values of the characteristic function by its maximum value, i.e., by the value of the function for the coalition of all players. This will modify the intensity but not the direction of the incentives motivating the players, so that in the absence of frictions, the strategic behavior of the players should be unaffected. This process produces, for constant-sum games, a characteristic function that is zero for the null set and for all one-person sets, and $+ 1$ for the coalition of all n players and for all coalitions of $n - 1$ players. For $n = 3$, this determines the characteristic function completely, confirming that there is only one type of essential three-person constant-sum game, all such games being strategically equivalent. In particular, in the example we have been discussing, normalization consists in deducting 4 from the values of all sets that include B, and then deducting 6 from all sets that include C, thus getting the symmetrical game in which one-person coalitions get 0, while all two- and three-person coalitions get 14. Dividing by 14 gives the normalized game.

Games with More Than Three Players

BUT WHILE there is only one type of essential three-person constant-sum game, and only one self-policing coherence (consisting of three imputations) emerging as a set of plausible outcomes, the situation rapidly becomes more complicated as the number of players is increased. For example, if we consider a four-person constant-sum game in its normalized unit-sum form, the characteristic function is already determined for coalitions of zero, one, three, and four players, but there remains a considerable variation in the possible values for the two-person coalitions, of which there are six altogether, consisting of three pairs of complements. If we take one coalition from each complementary pair, we can give the characteristic function for each such coalition any value from 0 to $+ 1$. Thus if we put $x = v(AB)$, $y = v(AC)$, and $z = v(AD)$, then because of the unit-sum condition we must have $v(CD) = 1 - x$, $v(BD) = 1 - y$, and $v(BC) = 1 - z$, so that we have no further freedom in specifying the characteristic function. But x, y, and z can each independently be given any values from 0 to 1, and for each choice of parameters we will have an essentially different game (except that some may be equivalent to others through permutation of the players). As the number of players increases, the complexities mount rapidly and in many cases qualitatively new phenomena appear: for five players, there are ten degrees of freedom in the characteristic function; for ten players, there are 501. Naturally, only a minute fraction of these possibilities has been explored, indeed even the four-person games have not all yet been analyzed.

The transition from the constant-sum game to the variable-sum or "general" game is in principle quite simple, although some rather serious questions arise as to whether the procedure is meaningful. For an n-person variable-sum game can be converted into an $(n + 1)$-person zero-sum game by the introduction of an additional "dummy" player who will in every case lose (or gain) what the "active" players in the aggregate gain (or lose), and who will be unable to have any choice of strategies (he has, in effect, only a single strategy available to him) or make any side payments to fellow members of a coalition. The n-person general game is then just a special case of the $(n + 1)$-person constant-sum game.

For example, if we consider the Cournot duopoly case, we can convert this into a three-person constant-sum game by introducing a dummy who will be required to pay the other two the amount of profits indicated by the outputs that they decide to market. (Note, however, that this "dummy" is not to be identified with the "public" in that the impairment of the consumers' surplus does not in general correspond to the profits of the duopolists.) If the two duopolists form a coalition, they will be able to agree to market in the aggregate the monopoly volume of product and so obtain the monopoly amount of profit to split between them in some way. Since coalitions involving the dummy are outlawed, and since the best that each duopolist can insure for himself, acting independently, is zero (considering the possibility that his competitor might insist on marketing so much as to bring the price down to cost), no other imputation can dominate any of the ones involving securing the monopoly profit, and these imputations taken together form the coherence in this case. Here stability is secured through the fact that the imputations in the coherence are undominated by any other, and there is thus within the theory no tendency to depart from a conforming imputation, once one has been reached. But on the other hand, there is nothing to indicate which one will be reached, or even what the probabilities are of various distributions of the monopoly profits between the two sellers.

Now it can be shown in general that no coherences exist that include imputations that involve anything but the maximum loss to the "dummy." In other words, it is implied that complete knowledge and rational behavior would lead in any case to an "efficient" result, in the sense that no system of rearrangements and compensations would be possible which would leave all parties better off. This is equivalent to saying that if there is any case of a failure to come to terms, such as in a strike, or when buyer and seller fail to reach an agreement when a possible agreement exists, this is necessarily the result of either ignorance or irrationality. Or further, if we consider the economic system as a game in which the entire population are players, the von Neumann "solutions" or coherences consist entirely of imputations that satisfy the Pareto condition, or in other words that lie on the generalized contract curve where there is no possibility of improving the lot of some without worsening the lot of others.

364]

But this says relatively little about the real world, for in fact we have to deal with persons who are often less than perfectly rational, and are usually less than omniscient. Indeed, for the results of the theory of games to be strictly applicable, we would have to assume participants whose ability to analyze combinatorial possibilities exceeded that of the champion chess player, and whose knowledge of the theory of games at times must be required to exceed that of von Neumann and Morgenstern. To be sure, some of the results predicted by the theory may be achieved by a trial-and-error process or by the interaction of intuitive hunches; in most cases, however, the results produced by such a process would differ substantially from those resulting from the type of rationality postulated in the theory of games.

Thus while we are in principle able to delineate possible results of rational behavior where each participant takes account of the reactions and probable strategies of the others, this is done only at the expense of making drastic and unrealistic assumptions concerning the knowledge, rationality, and analytic ability of the participants. And even so, the answers obtained are in terms of a multiplicity of sets of possible results, rather than in terms of a unique solution, so that the contribution of the theory of games lies not in pointing out specific answers, but rather in merely ruling out some possible results and pointing out many new possible results that might otherwise have been overlooked in the application of the less thorough methods of analysis.

Indeed, many of the more recent writers in this area have shown a tendency to retreat from the rigor of the von Neumann and Morgenstern approach, in favor of reintroducing some of the realism and atmosphere that was eliminated in the process of "normalizing" the game situation. Indeed, while in the zero-sum or "strictly adversary" situation the theory of games seems to indicate that in general one of the objectives is to conceal one's strategy and to avoid being "found out," in the non-zero-sum situation, particularly where there are impediments to communication and to the making of compensatory side payments, the problem is very often the reverse one of communicating convincingly one's intentions to the other party, and of being reciprocally certain of the completeness of the communication. The possibility of such communication may depend crucially on the atmosphere of the situation as distinguished from its formal structure. If, for example, two strangers are each asked, without prior communication, to pick a meeting place in New York from a list of, say, 1,000 such places, with the promise of a prize if they both pick the same spot, their expectations may be considered at first sight fairly low, especially if it is specified that the list of spots will be reshuffled before being presented to the second party. But if the list contains one or more such salient spots as the information booth in Grand Central, the likelihood of successful coincidence may become quite high.

Or, in the 2 × 2 variable-sum game with the payoff:

	C	c
R	5 7	o o
r	o o	7 5

if "Row" can effectively commit himself to strategy *R and* can manage to communicate this commitment to "Column" before "column" has become committed, "Row" obtains the best result for himself at *R, C*. But symmetrically "Column" has an incentive to try to commit himself to *c*, provided he can communicate this commitment to "Row" before "Row" has committed himself. However, to commit oneself and fail to communicate this commitment in time leads to a worse result than merely to leave the initiative to the opposite party. The crux of the game becomes not the choice of formal strategy in the matrix, but rather the pregame maneuvers. Attempts have been made to deal with such situations by formalizing the bargaining and other pregame maneuvers so as to incorporate them as additional moves in a super-game, but this again abstracts from the important fact that in many instances the field of possible pregame maneuvers may be very poorly defined, depending in good measure on the entire situational context, and on the ingenuity and temperament of the players. One can indeed distinguish certain fairly well-defined types of maneuver, such as the "threat," i.e., a commitment that binds the threatener to do something he would not normally do in the event of a given action on the part of his opposite number, with the aim of deterring him from this action; the "promise," being similar to the threat except that the aim is to encourage the specified action, so that the action promised will take place, whereas the threat is made in the hope that it will not be executed; establishment or interruption of communication: if in the above example "Row" departs conspicuously for a camping trip, "Column" will have no way to communicate any commitment he might make, so that if "Column" is tied to his office, "Row" will be able to make his commitment and communicate it to "Column" at his leisure. In other circumstances delegation or decentralization of the authority to make certain decisions may be advantageous game maneuvers. The possible variations and combinations that could be examined rapidly become overwhelming.

Thus none of the analytical tools that we have been able to develop and apply to the problem of imperfect competition seem to be outstandingly successful; the best we seem to be able to do with any precision is to frame a multitude of extremely rigid and restricted hypotheses and pursue the results for some fairly narrow special cases. In the analysis of perfect competition, however, one could with considerable confidence expect that moderate differences between the assumptions of the model and the facts of the real world would produce correspondingly moderate differences in the results. But here it seems that even very small changes in the basic assumptions can on occasion produce drastic changes in the results, so that generalization from the special tractable examples to more complex and realistic cases is fraught with considerably greater uncertainties than is the case in the analysis of perfect competition, if not with dangers of serious error. Beyond this point the analysis is likely to require collaboration from students of individual psychology and social institutions if much progress is to be made toward a more realistic structure. But as findings in these other fields are in general much less precise and axiomatized than those in pure economic analysis, some precision necessarily will be lost in the process of gaining realism in this way.

EXERCISES

1. Determine the minimax "mixed strategies" for "Column" and for "Row" in the two-person zero-sum game with the following payoff matrix giving the amounts to be paid by "Column" to "Row":

	C	c
R	4	−2
r	−6	3

What are the probabilities of the four outcomes? What is the value of the game to "row"?

2. Derive the Shapley values for the game of FIGURE 87.

3. What becomes of the game of FIGURE 86 if the two sellers are free to locate at any point, rather than merely at 3, 8, or 11? (Hint: Certain locations can be excluded as being inferior to some other location for every possible location of the competitor; they are "dominated" by another location. After thus excluding some locations, still others may be excluded by an iteration of the same reasoning.)

4. If there are three competitors in the situation of FIGURE 86, restricted to the three given locations, and if it is assumed that if two locate in the same spot they share the trade for that spot equally, what are the strategies and outcomes that correspond to the points p, m, n of FIGURE 87? What happens if the symmetry of the situation is destroyed by assuming that one of the sellers, say A, while selling his full share if he is alone at a location, is only half as effective as the others in attracting trade if he shares a location, obtaining one-third or one-fifth of the total trade at a location if he shares it with one or two others?

READINGS AND REFERENCES

PERIODICALS CITED

Accounting Review	*Acctg R*
American Economic Review	*AER*
———, Supplement (Papers and Proceedings, American Economic Association, Annual Meetings)	*AER/S*
American Journal of Economics and Sociology	*AJES*
American Journal of Sociology	*AJS*
American Sociological Review	*ASR*
American Statistician	*AmStat*
Annals of the Hitotsubashi Academy	*AnHit*
Applied Statistics (Royal Statistical Society)	*AppStat*
Cahiers du Séminaire d'Économetrie	*CSE*
Canadian Journal of Economic and Political Science	*CJEPS*
Comparative Psychology Monographs	*CPM*
The Controller	*Controller*
Current Economic Comment (Urbana, Illinois)	*CEC*
Dun's Review	*Dun's*
Econometrica	*Ecomet*
Economia Internazionale	*EcInt*
Economic Journal (Royal Economic Society)	*EcJ*
Economic Record (Australia)	*EcR*
———, Supplement	*EcR/S*
Economica, New Series	*Eca*
Économie Appliquée	*EA*
De Economist	*Economist*
Federal Reserve Bulletin	*FRBull*
Finanzarchiv	*Finanz*
Giornale degli Economisti e Annali di Economia	*GdE*
Harvard Business Review	*HBR*
Indian Journal of Economics	*IJE*
L'Industria	*L'Industria*
International Economic Papers	*IEP*
International Social Science Journal (Bulletin International des Sciences Sociales)	*ISSB*
Investigación Económica	*IE*
International Labour Review	*ILR*
Jahrbücher für Nationalökonomie und Statistik	*JNOS*
Journal of the American Statistical Association	*JASA*
Journal of Applied Psychology	*JAP*
Journal of Business (of the University of Chicago)	*JBUC*

Journal of Conflict Resolution	*JCR*
Journal of Farm Economics	*JFE*
Journal of Finance	*JFin*
Journal of Law and Economics	*JLE*
Journal of Marketing	*JM*
Journal of Political Economy	*JPE*
Journal of the Royal Statistical Society (Series A)	*JRSS (A)*
Kyklos	*Kyklos*
Land Economics (formerly Journal of Land and Public Utility Economics)	*LEc*
Lloyds Bank Review	*LBR*
Manchester School of Economic and Social Studies	*MSchl*
Metroeconomica	*Met*
Metron	*Metron*
Michigan Business Review	*MBusR*
Michigan Law Review	*MLawR*
Monthly Labor Review	*MLR*
National Association of Cost Accountants Bulletin	*NACA Bull*
Nationalökonomisk Tidsskrift	*NT*
Osaka Economic Papers	*OEP*
Oxford Economic Papers	*OxEP*
Oxford University Institute of Statistics Bulletin	*BOUIS*
Political Science Quarterly	*PSQ*
Psychometrika	*Psychomet*
Public Finance (Finances Publiques)	*PF*
Quarterly Journal of Economics	*QJE*
Review of Economic Studies	*RES*
Review of Economics and Statistics	*REStat*
Revista de Economía Política	*Revista*
Revue d'Économie Politique	*REP*
Revue Économique	*REc*
Revue de Sciences et Legislation Financière	*RSLF*
Rivista di Politica Economica	*RPE*
Sankhya: Indian Journal of Statistics	*Sankhya*
Schmollers Jahrbuch	*SJ*
Schweizerische Zeitschrift für Volkswirtschaft und Statistik	*SZVS*
Science and Society	*S & S*
Scottish Journal of Political Economy	*SJPE*
Social Psychology	*SP*
Social Research	*SocRes*
South African Journal of Economics	*SAJE*
Southern Economic Journal	*SEJ*
El Trimestre Económico	*Trim*
Weltwirtschaftliches Archiv	*WA*
Yale Law Journal	*YLJ*
Zeitschrift für die Gesamte Staatswissenschaft	*ZGS*
Zeitschrift für Nationalökonomie	*ZNO*

CHAPTER ONE

1.1. LIONEL ROBBINS, *An Essay on the Nature and Significance of Economic Science* (London: Macmillan, 1932; rev., 1935), xvi, 158 pp.

1.2. TERENCE W. HUTCHISON, *The Significance and Basic Postulates of Economic Theory* (London: Macmillan, 1938), 192 pp.

1.3. KENNETH E. BOULDING, *The Skills of the Economist* (Cleveland: Allen, 1958), vi, 193 pp.

1.4. MILTON FRIEDMAN, "The Methodology of Positive Economics," in his *Essays on Positive Economics* (Chicago: University of Chicago Press, 1953), pp. 3–43.

1.5. DENNIS ROBERTSON, "What Does the Economist Economize?" in his *Economic Commentaries* (London: Staples, 1956), pp. 147–54.

1.6. C. LOWELL HARRISS, *Selected Readings in Economics* (New York: Prentice-Hall, 1958). Sec. I, "What Is Economics?" pp. 1–18: selections from Ben W. Lewis, Alfred Marshall, I. M. D. Little, and J. M. Clark.

1.7. ARLEIGH P. HESS, JR., and OTHERS, *Outside Readings in Economics* (New York: Crowell, 1951) Sec. I, "What Is Economics?" pp. 1–35: selections from Oscar Lange, Kenneth E. Boulding, Ferdinand Zweig, and S. I. Hayakawa.

1.8. WALTER ADAMS and L. E. TRAYWICK, *Readings in Economics* (New York: Macmillan, 1948, 1950). Ch. 1, "The Scope and Method of Economics," pp. 6–30: selections from John Neville Keynes, H. J. Davenport, Lionel Robbins, A. C. Pigou, Thorstein Veblen, and M. J. Bowman.

Of the above, Nos. 6, 7, and 8 are excellent for providing a survey in brief compass of a number of points of view. No. 3 is an excellent elementary survey of the objectives of economics. No. 5 is perhaps a bit discursive, but delightful reading. Nos. 1, 2, and 4 are searching analyses, and might possibly be left to return to after some firsthand knowledge of economic theory has been acquired.

The following articles are also worth looking at:

1.9. DUNCAN BLACK, "The Unity of Economic and Political Science," *EcJ*, 60 (September 1950), 506–14.

1.10. KENNETH E. BOULDING, "In Defense of Statics," *QJE*, 69 (November 1955), 485–502.

1.11. ROY F. HARROD, "The Scope and Method of Economics," *EcJ*, 48 (September 1938), 383–412.

1.12. JOHN JEWKES, "The Economist and Public Policy," *LBR*, 28 (April 1953:2), 18–32.

1.13. FRITZ MACHLUP, "The Problem of Verification in Economics," *SEJ*, 22 (July 1955), 1–21.

1.14. JOSEPH A. SCHUMPETER, "Science and Ideology," *AER*, 39 (March 1949), 345–59.

1.15. RUTLEDGE VINING, "Methodological Issues in Quantitative Economics," *AER*, 40 (June 1950), 267–84.

The following references pertain to the problems of methodology in relation to other social sciences and to science in general:

1.16. EUGEN ALTSCHUL and ERWIN BISER, "Probability Models in Modern Physics and Their Methodological Significance for the Social Sciences," *JNOS*, 166 (February 1954), 20–27.

1.17. M. R. COHEN, *Reason and Nature: The Meaning of Scientific Method* (Glencoe, Ill: Free Press, 1953), 470 pp.

1.18. HERBERT FEIGL and MAY BRODBECK, *Readings in the Philosophy of Science* (New York: Appleton-Century-Crofts, 1958), 871 pp.

1.19. MELVILLE J. HERSKOVITZ, *Economic Anthropology* (New York: Knopf, 1952), 547 pp.

1.20. H. S. HOUTHAKKER, "Economics and Biology: Specialization and Speciation," *Kyklos*, 9 (1956), 181–89.

1.21. K. W. KAPP, "Economics and the Behavioral Sciences," *Kyklos*, 7 (1954), 205–25.

1.22. P. F. LAZARSFELD, ed., *The Language of Social Research* (Glencoe, Ill.: Free Press, 1954), 444 pp.

1.23. ———, *Mathematical Thinking in the Social Sciences* (Glencoe, Ill.: Free Press, 1955), 590 pp.

1.24. J. H. MADGE, *The Tools of Social Science* (New York: Longmans, Green, 1953), 308 pp.

1.25. R. K. MERTON, "The Bearing of Empirical Research upon the Development of Social Theory," *ASR*, 13 (October 1948), 505–15.

1.26. TALCOTT PARSONS, "The Prospects of Sociological Theory," *ASR*, 15 (February 1950), 3–16.

1.27. ROBERT REDFIELD, "The Art of Social Science," *AJS*, 54 (November 1948), 181–90.

1.28. DAVID RIESMAN, *Individualism Reconsidered and Other Essays* (Glencoe, Ill.: Free Press, 1954), 529 pp. Contains a chapter on "Problems of Method in the Social Sciences."

1.29. ARNOLD M. ROSE, *Theory and Method in the Social Sciences* (Minneapolis: University of Minnesota Press, 1954), 351 pp.

1.30. SIDNEY SCHOEFFLER, "Toward a General Definition of Rational Action," *Kyklos*, 7 (1954), 245–73.

1.31. G. J. STIGLER, "The Nature and Role of Originality in Scientific Progress," *Eca*, 22 (November 1955), 293–302.

1.32. N. S. TIMASHEFF, "Definitions in the Social Sciences," *AJS*, 53 (November 1947), 201–09.

1.33. W. A. WEISSKOPF, *The Psychology of Economics* (Chicago: University of Chicago Press, 1955), 266 pp.

1.34. ———, "Psychological Aspects of Economic Thought," *JPE*, 57 (August 1949), 304–14.

1.35. BARBARA WOOTON, "Terminology in the Social Sciences," *ISSB*, 1 (1950), 47–55.

1.36. W. ZAJDLIC, "The Limitations of Social Sciences," *Kyklos*, 9 (1956), 65–76.

1.37. H. L. ZETTERBERG, *On Theory and Verification in Sociology* (New York: Tressler Press, 1954), 78 pp.

1.38. HANS ALBERT, "Das Werturteilsproblem im Lichte der Logischen Analyse," *ZGS*, 112 (1956), 410–39.

1.39. A. A. ALCHIAN, "Uncertainty, Evolution and Economic Theory," *JPE*, 58 (June 1950), 211–21.

1.40. LOUIS BAUDIN, "Irrationality in Economics," *QJE*, 68 (November 1954), 487–502.

1.41. HANS BREMS and OTHERS, "Current Economic Thought and Its Application and Methodology: In Continental Europe (Brems), Japan (Bronfenbrenner), India (Millikan), Israel (Patinkin), Eastern Europe (Spulber)," *AER/S*, 46 (May 1956), 352–418.

1.42. J. F. CAIRNS, "The Use of Theory in History," *EcR*, 26 (December 1950), 239–53.

1.43. HENRI DENIS, "La théorie psychologique de la formation des prix devant la critique contemporaine," *REP*, 59 (March-April 1949), 166–82.

1.44. L. H. DUPRIEZ, "Du concept d'équilibre en économie politique," *REP*, 58 (May–June 1948), 337–65.

1.45. G. A. ELLIOTT, "On Some Fashions in Economic Theory," *CJEPS*, 20 (November 1954), 478–92.

1.46. L. M. FRASER, *Economic Thought and Language* (London: Black, 1937), 411 pp.

1.47. ———, "Economists and Their Critics," *EcJ*, 48 (June 1938), 196–210.

1.48. D. F. GORDON, "Operational Propositions in Economic Theory," *JPE* 58 (April 1955), 150–61.

1.49. L. P. GREEN, "The Nature of Economic Principles," *SAJE*, 19 (December 1951), 331–48.

1.50. DAVID HAMILTON, *Newtonian Classicism and Darwinian Institutionalism: A Study of Change in Economic Theory* (Albuquerque: University of New Mexico Press, 1953), 138 pp.

1.51. E. C. HARWOOD, "Scientific Method As Applied in Economics," *AJES*, 14 (January 1955), 113–22.

1.52. ———, "What Is Economic Knowledge?" *AJES*, 13 (January 1954), 113–27.

1.53. EDWARD HEIMANN, *Wirtschaftssysteme und Gesellschaftssysteme* (Tübingen: Mohr, 1954), xiv, 250 pp.

1.54. J. S. HERTZOG, "Homilía para futuros economistas," *IE*, 16 (1956).

1.55. JOHN NEVILLE KEYNES, *The Scope and Method of Political Economy* (London, 1891; rep. New York: Kelley and Millman, 1955), 382 pp.

1.56. F. H. KNIGHT, *On the History and Method of Economics—Selected Essays* (Chicago: University of Chicago Press, 1956), 309 pp.

1.57. L. M. LACHMAN, "Some Notes on Economic Thought," *SAJE*, 22 (March 1954), 22–31.

1.58. ———, "The Science of Human Action," *Eca*, 18 (November 1951), 412.

1.59. OSKAR LANGE, "The Scope and Method of Economics," *REStud*, 13 (1945–46), 19.

1.60. ANDRÉ MARCHAL, *Méthode scientifique et science économique II: Problèmes actuels de l'analyse économique—ses approches fondamentales* (Paris: Genin, 1955, 1959), 314 pp.

1.61. ROBERT MOSSÉ, "Economic Knowledge and the Problem of Method," *ISSB*, I, Nos. 3–4 (1949), 21–29.

1.62. D. P. MUKERJI, "Rationality in Economic Science and the Contributions of Robbins, Keynes, Marx, and Schumpeter," *IJE*, 35 (April 1955), 295–317.

1.63. BERTRAND NOGARO, *La valeur logique des théories économiques* (Paris: Presses Universitaires, 1947), 185 pp.

1.64. DAVID NOVICK, "Mathematics, Logic, Quantity and Method," with an introduction by P. A. Samuelson, comments by Samuelson, Klein, Duesenberry, Chipman, Tinbergen, Champernowne, Solow, Dorfman, Koopmans, and S. E. Harris, *REStat*, 36 (November 1954), 357–86.

1.65. HANS PETER, "'Grenz'-gesetze in der Nationalökonomie," *Kyklos*, 5 (1952), 165–79.

1.66. C. E. PHILBROOK, "'Realism' in Policy Espousal," *AER*, 43 (December 1953), 846–59.

1.67. F. L. POLAK, *Kennen en Keuren en de Sociale Warenschappen* (Objective and Subjective Judgments in Economics) (Leiden: Stenfert Kroese, 1948), 293 pp.

1.68. KENNETH RIVETT, "The Definition of Economics," *EcR*, 31 (November 1955), 215–31.

1.69. LEO ROGIN, *The Meaning and Validity of Economic Theory—An Historical Approach* (New York: Harper, 1956), 697 pp.

1.70. SIDNEY SCHOEFFLER, *The Failures of Economics: A Diagnostic Study* (Cambridge: Harvard University Press, 1955), 254 pp.

1.71. J. A. SCHUMPETER, *Economic Doctrine and Method: A Historical Sketch* (London: Allen & Unwin, 1954), 207 pp. Tr. by R. Aris from *Epochen der Dogmen—Und Methodengeschichte*, 1912.

1.72. G. L. S. SHACKLE, "A Chart of Economic Theory," *Met*, 5 (April 1953), 1–10.

1.73. G. J. STIGLER, "El método matemático en la economía," *Trim*, 18 (July–September 1951), 537–48.

1.74. OTTO VON MERING, "Some Problems of Methodology in Modern Economic Theory," *AER*, 34 (March 1944) 87–97. Comment by D. Dillard in *AER*, 34 (December 1944), 856–62; rejoinder by von Mering, *AER*, 35 (March 1945), 145–47; (September 1945), 667.

1.75. FREDERIK ZEUTHEN, *Economic Theory and Method* (Cambridge: Harvard University Press, 1955), 364 pp. Enlarged and revised translation of his *Økonomisk Teori og Metode* (Copenhagen: Nyt Nordisk Forlag, 1942).

1.76. A. B. WOLFE, "Neurophysiological Economics," *JPE*, 58 (April 1950), 97–110. A review of 1.77.

1.77. C. REINOLD NOYES, *Economic Man in Relation to His Natural Environment* (New York: Columbia University Press, 1948), 1443 pp.

CHAPTER TWO

The Background of Consumption Analysis

2.1. THORSTEIN VEBLEN, "Limitations of Marginal Utility," *JPE*, 17 (1909), 620–36.

2.2. EMIL KAUDER, "Genesis of the Marginal Utility Theory," *EcJ*, 63 (September 1953), 639–50.

2.3. J. A. LANAUZE, "The Conception of Jevons' Utility Theory," *Eca*, 20 (November 1953), 356–58.

2.4. E. F. SCHRODER, *Marginal Utility Theory in the U.S.A.* (Nijmegen: Centrale Drukkrij 1947), 121 pp.

2.5. NICHOLAS GEORGESCU-ROEGEN, "The Theory of Choice and the Constancy of Economic Laws," *QJE*, 64 (February 1950), 125–38.

2.6. C. R. NOYES, "What Kind of Psychology Does Economics Need?" *CJEPS*, 16 (May 1950), 210–15.

2.7. K. W. KAPP, "Political Economy and Psychology," *Kyklos*, 4 (1950), 291–316.

Consumer Behavior

2.8. GEORGE KATONA, *Psychological Analysis of Economic Behavior* (New York: McGraw-Hill, 1951), 347 pp.

2.9. GEORGE KATONA and R. W. MUELLER, *Consumer Attitudes and Demand* (Ann Arbor: University of Michigan Survey Research Center, 1953), 119 pp.

2.10. A. L. MACFIE, "Choice in Psychology and as an Economic Assumption," *EcJ*, 63 (June 1953), 352–67.

2.11. M. J. FARRELL, "Irreversible Demand Functions," *Ecomet*, 20 (April 1952), 171–86.

2.12. B. S. LOEB, "The Use of Engel's Laws as a Basis for Predicting Consumer Expenditure," *JM*, 20 (July 1955), 20–27.

2.13. J. B. WOLFE, "Food Tokens as Incentives for Learning by Chimpanzees," *CPM*, 14, No. 5 (1937), 96 pp.

2.14. ———, "Effectiveness of Token-Rewards for Chimpanzees," *CPM*, 12, No. 5 (1936), 72 pp.

2.15. W. J. BILKEY, "A Psychological Approach to Consumer Behavior Analysis," *JM*, 18 (July 1953), 18–25.

2.16. F. H. BENSON, "A Model for the Analysis of Consumer Preferences and an Exploratory Test," *JAP*, 39, No. 5 (1955), 375–38.

2.17. G. B. GREIG, "Some Varieties of Consumer Behavior Described in the Decisions of the Federal Trade Commission," *JBUC*, 20 (October 1947), 191–200.

2.18. A. R. OXENFELDT, "Consumer Knowledge, Its Measurement and Extent," *REStat*, 32 (November 1950), 300–14.

2.19. HARVEY LEIBENSTEIN, "Bandwagon, Snob, and Veblen Effects in the Theory of Consumer's Demand," *QJE*, 64 (May 1950), 183–207.

Utility

2.20. D. H. ROBERTSON, "Utility and All That," *MSchl*, 19 (May 1951), 111–42; also reprinted in *Utility and All That and Other Essays* (London: Macmillan, 1952).

2.21. LIONEL ROBBINS, "Robertson on Utility and Scope," *Eca*, 20 (May 1953), 99–111.

2.22. J. R. HICKS, "Robbins on Robertson on Utility," *Eca*, 21 (May 1954), 154–57.

2.23. D. H. ROBERTSON, "Utility and All What?" *EcJ*, 64 (December 1954), 665–78.

2.24. MILTON FRIEDMAN, "What All Is Utility?" *EcJ*, 65 (September 1955), 405–09. D. H. Robertson, "A Rejoinder," *EcJ*, 65 (September 1955), 410.

(The above sequence may also be read under the headings "Utility and Risk" and "The New Welfare Economics.")

2.25. W. E. ARMSTRONG, "Concerning Marginal Utility," *OxEP*, 7 (June 1955), 170–76.

2.26. CHARLES KENNEDY, "Concerning Utility," *Eca*, 21 (February 1954) 7–20.

2.27. WERNER STARK, "Diminishing Utility Reconsidered," *Kyklos*, 1 (1947), 321–44.

2.28. R. W. PFOUTS, "Prolegomena to the Testing of Utility Theory," *SEJ*, 22 (October 1955), 178–88.

2.29. R. J. LAMPMAN, "Making Utility Predictions Verifiable," *SEJ*, 22 (January 1956), 360–66.

2.30. P. A. SAMUELSON, "The Problem of Integrability in Utility Theory," *Eca*, 17 (November 1950), 355–85.

2.31. JEAN VILLE, "The Existence Conditions of a Total Utility Function," *REStud*, 19 (1951–52), 123–28.

2.32. GIAMPIETRO ZACCHERINI, "Determinatezza della Funzione dell' ofelimitzà. Curva storiche e curve dinamiche di domanda," *GdE*, 7 (March–April 1948), 176–86.

2.33. BRUNO DE FINETTI, "Sulla Preferibilità," *GdE*, 11 (November–December 1952), 685–709.

2.34. ERICH CARELL, "Der Ordinalismus in der Nutzentheorie," *ZGS*, 111 (1955), 176–86.

2.35. PLINIO PAGNI, "Le linée d'indifferenza e le funzioni indici nella matematica financiaria," *GdE*, 14 (July–August 1955), 349–74.

2.36. ALEXANDER MAHR, "Indifferenzcurven und Grenznutzenniveau," *ZNO*, 14 (September 1954), 325–40.

2.37. JEROME ROTHENBERG, "Welfare Comparisons and Changes in Tastes," *AER*, 43 (December 1953), 885–90.

2.38. SIDNEY SCHOEFFLER, "Note on Modern Welfare Economics," *AER*, 42 (December 1952), 880–87.

Revealed Preference

(The discussion under this heading tends to be somewhat hair-splitting, but the reading can be good intellectual exercise.)

2.39. P. A. SAMUELSON, "Consumption Theory in Terms of Revealed Preference," *Eca*, 15 (November 1948), 243–53.

376]

2.40. I. M. D. LITTLE, "A Reformulation of the Theory of Consumer's Behavior," *OxEP*, 1 (January 1949), 90–99.

2.41. W. E. ARMSTRONG, "A Note on the Theory of Consumer's Behavior," *OxEP*, 2 (January 1950), 119–22.

2.42. I. M. D. LITTLE, "The Theory of Consumer's Behavior: A Comment," *OxEP*, 2 (January 1950), 132–35.

2.43. CHARLES KENNEDY, "The Common Sense of Indifference Curves," *OxEP*, 2 (January 1950), 123–31.

2.44. H. S. HOUTHAKKER, "Revealed Preference and the Utility Function," *Eca*, 17 (May 1950), 159-74.

2.45. W. J. CORLETT and P. K. NEWMAN, "A Note on Revealed Preference and the Transitivity Condition," *REStud*, 20 (1952–53), 146–58.

2.46. V. C. WALSH, "On Descriptions of Consumers' Behavior," *Eca*, 21 (August 1954), 244.

2.47. P. A. SAMUELSON, "Consumption Theorems in Terms of Overcompensation Rather Than Indifference Comparisons," *Eca*, 20 (February 1953) 1–9.

2.48. NICHOLAS GEORGESCU-ROEGEN, "Choice and Revealed Preference," *SEJ*, 21 (October 1954), 119–30.

2.49. P. K. NEWMAN, "The Foundations of Revealed Preference Theory," *OxEP*, 7 (June 1955), 151–69.

Characteristics of Indifference Maps

2.50. F. H. KNIGHT, "Realism and Relevance in the Theory of Demand," *JPE*, 52 (December 1944), 289–318.

2.51. J. M. CLARK, "Realism and Relevance in the Theory of Demand," *JPE*, 54 (August 1946), 347–53.

2.52. A. G. HART, "Peculiarities of Indifference Maps Involving Money," *REStud*, 8 (February 1941), 126–28.

2.53. J. A. GALBRAITH, "Indifference Maps for Indispensable Goods," *REStud*, 20 (1952–53), 152–55.

2.54. JOHN AITCHISON and J. A. C. BROWN, "A Synthesis of Engel Curve Theory," *REStud*, 22 (1954–55), 35–46.

2.55. L. L. THURSTONE, "The Indifference Function," *SP*, 2 (1931), 139.

2.56. MILTON FRIEDMAN and W. A. WALLIS, "The Empirical Derivation of Indifference Functions," in *Studies in Mathematical Economics and Econometrics in Memory of H. Schultz*, Lange, McIntyre, and Yntema, eds. (Chicago: University of Chicago Press, 1942), pp. 175–89.

2.57. A. G. HART and STEPHEN ROUSSEAS, "Experimental Verification of a Composite Indifference Map," *JPE*, 59 (August 1951), 288–318.

2.58. K. J. ARROW, "The Determination of a Many-Commodity Preference Scale by Two-Commodity Comparisons," *Met*, 4 (December 1952), 105–15.

Complementarity and Substitution

2.59. EUGEN SLUTSKY, "On the Theory of the Budget of the Consumer," in *AEA Readings in Price Theory*, G. J. Stigler and Kenneth E. Boulding, eds. (Homewood, Ill.: Irwin, 1952), pp. 27–56 (translated from the original Italian of *GdE*, 1915; this article is a famous "sleeper").

2.60. R. G. D. ALLEN, "The Substitution Effect in Value Theory," *EcJ*, 60 (December 1950), 675–85.

2.61. RENÉ ROY, "Les élasticités de demande relative aux biens et aux groupes de biens," *Ecomet*, 20 (July 1952), 391–405.

2.62. NICHOLAS GEORGESCU-ROEGEN, "A Diagrammatic Analysis of Complementarity," *SEJ*, 19 (July 1952), 1–20.

2.63. MICHIO MORISHIMA, "Some Laws of Complementary and Substitutive Goods," *OEP*, 2 (March 1954), 53–57.

2.64. ———, "A Note on Definitions of Related Goods," *REStud*, 23 (1955–56), 132–34.

2.65. SHINICHI ICHIMURA, "A Critical Note on the Definition of Related Goods," *REStud*, 18 (1950–51), 179–83.

2.66. R. L. BASMANN, "A Note on Mr. Ichimura's Definition of Related Goods," *REStud*, 22 (1954–55), 67–69.

2.67. H. HALLER, "Indifferenzlinien, Komplimentarietät und Substituierbarkeit," *ZGS*, 109 (1953), 115–39.

2.68. GERHARD TINTNER, "Complementarity and Shifts in Demand," *Met*, 4 (April 1952), 1–4.

2.69. H. VILLAR, "El proceso de ajuste de los precios de los bienes de demandas conexas," *Revista*, 5 (September–December 1955), 1–28.

2.70. IRVING MORRISSETT, "Some Recent Uses of Elasticity of Substitution: A Survey," *Ecomet*, 21 (January 1953), 41–62.

2.71. ITALO CUTULO, "Evoluzione della legge di domanda di due beni di cui uno strumentale dell' altro," *GdE*, 13 (September–October 1954), 559–77.

Consumer's Surplus

2.72. ALFRED MARSHALL, *Principles of Economics*, 8th ed. (London: Macmillan, 1920), Bk. III, Ch. 6, pp. 124–33. This is the definition that started the modern discussion.

2.73. JULES DUPUIT, *De l'utilité et de sa mesure*. First published in 1844; rep. with comments by Mario de Bernardi and Luigi Einaudi (Turin: La Riforma Soziale, 1942). The first application to a practical problem.

2.74. J. R. HICKS, "The Rehabilitation of Consumer's Surplus," *REStud*, 8 (February 1941), 108–16.

2.75. A. M. HENDERSON, "Consumer's Surplus and the Compensating Variation," *REStud*, 8 (February 1941), 117–21.

2.76. J. R. HICKS, "The Four Consumer's Surpluses," *REStud*, 12 (1944), 31–41.

2.77. E. J. MISHAN, "Realism and Relevance in Consumer's Surplus," *REStud*, 15 (1947–48), 27–33.

The above four items trace the development of consumer's surplus in its less mathematical form.

2.78. J. R. Hicks, "The Generalized Theory of Consumer's Surplus," *REStud*, 13 (1945–46), 68–74.

2.79. Harold Hotelling, "The General Welfare in Relation to Problems of Taxation and of Railway and Utility Rates," *Ecomet*, 6 (July 1938), 242–69.

The above two items illustrate the extension of the theory of consumer's surplus with the aid of mathematics to cover cases of numerous interrelated goods.

2.80. R. L. Bishop, "Consumer's Surplus and Cardinal Utility," *QJE*, 57 (May 1943), 421–49.

2.81. J. N. Morgan, "The Measurement of Gains and Losses," *QJE*, 62 (February 1948), 287–308.

2.82. R. W. Pfouts, "A Critique of Some Recent Contributions to the Theory of Consumer's Surplus," *SEJ*, 19 (January 1953), 315–33.

2.83. A. A. Crosara, "Sopravalori psicologici colleganti curve di indifferenza di Edgeworth e curva di esborso," *EcInt* 4 (August 1951), 599–605.

2.84. George D. Bodenhorn, A Modification of Consumer's Surplus, dissertation, University of Chicago, 1953.

Cost-of-Living Indexes

2.85. Irving Fisher, *The Making of Index Numbers*, 3rd. ed., rev. (New York: Houghton Mifflin, 1927), 538 pp.

2.86. Gottfried Haberler, *Der Sinn der Indexzahlen* (Tübingen: Mohr, 1927), 134 pp. The start of the modern theory.

2.87. M. J. Ulmer, *The Economic Theory of Cost of Living Index Numbers*, doctoral thesis (New York: Columbia University Press, 1949), 105 pp. A good summary and some suggestions.

2.88. Ragnar Frisch, "The Problem of Index Numbers," *Ecomet*, 4 (January 1936), 1–38.

2.89. R. G. D. Allen, "The Economic Theory of Index Numbers," *Eca*, 16 (August 1949), 197–203.

2.90. Ragnar Frisch, "Some Basic Principles of Price of Living Measurements," *Ecomet*, 22 (October 1954), 407–21.

2.91. A. A. Konüs, "The Problem of the True Index of the Cost of Living," *Ecomet*, 7 (January 1939), 10–29.

2.92. Bruce Mudgett, "The Konüs Condition," *Ecomet*, 13 (April 1945), 171–81.

2.93. Hans Staehle, "A Development of the Economic Theory of Price Index Numbers," *REStud*, 2 (June 1935), 163–88.

2.94. J. R. Hicks, "Consumer's Surplus and Index Numbers," *REStud*, 9 (1941–42), 126–37.

2.95. A. C. Pigou, "Real Income and Economic Welfare," *OxEP*, 3 (February 1951), 16–20.

2.96. M. H. Dobb, "A Note on Index Numbers and Compensation Criteria," *OxEP*, 8 (February 1956), 78–79.

Items 86–95 are discussions of various aspects of the general theory of index numbers. The following 12 items pursue various detailed aspects of the theory.

2.97. HANS STAEHLE, "A General Method for the Comparison of the Price of Living," *REStud*, 4 (June 1937), 205–14.

2.98. ———, "The International Comparison of Real National Income—A Note on Methods," *Studies in Income and Wealth*, Vol. II (New York: National Bureau of Economic Research, 1949), pp. 223–51. Comments by Abram Bergson, D. S. Brady, E. M. Snyder, M. H. Copeland, and William Vickrey, pp. 252–72.

2.99. RICHARD STONE and S. J. PRAIS, "Systems of Aggregative Index Numbers and Their Compatibility," *EcJ*, 62 (September 1952), 565–83.

2.100. L. R. KLEIN and H. RUBIN, "A Constant Utility Index of the Cost of Living," *REStud*, 18 (1949–50), 84–87.

2.101. R. C. GEARY, "A Note on a Constant Utility Index of the Cost of Living," *REStud*, 18 (1949–50), 65–66.

2.102. ABRAHAM WALD, "A New Formula for the Index of the Cost of Living," *Ecomet*, 7 (October 1939), 319–31.

2.103. K. S. BANERJEE, "Simplification of the Derivation of Wald's Formula for the Cost of Living Index," *Ecomet*, 24 (July 1956), 296–98.

2.104. WASSILY LEONTIEFF, "Composite Commodities and the Problem of Index Numbers," *Ecomet*, 4 (1936), 39–59.

2.105. CORRADO GINI, "On the Circular Test of Index Numbers," *Metron*, 9, No. 2 (August 1931), 3–24.

2.106. ———, "Quelques considérations au sujet de la construction des nombres indices," *Metron*, 4 (1924), 1–194.

2.107. PIERRE GORRA, "Une méthode d'élaboration de nombres indices permanents," *Met*, 5 (April 1953), 31–34.

2.108. R. S. G. RUTHERFORD, "The Principal Factors Approach to Index Number Theory," *EcR*, 30 (November 1954), 200–08.

2.109. ISAMU YAMADA, "A Measurement of Money Utility and Functional Values of the Cost of Living Index," *AnHit*, 1 (October 1950), 34–42.

Some of the more practical aspects of index number construction are brought to the fore in the following 11 items:

2.110. I. O. SCOTT, JR., "The Gerschenkron Hypothesis of Index-Number Bias," *REStat*, 34 (November 1952), 386–87.

2.111. W. C. MITCHELL, *The Making and Using of Index Numbers*, United States Department of Labor Bulletin, 656 (1938).

2.112. DUDLEY SEERS, "Is There Bias in the Interim Index of Retail Prices?" *BOUIS*, 11 (January 1949), 1–8.

2.113. AMERICAN STATISTICAL ASSOCIATION, "An Appraisal of the U.S.B.L.S. Index," *JASA*, 38 (December 1943), 387–405.

2.114. *The Consumer Price Index: A Short Description of the Index As Revised* (Washington, D.C.: United States Bureau of Labor Statistics, 1953), 10 pp.

2.115. "Taxes and the Consumer Price Index," *MLR*, 76 (January 1953), 53–57.

2.116. "The Revised Consumer Price Index," *MLR*, 76 (February 1953), 162–75.

2.117. A. P. RUDERMAN, "A Neglected Point in the Construction of Price Index Numbers," *AppStat*, 3 (March 1954), 44–47.

2.118. R. B. HEFLEBOWER, "An Economic Appraisal of Price Measures," *JASA*, 46 (December 1951), 461–79.

2.119. COLIN CLARK, "International Comparisons in Economics," *ISSB*, 7 (1955), 615–21.

Special Topics in Consumption Theory

2.120. J. D. CAPPOCK, "Indifference Curve Analysis Applied to the Food Stamp Plan," *AER*, 35 (March 1945), 99–110.

2.121. SIDNEY WEINTRAUB, "The Theory of Consumer Monopsony," *REStud*, 17 (1949–50), 168–78.

2.122. G. J. STIGLER, "Notes on the History of the Giffen Paradox," *JPE*, 55 (April 1947), 152–56.

2.123. MILTON FRIEDMAN, "The Marshallian Demand Curve," *JPE*, 57 (December 1949), 463–95.

2.124. M. J. BAILEY, "The Marshallian Demand Curve," *JPE*, 62 (June 1954), 255–61. Reply by Milton Friedman, *JPE*, 62 (June 1954), 261–66.

2.125. MAURICE McMANUS, "Points Rationing and the Consumer," *Met*, 8 (August 1956), 118–34.

2.126. P. A. SAMUELSON, "Comparative Statics and the Logic of Economic Maximizing," *REStud*, 14 (1946–47), 41–43.

2.127. H. S. HOUTHAKKER, "Demand Analysis," *JASA*, 49 (March 1954), 88–96. A review of Herman Wold's *Demand Analysis* (2.131).

2.128. R. L. BASMANN, "A Theory of Demand with Variable Consumer Preference," *Ecomet*, 24 (January 1956), 47–58.

General References

2.129. J. R. HICKS, *Value and Capital* (London: Oxford University Press, 1939), xi, 331 pp; especially Chs. 1–3, pp. 11–52.

2.130. J. R. HICKS, *A Revision of Demand Theory* (London: Oxford University Press, 1945), 196 pp.

2.131. HERMAN WOLD and LARS JURÉEN, *Demand Analysis* (New York: Wiley, 1953), xiv, 358 pp.

2.132. F. Y. EDGEWORTH, *Mathematical Psychics* (London: Kegan Paul, 1881), viii, 150 pp.

2.133. R. T. NORRIS, *The Theory of Consumer's Demand* (New Haven: Yale University Press, 1941), 237 pp.

2.134. P. A. SAMUELSON, *Foundations of Economic Analysis* (Cambridge: Harvard University Press, 1947), xii, 447 pp.; especially Chs. 3, 5, 6, and 7, pp. 21–56 and 90–202.

CHAPTER THREE

Most modern discussions of the pure theory of exchange are concerned with special applications to welfare economics, which will be taken up later in Chapter

6, or with international trade theory, which involves an admixture of other complicating elements. A summary of the Walrasian approach to general exchange equilibrium can be found in LEON WALRAS, *Abrégé des éléments d'économie politique pure* (Paris: Lausanne, 1938), pp. 117–53. A more strictly mathematical development is found in A. L. BOWLEY, *Mathematical Groundwork of Economics* (London: Oxford University Press, 1924), pp. 19–27 and 47–54. See also the discussion in J. R. HICKS, *Value and Capital* (London: Oxford University Press, 1939), pp. 55–77. A more recent mathematical exposition is given in R. G. D. ALLEN, *Mathematical Economics* (London: Macmillan, 1956), pp. 314–42; also in JAMES M. HENDERSON and RICHARD E. QUANDT, *Microeconomic Theory* (New York: McGraw-Hill, 1958), pp. 6–41.

CHAPTER FOUR

General Theory of Production and the Firm

4.1. KENNETH E. BOULDING, *Economic Analysis*, 3rd ed. (New York: Harper 1955), pp. 489–604.

4.2. A. W. STONIER and D. C. HAGUE, *Textbook of Economic Theory* (New York: Longmans, Green, 1953), pp. 87–161 and 210–58.

4.3. P. J. WILES, *Price, Cost, and Output* (Oxford: Blackwell, 1956, 1961), xiv, 313 pp.

4.4. G. J. STIGLER, *Theory of Price* (New York: Macmillan, 1946), pp. 102–93.

The Nature, Identity, and Role of the Firm

4.5. LIONEL ROBBINS, "The Representative Firm," *EcJ*, 38 (September 1938), 387–404.

4.6. J. N. WOLFE, "The Representative Firm," *EcJ*, 64 (June 1954), 337–49.

4.7. R. H. COASE, "The Nature of the Firm," *Eca*, 4 (November 1937), 386–405.

4.8. A. G. PAPANDREOU, "Some Basic Problems in the Theory of the Firm," with comments by R. B. Heflebower and E. S. Mason, in B. F. Haley, ed., *Survey of Contemporary Economics*, Vol. II (Homewood, Ill.: Irwin, 1952), pp. 183–222.

4.9. GUNNAR LINDGREN, "How Long Does a Company Live?" *OxEP*, 5 (October 1953), 235–47.

4.10. DAVID SCHWARTZMAN, "Multiple Company Mergers and the Theory of the Firm," *OxEP*, 7 (June 1955), 197–214.

4.11. K. S. KRISHNASWAMY, "The Firm's Decisions and Factors Affecting Them," *IJE*, 1 (January 1954), 253–69.

4.12. H. A. SIMON, *Administrative Behavior: A Study of Decision Making Processes in Administrative Organization* (New York: Macmillan, 1957), 259 pp.

4.13. H. R. BOWEN, *The Business Enterprise as a Subject for Research* (New York: Social Science Research Council, 1955), 103 pp.

4.14. R. A. LESTER, "Equilibrium of the Firm," *AER*, 39 (March 1949), 478–84.

4.15. THOMAS WILSON, "The Inadequacy of the Theory of the Firm as a Branch of Welfare Economics," *OxEP*, 4 (February 1952), 18–44.

4.16. M. J. FARRELL, "Deductive Systems and Empirical Generalizations in the Theory of the Firm," *OxEP*, 4 (February 1952), 45–49.

4.17. W. W. COOPER, "Theory of the Firm: Some Suggestions for Revision," *AER*, 39 (December 1949), 1204–22.

4.18. JAN TINBERGEN, *Centralization and Decentralization in Economic Policy* (Amsterdam: North Holland, 1954), 78 pp.

4.19. H. A. SIMPSON, "A Comparison of Organization Theories," *REStud*, 20 (1952–53), 40–48.

4.20. W. W. COOPER, "A Proposal for Extending the Theory of the Firm," *QJE*, 65 (February 1951), 87–109.

4.21. J. J. KRUIDINGA, ed., *The Balance Between Centralization and Decentralization in Managerial Control* (Leiden: Stenfert Kroese, 1954), 119 pp.

The Nature and Role of Profit

4.22. R. G. HAWTREY, "The Nature of Profit," *EcJ*, 61 (September 1951), 489–504.

4.23. VICTOR EDELBERG, "The Ricardian Theory of Profit," *Eca*, 13 (February 1933), 51–74.

4.24. P. L. BERNSTEIN, "Profit Theory: Where Do We Go from Here?" *QJE*, 67 (August 1953), 407–22.

4.25. J. F. WESTON, "The Profit Concept and Theory: A Restatement," *JPE*, 62 (April 1954), 152–70.

4.26. G. D. BAILEY, "Concepts of Income," *HBR*, 26 (November 1948), 680–92.

4.27. R. A. FOULKE, "The Relativity of Net Profits," *Dun's*, Pt. I (January 1949), p. 11; Pt. II (February 1949), p. 13.

4.28. G. C. HARRISON, "The Practical Economist's Profit and Loss Statement," *NACA Bull*, Sec. I (December 14, 1948), 443–56.

Profit Maximization and Marginal Analysis

4.29. TIBOR SCITOVSKY, "A Note on Profit Maximization and Its Implications," *REStud*, 11 (1943–44), 57–60; rep. in Stigler and Boulding, eds., *Readings in Price Theory*, pp. 352–58.

4.30. ———, "Sur deux principes de maximation du profit et quelques-unes de leurs implications," *REc* (May 1955), 368–86.

4.31. W. M. CORDEN, "The Maximization of Profit by a Newspaper," *REStud*, 20 (1952–43), 181–90.

4.32. W. J. BAUMOL and HELEN MAKOWER, "The Analogy Between Consumer and Producer Equilibrium Analysis," *Eca*, 17 (February 1950), 63–68.

4.33. FRITZ MACHLUP, "Marginal Analysis and Empirical Research," *AER*, 36 (September 1946), 519–55.

4.34. H. M. OLIVER, "Marginal Theory and Business Behavior," *AER*, 37 (June 1947), 375–83.

4.35. P. W. Cartwright, "Marginalism and Price Theory Reconsidered," *CJEPS*, 17 (November 1951), 543–50.

4.36. P. W. S. Andrews, "A Reconsideration of the Theory of the Individual Business," *OxEP*, 3 (February 1940), 32–73.

4.37. D. C. Hague, "Economic Theory and Business Behavior," *REStud*, 16 (1949–50), 144–57.

4.38. J. S. Early, "Recent Developments in Cost Accounting and the Marginal Analysis," *JPE*, 63 (June 1955), 227–42.

4.39. M. W. Reder, "A Reconsideration of Marginal Productivity Theory," *JPE*, 55 (October 1947), 450–58.

4.40. André Gabor and I. F. Pearce, "A New Approach to the Theory of the Firm," *OxEP*, 4 (October 1952), 252–65.

4.41. F. M. Westerfield, "Marginal Analysis, Multi-plant Firms, and Business Practice: An Example," *QJE*, 69 (May 1955), 253–68.

Production Functions

4.42. J. M. Cassels, "On the Law of Variable Proportions," from *Explorations in Economics* (New York: McGraw-Hill, 1936), pp. 223–36; rep. in *Readings in the Theory of Income Distribution*, pp. 158–74.

4.43. Fritz Machlup, "On the Meaning of the Marginal Product," from *Explorations in Economics* (New York: McGraw-Hill, 1936), pp. 250–63; rep. in *Readings in the Theory of Income Distribution*, pp. 158–74.

4.44. R. W. Shephard, *Costs and Production Functions* (Princeton: Princeton University Press, 1952), 104 pp.

4.45. P. H. Douglas, "Are There Laws of Production?" *AER*, 38 (March 1948), 1–41.

4.46. C. E. V. Leser, "Production Functions for the British Industrial Economy," *AppStat*, 3 (November 1954), 174–83.

4.47. V. E. Smith, "Continuous and Discontinuous Factor Substitution," *SEJ*, 22 (October 1955), 189–201.

4.48. R. M. Solow, "Technical Change and the Aggregate Production Function," *REStat*, 39 (August 1957), 312–20.

4.49. P. B. Simpson, "Transformation Functions in the Theory of Production Indexes," *JASA*, 46 (June 1951), 225–32.

4.50. Felice Villani, "L'impiego delle curve di indifferenza in alcune analisi finanziane ed il 'paradosso de Giffen,'" *RPE*, 42 (February 1952), 149–75.

4.51. R. L. Mighell, "What Is the Place of the Equal Product Function?" *JFE*, 35 (February 1953), 29–43.

4.52. W. J. Eiteman, "The Equilibrium of the Firm in Multi-Process Industries," *QJE*, 59 (February 1945), 280–86.

4.53. J. C. Weldon, "The Multi-product Firm," *CJEPS*, 14 (May 1948), 176–90.

4.54. E. O. Heady, "A Production Function and Marginal Rates of Substitution in the Utilization of Feed Resources by Dairy Cows," *JFE*, 33 (November 1951), 485–98.

4.55. ——, "An Econometric Investigation of the Technology of Agricultural Production Functions," *Ecomet*, 25 (April 1957), 249–68.

4.56. R. H. ALEXANDER and R. F. HUTTON, "Determining Least Cost Combinations," *JFE*, 39 (November 1957), 936–41.

4.57. BURGESS CAMERON, "The Production Function in Leontieff Models," *REStud*, 20 (1952–53), 62–69.

Costs and Cost Curves

4.58. W. E. PAULSON, "Characteristics of the Marginal Cost Curve," *JFE*, 30 (August 1948), 467–99.

4.59. ——, "Diagrammatic Economics," *JFE*, 28 (August 1946), 687–722.

4.60. P. J. WILES, "Empirical Research and Marginal Analysis," *EcJ*, 60 (September 1950), 513–30.

4.61. HANS STAEHLE, "The Measurement of Statistical Cost Functions: An Appraisal of Some Recent Contributions," *AER*, 32 (June 1942), 321–33; rep. in Stigler and Boulding, eds., *Readings in Price Theory*, pp. 264–79.

4.62. J. R. MAYER, A. R. FERGUSON, and G. H. BORTS, "Statistical Cost Function," *AER/S*, 48 (May 1958), 209–38.

4.63. F. S. BRAY, "An Accountant's Comments on the Subjective Theory of Value and Accounting Cost, *Eca*, 13 (November 1946), 295–99.

4.64. L. T. LITTLE, "Replacement Costs, An Economist's View," *Acctg R*, 1 (November 1948), 58–78.

4.65. W. H. FRANKLIN, "Productivity in Relation to Costs," *NACA Bull* (March 1947), 859–68.

4.66. M. J. BECKMAN, "Fixed Technological Cost Coefficients and the Short-run Cost Curve," *Kyklos*, 9 (1956), 384–86.

Cost Curves and Capacity

4.67. J. M. CLARK, *Studies in the Economics of Overhead Costs* (Chicago: University of Chicago Press, 1923), xiii, 502 pp.

4.68. W. A. LEWIS, *Overhead Costs* (New York: Rinehart, 1949), 200 pp.

4.69. ——, "Fixed Costs," *Eca*, 13 (November 1946), 231–58.

4.70. W. J. EITEMAN and G. E. GUTHRIE, "The Shape of Average Cost Curves," *AER*, 42 (December 1952), 832–38. Comments by L. S. Ritter, M. Kaplan, and Martin Bronfenbrenner and rejoinder by Eiteman, *AER*, 43 (September 1953), 620–30.

4.71. HANS BREMS, "A Discontinuous Cost Function," *AER*, 43 (September 1952), 577–86.

4.72. W. J. EITEMAN, "Factors Determining the Location of the Least Cost Point," *AER*, 37 (December 1947), 910–18.

4.73. R. L. BISHOP, "Cost Discontinuities, Declining Costs, and Marginal Analysis," *AER*, 38 (September 1948), 607–17.

4.74. W. W. HAINES, "Capacity Production and the Least Cost Point," *AER*, 38 (September 1948), 617–24.

4.75. W. J. EITEMAN, "The Least Cost Point, Capacity, and Marginal Analysis," *AER*, 38 (December 1948), 899–904.

4.76. K. TAKADA, "Step Cost (Springkosten)," *OEP*, 6 (February 1958), 31–38.
4.77. HANS APEL, "Marginal Cost Constancy and Its Implications," *AER*, 38 (December 1948), 870–85.

Increasing and Decreasing Returns

4.78. J. H. CLAPHAM, "Of Empty Economic Boxes," *EcJ*, 32 (March 1922), 305–14.
4.79. A. C. PIGOU, "Empty Economic Boxes, a Reply," *EcJ*, 32 (December 1922), 458–65.
4.80. J. H. CLAPHAM, "The Empty Boxes, Rejoinder," *EcJ*, 32 (December 1922), 560–63.
4.81. D. H. ROBERTSON, "Those Empty Boxes," *EcJ*, 34 (March 1924), 16–31.
4.82. PIERO SRAFFA, "The Laws of Returns Under Competitive Conditions," *EcJ*, 36 (December 1926), 535–50.
4.83. JOAN ROBINSON, "Rising Supply Price," *Eca*, 8 (February 1941), 1–8.
4.84. JACOB VINER, "Cost Curves and Supply Curves," *ZNO*, 3 (September 1931), 23–46.

The above seven items, with notes by Robertson and Viner and changes by Robinson, are also in Stigler and Boulding, eds., *Readings in Price Theory*, pp. 119–59 and 180–241.

4.85. E. H. CHAMBERLIN, "Proportionality, Divisibility, and Economies of Scale," *QJE*, 62 (February 1948), 229–62.
4.86. JOSEPH LERNER, "Constant Proportions, Fixed Plant, and the Optimum Conditions of Production," *QJE*, 63 (August 1948), 361–70.
4.87. N. S. ROSS, "Management and the Size of the Firm," *REStud*, 19 (1952–53), 148–54.
4.88. A. C. PIGOU, "The Laws of Diminishing Returns and Increasing Costs," *EcJ*, 37 (June 1927), 188–97.
4.89. R. B. HEFLEBOWER, "Economics of Size," *JBUC*, 24 (October 1951), 253–68.
4.90. T. M. WHITIN and M. H. PRESTON, "Random Variations, Risk, and Returns to Scale," *QJE*, 68 (November 1954), 603–12.
4.91. JOSEPH JOHNSON, "Labor Productivity and the Size of Establishments," *BOUIS*, 16 (November-December 1954), 339–61.
4.92. Q. H. SIDDIQI, "Laws of Returns and the Competitive Average Cost," *IJE* 35 (July 1954), 21–30.
4.93. F. E. BALDERSTON, "Scale of Output and Internal Organization of the Firm," *QJE*, 69 (February 1955), 45–70.
4.94. H. R. EDWARDS, "Price Formation in Manufacturing Industry and Excess Capacity," *OxEP*, 7 (February 1955), 94–118.
4.95. J. K. MEHTA, "Elasticity of Substitution in Relation to the Laws of Returns," *IJE*, 34 (April 1954), 273–84.
4.96. SEYMOUR MELMAN, "Production and Administration Cost in Relation to Size of Firm," *AppStat*, 3 (March 1954), 1–11.

4.97. S. S. ALEXANDER, "The Effect of Size of Manufacturing Corporations on the Distribution of the Rate of Return," *REStat*, 31 (August 1949), 225–39.

4.98. E. O. HEADY, G. L. Johnson, and L. S. Hardin, eds., *Resource Productivity, Returns to Scale, and Farm Size* (Ames: Iowa State University, 1956), 203 pp.

4.99. H. B. CHENERY, "Engineering Production Functions," *QJE*, 63 (November 1949), 507–31.

4.100. E. H. PHELPS-BROWN, "Cost Categories and the Total Cost Function," *Ecomet*, 4 (July 1936), 242–63.

4.101. W. BALDAMUS, "Mechanization, Utilization, and Size of Plant," *EcJ*, 63 (March 1953), 50–69.

4.102. E. O. HEADY, "Technical Scale Relationships and Farm Size Policy," *SEJ*, 19 (January 1953), 353–64.

4.103. J. S. BAIN, "Economies of Scale, Concentration, and the Conditions of Entry in Twenty Manufacturing Industries," *AER*, 44 (March 1954), 15–39.

4.104. R. M. SOLDOVSKY, "The Cost of Capital Function for a Firm," *Controller*, 26 (June 1958), 263–68.

4.105. DAVID SCHWARTZMAN, "The Methodology of the Theory of Return to Scale," *OxEP*, 10 (February 1958), 98–105.

4.106. HARVEY LEIBENSTEIN, "The Proportionality Controversy and the Theory of Production," *AJE*, 69 (November 1955), 619–25.

4.107. J. S. CHIPMAN, "Returns to Scale and Substitution," *CJEPS*, 16 (May 1950), 215–21.

CHAPTER FIVE

5.1. TIBOR SCITOVSKY, "The State of Welfare Economics," *AER*, 41 (June 1951), 303.

5.2. A. C. PIGOU, *Economics of Welfare*, 4th ed. (London: Macmillan, 1920, 1932), xxxi, 837 pp.

5.3. A. P. LERNER, *The Economics of Control* (New York: Macmillan, 1944), xxii, 428 pp.

5.4. U. HLA MYINT, *Theories of Welfare Economics* (Cambridge: Harvard University Press, 1948), xiii, 240 pp. (Listed under "Hla")

5.5. W. J. BAUMOL, *Welfare Economics and the Theory of the State* (Cambridge: Harvard University Press, 1952), 171 pp.

5.6. M. W. REDER, *Studies in the Theory of Welfare Economics* (New York: Columbia University Press, 1947), 208 pp.

5.7. J. E. MEADE, *Planning and the Price Mechanics* (London: Allen & Unwin, 1948), xiv, 130 pp.

5.8. TIBOR SCITOVSKY, *Welfare and Competition* (Chicago: Irwin, 1951), 457 pp.

5.9. J. DE V. GRAAFF, *Theoretical Welfare Economics* (Cambridge: University Press, 1957), 187 pp.

Marginal-cost Pricing

5.10. GABRIEL DESSUS, "General Principles of Rate Fixing in Public Utilities," *IEP*, 1 (1951), 4–22.

5.11. WILLIAM VICKREY, "Some Objections to Marginal Cost Pricing," *JPE*, 56 (June 1948), 218.

5.12. H. S. HOUTHAKKER, "Electricity Tariffs in Theory and Practice," *EcJ*, 61 (March 1951), 1–25.

5.13. NANCY RUGGLES, "The Welfare Basis of the Marginal Cost Pricing Principle," *REStud*, 17 (1949–50), 29.

5.14. ———, "Recent Developments in the Theory of Marginal Cost Pricing," *REStud*, 17 (1949–50), 107.

5.15. MARCEL BOITEUX, "La tarification au coût marginal et la demande aléatoire," *CSE*, No. 1 (1952), 56–69.

5.16. B. P. BECKWITH, *The Economic Theory of a Socialist Economy* (Stanford: Stanford University Press, 1949), viii, 444 pp.

5.17. ———, *Marginal Cost Price-Output Control* (New York: Columbia University Press, 1955), 283 pp.

5.18. C. J. OORT, *Decreasing Costs as a Problem of Welfare Economics* (Amsterdam: Drukkerij Holland, 1958), 187 pp.

Items 5.13 and 5.18 have extensive bibliographies for further inquiry.

5.19. F. M. BATOR, "The Simple Analytics of Welfare Maximization," *AER*, 47 (March 1957), 22–59.

5.20. P. B. KENEN, "On the Geometry of Welfare Economics," *QJE*, 72 (August 1957), 426–47.

5.21. JULIUS MARGOLIS, "Welfare Criteria, Pricing, and the Decentralization of a Public Service," *QJE*, 71 (August 1957), 448–63.

5.22. K. W. KAPP, *The Social Costs of Private Enterprise* (Cambridge: Harvard University Press, 1950), xii, 287 pp.

5.23. R. G. LIPSEY and R. K. LANCASTER, "The General Theory of Second Best," *REStud*, 24 (1956–57), 11–32.

CHAPTER SIX

The "New" Welfare Economics

6.1. D. H. ROBERTSON, *Utility and All That and Other Essays* (London: Allen & Unwin, 1952), 206 pp.

6.2. I. M. D. LITTLE, *A Critique of Welfare Economics* (Oxford: Clarendon Press, 1950), 275 pp.

6.3. ———, "The Foundations of Welfare Economics," *OxEP*, 1 (June 1949), 227–46.

6.4. K. J. ARROW, "Little's Critique of Welfare Economics," *AER*, 41 (December 1951), 923–34.

6.5. KINGSLEY LAFFER, "The Foundations of Welfare Economics," *EcR*, 27 (December 1951), 213–19.

The Compensation Principle

6.6. NICHOLAS KALDOR, "Welfare Propositions in Economics and Interpersonal Comparisons of Utility," *EcJ*, 49 (September 1939), 549–52.

6.7. TIBOR SCITOVSKY, "A Note on Welfare Propositions in Economics," *REStud*, 9 (1941), 77–88.

6.8. R. E. BALDWIN, "A Comparison of Welfare Criteria," *REStud*, 21 (1953–54), 154–61.

6.9. CHARLES KENNEDY, "The Economic Welfare Function and Little's Criterion," *REStud*, 20 (1952–53), 137–42.

6.10. M. J. BAILEY, "The Interpretation and Application of the Compensation Principle," *EcJ*, 64 (March 1954), 39–52.

6.11. E. J. MISHAN, "The Principle of Compensation Reconsidered," *JPE*, 60 (August 1952), 312–22.

6.12. ———, "A Reappraisal of the Principles of Resource Allocation," *Eca*, 24 (November 1957), 324–42.

6.13. F. M. BATOR, "The Simple Analytics of Welfare Maximization," *AER*, 47 (March 1957), 22–59.

Social Welfare Functions and Community Indifference Curves

6.14. A. BURK, "A Reformulation of Certain Aspects of Welfare Economics," *QJE*, 52 (February 1937), 310–34.

6.15. GERHARD TINTNER, "A Note on Welfare Economics," *Ecomet*, 14 (January 1945), 69–78.

6.16. J. M. FLEMING, "A Cardinal Concept of Welfare," *QJE*, 66 (August 1952), 366–84.

6.17. JEROME ROTHENBERG, "Conditions for a Social Welfare Function," *JPE*, 61 (October 1953), 389–405.

6.18. W. J. BAUMOL, "The Community Indifference Map: A Construction," *REStud*, 17 (1949–50), 189–97.

6.19. W. M. GORMAN, "Community Preference Fields," *Ecomet*, 21 (January 1953), 63–80.

Social Choice in Terms of Individual Rankings

6.20. K. J. ARROW, "A Difficulty in the Concept of Social Welfare," *JPE*, 58 (August 1950), 328–46.

6.21. ———, *Social Choice and Individual Values* (New York: Wiley, 1951), xi, 99 pp.

6.22. R. D. LUCE and HOWARD RAIFFA, *Games and Decisions* (New York: Wiley, 1957), pp. 327–70.

6.23. K. J. ARROW, "Le principe de la rationalité dans les décisions collectives," *EA*, 5 (October–December 1952), 469–84.

6.24. W. J. BAUMOL, "Social Choice and Individual Values," *Ecomet*, 20 (January 1952), 110–11.

6.25. D. B. SUITS, "A Note on the Theory of Social Choice," *Kyklos*, 5 (1951–52), 213–18.

6.26. I. M. D. LITTLE, "Social Choice and Individual Values," *JPE*, 60 (October 1952), 422–32.

6.27. G. T. GUILBAUD, "Les théories de l'intérêt général et le problème logique de l'agrégation," *EA*, 5 (October-December 1952), 501–84.

6.28. CLIFFORD HILDRETH, "Alternative Conditions for Social Orderings," *Ecomet*, 21 (January 1953), 81–94.

6.29. L. A. GOODMAN and H. W. MARKOWITZ, "Social Functions Based on Individual Rankings," *AJS*, 58 (November 1952), 257.

6.30. M. C. KEMP and A. ASIMAKOPOLOUS, "A Note on Social Welfare Functions and Cardinal Utility," *CJEPS*, 18 (May 1952), 195–200.

6.31. JEROME ROTHENBERG, "Welfare Comparisons and Changes in Taste," *AER*, 43 (December 1953), 885–90.

6.32. SIDNEY SCHOEFFLER, "Note on Modern Welfare Economics," *AER*, 42 (December 1952), 880–87.

6.33. K. O. MAY, "Transitivity, Utility and Aggregation in Preference Patterns," *Ecomet*, 22 (January 1954), 1–13.

6.34. ABRAM BERGSON, "On the Concept of Social Welfare," *QJE*, 68 (May 1954), 233–52.

6.35. J. M. BUCHANAN, "Social Choice, Democracy, and Free Markets," *JPE*, 62 (April 1954), 114–23.

6.36. A. L. MACFIE, "Choice in Psychology and as an Economic Assumption," *EcJ*, 63 (January 1953), 352–67.

6.37. H. R. BOWEN, "The Interpretation of Voting in the Allocation of Resources," *QJE*, 48 (November 1943), 27–48.

6.38. GÖRAN NYBLÉN, "Quelques réfléctions sur le vieux problème de l'avantage collectif à la lumière des développements récents," *EA*, 5 (October-December 1952), 485–99.

CHAPTER SEVEN

7.1. ALFRED MARSHALL, *Principles of Economics*, 8th ed. (London: Macmillan, 1920), Ch. 14, pp. 477–95.

7.2. KENNETH E. BOULDING, *Economic Analysis*, 3rd ed. (New York: Harper, 1955), Ch. 29, pp. 605–27.

7.3. G. J. STIGLER, *Theory of Price* (New York: Macmillan, 1946), Chs. 11–15, pp. 197–302.

7.4. A. W. STONIER and D. C. HAGUE, *A Textbook of Economic Theory* (London: Longmans, Green, 1953), Ch. 8, pp. 162–81.

7.5. JOAN ROBINSON, *The Economics of Imperfect Competition* (London: Macmillan, 1946), especially Chs. 3, 4, 5, 15, 16, 17, and 18, pp. 47–84, and 179–234.

7.6. E. A. LEVER, *Advertising and Economic Theory* (London: Oxford University Press, 1947), xi, 132 pp.

7.7. NICHOLAS KALDOR, "The Economic Aspects of Advertising," *REStud*, 18 (1949–50), 1–27.

7.8. ALFRED SHERRARD, "Advertising, Product Variation, and the Limits of Economics," *JPE*, 59 (April 1951), 126–42.

7.9. L. A. DOW, "Marketing Costs and Economic Theory," *JM*, 19 (April 1955), 346–50.

7.10. FRITZ MACHLUP, *The Political Economy of Monopoly* (Baltimore: Johns Hopkins Press, 1952), 544 pp.

7.11. E. O. EDWARDS, "The Analysis of Output Under Discrimination," *Ecomet*, 18 (April 1950), 162–72.

7.12. E. W. CLEMENS, "The Marginal Revenue Curve Under Price Discrimination," *AER*, 38 (June 1948), 388–90.

7.13. J. E. ANDRIESSEN, "Lerners Monopoliegraad Onbruikbar?" *Economist*, 104 (June 1956), 403–13.

7.14. F. J. DEJONG, "Heertje over de Monopoliegraad van Lerner," *Economist*, 104 (June 1956), 414–26.

7.15. C. L. JAMISON, "How Good Are the Reasons for Mergers?" *MBusR*, 7 (November 1955), 8–13.

7.16. MICHAEL POLANYI, "Patent Reform," *REStud*, 11 (Summer 1944), 61–76.

7.17. H. G. FOX, "Patents in Relation to Monopoly," *CJEPS*, 13 (February 1947), 68–80.

7.18. L. S. ORD, *Secrets of Industry* (London: Allen & Unwin, 1945), 160 pp.

7.19. ANDREW MARTIN, *Restrictive Trade Practices and Monopolies* (London: Routledge and Kegan Paul, 1957), 264 pp.

7.20. E. S. MASON, *Economic Concentration and the Monopoly Problem* (Cambridge: Harvard University Press, 1957), 411 pp.

7.21. WALTER ADAMS and H. M. GRAY, *Monopoly in America: The Government as Promoter* (New York: Macmillan, 1955), 221 pp.

7.22. O. W. MAIN, *The Canadian Nickel Industry: A Study in Market Control and Public Policy* (Toronto: University of Toronto Press, 1955), 168 pp.

CHAPTER EIGHT

Imperfect Competition Generally

8.1. E. H. CHAMBERLIN, *The Theory of Monopolistic Competition* (Cambridge: Harvard University Press, 1933, 1942), 282 pp.

8.2. J. F. DUE, *Intermediate Economic Analysis* (Homewood, Ill., Irwin, 1947), Chs. 6 and 7, pp. 150–218.

8.3. KENNETH E. BOULDING, *Economic Analysis* (New York: Harper, 1955), Chs. 30 and 31, pp. 628–79.

8.4. ROBERT TRIFFIN, *Monopolistic Competition and General Equilibrium Theory* (Cambridge: Harvard University Press, 1947), 195 pp.

8.5. FRITZ MACHLUP, *The Economics of Sellers' Competition* (Baltimore: Johns Hopkins Press, 1952), 582 pp.

8.6. WILLIAM FELLNER, *Competition Among the Few* (New York: Knopf, 1949), 328 pp.

Duopoly

8.7. A. C. PIGOU, "A Comment on Duopoly," *Eca*, 15 (November 1948), 254–58.

8.8. MARTIN SHUBIK, "A Comparison of Treatments of a Duopoly Problem," *Ecomet*, 21 (January 1953), 141–54; 23 (October 1955), 417–31.

8.9. A. M. HENDERSON, "The Theory of Duopoly," *QJE*, 68 (November 1954), 565–84.

Oligopoly

8.10. FRITZ MACHLUP, "The Characteristics and Classifications of Oligopoly," *Kyklos*, 5 (1951–52), 145–63.

8.11. ———, "Oligopolistic Indeterminacy," *WA*, 68 (1952), 1–19.

8.12. WILLIAM FELLNER, "Une théorie de l'oligopole," *EA*, 5 (April-September 1952), 197–223.

8.13. E. G. DOWDELL, "Oligopoly and Imperfect Competition," *OxEP*, 1 (June 1949), 217–26.

8.14. K. W. ROTHSCHILD, "Price Theory and Oligopoly," *EcJ*, 57 (September 1947), 299–320.

8.15. R. W. PFOUTS, "Distribution Theory in a Certain Case of Oligopoly and Oligopsony," *Met*, 7 (December 1955), 137–46.

8.16. R. M. CYERT and J. G. MARCH, "Organizational Factors in the Theory of Oligopoly," *QJE*, 70 (February 1956), 44–64.

8.17. FREDERIK ZEUTHEN and OTHERS, "L'oligopole," *EA*, 8 (July-December 1955), 327–552.

8.18. J. N. WOLFE, "Oligopoly and Its Problems," *REStud*, 23 (1955–56), 163–64.

Monopolistic Competition

8.19. E. H. CHAMBERLAIN, "Monopolistic Competition Revisited," *Eca*, 18 November 1951), 343–62.

8.20. JOAN ROBINSON, "Imperfect Competition Revisited," *EcJ*, 63 (September 1953), 579–93.

8.21. HANS BREMS, "Employment, Prices, and Monopolistic Competition," *REStud*, 34 (November 1952), 314–25.

8.22. F. H. HAHN, "Excess Capacity and Imperfect Competition," *OxEP*, 7 (October 1955), 229–40.

8.23. M. E. PAUL, "Notes on Excess Capacity," *OxEP*, 6 (February 1954), 33–40.

8.24. P. M. GREGORY, "Fashion and Monopolistic Competition," *JPE*, 56 February 1948), 69–75.

8.25. C. C. RENWICK, "The Equilibrium of the Firm in Monopolistic and Imperfect Competition Theories," *EcR*, 24 (June 1948), 32–41.

Imperfect Competition

8.26. BURKHARDT ROPER, *Die Konkurrenz und ihre Fehlentwicklung: Untersuchung über Störung der Marktwirtschaft* (Berlin: Duncker & Humblot, 1952), 243 pp.

8.27. J. W. MARKHAM, "An Alternative Approach to the Concept of Workable Competition," *AER*, 40 (June 1950), 349–61.

8.28. J. R. HICKS, "The Process of Imperfect Competition," *OxEP*, 6 (February 1954), 41–54.

8.29. MARTIN BRONFENBRENNER, "Imperfect Competition on a Long-run Basis," *JBUC*, 23 (April 1950), 81–93.

8.30. C. M. BIRCH, "A Revised Classification of Forms of Competition," *CJEPS*, 20 (May 1954), 157–65.

8.31. W. D. ARANT, "Competition of the Few Among the Many," *QJE*, 70 (August 1956), 327–45.

8.32. ALFRED NICOLS, "The Rehabilitation of Price Competition," *QJE*, 62 (November 1947), 31–63.

8.33. E. H. CHAMBERLAIN, "An Experimental Imperfect Market," *JPE*, 56 (April 1948), 95–108.

8.34. MARTIN BRONFENBRENNER, "Price Control Under Imperfect Competition: The Joint Production Problem," *CJEPS*, 15 (May 1949), 210–16.

8.35. MICHAEL MICHAELY, "A Geometrical Analysis of Black Market Behavior," *AER*, 44 (September 1954), 627–36.

Kinky Demand and Full-cost Pricing

8.36. P. M. SWEEZY, "Demand Under Conditions of Oligopoly," *JPE*, 47 (August 1939), 568–73.

8.37. MARTIN BRONFENBRENNER, "Applications of the Discontinuous Oligopoly Demand Curve," *JPE*, 48 (June 1940), 420–27.

8.38. H. M. OLIVER, "Average Cost and the Long-run Elasticity of Demand," *JPE*, 55 (June 1947), 212–21.

8.39. G. J. STIGLER, "The Kinky Oligopoly Demand Curve and Rigid Prices," *JPE*, 55 (October 1947), 432–49.

8.40. WILLIAM FELLNER, "Average Cost Pricing and the Theory of Uncertainty," *JPE*, 56 (June 1948), 249–52.

8.41. J. W. MARKHAM, "The Nature and Significance of Price Leadership," *AER*, 41 (December 1951), 891–905.

8.42. A. R. OXENFELDT, "Professor Markham on Price Leadership: Some Unanswered Questions," *AER*, 42 (June 1952), 380–84.

8.43. KINGSLEY LAFFER, "A Note on some Marginalist and Other Explanations of Full Cost Price Theory," *EcR*, 29 (May 1953), 51–62.

8.44. RON NIESER, "A Kinked Demand Curve for Monopolistic Competition," *EcR*, 29 (May 1953), 19–34.

8.45. C. W. EFROYMSON, "The Kinked Demand Curve Reconsidered," *QJE*, 69 (February 1955), 119–36.

Geographic Competition

8.46. HAROLD HOTELLING, "Stability in Competition," *EcJ*, 39 (March 1929), 41–57.

8.47. FREDERIK ZEUTHEN, "Theoretical Remarks on Price Policy: Hotelling's Case with Variations," *QJE*, 47 (February 1933), 231–53.

8.48. A. P. LERNER and H. W. SINGER, "Some Notes on Duopoly and Spatial Competition," *JPE*, 45 (April 1937).

8.49. ARTHUR SMITHIES, "Optimum Location in Spatial Competition," *JPE*, 49 (June 1941), 423–39.

8.50. AUGUST LOSCH, *The Economics of Location* (New Haven: Yale University Press, 1954), 520 pp.

8.51. WALTER ISARD, *Location and Space Economy: A General Theory Relating to Industrial Location, Market Areas, Land Use, and Urban Structure* (New York: Wiley, 1956), 350 pp.

8.52. FRITZ MACHLUP, *The Basing Point System: An Economic Analysis of a Controversial Pricing Practice* (Philadelphia: Blakiston, 1949).

8.53. J. M. CLARK, "Machlup on the Basing Point System," *QJE*, 58 (August 1949), 315–21.

8.54. ———, "The Law and Economics of Basing Points: Appraisal and Proposals," *AER*, 39 (March 1949), 430–47.

8.55. CARL KAYSEN, "Basing Point Price Policy and Public Policy," *QJE*, 58 (August 1949), 289–314.

8.56. "Price Systems: The Basing Point Issues," *YLJ*, 58 (February 1949), 426–56.

8.57. EARL LATHAM, "Giantism and Basing Points: A Political Analysis," *YLJ*, 58 (February 1949), 383–99.

8.58. P. B. MCALLISTER and M. T. QUIGG, "The Art of Selecting and Exploiting Half-Truths: A Reply to 'Giantism and Basing Points,' " *YLJ*, 58 (June 1949), 1068–78.

8.59. G. J. STIGLER, "A Theory of Delivered Price Systems," *AER*, 39 (December 1949), 1143–59.

8.60. G. W. STOCKING, *Basing Point Pricing and Regional Development* (Chapel Hill: University of North Carolina Press, 1954), 274 pp.

8.61. DONALD DEWEY, "A Reappraisal of FOB Pricing and Freight Absorption," *SEJ*, 22 (July 1955), 48–54.

8.62. J. S. MCGEE, "Cross-Hauling: A Symptom of Incomplete Collusion under Basing Point Systems," *SEJ*, 20 (April 1954), 369–79.

8.63. E. B. GEORGE, "The Law and Economics of Basing Points," *Dun's* (September 1948), pp. 14 ff.; (October 1948), pp. 11 ff.

Miscellaneous

8.64. R. L. BISHOP, "Elasticities, Cross Elasticities, and Market Relationships," *AER*, 42 (December 1952), 779–803.

CHAPTER NINE

9.1. R. D. LUCE and HOWARD RAIFFA, *Games and Decisions* (New York: Wiley, 1957), 509 pp.

9.2. R. B. BRAITHWAITE, *Theory of Games as a Tool for the Moral Philosopher* (Cambridge: University Press, 1955), 75 pp.

9.3. T. C. SCHELLING, "The Strategy of Conflict: Prospectus for a Reorientation of Game Theory," *JCR*, 2 (September 1958), 203–64.

9.4. J. R. N. STONE, "The Theory of Games," *EcJ*, 58 (June 1948), 186–201.

9.5. HANS NEISSER, "The Strategy of Expecting the Worst," *Soc Res*, 19 (September 1952), 346–63.

9.6. J. D. WILLIAMS, *The Compleat Strategyst, Being a Primer on the Theory of Games of Strategy* (New York: McGraw-Hill, 1954), 234 pp.

9.7. G. T. GUILBAUD, "The Theory of Games," *IEP*, 1 (1951), 37–65.

9.8. CARL KAYSEN, "A Revolution in Economic Theory?" *REStud*, 14 (1946–47), 1–15.

9.9. J. C. C. MCKINSEY, *Introduction to the Theory of Games* (New York: McGraw-Hill, 1952), 371 pp.

9.10. JOHN VON NEUMANN and OSKAR MORGENSTERN, *Theory of Games and Economic Behavior* (Princeton: Princeton University Press, 1944, 1947, 1953), 541 pp.

9.11. J. C. HARSANYI, "Approaches to the Bargaining Problem Before and After the Theory of Games: A Critical Discussion of Zeuthen's, Hicks', and Nash's Theories," *Ecomet*, 24 (April 1956), 144–57.

9.12. H. W. KUHN and A. W. TUCKER, eds., *Contributions to the Theory of Games*, Vols. I–IV (Princeton: Princeton University Press, 1950–59).

9.13. HANS NEISSER, "L'oligopole, les anticipations et la théorie des jeux," *EA*, 5 (April-September 1952), 225–59.

9.14. G. T. GUILBAUD, "Les problèmes de partage," *EA*, 5 (January–March 1952), 93-137.

9.15. H. A. SIMON, "A Comparison of Game Theory and Learning Theory," *Psychomet*, 21 (September 1956), 267–72; rep. in H. A. Simon, *Models of Man* (New York: Wiley, 1957), pp. 274–79.

9.16. WILLIAM VICKREY, "Counterspeculation, Auctions, and Competitive Sealed Tenders," *JFin*, 16 (March 1961), 8–37.

9.17. ———, "Auction and Bidding Games," in *Recent Advances in Game Theory* (Princeton: Princeton University Conference, 1962), pp. 15–27.

INDEX

A

Accounting: internal, 181; and marginal cost, 232
Adjustment, instantaneous, 18
Adjustment of plant, 195–98
Administrative inertia, 256
Admissible perference rankings, 276–78
Advance reservations, 236, 245
Advertising, 24, 217, 298, 314; economies of scale in, 252; uniqueness of, 337
Advice, purchase of, 24, 218
Agency, self-liquidating, 224, 249, 265
Aggregation, 83; of commodities, 35; of demand, 316
Agriculture, diminishing returns in, 154
Alcoholics, 24, 40
Alienation of land, obstacles to, 142
All-purpose indexes, 82
Allocation: of capital costs over time, 256; of current overhead, 231; of demand among sellers, 304; optimal, 212, of production, 177; of resources, 2, 259, 336; of total cost among products, 194
Alternatives; certain, 31; dominating, 279; range of, 280
Alternatives, irrelevant, in social welfare, 276, 281
Altruism, 11
Antitrust action, 146, 214, 298
Approximations, successive, 7, 17
Arbiter, of social-welfare function, 275
Arbitrage, 97
Arrow, Kenneth, 272, 282
Artificial differentiation of products, 314
Assumptions: of competitive model, 209; extreme, 8; of optimality theorem, 212; selection of, 8
Asymptotic indifference curves, 44
Auditing, 180
Australian railroads, gauge of, 198
Auxiliary services, 315
Average cost, 161, 175, 177, 214, 249, 254, 256, 265, 316, 319; flexible plant, 199; meaninglessness of, in multi-product case, 184; to purchaser, 291, 292; short-run and long-run, 192; to supplying industry, 291, 292
Average current cost, 195
Average fixed cost, 164
Average marginal revenue, 289
Average net revenue-product, 294
Average product, 150; creased, 188; meaninglessness of, 184
Average revenue, 288; and elasticity, 291; of flexible plant, 200
Average value-product, 157, 158; *see also* Value of average product
Average variable cost, 195
Avoidable costs, 195, 196

B

Bank loans, 182
Bargaining, 115, 176; locus, 59; procedures, 116
Barter, 96
Base demand, 236
Base period, for index, 76
Behavior, competitive, 209, 212
Behavior assumed by duopolists, 306
Benefits, marginal, 228; splitting of, 115
Bentham, Jeremy, 280
Bilateral monopoly, 115, 164, 288
Bonds, as capital, 140
Bonus payments, in game theory, 353, 355, 361
Branding, 314
Break-even price, 241
Breakdown, reserves for, 179
Bribes, *see* Bonus payments, Compensation
Bribing of gainers by losers, 271
Budget constraint, 124
Budget equations, 120
Budget line, 51, 52, 76, 172
Buridan's ass, 55
Business demand, 236
Buyer's average cost, 292
Buyer's marginal cost, 292
By-product services, 230
By-products, 184

C

Calories, in food, 44
Capacity, 227; adjustment of, 244; costs, 231; difficulties in definition of, 200; exceeded by demand, 237; restraint on duopolists, 310; and risk of emergency shortage, 245; of seller, 303; utilization of, 244
Capital: as a factor, 138, 139; inexhaustible, 140; as a joint cost, 256; market for, 221; provision of, 142; rationing, 181, 182
Capitalism, economics of, 11
Cardinal utility, 32, 48
Carnot cycle, 7
Carrying charges, 243
Carrying costs, 225
Cartels, 145
Catallactic system, 19
Cement, economies of scale in, 251
Centralized traffic control, 250
Certain alternatives, 31
Ceteris paribus, 36
Chain index numbers, *see* Linked relatives
Chain stores; 220
Chamberlin, E. H., 315
Chance variables, 343
Changes: compensated, 130; dynamic, 334
Changing tastes, 23, 24
Characteristic function, 353, 362, 363
Charging what the traffic will bear, 232, 297

4
B 5
C 6
D 7
E 8
F 9
G 0
H 1
I 2
J 3